JavaScript Frameworks for Modern Web Development

The Essential Frameworks, Libraries, and Tools to Learn Right Now

Second Edition

Sufyan bin Uzayr

Nicholas Cloud

Tim Ambler

Apress®

JavaScript Frameworks for Modern Web Development

Sufyan bin Uzayr
Al Manama, United Arab Emirates

Nicholas Cloud
Florissant, MO, USA

Tim Ambler
Nashville, TN, USA

ISBN-13 (pbk): 978-1-4842-4994-9
https://doi.org/10.1007/978-1-4842-4995-6

ISBN-13 (electronic): 978-1-4842-4995-6

Managing Director, Apress Media LLC: Welmoed Spahr
Acquisitions Editor: Louise Corrigan
Development Editor: James Markham
Coordinating Editor: Nancy Chen

Cover designed by eStudioCalamar

Distributed to the book trade worldwide by Springer Science+Business Media New York, 233 Spring Street, 6th Floor, New York, NY 10013. Phone 1-800-SPRINGER, fax (201) 348-4505, e-mail orders-ny@springer-sbm.com, or visit www.springeronline.com. Apress Media, LLC is a California LLC and the sole member (owner) is Springer Science + Business Media Finance Inc (SSBM Finance Inc). SSBM Finance Inc is a **Delaware** corporation.

For information on translations, please e-mail rights@apress.com, or visit http://www.apress.com/rights-permissions.

Apress titles may be purchased in bulk for academic, corporate, or promotional use. eBook versions and licenses are also available for most titles. For more information, reference our Print and eBook Bulk Sales web page at http://www.apress.com/bulk-sales.

Any source code or other supplementary material referenced by the author in this book is available to readers on GitHub via the book's product page, located at www.apress.com/9781484249949. For more detailed information, please visit http://www.apress.com/source-code.

Printed on acid-free paper

For Anza
—Sufyan bin Uzayr

Table of Contents

About the Authors

Sufyan bin Uzayr is a web developer with over 10 years of experience in the industry. He specializes in a wide variety of technologies, including JavaScript, WordPress, Drupal, PHP, and UNIX/Linux shell and server management, and is the author of five previous books. Sufyan is the Director of Parakozm, a multinational design and development consultancy firm that offers customized solutions to a global clientele. He is also the CTO at Samurai Servers, a server management and security company catering mainly to enterprise-scale audience. He takes a keen interest in technology, politics, literature, history, and sports, and in his spare time he enjoys teaching coding and English to students. Read more about his works at www.sufyanism.com.

Nicholas Cloud is a software developer who lives in the very humid city of St. Louis. For over a decade, he has forged his skills into a successful career. He has developed web applications, web services, and desktop software on diverse platforms with JavaScript, C#, and PHP. A strong proponent of open source software, Nicholas contributes to userland projects and has written several of his own open source libraries. He speaks at a variety of user groups and conferences and writes books, technical articles, and blog posts in his spare time. He opines on Twitter at @nicholascloud.

ABOUT THE AUTHORS

Tim Ambler is a software engineer from Nashville, Tennessee. His passion for programming follows in the footsteps of his father, who introduced him to computers at a young age with a Commodore 64. Tim is the author of several popular open source projects, one of which (whenLive) has been featured by GitHub's staff. An occasional conference speaker and frequent writer, Tim has been referenced multiple times in online publications such as *JavaScript Weekly* and *Node Weekly*. He currently lives in the 12 South area with his wife, Laura, and two cats. You can follow him on Twitter at @tkambler.

About the Technical Reviewer

Aleemullah Samiullah is a seasoned developer with over 10+ years of experience in front-end technologies. He is a senior engineer at Software AG and has previously worked at Publicis Sapient and Infosys, gaining considerable expertise, working with major brands such as Tesco, Target, and Holt Renfrew. He enjoys crafting digital experiences based on human-centered design, with a keen focus on usability and accessibility. In his career, Aleem has used various JavaScript libraries, including React, Angular, Backbone, ExtJS, jQuery, and so on. He is passionate about the latest technologies and actively participates in JS meetups and conferences. When he's not coding, he likes to travel, write blog posts, and spend time with family.

Aleem can be found on LinkedIn at `www.linkedin.com/in/aleemullah/`.

Acknowledgments

There are several people who deserve to be on this page because this book would not have come into existence without their support. That said, some names deserve a special mention, and I am genuinely grateful to

- My mom and dad, for everything they have done for me

- Faisal Fareed and Sadaf Fareed, my siblings, for helping with things back home

- Nancy Chen, Content Development Editor for this book, for keeping track of everything and for being very patient as I kept missing one deadline or the other

- The Apress team, especially Louise Corrigan, Jade Scard, and James Markham, for ensuring that the book's content, layout, formatting, and everything else remains perfect throughout

- The coauthors of this book's first edition and the tech reviewer, for going through the manuscript and providing his insight and feedback

- Typesetters, cover designers, printers, and everyone else, for their part in the development of this book

- All the folks associated with Parakozm, either directly or indirectly, for their help and support

- The JavaScript community at large, for all their hard work and efforts

—Sufyan bin Uzayr

Introduction

They tell me we're living in an information age, but none of it seems to be the information I need or brings me closer to what I want to know. In fact (I'm becoming more and more convinced) all this electronic wizardry only adds to our confusion, delivering inside scoops and verdicts about events that have hardly begun: a torrent of chatter moving at the speed of light, making it nearly impossible for any of the important things to be heard.

—Matthew Flaming, *The Kingdom of Ohio*

The notion that "technology moves quickly" is a well-worn aphorism, and with good reason: technology does move quickly. But at this moment, JavaScript in particular is moving very quickly indeed—much like that "torrent of chatter moving at the speed of light" that Matthew Flaming refers to in *The Kingdom of Ohio*. The language is in the midst of what many have called a renaissance, brought about by the rapidly increasing sophistication of browser-based applications and the rising popularity of JavaScript on the server, thanks to Node.js.

An almost feverish pace of innovation is occurring within the JavaScript community that, while endlessly fascinating to follow, also presents some unique challenges of its own. JavaScript's ecosystem of libraries, frameworks, and utilities has grown dramatically. Where once a small number of solutions for any given problem existed, many can now be found, and the options continue to grow by the day. As a result, developers find themselves faced with the increasingly difficult task of choosing the appropriate tools from among many seemingly good options.

If you've ever found yourself wondering why JavaScript seems to be attracting so much attention, as we have, it's worth stopping for a moment to consider the fact that JavaScript, a language that was created by one person in 10 days, now serves as the foundation upon which much of the Web as we know it sits. A language that was originally created to solve relatively simple problems is now being applied in new and innovative ways that were not originally foreseen. What's more, JavaScript is a beautifully expressive language, but it's not without its share of rough edges and potential pitfalls.

While flexible, efficient, and ubiquitous, JavaScript concepts such as the event loop and prototypal inheritance can prove particularly challenging for those coming to the language for the first time.

For these and many other reasons, the development community at large is still coming to terms with how best to apply the unique features that JavaScript brings to the table. We've no doubt only scratched the surface of what the language and the community behind it are capable of. For those with an insatiable appetite for knowledge and a desire to create, now is the perfect time to be a JavaScript developer.

We have written *JavaScript Frameworks for Modern Web Development* to serve as your guide to a wide range of popular JavaScript tools that solve difficult problems at both ends of the development stack: in the browser and on the server. The tutorials and downloadable code examples contained within this book illustrate the usage of tools that manage dependencies, structure code in a modular fashion, automate repetitive build tasks, create specialized servers, structure client-side applications, facilitate horizontal scaling, perform event logging, and interact with disparate data stores.

The libraries and frameworks covered include Grunt, Yeoman, PM2, RequireJS, Browserify, Knockout, Angular, Kraken, Mongoose, Knex, Bookshelf, Async.js, Underscore, Lodash, React, and Vue.js.

In writing *JavaScript Frameworks for Modern Web Development*, our goal was to create a filter for the "torrent of chatter" that often seems to surround JavaScript and, in so doing, to allow what we believe are some important things to be heard. We hope the information contained within these pages proves as useful to you as it has to us.

Who This Book Is For

This book is intended for web developers who are already confident with JavaScript, but also frustrated with the sheer number of solutions that exist for seemingly every problem. This book helps lift the fog, providing the reader with an in-depth guide to specific libraries and frameworks that well-known organizations are using right now with great success. Topics pertaining to both client-side and server-side development are covered. As a result, readers will gain the most benefit from this book if they already have at least an intermediate familiarity with both the web browser Document Object Model (DOM), common client-side libraries like jQuery, and Node.js.

How This Book Is Structured

This book covers a wide selection of JavaScript tools that are applicable throughout the entire development process, from a project's first commit to its first release and beyond. To that end, the chapters have been grouped into the following parts.

Part 1: Development Tools
Grunt

Larry Wall, the creator of Perl, describes the three virtues of a great programmer as laziness, impatience, and hubris. In this chapter, we'll focus on a tool that will help you strengthen the virtue of laziness—Grunt. This popular task runner provides developers with a framework for creating command-line utilities that automate repetitive build tasks such as running tests, concatenating files, compiling SASS/LESS stylesheets, checking for JavaScript errors, and more. After reading this chapter, you'll know how to use several popular Grunt plugins as well as how to go about creating and sharing your own plugins with the community.

Yeoman

Yeoman provides JavaScript developers with a mechanism for creating reusable templates ("generators") that describe the overall structure of a project (initially required dependencies, Grunt tasks, etc.) in a way that can be easily reused over and over. Broad community support also allows you to take advantage of a wide variety of preexisting templates. In this chapter, we'll walk through the process of installing Yeoman and using several popular preexisting generators. Finally, we'll take a look at how we can create and share our own templates with the community.

PM2

In this chapter, we will close out our discussion of development tools by taking a look at PM2, a command-line utility that simplifies many of the tasks associated with running Node applications, monitoring their status, and efficiently scaling them to meet increasing demand.

Part 2: Module Loaders
RequireJS and Browserify

JavaScript lacks a native method for loading external dependencies in the browser—a frustrating oversight for developers. Fortunately, the community has stepped in to fill this gap with two very different and competing standards: the Asynchronous Module Definition (AMD) API and CommonJS. We'll dive into the details of both and take a look at widely used implementations of each: RequireJS and Browserify. Each has its merits, which we'll discuss in detail, but both can have a profoundly positive impact on the way in which you go about structuring your applications.

Part 3: Client-Side Frameworks
Knockout and Angular

In recent years, web developers have witnessed a sharp rise in popularity of so-called "single-page apps." Such applications exhibit behavior once available only on the desktop, but at the expense of increased code complexity within the browser. In this section, we'll dive into two widely used front-end frameworks that help minimize that complexity by providing proven patterns for solving frequently encountered problems: Knockout and Angular. Knockout focuses on the relationship between view and data, but otherwise leaves the application architecture and plumbing to the developer's discretion. Angular takes a more prescriptive approach, covering the view, data transfer, Dependency Injection, and so on.

Part 4: Server-Side Frameworks
Kraken

Client-side applications aren't very useful without a server with which to interact. In this chapter, we'll take a look at one popular framework that supports developers in the creation of back-end applications: Kraken.

Part 5: Managing Database Interaction
Mongoose, Knex, and Bookshelf

At the core of every application lies the most important component of any development stack—the data that our users seek. In this section, we'll become familiar with two libraries that help simplify some of the complexity that's often experienced when interacting with popular storage platforms such as MongoDB, MySQL, PostgreSQL, and SQLite. After reading this section, you'll be comfortable defining schemas, associations, lifecycle "hooks," and more.

Part 6: Managing Control Flow
Async.js

The asynchronous nature of JavaScript provides developers with a significant degree of flexibility—as opposed to forcing developers to execute their code in a linear fashion, JavaScript allows developers to orchestrate multiple actions simultaneously. Unfortunately, along with this flexibility comes a significant degree of additional complexity—what many developers refer to as "callback hell" or the "pyramid of doom."

Part 7: Further Useful Libraries

A number of wonderfully useful libraries exist that this book would be remiss not to cover, but for which additional parts are not necessarily warranted. This part will cover such libraries.

Underscore and Lodash

Underscore (and its successor, Lodash) is an incredibly useful collection of functions that simplifies many frequently used patterns that can be tedious to implement otherwise. This brief chapter will bring these libraries to your attention, along with some of the more popular extensions that can also be included to enhance their usefulness even further. Examples are included that highlight some of the most frequently used portions of these libraries.

Part 8: Front-End Development
React and Vue.js

In this section, we will cover JavaScript frameworks that are geared for front-end development, such as React and Vue.js.

React, having the backing of Facebook, has risen in popularity in a very short span of time and continues to be a preferred choice for many developers.

On the other hand, Vue.js is a slightly less popular name in the field, but it has been gaining a steady and very loyal following, primarily due to its ease of use and simplicity.

Downloading the Code

Each chapter in this book contains many examples, the source code for which may be downloaded from `www.apress.com/9781484249949` in zipped form.

Most examples are run with the Node.js runtime, which may be obtained from `https://nodejs.org`. Chapters with additional prerequisites will explain the necessary procedures for downloading and installing the examples. (For example, MongoDB is necessary to run examples in Chapter 9, which covers Mongoose.)

Any additional steps necessary for running code examples (e.g., executing curl requests) or interacting with a running example (e.g., opening a web browser and navigating to a specific URL) are explained alongside each listing.

PART I

Development Tools

CHAPTER 1

Grunt

I'm lazy. But it's the lazy people who invented the wheel and the bicycle because they didn't like walking or carrying things.

—Lech Walesa, former president of Poland

In his book *Programming Perl*, Larry Wall (the well-known creator of the language) puts forth the idea that all successful programmers share three important characteristics: laziness, impatience, and hubris. At first glance, these traits all sound quite negative, but dig a little deeper, and you'll find the hidden meaning in his statement:

> Laziness: Lazy programmers hate to repeat themselves. As a result, they tend to put a lot of effort into creating useful tools that perform repetitive tasks for them. They also tend to document those tools well, to spare themselves the trouble of answering questions about them later.

> Impatience: Impatient programmers have learned to expect much from their tools. This expectation teaches them to create software that doesn't just react to the needs of its users, but that actually attempts to anticipate those needs.

> Hubris: Good programmers take great pride in their work. It is this pride that compels them to write software that others won't want to criticize—the type of work that we should all be striving for.

In this chapter, we'll focus on the first of these three characteristics, laziness, along with Grunt, a popular JavaScript "task runner" that supports developers in nurturing this trait by providing them with a toolkit for automating the repetitive build tasks that often accompany software development, such as

© Sufyan bin Uzayr, Nicholas Cloud, Tim Ambler 2019
S. bin Uzayr et al., *JavaScript Frameworks for Modern Web Development*,
https://doi.org/10.1007/978-1-4842-4995-6_1

- Script and stylesheet compilation and minification

- Testing

- Linting

- Database migrations

- Deployments

In other words, Grunt helps developers who strive to work smarter, not harder. If that idea appeals to you, read on. After you have finished this chapter, you will be well on your way toward mastering Grunt. You'll learn how to do the following in this chapter:

- Create configurable tasks that automate the repetitive aspects of software development that accompany nearly every project

- Interact with the file system using simple yet powerful abstractions provided by Grunt

- Publish Grunt plugins from which other developers can benefit and to which they can contribute

- Take advantage of Grunt's preexisting library of community-supported plugins

Installing Grunt

Before continuing, you should ensure that you have installed Grunt's command-line utility. Available as an npm package, the installation process is shown in Listing 1-1.

Listing 1-1. Installing the grunt Command-Line Utility via npm

```
$ npm install -g grunt-cli
$ grunt —version
grunt-cli v1.3.2
```

How Grunt Works

Grunt provides developers with a toolkit for creating command-line utilities that perform repetitive project tasks. Examples of such tasks include the minification of JavaScript code and the compilation of Sass stylesheets, but there's no limit to how Grunt can be put to work. Grunt can be used to create simple tasks that address the specific needs of a single project—tasks that you don't intend to share or reuse—but Grunt's true power derives from its ability to package tasks as reusable plugins that can then be published, shared, used, and improved upon by others.

Four core components make Grunt tick, which we will now cover.

Gruntfile.js

At Grunt's core lies the *Gruntfile*, a Node module saved as `Gruntfile.js` (see Listing 1-2) at the root of your project. It's within this file that we can load Grunt plugins, create our own custom tasks, and configure them according to the needs of our project. Each time Grunt is run, its first order of business is to retrieve its marching orders from this module.

Listing 1-2. Sample Gruntfile

```
// example-starter/Gruntfile.js

module.exports = function(grunt) {

    /**
     * Configure the various tasks and plugins that we'll be using
     */
    grunt.initConfig({
        /* Grunt's 'file' API provides developers with helpful abstractions for
        interacting  with the file system. We'll take a look at these in
        greater detail later in the chapter. */
        'pkg': grunt.file.readJSON('package.json'),
        'uglify': {
            'development': {
                'files': {
                    'build/app.min.js': ['src/app.js', 'src/lib.js']
                }
            }
        }
    });
```

```
    /**
     * Grunt plugins exist as Node packages, published via npm. Here, we
       load the
     * 'grunt-contrib-uglify' plugin, which provides a task for merging and
       minifying
     * a project's source code in preparation for deployment.
     */
    grunt.loadNpmTasks('grunt-contrib-uglify');

    /**
     * Here we create a Grunt task named 'default' that does nothing more
       than call
     * the 'uglify' task. In other words, this task will serve as an alias to
     * 'uglify'. Creating a task named 'default' tells Grunt what to do
       when it is
     * run from the command line without any arguments. In this example,
       our 'default'
     * task calls a single, separate task, but we could just as easily have
       called
     * multiple tasks (to be run in sequence) by adding multiple entries to
       the array
     * that is passed.
     */
    grunt.registerTask('default', ['uglify']);

    /**
     * Here we create a custom task that prints a message to the console
       (followed by
     * a line break) using one of Grunt's built-in methods for providing
       user feedback.
     * We'll look at these in greater detail later in the chapter.
     */
    grunt.registerTask('hello-world', function() {
        grunt.log.writeln('Hello, world.');
    });

};
```

Tasks

Tasks are the basic building blocks of Grunt and are nothing more than functions that are registered with assigned names via Grunt's `registerTask()` method. In Listing 1-2, a simple `hello-world` task is shown that prints a message to the console. This task can be called from the command line as shown in Listing 1-3.

Listing 1-3. Running the `hello-world` Task Shown in Listing 1-2

```
$ grunt hello-world
Running "hello-world" task
Hello, world.

Done, without errors.
```

Multiple Grunt tasks can also be run in sequence with a single command, as shown in Listing 1-4. Each task will be run in the order in which it was passed.

Listing 1-4. Running Multiple Grunt Tasks in Sequence

```
$ grunt hello-world uglify
Running "hello-world" task
Hello, world.

Running "uglify:development" (uglify) task
>> 1 file created.

Done, without errors.
```

The `hello-world` task that we've just seen serves as an example of a basic, stand-alone Grunt task. Such tasks can be used to implement simple actions specific to the needs of a single project that you don't intend to reuse or share. Most of the time, however, you will find yourself interacting not with stand-alone tasks, but instead with tasks that have been packaged as Grunt plugins and published to npm so that others can reuse them and contribute to them.

Plugins

A Grunt plugin is a collection of configurable tasks (published as an npm package) that can be reused across multiple projects. Thousands of such plugins exist. In Listing 1-2, Grunt's `loadNpmTasks()` method is used to load the `grunt-contrib-uglify` Node module, a Grunt plugin that merges a project's JavaScript code into a single, minified file that is suitable for deployment.

Note   A list of all available Grunt plugins can be found at `http://gruntjs.com/plugins`. Plugins whose names are prefixed with `contrib-` are officially maintained by the developers behind Grunt. In the repository, officially maintained plugins are now also marked by a "star" icon, making them easier to differentiate from third-party developers' plugins.

Configuration

Grunt is known for emphasizing "configuration over code": the creation of tasks and plugins whose functionality is tailored by configuration that is specified within each project. It is this separation of code from configuration that allows developers to create plugins that are easily reusable by others. Later in the chapter, we'll take a look at the various ways in which Grunt plugins and tasks can be configured.

Adding Grunt to Your Project

Earlier in the chapter, we installed Grunt's command-line utility by installing the `grunt-cli` npm package as a global module. We should now have access to the `grunt` utility from the command line, but we still need to add a local `grunt` dependency to each project we intend to use it with. The command to be called from within the root folder of your project is shown next. This example assumes that npm has already been initialized within the project and that a `package.json` file already exists.

```
$ npm install grunt --save-dev
```

Our project's `package.json` file should now contain a `grunt` entry similar to that shown in Listing 1-5.

Listing 1-5. Our Project's Updated package.json File

```
// example-tasks/package.json

{
    "name": "example-tasks",
    "version": "1.0.0",
    "devDependencies": {
        "grunt": "1.0.3"
    }
}
```

The final step toward integrating Grunt with our project is the creation of a Gruntfile (see Listing 1-6), which should be saved within the root folder of the project. Within our Gruntfile, a single method is called, loadTasks(), which is discussed in the upcoming section.

Listing 1-6. Contents of Our Project's Gruntfile

```
// example-tasks/Gruntfile.js

module.exports = function(grunt) {
    grunt.loadTasks('tasks');
};
```

Maintaining a Sane Grunt Structure

We hope that by the time you have finished this chapter, you will have found Grunt to be a worthwhile tool for automating many of the repetitive, tedious tasks that you encounter during the course of your daily workflow. That said, we'd be lying if we told you that our initial reaction to Grunt was positive. In fact, we were quite turned off by the tool at first. To help explain why, let's take a look at the Gruntfile that is prominently displayed within Grunt's official documentation (see Listing 1-7).

Listing 1-7. Example Gruntfile Provided by Grunt's Official Documentation

```
module.exports = function(grunt) {

    grunt.initConfig({
        pkg: grunt.file.readJSON('package.json'),
        concat: {
            options: {
                separator: ';'
            },
            dist: {
                src: ['src/**/*.js'],
                dest: 'dist/<%= pkg.name %>.js'
            }
        },
        uglify: {
            options: {
                banner: '/*! <%= grunt.template.today("dd-mm-yyyy") %> */\n'
            },
            dist: {
                files: {
                    'dist/<%= pkg.name %>.min.js': ['<%= concat.dist.dest %>']
                }
            }
        },
        qunit: {
            files: ['test/**/*.html']
        },
        jshint: {
            files: ['Gruntfile.js', 'src/**/*.js', 'test/**/*.js'],
            options: {
                // options here to override JSHint defaults
                globals: {
                    jQuery: true,
                    console: true,
                    module: true,
```

```
                document: true
              }
          }
      },
      watch: {
          files: ['<%= jshint.files %>'],
          tasks: ['jshint', 'qunit']
      }
  });

  grunt.loadNpmTasks('grunt-contrib-uglify');
  grunt.loadNpmTasks('grunt-contrib-jshint');
  grunt.loadNpmTasks('grunt-contrib-qunit');
  grunt.loadNpmTasks('grunt-contrib-watch');
  grunt.loadNpmTasks('grunt-contrib-concat');

  grunt.registerTask('test', ['jshint', 'qunit']);

  grunt.registerTask('default', ['jshint', 'qunit', 'concat', 'uglify']);

};
```

The Gruntfile shown in Listing 1-7 is for a relatively simple project. We already find this example to be slightly unwieldy, but within larger projects we have seen this file balloon to many times this size. The result is an unreadable and difficult-to-maintain mess. Experienced developers would never write their code in a way that combines functionality from across unrelated areas into a single, monolithic file, so why should we approach our task runner any differently?

The secret to maintaining a sane Grunt structure lies with Grunt's `loadTasks()` function, as shown in Listing 1-6. In this example, the `tasks` argument refers to a `tasks` folder relative to our project's Gruntfile. Once this method is called, Grunt will load and execute each Node module it finds within this folder, passing along a reference to the `grunt` object each time. This behavior provides us with the opportunity to organize our project's Grunt configuration as a series of separate modules, each responsible for loading and configuring a single task or plugin. An example of one of these smaller modules is shown in Listing 1-8. This task can be executed by running `grunt uglify` from the command line.

Listing 1-8. Example Module (uglify.js) Within Our New tasks Folder

```
// example-tasks/tasks/uglify.js

module.exports = function(grunt) {

    grunt.loadNpmTasks('grunt-contrib-uglify');

    grunt.config('uglify', {
        'options': {
            'banner': '/*! <%= grunt.template.today("dd-mm-yyyy") %> */\n'
        },
        'dist': {
            'files': {
                'dist/app.min.js': ['src/index.js']
            }
        }
    });

};
```

Working with Tasks

As previously mentioned, tasks serve as the foundation on which Grunt is built—everything begins here. A Grunt plugin, as you'll soon discover, is nothing more than one or more tasks that have been packaged into a Node module and published via npm. We've already seen a few examples that demonstrate the creation of basic Grunt tasks, so let's take a look at some additional features that can help us get the most out of them.

Managing Configuration

Grunt's config() method serves as both a "getter" and a "setter" for configuration. In Listing 1-9, we see how a basic Grunt task can access its configuration through the use of this method.

Listing 1-9. Managing Configuration Within a Basic Grunt Task

```
module.exports = function(grunt) {

    grunt.config('basic-task', {
        'message': 'Hello, world.'
    });

    grunt.registerTask('basic-task', function() {
        grunt.log.writeln(grunt.config('basic-task.message'));
    });

};
```

Note   In Listing 1-9, "dot notation" is used for accessing nested configuration values. In the same way, dot notation can be used to set nested configuration values. If at any point Grunt encounters a path within the configuration object that does not exist, Grunt will create a new, empty object without throwing an error.

Task Descriptions

Over time, projects have a tendency to grow in complexity. With this additional complexity often come new Grunt tasks. As new tasks are added, it's often easy to lose track of what tasks are available, what they do, and how they are called. Fortunately, Grunt provides us with a way to address this problem by assigning descriptions to our tasks, as shown in Listing 1-10.

Listing 1-10. Assigning a Description to a Grunt Task

```
// example-task-description/Gruntfile.js

module.exports = function(grunt) {

    grunt.config('basic-task', {
        'message': 'Hello, world.'
    });

    grunt.registerTask('basic-task', 'This is an example task.', function() {
```

```
        grunt.log.writeln(grunt.config('basic-task.message'));
    });

    grunt.registerTask('default', 'This is the default task.', ['basic-task']);
};
```

By passing an additional argument to the registerTask() method, Grunt allows us to provide a description for the task being created. Grunt helpfully provides this information when help is requested from the command line, as shown in Listing 1-11, which includes an excerpt of the information Grunt provides.

Listing 1-11. Requesting Help from the Command Line

```
$ grunt -help
...
Available tasks
    basic-task  This is an example task.
       default  This is the default task.
...
```

Asynchronous Tasks

By default, Grunt tasks are expected to run synchronously. As soon as a task's function returns, it is considered finished. There will be times, however, when you find yourself interacting with other asynchronous methods within a task, which must first complete before your task can hand control back over to Grunt. The solution to this problem is shown in Listing 1-12. Within a task, a call to the async() method will notify Grunt that it executes asynchronously. The method will return a callback function to be called when our task has completed. Until this is done, Grunt will hold the execution of any additional tasks.

Listing 1-12. Asynchronous Grunt Task

```
// example-async/tasks/list-files.js

var glob = require('glob');

module.exports = function(grunt) {
```

```
grunt.registerTask('list-files', function() {

    /**
     * Grunt will wait until we call the `done()` function to indicate
       that our
     * asynchronous task is complete.
     */
    var done = this.async();

    glob('*', function(err, files) {
        if (err) {
            grunt.fail.fatal(err);
        }
        grunt.log.writeln(files);
        done();
    });

});
};
```

Task Dependencies

Complicated Grunt workflows are best thought of as a series of steps that work together to produce a final result. In such situations, it can often be helpful to specify that a task requires one or more separate tasks to precede it, as shown in Listing 1-13.

Listing 1-13. Declaring a Task Dependency

```
// example-task-dependency/tasks/step-two.js

module.exports = function(grunt) {
    grunt.registerTask('step-two', function() {
        grunt.task.requires('step-one');
    });
};
```

In this example, the step-two task requires that the step-one task run first before it can proceed. Any attempt to call step-two directly will result in an error, as shown in Listing 1-14.

Listing 1-14. Grunt Reporting an Error When a Task Is Called Before Any Tasks on Which It Depends Have Run

```
$ grunt step-two
Running "step-two" task
Warning: Required task "step-one" must be run first. Use --force to continue.

Aborted due to warnings.
```

Multi-Tasks

In addition to basic tasks, Grunt offers support for what it calls "multi-tasks." Multi-tasks are easily the most complicated aspect of Grunt, so if you find yourself confused at first, you're not alone. After reviewing a few examples, however, their purpose should start to come into focus—at which point you'll be well on your way toward mastering Grunt.

Before we go any further, let's take a look at a brief example (see Listing 1-15) that shows a Grunt multi-task, along with its configuration.

Listing 1-15. Grunt Multi-Task

```
// example-list-animals/tasks/list-animals.js

module.exports = function(grunt) {

    /**
     * Our multi-task's configuration object. In this example, 'mammals'
     * and 'birds' each represent what Grunt refers to as a 'target.'
     */
    grunt.config('list-animals', {
        'mammals': {
            'animals': ['Cat', 'Zebra', 'Koala', 'Kangaroo']
        },
        'birds': {
            'animals': ['Penguin', 'Sparrow', 'Eagle', 'Parrot']
```

```
        }
    });

    grunt.registerMultiTask('list-animals', function() {
        grunt.log.writeln('Target:', this.target);
        grunt.log.writeln('Data:', this.data);
    });

};
```

Multi-tasks are extremely flexible, in that they are designed to support multiple configurations (referred to as "targets") within a single project. The multi-task shown in Listing 1-15 has two targets: mammals and birds. This task can be run against a specific target as shown in Listing 1-16.

Listing 1-16. Running the Grunt Multi-Task Shown in Listing 1-15 Against a Specific Target

```
$ grunt list-animals:mammals
Running "list-animals:mammals" (list-animals) task
Target: mammals
Data: { animals: [ 'Cat', 'Zebra', 'Koala', 'Kangaroo' ] }

Done, without errors.
```

Multi-tasks can also be called without any arguments, in which case they are executed multiple times, once for each available target. Listing 1-17 shows the result of calling this task without specifying a target.

Listing 1-17. Running the Multi-Task Shown in Listing 1-15 Without Specifying a Target

```
$ grunt list-animals
Running "list-animals:mammals" (list-animals) task
Target: mammals
Data: { animals: [ 'Cat', 'Zebra', 'Koala', 'Kangaroo' ] }

Running "list-animals:birds" (list-animals) task
Target: birds
Data: { animals: [ 'Penguin', 'Sparrow', 'Eagle', 'Parrot' ] }
```

In this example, our multi-task ran twice, once for each available target (`mammals` and `birds`). Notice in Listing 1-15 that within our multi-task we referenced two properties: `this.target` and `this.data`. These properties allow our multi-task to fetch information about the target that it is currently running against.

Multi-Task Options

Within a multi-task's configuration object, any values stored under the `options` key (see Listing 1-18) receive special treatment.

Listing 1-18. Grunt Multi-Task with Configuration Options

```
// example-list-animals-options/tasks/list-animals.js

module.exports = function(grunt) {

    grunt.config('list-animals', {
        'options': {
            'format': 'array'
        },
        'mammals': {
            'options': {
                'format': 'json'
            },
            'animals': ['Cat', 'Zebra', 'Koala', 'Kangaroo']
        },
        'birds': {
            'animals': ['Penguin', 'Sparrow', 'Eagle', 'Parrot']
        }
    });

    grunt.registerMultiTask('list-animals', function() {

        var options = this.options();

        switch (options.format) {
            case 'array':
                grunt.log.writeln(this.data.animals);
            break;
```

```
        case 'json':
            grunt.log.writeln(JSON.stringify(this.data.animals));
        break;
        default:
            grunt.fail.fatal('Unknown format: ' + options.format);
        break;
    }

  });

};
```

Multi-task options provide developers with a mechanism for defining global options for a task, which can then be overridden at the target level. In this example, a global format in which to list animals (`'array'`) is defined at the task level. The mammals target has chosen to override this value (`'json'`), while the birds task has not. As a result, mammals will be displayed as JSON, while birds will be shown as an array due to its inheritance of the global option.

The vast majority of Grunt plugins that you will encounter are configurable as multi-tasks. The flexibility afforded by this approach allows you to apply the same task differently under different circumstances. A frequently encountered scenario involves the creation of separate targets for each build environment. For example, when compiling an application, you may want to modify the behavior of a task based on whether you are compiling for a local development environment or in preparation for release to production.

Configuration Templates

Grunt configuration objects support the embedding of template strings, which can then be used to reference other configuration values. The template format favored by Grunt follows that of the Lodash and Underscore utility libraries, which are covered in further detail in a later chapter. For an example of how this feature can be put to use, see Listings 1-19 and 1-20.

Listing 1-19. Sample Gruntfile That Stores the Contents of Its Project's `package.json` File Under the `pkg` Key Within Grunt's Configuration Object

```
// example-templates/Gruntfile.js

module.exports = function(grunt) {
    grunt.initConfig({
        'pkg': grunt.file.readJSON('package.json')
    });
    grunt.loadTasks('tasks');
    grunt.registerTask('default', ['test']);
};
```

Listing 1-20. A Subsequently Loaded Task with Its Own Configuration That Is Able to Reference Other Configuration Values Through the Use of Templates

```
// example-templates/tasks/test.js

module.exports = function(grunt) {
    grunt.config('test', {
        'banner': '<%= pkg.name %>-<%= pkg.version %>'
    });
    grunt.registerTask('test', function() {
        grunt.log.writeln(grunt.config('test.banner'));
    });
};
```

Listing 1-19 shows a sample Gruntfile that loads the contents of the project's `package.json` file using one of several built-in methods for interacting with the file system that are discussed in further detail later in the chapter. The contents of this file are then stored under the `pkg` key of Grunt's configuration object. In Listing 1-20, we see a task that is able to directly reference this information through the use of configuration templates.

Command-Line Options

Additional options can be passed to Grunt using the following format:

```
$ grunt count --count=5
```

The example shown in Listing 1-21 demonstrates how a Grunt task can access this information via the `grunt.option()` method. The result of calling this task is shown in Listing 1-22.

Listing 1-21. Simple Grunt Task That Counts to the Specified Number

```
// example-options/tasks/count.js

module.exports = function(grunt) {

    grunt.registerTask('count', function() {
        var limit = parseInt(grunt.option('limit'), 10);
        if (isNaN(limit)) grunt.fail.fatal('A limit must be provided (e.g.
        --limit=10)');
        console.log('Counting to: %s', limit);
        for (var i = 1; i <= limit; i++) console.log(i);
    });

};
```

Listing 1-22. Result of Calling the Task Shown in Listing 1-21

```
$ grunt count --limit=5
Running "count" task
Counting to: 5
1
2
3
4
5

Done, without errors.
```

Providing Feedback

Grunt provides a number of built-in methods for providing feedback to users during the execution of tasks, a few of which you have already seen used throughout this chapter. While we won't list all of them here, several useful examples can be found in Table 1-1.

Table 1-1. *Useful Grunt Methods for Displaying Feedback to the User*

Method	Description
grunt.log.write()	Prints a message to the console
grunt.log.writeln()	Prints a message to the console, followed by a newline character
grunt.log.oklns()	Prints a success message to the console, followed by a newline character
grunt.log.error()	Prints an error message to the console, followed by a newline character
grunt.log.subhead()	Prints a bold message to the console, followed by a newline character
grunt.log.debug()	Prints a message to the console only if the - -debug flag was passed

Handling Errors

During the course of task execution, errors can occur. When they do, it's important to know how to appropriately handle them. When faced with an error, developers should make use of Grunt's error API, which is easy to use, as it provides just two methods, shown in Table 1-2.

Table 1-2. *Methods Available via Grunt's* error *API*

Method	Description
grunt.fail.warn()	Displays a warning and aborts Grunt immediately. Tasks will continue to run if the - -force option is passed
grunt.fail.fatal()	Displays a warning and aborts Grunt immediately

Interacting with the File System

As a build tool, it comes as no surprise that the majority of Grunt's plugins interact with the file system in one way or another. Given its importance, Grunt provides helpful abstractions that allow developers to interact with the file system with a minimal amount of boilerplate code.

While we won't list all of them here, Table 1-3 shows several of the most frequently used methods within Grunt's file API.

Table 1-3. *Useful Grunt Methods for Interacting with the File System*

Method	Description
grunt.file.read()	Reads and returns file's contents
grunt.file.readJSON()	Reads a file's contents, parsing the data as JSON, and returns the result
grunt.file.write()	Writes the specified contents to a file, creating intermediate directories, if necessary
grunt.file.copy()	Copies a source file to a destination path, creating intermediate directories, if necessary
grunt.file.delete()	Deletes the specified file path; deletes files and folders recursively
grunt.file.mkdir()	Creates a directory, along with any missing intermediate directories
grunt.file.recurse()	Recurses into a directory, executing a callback for every file that is found

Source-Destination Mappings

Many Grunt tasks that interact with the file system rely heavily on the concept of source-destination mappings, a format that describes a set of files to be processed and a corresponding destination for each. Such mappings can be tedious to construct, but thankfully Grunt provides helpful shortcuts that address this need.

Imagine for a moment that you are working on a project with a public folder located at its root. Within this folder are the files to be served over the Web once the project is deployed, as shown in Listing 1-23.

Listing 1-23. Contents of an Imaginary Project's public Folder

```
// example-iterate1
```

```
.
└── public
    └── images
        ├── cat1.jpg
        ├── cat2.jpg
        └── cat3.png
```

As you can see, our project has an images folder containing three files. Knowing this, let's take a look at a few ways in which Grunt can help us iterate through these files.

In Listing 1-24, we find a Grunt multi-task similar to those we've recently been introduced to. The key difference here is the presence of an src key within our task's configuration. Grunt gives special attention to multi-task configurations that contain this key, as we'll soon see. When the src key is present, Grunt provides a this.files property within our task that provides an array containing paths to every matching file that is found via the node-glob module. The output from this task is shown in Listing 1-25.

Listing 1-24. Grunt Multi-Task with a Configuration Object Containing an src Key

```
// example-iterate1/tasks/list-files.js

module.exports = function(grunt) {

    grunt.config('list-files', {
        'images': {
            'src': ['public/**/*.jpg', 'public/**/*.png']
        }
    });

    grunt.registerMultiTask('list-files', function() {
        this.files.forEach(function(files) {
            grunt.log.writeln('Source:', files.src);
        });
    });

};
```

Listing 1-25. Output from the Grunt Task Shown in Listing 1-24

```
$ grunt list-files
Running "list-files:images" (list-files) task
Source: [ 'public/images/cat1.jpg',
  'public/images/cat2.jpg',
  'public/images/cat3.png' ]

Done, without errors.
```

The combination of the `src` configuration property and the `this.files` multi-task property provides developers with a concise syntax for iterating over multiple files. The contrived example that we've just looked at is fairly simple, but Grunt also provides additional options for tackling more complex scenarios. Let's take a look.

As opposed to the src key that was used to configure our task in Listing 1-24, the example in Listing 1-26 demonstrates the use of the files array—a slightly more verbose, but more powerful format for selecting files. This format accepts additional options that allow us to more finely tune our selection. Of particular importance is the expand option, as you'll see in Listing 1-27. Pay close attention to how the output differs from that of Listing 1-26, due to the use of the expand option.

Listing 1-26. Iterating Through Files Using the "Files Array" Format

```
// example-iterate2/tasks/list-files.js

module.exports = function(grunt) {

    grunt.config('list-files', {
        'images': {
            'files': [
                {
                    'cwd': 'public',
                    'src': ['**/*.jpg', '**/*.png'],
                    'dest': 'tmp',
                    'expand': true
                }
            ]
        }
    });

    grunt.registerMultiTask('list-files', function() {
        this.files.forEach(function(files) {
            grunt.log.writeln('Source:', files.src);
            grunt.log.writeln('Destination:', files.dest);
        });
    });

};
```

Listing 1-27. Output from the Grunt Task Shown in Listing 1-26

```
$ grunt list-files
Running "list-files:images" (list-files) task
Source: [ 'public/images/cat1.jpg' ]
Destination: tmp/images/cat1.jpg
Source: [ 'public/images/cat2.jpg' ]
Destination: tmp/images/cat2.jpg

Done, without errors.
```

The expand option, when paired with the dest option, instructs Grunt to iterate through our task's this.files.forEach loop once for every entry it finds, within which we can find a corresponding dest property. Using this approach, we can easily create source-destination mappings that can be used to copy (or move) files from one location to another.

Watching for File Changes

One of Grunt's most popular plugins, grunt-contrib-watch, gives Grunt the ability to run predefined tasks whenever files that match a specified pattern are created, modified, or deleted. When combined with other tasks, grunt-contrib-watch enables developers to create powerful workflows that automate actions such as

- Checking JavaScript code for errors (i.e., "linting")
- Compiling Sass stylesheets
- Running unit tests

Let's take a look at a few examples that demonstrate such workflows put into action.

Automated JavaScript Linting

Listing 1-28 shows a basic Grunt setup similar to those already shown in this chapter. A default task is registered which serves as an alias to the watch task, allowing us to start watching for changes within our project by simply running $ grunt from the command line. In this example, Grunt will watch for changes within the src folder. As they occur, the jshint task is triggered, which will scan our project's src folder in search of JavaScript errors.

Listing 1-28. Automatically Checking for JavaScript Errors As Changes Occur

```javascript
// example-watch-hint/Gruntfile.js

module.exports = function(grunt) {
    grunt.loadTasks('tasks');
    grunt.registerTask('default', ['watch']);
};

// example-watch-hint/tasks/jshint.js

module.exports = function(grunt) {

    grunt.loadNpmTasks('grunt-contrib-jshint');

    grunt.config('jshint', {
        'options': {
            'globalstrict': true,
            'node': true,
            'scripturl': true,
            'browser': true,
            'jquery': true
        },
        'all': [
            'src/**/*.js'
        ]
    });

};

// example-watch-hint/tasks/watch.js

module.exports = function(grunt) {

    grunt.loadNpmTasks('grunt-contrib-watch');

    grunt.config('watch', {
        'js': {
            'files': [
                'src/**/*'
```

```
            ],
            'tasks': ['jshint'],
            'options': {
                'spawn': true
            }
        }
    });
};
```

Automated Sass Stylesheet Compilation

Listing 1-29 shows an example in which Grunt is instructed to watch our project for changes. This time, however, instead of watching our JavaScript, Grunt is configured to watch our project's Sass stylesheets. As changes occur, the `grunt-contrib-compass` plugin is called, which compiles our stylesheets into their final form.

Listing 1-29. Automatically Compiling Sass Stylesheets As Changes Occur

```
// example-watch-sass/Gruntfile.js

module.exports = function(grunt) {
    grunt.loadTasks('tasks');
    grunt.registerTask('default', ['watch']);
};

// example-watch-sass/tasks/compass.js

module.exports = function(grunt) {

    grunt.loadNpmTasks('grunt-contrib-compass');

    grunt.config('compass', {
        'all': {
            'options': {
                'httpPath': '/',
                'cssDir': 'public/css',
                'sassDir': 'scss',
                'imagesDir': 'public/images',
                'relativeAssets': true,
```

```
            'outputStyle': 'compressed'
        }
    }
    });

};

// example-watch-compass/tasks/watch.js

module.exports = function(grunt) {

    grunt.loadNpmTasks('grunt-contrib-watch');

    grunt.config('watch', {
        'scss': {
            'files': [
                'scss/**/*'
            ],
            'tasks': ['compass'],
            'options': {
                'spawn': true
            }
        }
    });

};
```

Note   In order for this example to function, you must install Compass, an open source CSS authoring framework. You can find additional information on how to install Compass at `http://compass-style.org/install`.

Automated Unit Testing

Our final example regarding `grunt-contrib-watch` concerns unit testing. In Listing 1-30, we see a Gruntfile that watches our project's JavaScript for changes. As these changes occur, our project's unit tests are immediately triggered with the help of Grunt's `grunt-mocha-test` plugin.

Listing 1-30. Automatically Running Unit Tests As Changes Occur

```javascript
// example-watch-test/Gruntfile.js

module.exports = function(grunt) {
    grunt.loadTasks('tasks');
    grunt.registerTask('default', ['watch']);
};

// example-watch-test/tasks/mochaTest.js

module.exports = function(grunt) {

    grunt.loadNpmTasks('grunt-mocha-test');

    grunt.config('mochaTest', {
        'test': {
            'options': {
                'reporter': 'spec'
            },
            'src': ['test/**/*.js']
        }
    });

};


// example-watch-test/tasks/watch.js

module.exports = function(grunt) {

    grunt.loadNpmTasks('grunt-contrib-watch');

    grunt.config('watch', {
        'scss': {
            'files': [
                'src/**/*.js'
            ],
            'tasks': ['mochaTest'],
            'options': {
                'spawn': true
```

```
        }
      }
   });
};
```

Creating Plugins

A large library of community-supported plugins is what makes Grunt truly shine—a library that will allow you to start benefitting from Grunt immediately, without the need to create complex tasks from scratch. If you need to automate a build process within your project, there's a good chance that someone has already done the "grunt" work (zing!) for you.

In this section, you'll discover how you can contribute back to the community with Grunt plugins of your own creation.

Getting Started

One of the first things you'll want to do is create a public GitHub repository in which to store your new plugin. The example that we will be referencing is included with the source code that accompanies this book.

Once your new repository is ready, clone it to your computer. Next, initialize Grunt within it by following the same steps that were outlined earlier in this chapter's "Adding Grunt to Your Project" section. Afterward, the file structure of your new Grunt plugin should resemble that shown in Listing 1-31.

Listing 1-31. File Structure of Your New Grunt Plugin

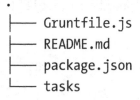
```
.
├── Gruntfile.js
├── README.md
├── package.json
└── tasks
```

Note   The most important point to note here is that there is no special structure or knowledge required (apart from what has already been covered in this chapter) for the creation of Grunt plugins. The process mirrors that of integrating Grunt into an existing project—the creation of a Gruntfile that loads tasks, along with the tasks themselves. Once published to npm, other Grunt projects will be able to load your plugin in the same way that other plugins have been referenced throughout this chapter.

Creating the Task

By way of an example, let's create a Grunt plugin capable of generating a report that details the type, size, and number of files contained within a project. An example demonstrating the configuration for this plugin is shown in Listing 1-32.

Listing 1-32. Example Demonstrating the Configuration of Our Plugin

```
// example-plugin/Gruntfile.js

module.exports = function(grunt) {

    grunt.config('file-report', {
        'options': {
        },
        'public': {
            'src': ['public/**/*']
        },
        'images': {
            'src': ['public/**/*.jpg', 'public/**/*.png', 'public/**/*.gif']
        }
    });

    grunt.loadNpmTasks('grunt-file-reporter');
    grunt.registerTask('default', ['file-report']);

};
```

The source code for our plugin is shown in Listing 1-33. Within our plugin, a Grunt multi-task named `file-report` is registered. When called, the task will iterate through the various target files that were specified in Listing 1-32. As it does so, the plugin will compile a report that details the type, number, and size of the files it finds.

Listing 1-33. Source Code for Our Plugin

```
// example-plugin/node_modules/grunt-file-reporter/Gruntfile.js

var fs = require('fs');
var filesize = require('filesize');
var _ = require('lodash');
_.mixin(require('underscore.string'));

module.exports = function(grunt) {

    var mime = require('mime');
    var Table = require('cli-table');

    grunt.registerMultiTask('file-report', 'Generates a report of file
    types & sizes used within a project', function() {

        var report = {
            'mimeTypes': {},
            'largest': null,
            'smallest': null
        };

        var table = new Table({
            'head': ['Content Type', 'Files Found', 'Total Size',
            'Average Size', 'Largest', 'Smallest']
        });
        var addFile = function(file) {
            if (grunt.file.isDir(file)) return;
            var mimeType = mime.lookup(file);
            if (!report.mimeTypes[mimeType]) {
                report.mimeTypes[mimeType] = {
                    'count': 0,
                    'sizes': [],
```

```
                        'largest': null,
                        'smallest': null,
                        'oldest': null,
                        'newest': null
                };
        }
        var details = report.mimeTypes[mimeType];
        details.count++;
        var stats = fs.statSync(file);
        details.sizes.push(stats.size);
        if (!details.largest || stats.size > details.largest.size) {
                details.largest = { 'file': file, 'size': stats.size };
        }
        if (!report.largest || stats.size > report.largest.size) {
                report.largest = { 'file': file, 'size': stats.size };
        }
        if (!details.smallest || stats.size < details.smallest.size) {
                details.smallest = { 'file': file, 'size': stats.size };
        }
        if (!report.smallest || stats.size < report.smallest.size) {
                report.smallest = { 'file': file, 'size': stats.size };
        }
};

var sum = function(arr) {
        return arr.reduce(function(a, b) {
                return a + b;
        });
};

var displayReport = function() {
        var totalSum = 0;
        var totalFiles = 0;
        var totalSizes = [];
        _.each(report.mimeTypes, function(data, mType) {
                var fileSum = sum(data.sizes);
```

```
            totalSum += fileSum;
            totalFiles += data.sizes.length;
            totalSizes = totalSizes.concat(data.sizes);
            table.push([mType, data.count, filesize(fileSum),
                filesize(fileSum / data.sizes.length),
                _.sprintf('%s (%s)', data.largest.file, filesize(data.
                largest.size)),
                _.sprintf('%s (%s)', data.smallest.file, filesize(data.
                smallest.size)),
            ]);
        });
        table.push(['-', totalFiles, filesize(totalSum),
            filesize(totalSum / totalSizes.length),
            _.sprintf('%s (%s)', report.largest.file, filesize(report.
            largest.size)),
            _.sprintf('%s (%s)', report.smallest.file, filesize(report.
            smallest.size)),
        ]);
        console.log(table.toString());
    };

    this.files.forEach(function(files) {
        files.src.forEach(addFile);
    });

    displayReport();

  });

};
```

The output generated by our plugin's file-report task is shown in Figure 1-1.

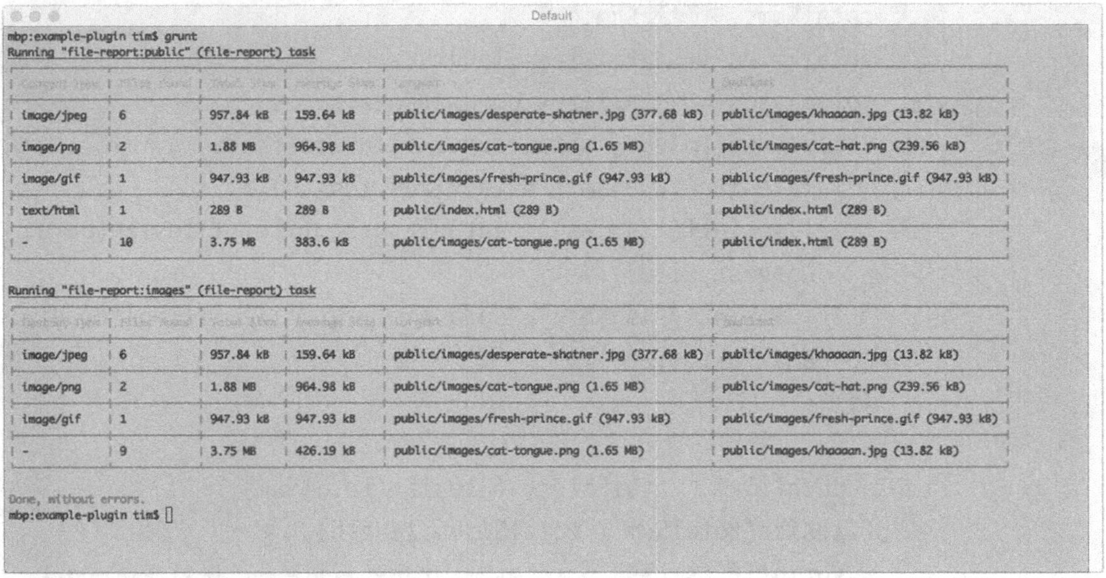

Figure 1-1. *The output generated by the* file-report *task*

Publishing to npm

Once our plugin is ready and our Git repository is updated with the latest code, the final step toward making it available to others is publishing it via npm:

```
$ npm publish
```

Note   If this is your first time publishing a module to npm, you will be asked to create an account.

Summary

In this chapter, we've looked at how Grunt provides developers with a powerful toolkit for automating many of the repetitive, tedious tasks that often accompany software development. You've discovered

- What makes Grunt tick (tasks, plugins, and configuration objects)
- How to configure tasks and plugins

- How to use many of the helpful built-in utilities that Grunt makes available for providing user feedback and interacting with the file system

- How to create and share your own Grunt plugins

Related Resources

- Grunt: `http://gruntjs.com`

- JSHint: `http://jshint.com`

- grunt-contrib-watch: `https://github.com/gruntjs/grunt-contrib-watch`

- grunt-contrib-jshint: `https://github.com/gruntjs/grunt-contrib-jshint`

- grunt-contrib-uglify: `https://github.com/gruntjs/grunt-contrib-uglify`

- grunt-contrib-compass: `https://github.com/gruntjs/grunt-contrib-compass`

- grunt-mocha-test: `https://github.com/pghalliday/grunt-mocha-test`

- Syntactically Awesome Stylesheets (Sass): `http://sass-lang.com`

- Compass: `http://compass-style.org`

CHAPTER 2

Yeoman

One only needs two tools in life: WD-40 to make things go, and duct tape to make them stop.

—G. Weilacher

The development community has witnessed a role reversal of sorts take place in recent years. Web applications, once considered by many to be second-class citizens in comparison to their native counterparts, have largely supplanted traditional desktop applications, thanks in large part to the widespread adoption of modern web development technologies and the rise of the mobile Web. But as web applications have grown increasingly sophisticated, so too have the tools on which they rely and the steps required to bootstrap them into existence.

The topic of this chapter, Yeoman, is a popular project "scaffolding" tool that helps to alleviate this problem by automating the tedious tasks associated with bootstrapping new applications off the ground. Yeoman provides a mechanism for creating reusable templates that describe a project's initial file structure, HTML, third-party libraries, and task runner configurations. These templates, which can be shared with the wider development community via npm, allow developers to bootstrap new projects that follow agreed-upon best practices in a matter of minutes.

In this chapter, you will learn how to

- Install Yeoman

- Take advantage of Yeoman generators that have already been published by the community

- Contribute back to the community with your own Yeoman generators

© Sufyan bin Uzayr, Nicholas Cloud, Tim Ambler 2019
S. bin Uzayr et al., *JavaScript Frameworks for Modern Web Development*,
https://doi.org/10.1007/978-1-4842-4995-6_2

Installing Yeoman

Yeoman's command-line utility, yo, is available via npm. If you have not already installed Yeoman, you should do so before you continue, as shown in Listing 2-1.

Listing 2-1. Installing the yo Command-Line Utility via npm

```
$ npm install -g yo
$ yo –version
2.0.5
```

Creating Your First Project

Yeoman allows developers to quickly create the initial structure of an application through the use of reusable templates, which Yeoman refers to as "generators." To better understand how this process can improve your workflow, let's create a new project with the help of the modernweb generator that was created specifically for this chapter. Afterward, we will look at how this generator was created, providing you with the knowledge you need to create and share your own custom Yeoman generators with the wider development community.

The generator we will be using will create the initial foundations of a project that uses the following tools and libraries:

- Grunt

- Bower

- jQuery

- AngularJS

- Browserify

- Compass

Yeoman generators are installed as global npm modules. That being the case, the command for installing our generator should look familiar:

```
$ npm install -g generator-modernweb
```

Note   This generator's name is prefixed with `generator-`, which is an important convention that all Yeoman generators must follow. At runtime, Yeoman will determine what (if any) generators have been installed by searching for global modules whose names follow this format.

With our generator now installed, we can move forward with setting up our first project. First, we create a new folder to contain it. Afterward, we instruct Yeoman to create a new project based on the generator that we just installed. Listing 2-2 shows these steps in action, along with several questions the generator is designed to prompt you with.

Listing 2-2. Creating Our First Project with the modernweb Generator

```
$ mkdir my-app
$ cd my-app
$ yo modernweb

? Project Title: My Project
? Package Name: my-project
? Project Description: My awesome project
? Project Author: John Doe
? Express Port: 7000
```

After responding to the generator's questions (you can safely accept the defaults), Yeoman will move forward with creating the project. Afterward, we can easily build and launch it using the project's default Grunt task, which our generator has conveniently set up for us (see Listing 2-3).

Listing 2-3. Our New Project's Default Grunt Task Will Trigger Various Build Steps and Open the Project Within Our Browser

```
$ grunt
Running "concat:app" (concat) task
File public/dist/libs.js created.

Running "compass:app" (compass) task
unchanged scss/style.scss
Compilation took 0.002s
```

41

```
Running "browserify" task

Running "concurrent:app" (concurrent) task
Running "watch" task
Waiting...
Running "open:app" (open) task
Running "server" task
Server is now listening on port: 7000

Done, without errors.
```

As you can see, our new project's default Grunt task executes several additional build steps for us:

- JavaScript libraries are compiled into a single, minified script.

- Sass stylesheets are compiled.

- The source code of the application itself is compiled via Browserify.

- An instance of Express is created to serve our project.

- Various watch scripts are initialized that will automatically recompile our project as changes are made.

The final action of our project's default Grunt task will be to launch our project within a new browser window, as shown in Figure 2-1.

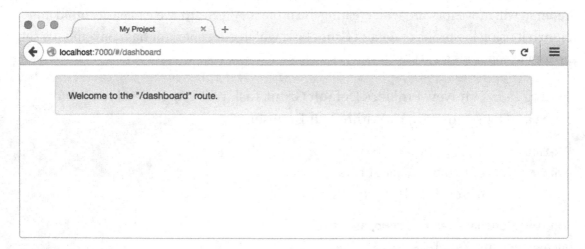

Figure 2-1. *Our new project's home page, opened for us by the default Grunt task*

Now that our new project is ready for further development, let's take a few moments to become familiar with the various templates, scripts, and Grunt tasks that our generator has put in place for us, paying special attention to the contents of these files:

- `bower.json`

- `Gruntfile.js`

- `package.json`

- `public/index.html`

With the help of Yeoman's support for user prompts and templates (which we will discuss in more detail in the next section), the generator has merged our answers to its initial questions with the contents of our project's files, where appropriate. For instance, the values for `name`, `description`, and `author` within our project's `package.json` file have been set for us (see Listing 2-4).

Listing 2-4. Contents of Our Project's `package.json` File

```
// package.json

{
  "name": "my-project",
  "description": "My awesome project",
  "author": "John Doe",
  "files": [],
  "keywords": [],
  "dependencies": {},
  "browserify": {
    "transform": [
      "brfs",
      "bulkify",
      "folderify"
    ]
  },
  "browser": {}
}
```

Subcommands

In their simplest form, generators act as configurable project templates that simplify the creation of new projects, but that's not their only purpose. In addition to assisting with the initial creation of new projects, generators can also include other commands that project maintainers will find useful throughout development.

In Listing 2-2, we used the `modernweb` generator to create a new single-page application built using the AngularJS framework. If you are unfamiliar with Angular, don't worry—the particulars of this framework are unimportant for now. What is important, however, is the contents of the project's `public/app/routes` folder. Notice that a single folder, `dashboard`, has been created for us at this location. The contents of this folder are shown in Listing 2-5.

Listing 2-5. Contents of Our Project's `public/app/routes/dashboard` Folder

```
.
├── index.js
└── template.html
```

```
// public/app/routes/dashboard/index.js
```

```javascript
module.exports = {
    'route': '/dashboard',
    'controller': function() {
    },
    'templateUrl': '/app/routes/dashboard/template.html',
    'resolve': {}
};
```

```
// public/app/routes/dashboard/template.html
```

```html
<div class="well">
    Welcome to the "/dashboard" route.
</div>
```

This project has been set up such that each folder within `public/app/routes` defines a different "hashbang" route within the application. In this example, the project's `dashboard` folder defines a route that can be accessed at `http://localhost:7000/#/dashboard`. Knowing this, suppose that we wanted to add a new `users` route to our application. To do so, we could manually create the necessary files at the appropriate location. Alternatively, we could use an additional command provided by our generator that simplifies this process (see Listing 2-6).

Listing 2-6. Example of Calling the `route` Sub-generator to Automate the Process of Creating New Routes Within Our Angular Application

```
$ yo modernweb:route users
   create public/app/routes/users/index.js
   create public/app/routes/users/template.html
Route `users` created.
```

After running this command, refer to the project's `/public/app/routes` folder and note the existence of a new folder named `users`. Within this folder, our Yeoman generator has taken care of creating the appropriate files for us. If you happen to still have the server that we created in Listing 2-3 running, you should also be able to see that the watch scripts that were started for us have detected this change and automatically recompiled our application (see Listing 2-7).

Listing 2-7. Grunt Automatically Recompiles Application As Changes Are Made

```
>> File "public/app/routes/users" added.
Running "browserify" task
Done, without errors.
```

Creating Your First Generator

The remainder of this chapter will focus on the creation of a custom Yeoman generator—the same one used in the previous section to bootstrap a new project built around AngularJS (among other tools). Afterward, you will be well prepared to begin creating your own generators that will allow you to quickly get up and running with workflows that meet your specific needs.

Yeoman Generators Are Node Modules

A Yeoman generator is nothing more than a simple Node module that follows Yeoman's prescribed guidelines. As such, the first step in creating a generator is the creation of a new Node module. Listing 2-8 shows the required commands, along with the resulting `package.json` file.

Listing 2-8. Creating a New Node Module to Contain the Contents of Our First Yeoman Generator

```
$ mkdir generator-example
$ cd generator-example
$ npm init

// generator-example/package.json
{
  "name": "generator-example",
  "version": "1.0.0",
  "description": "An example Yeoman generator",
  "files": [],
  "keywords": [
    "yeoman-generator"
  ],
  "dependencies": {}
}
```

> **Note**   Although we are following the same steps that were used to create the `modernweb` generator that was referenced earlier in this chapter, we are assigning a different name to our new module, so as not to conflict with the one that has already been installed. Also note the inclusion of `yeoman-generator` within our module's list of keywords. Yeoman's web site maintains a list of every generator available within npm, making it easy for developers to find preexisting generators to suit their needs. If a generator is to be included within this list, it must include this keyword, along with a description in its `package.json` file.

Yeoman generators have the option of relying on external dependencies, as is the case with any other Node module. At a bare minimum, however, every generator must specify the `yeoman-generator` module as a local dependency. This module will provide us with the core functionality provided by Yeoman for creating user interactions, interacting with the file system, and other important tasks. This module is installed as a local dependency using the following command:

```
$ npm install yeoman-generator --save
```

Sub-generators

Yeoman generators consist of one or more commands, each of which can be called separately from the command line. These commands, which Yeoman refers to as "sub-generators," are defined within folders that exist at the root level of the module. For some additional context, refer back to Listing 2-2, in which we created a new project based off of the `modernweb` generator by running `$ yo modernweb` from the command line. In that example, we did not specify a command—we simply passed Yeoman the name of a generator. As a result, Yeoman executed that generator's *default* sub-generator, which by convention is always named `app`. We could have accomplished the same thing by running this command:

```
$ yo modernweb:app
```

To better understand how this works, let's move forward with creating our generator's default `app` sub-generator. We do so in four steps:

1. Create a folder named `app` at the root level of our module.

2. Create a folder named `templates` within our new `app` folder.

3. Place various files within our `templates` folder that we want to copy into the target project (e.g., HTML files, Grunt tasks, etc.).

4. Create the script shown in Listing 2-9, which is responsible for driving the functionality for this command.

Listing 2-9. Contents of Our Generator's Default app Command ("Sub-generator")

```javascript
// generator-example/app/index.js

var generators = require('yeoman-generator');

/**
 * We create our generator by exporting a class that extends
 * from Yeoman's `Base` class.
 */
module.exports = generators.Base.extend({

    'prompting': function() {

    /**
     * Indicates that this function will execute asynchronously. Yeoman
     * will wait until we call the `done()` function before continuing.
     */
        var done = this.async();

    /**
     * Our generator's `prompt` method (inherited from Yeoman's `Base`
     * class) allows us to define a series of questions to prompt the
     * user with.
     */
        this.prompt([
            {
                'type': 'input',
                'name': 'title',
                'message': 'Project Title',
                'default': 'My Project',
                'validate': function(title) {
                    return (title.length > 0);
                }
            },
            {
                'type': 'input',
                'name': 'package_name',
```

```
        'message': 'Package Name',
        'default': 'my-project',
        'validate': function(name) {
            return (name.length > 0 && /^[a-z0-9\-]+$/i.test(name));
        },
        'filter': function(name) {
            return name.toLowerCase();
        }
    },
    {

        'type': 'input',
        'name': 'description',
        'message': 'Project Description',
        'default': 'My awesome project',
        'validate': function(description) {
            return (description.length > 0);
        }
    },
    {

        'type': 'input',
        'name': 'author',
        'message': 'Project Author',
        'default': 'John Doe',
        'validate': function(author) {
            return (author.length > 0);
        }
    },
    {

        'type': 'input',
        'name': 'port',
        'message': 'Express Port',
        'default': 7000,
        'validate': function(port) {
            port = parseInt(port, 10);
            return (!isNaN(port) && port > 0);
```

```
            }
        }
    ], function(answers) {
        this._answers = answers;
        done();
    }.bind(this));

},

'writing': function() {

  /**
    * Copies files from our sub-generator's `templates` folder to the target
    * project. The contents of each file is processed as a Lodash template
    * before being written to the disk.
    */
    this.fs.copyTpl(
    this.templatePath('**/*'),
    this.destinationPath(),
    this._answers
     );

    this.fs.copyTpl(
        this.templatePath('pkg.json'),
        this.destinationPath('package.json'),
        this._answers
    );

    this.fs.delete(this.destinationPath('pkg.json'));

    this.fs.copyTpl(
     this.templatePath('.bowerrc'),
     this.destinationPath('.bowerrc'),
     this._answers
    );
```

```
/**
 * Writes a Yeoman configuration file to the target project's folder.
 */
    this.config.save();

},

'install': function() {

 /**
  * Installs various npm modules within the project folder and updates
  * `package.json` accordingly.
  */
    this.npmInstall([
        'express', 'lodash', 'underscore.string', 'browserify',
        'grunt', 'grunt-contrib-concat', 'grunt-contrib-watch',
        'grunt-contrib-compass', 'grunt-concurrent', 'bulk-require',
        'brfs', 'bulkify', 'folderify', 'grunt-open'
    ], {
        'saveDev': false
    });
 /**
  * Installs dependencies defined within `bower.json`.
  */
    this.bowerInstall();

},

'end': function() {
    this.log('Your project is ready.');
}

});
```

The contents of our generator's app folder are shown in Figure 2-2.

Figure 2-2. *The contents of our generator's app folder. The contents of the* `templates` *folder will be copied into the target project.*

In Listing 2-9, our generator's default `app` command is created by exporting a class that extends from Yeoman's `Base` class. Within this class, four instance methods are defined:

- `prompting()`

- `writing()`

- `install()`

- `end()`

These method names play an important role during execution (they were not arbitrarily chosen). When Yeoman runs a generator, it searches for prototype methods whose names match those listed here:

- `initializing()`: Initialization methods (checking project state, getting configs).

- `prompting()`: Prompting the user for information.

- `configuring()`: Saving configuration files.

- `default()`: Prototype methods with names *not* included within this list will be executed during this step.

- `writing()`: Write operations specific to this generator occur here.

- `conflicts()`: Conflicts are handled here (used internally by Yeoman).

- `install()`: Installation procedures occur here (npm, bower).

- `end()`: Last function to be called. Cleanup/closing messages.

Once Yeoman has compiled a list of the various prototype methods that exist within our generator, it will execute them in the priority shown in the preceding list.

Lodash Templates

In Listing 2-9, Yeoman's `fs.copyTpl()` method was used to copy files from our sub-generator's `templates` folder to the target project. This method differs from Yeoman's `fs.copy()` method, in that it also processes each file it finds as a Lodash template. Listing 2-10 shows the contents of our sub-generator's `templates/pkg.json` file, which will be processed in this way before being saved to the folder of the new project as `package.json`.

Listing 2-10. Contents of Our Sub-generator's `templates/pkg.json` File

```
// generator-example/app/templates/pkg.json

{
  "name": "<%= package_name %>",
  "description": "<%= description %>",
  "author": "<%= author %>",
  "files": [],
  "keywords": [],
  "dependencies": {},
  "browserify": {
    "transform": [
      "brfs",
      "bulkify",
      "folderify"
    ]
```

```
  },
  "browser": {}
}
```

Note   The process by which Yeoman generators can modify their behavior and alter the contents of templates based on a user's answers to prompts opens up a lot of exciting possibilities. It allows for the creation of new projects that are dynamically configured according to a user's specific needs. It's this aspect of Yeoman, more than any other, that makes the tool truly useful.

We're now ready to create our first project using our new generator. To do so, open a new terminal window and create a folder to contain it. Next, move into the new folder and run the generator, as shown in Listing 2-11.

Listing 2-11. Running Our New Generator for the First Time

```
$ mkdir new-project
$ cd new-project
$ yo example

Error example

You don't seem to have a generator with the name example installed.
You can see available generators with npm search yeoman-generator and then
install the
with npm install [name].
```

Obviously, this isn't the result we were hoping for. To understand what caused this error, recall from earlier in the chapter that when Yeoman is called, it locates generators by searching for modules whose names begin with generator- that have been installed in the global context. As a result, Yeoman is currently unaware of the existence of our new generator. Fortunately, npm provides a handy command that will solve this problem for us. The npm link command creates a symbolic link (symlink) between our new module and Node's global modules folder. The command is executed at the root level of our new module (see Listing 2-12).

Listing 2-12. Creating a Symbolic Link with the npm link Command

```
$ npm link
/Users/tim/.nvm/v0.10.33/lib/node_modules/generator-example -> /opt/
generator-example
```

Npm's link command creates a symbolic link between the folder in which it is run and the folder in which globally installed Node modules are stored. By running this command, we place a reference to our new generator in a location that Yeoman can find. With this link in place, let's run our generator again (see Listing 2-13).

Listing 2-13. Successfully Running Our New Generator for the First Time

```
$ yo example

? Project Title: My Project
? Package Name: my-project
? Project Description: My awesome project
? Project Author: John Doe
? Express Port: 7000
```

After responding to the generator's questions, Yeoman will move forward with building our new project, just as it did with the modernweb generator that we used in the first half of this chapter. Once this process is finished, run Grunt's default task—$ grunt—to build and launch the project.

Defining Secondary Commands

In the first half of this chapter, you learned that multiple commands can be included with Yeoman generators—commands whose usefulness can extend well beyond the initial creation of a new project. The modernweb generator demonstrated this by including a route command that automated the process of creating new routes within an Angular application (refer to Listing 2-6 earlier in the chapter). The steps involved in creating this command closely follow those we took when we created our generator's default app command:

1. Create a folder named route at the root level of our module.

2. Create a folder named templates within our new route folder.

3. Place various files within our `templates` folder that we want to copy into the target project.

4. Create the script shown in Listing 2-14, which is responsible for driving the functionality for the `route` command.

Listing 2-14. A route Sub-generator That Automates the Creation of New Angular Routes

```
// generator-example/route/index.js

var generators = require('yeoman-generator');

/*
Our generator's default `app` command was created by extending Yeoman's
`Base` class. In this example, we extend the `NamedBase` class, instead.
Doing so alerts Yeoman to the fact that this command expects one or more
arguments. For example: $ yo example:route my-new-route
*/
module.exports = generators.NamedBase.extend({

    'constructor': function(args) {
        this._opts = {
            'route': args[0]
        };
        generators.NamedBase.apply(this, arguments);
    },

    'writing': function() {

        this.fs.copyTpl(
            this.templatePath('index.js'),
            this.destinationPath('public/app/routes/' + this._opts.route +
            '/index.js'),
            this._opts
        );

        this.fs.copyTpl(
            this.templatePath('template.html'),
```

```
        this.destinationPath('public/app/routes/' + this._opts.route +
        '/template.html'),
        this._opts
    );

  },

  'end': function() {
      this.log('Route `' + this._opts.route + '` created.');
  }

});
```

The script shown in Listing 2-14 looks very similar to that shown in Listing 2-9, the primary difference being the use of Yeoman's `NamedBase` class. By creating a sub-generator that extends from `NamedBase`, we alert Yeoman to the fact that this command expects to receive one or more arguments.

Listing 2-15 demonstrates the use of our generator's new `route` command.

Listing 2-15. Creating a New Angular Route Using Our Generator's `route` Command

```
$ yo example:route users
   create public/app/routes/users/index.js
   create public/app/routes/users/template.html
Route `users` created.
```

Composability

When creating Yeoman generators, it is not uncommon to encounter situations in which having the ability to execute one sub-generator from within another would be useful. For example, consider the generator that we just created. It's easy to imagine a scenario in which we might want our generator to automatically create several default routes when run. To accomplish that goal, it would be helpful if we had the ability to call our generator's `route` command from *within* its `app` command. Yeoman's `composeWith()` method exists for this very reason (see Listing 2-16).

Listing 2-16. Yeoman's `composeWith()` Method Allows One Sub-generator to Call Another

```
// generator-example/app/index.js (excerpt)

'writing': function() {
    this.fs.copyTpl(
        this.templatePath('**/*'),
        this.destinationPath(),
        this._answers
    );

    this.fs.copy(
        this.templatePath('.bowerrc'),
        this.destinationPath('.bowerrc'),
        this._answers
    );

    /*
    Yeoman's `composeWith` method allows us to execute external generators.
    Here, we trigger the creation of a new route named "dashboard".
    */
    this.composeWith('example:route', {
        'args': ['dashboard']
    });

    this.config.save();
}
```

With the help of Yeoman's `composeWith()` method, simple sub-generators can be combined (i.e., "composed") with one another to create fairly sophisticated workflows. By taking advantage of this method, developers can create complex, multicommand generators while avoiding the use of duplicate code across commands.

Lastly, it is worth noting that if you are stuck somewhere when developing with Yeoman, or, let us say, your Yeoman generator does not seem to be functioning as desired, there is a built-in troubleshooting command that you can make use of to diagnose and figure out code issues, compatibility issues, and more:

yo doctor

Summary

Yeoman is a simple but powerful tool that automates the tedious tasks associated with bootstrapping new applications into existence, speeding up the process by which developers can move from concept to prototype. When used, it allows developers to focus their attention where it matters most—on the applications themselves.

Thousands of Yeoman generators have been published to npm, making it easy for developers to experiment with a wide variety of tools, libraries, frameworks, and design patterns (e.g., Bower, Grunt, AngularJS, Knockout, React) with which they may not have experience.

Related Resources

- Yeoman: `http://yeoman.io/`

- Yeoman on npm: `www.npmjs.com/package/yo`

CHAPTER 3

PM2

Do not wait; the time will never be "just right." Start where you stand, and work with whatever tools you may have at your command, and better tools will be found as you go along.

—George Herbert

The previous chapters within this section have covered a variety of useful web development tools, with our primary focus placed on client-side development. In this chapter, we will round out our coverage of development tools by shifting our focus to the server. We will be exploring PM2, a command-line utility that simplifies many of the tasks associated with running Node applications, monitoring their status, and efficiently scaling them to meet increasing demand. Topics covered include

- Working with processes
- Monitoring logs
- Monitoring resource usage
- Advanced process management
- Load balancing across multiple processors
- Zero downtime deployments

Installation

PM2's command-line utility, pm2, is available via npm. If you have not already installed PM2, you should do so before you continue, as shown in Listing 3-1.

© Sufyan bin Uzayr, Nicholas Cloud, Tim Ambler 2019
S. bin Uzayr et al., *JavaScript Frameworks for Modern Web Development*,
https://doi.org/10.1007/978-1-4842-4995-6_3

Listing 3-1. Installing the pm2 Command-Line Utility via npm

```
$ npm install -g pm2
$ pm2 --version
3.2.9
```

Note   Node's package manager (npm) allows users to install packages in one of two contexts: locally or globally. In this example, pm2 is installed within the global context, which is typically reserved for command-line utilities.

Working with Processes

Listing 3-2 shows the contents of a simple Node application that will form the basis of our first several interactions with PM2. When accessed, it does nothing more than display the message "Hello, world." to users.

Listing 3-2. Simple Express Application

```
// my-app/index.js

var express = require('express');
var morgan = require('morgan');
var app = express();
app.use(morgan('combined'));

app.get('/', function(req, res, next) {
    res.send('Hello, world.\n');
});

app.listen(8000);
```

Figure 3-1 demonstrates the process by which we can launch this application with the help of the pm2 command-line utility. In this example, we instruct PM2 to start our application by executing its index.js script. We also provide PM2 with an optional name for our application (my-app), making it easier for us to reference it at a later time. Before doing so, be sure you install the project's dependencies by running $ npm install.

```
● ○ ○                                          Default
Tims-MacBook-Pro:my-app tim$ pm2 start index.js --name my-app
[PM2] Spawning PM2 daemon
[PM2] PM2 Successfully daemonized
[PM2] Process index.js launched

| App name | id | mode | pid   | status | restart | uptime | memory    | watching |
+----------+----+------+-------+--------+---------+--------+-----------+----------+
| my-app   | 0  | fork | 57203 | online | 0       | 0s     | 23.488 MB | disabled |

Use `pm2 show <id|name>` to get more details about an app
Tims-MacBook-Pro:my-app tim$ ▌
```

Figure 3-1. *Launching the application shown in Listing 3-2 with PM2*

After calling PM2's start command, PM2 helpfully displays a table containing information about every Node application it is currently aware of before returning us to the command prompt. The meaning of the columns that we see in this example is summarized in Table 3-1.

Table 3-1. *Summary of Columns Shown in Figure 3-1*

Heading	Description
App name	The name of the process. Defaults to the name of the script that was executed.
id	A unique ID assigned to the process by PM2. Processes can be referenced by name or ID.
mode	The method of execution (fork or cluster). Defaults to fork. Explored in more detail later in the chapter.
pid	A unique number assigned by the operating system to the process.
status	The current status of the process (e.g., online, stopped, etc.).
restart	The number of times the process has been restarted by PM2.
uptime	The length of time the process has been running since last being restarted.
memory	The amount of memory consumed by the process.
watching	Indicates whether PM2 will automatically restart the process when it detects changes within a project's file structure. Particularly useful during development. Defaults to disabled.

As indicated by the output provided by PM2 in Listing 3-3, our application is now online and ready for use. We can verify this by calling our application's sole route using the `curl` command-line utility, as shown in Figure 3-2.

```
Tims-MacBook-Pro:my-app tim$ curl http://localhost:8000
Hello, world.
Tims-MacBook-Pro:my-app tim$ █
```

Figure 3-2. *Accessing the sole route defined by our Express application*

Note   Figure 3-2 assumes the existence of the `curl` command-line utility within your environment. If you happen to be working in an environment where this utility is not available, you could also verify the status of this application by opening it directly within your web browser.

In addition to the `start` command, PM2 also provides a number of useful commands for interacting with processes that PM2 is already aware of, the most common of which are shown in Table 3-2.

Table 3-2. *Frequently Used Commands for Interacting with PM2 Processes*

Command	Description
list	Displays an up-to-date version of the table shown in Listing 3-4
stop	Stops the process, without removing it from PM2's list
restart	Restarts the process
delete	Stops the process and removes it from PM2's list
show	Displays details regarding the specified process

Simple commands such as `stop`, `start`, and `delete` require no additional commentary. Figure 3-3, on the other hand, shows the information you can expect to receive when requesting information about a specific PM2 process via the `show` command.

```
Tims-MacBook-Pro:my-app tim$ pm2 show my-app
Describing process with id 0 - name my-app

| status             | online                                                                   |
| name               | my-app                                                                   |
| id                 | 0                                                                        |
| path               | /Users/tim/repos/pro-javascript-frameworks/code/pm2/my-app/index.js      |
| args               |                                                                          |
| exec cwd           | /Users/tim/repos/pro-javascript-frameworks/code/pm2/my-app               |
| error log path     | /Users/tim/.pm2/logs/my-app-error-0.log                                  |
| out log path       | /Users/tim/.pm2/logs/my-app-out-0.log                                    |
| pid path           | /Users/tim/.pm2/pids/my-app-0.pid                                        |
| mode               | fork_mode                                                                |
| node v8 arguments  |                                                                          |
| watch & reload     | ✗                                                                        |
| interpreter        | node                                                                     |
| restarts           | 0                                                                        |
| unstable restarts  | 0                                                                        |
| uptime             | 5m                                                                       |
| created at         | 2015-07-27T13:02:22.410Z                                                 |

Revision control metadata

| revision control | git                                                         |
| remote url       | git@github.com:tkambler/pro-javascript-frameworks.git       |
| repository root  | /Users/tim/repos/pro-javascript-frameworks                  |
| last update      | 2015-07-27T13:07:22.000Z                                    |
| revision         | 5b437670e51606d68e1184051ebbba8e194a0034                    |
| comment          | Replaces absolute path with relative path                   |
| branch           | pm2                                                         |

Tims-MacBook-Pro:my-app tim$
```

Figure 3-3. *Viewing details for a specific PM2 process*

Recovering from Errors

At this point, you are now familiar with some of the basic steps involved in interacting with PM2. You've learned how to create new processes with the help of PM2's start command. You've also discovered how you can subsequently manage running processes with the help of commands such as list, stop, restart, delete, and show. We've yet to discuss, however, much of the real value that PM2 brings to the table in regard to managing Node processes. We'll begin that discussion by discovering how PM2 can assist Node applications in automatically recovering from fatal errors.

Listing 3-3 shows a modified version of the application we originally saw in Listing 3-2. In this version, however, an uncaught exception is thrown at a regular interval.

Listing 3-3. Modified Version of Our Original Application That Throws an Uncaught Exception Every 4 Seconds

```
// my-bad-app/index.js

var express = require('express');
```

65

```
var morgan = require('morgan');
var app = express();
app.use(morgan('combined'));

app.get('/', function(req, res, next) {
    res.send('Hello, world.\n');
});

setInterval(function() {
    throw new Error('Uh oh.');
}, 4000);

app.listen(8000);
```

If we were to start this application without the help of PM2 by passing it directly to the node executable, we would quickly find ourselves out of luck the moment our first error was thrown. Node would simply print the error message to the console before dumping us back to the command prompt, as shown in Figure 3-4.

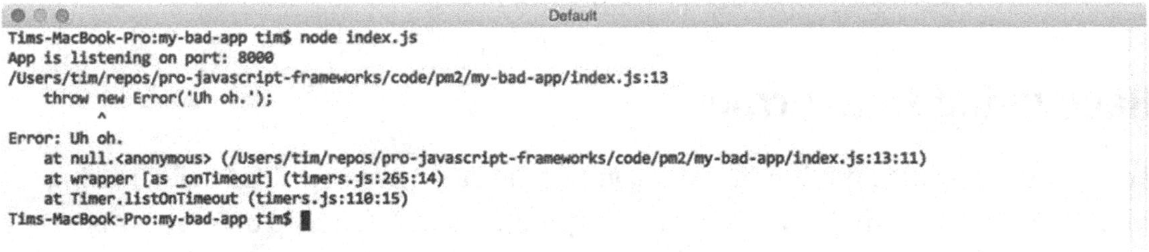

Figure 3-4. *Output provided by Node after crashing from the error shown in Listing 3-3*

Such behavior won't get us very far in a real usage scenario. Ideally, an application that has been released to a production environment should be thoroughly tested and devoid from such uncaught exceptions. However, in the event of such a crash, an application should at the very least be able to bring itself back online without requiring manual intervention. PM2 can help us accomplish this goal.

In Figure 3-5, we remove our existing process from PM2's list via the delete command and create a new instance of the poorly written application shown in Listing 3-3. Afterward, we wait several seconds before requesting an up-to-date process list from PM2.

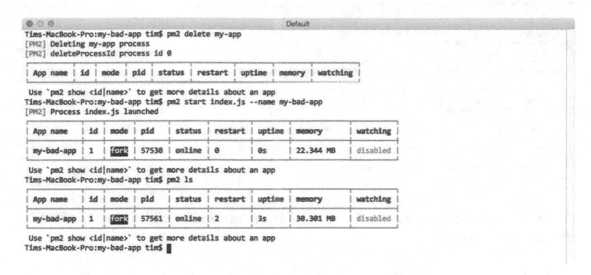

Figure 3-5. *PM2 helps Node applications recover from fatal errors*

Notice anything interesting here? Based on the values within the `status`, `restart`, and `uptime` columns, we can see that our application has crashed three times already. Each time, PM2 has helpfully stepped in and restarted it for us. The most recent process has been running for a total of 2 seconds, which means we can expect another crash (and automatic restart) 2 seconds from now.

PM2's ability to assist applications in recovering from fatal errors in a production environment, while useful, is just one of several useful features the utility provides. PM2 is also equally useful within development environments, as we'll soon see.

Responding to File Changes

Imagine a scenario in which you've recently begun work on a new Node project. Let's assume it's a web API built with Express. Without the help of additional tools, you must manually restart the related Node process in order to see the effects of your ongoing work—a frustrating chore that quickly grows old. PM2 can assist you in this situation by automatically monitoring the file structure of your project. As changes are detected, PM2 can automatically restart your application for you, if you instruct it to do so.

Figure 3-6 demonstrates this process. In this example, we first remove our currently running instance of `my-bad-app`. Next, we create a new instance of the application that was shown in our original example (see Listing 3-2). This time, however, we pass an additional flag, `--watch`, which instructs PM2 to monitor our project for changes and to respond accordingly.

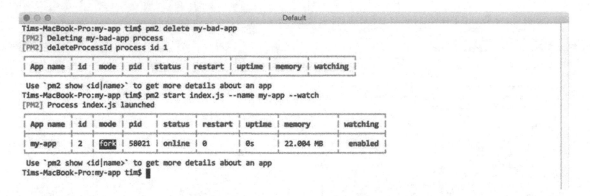

Figure 3-6. *Creating a new PM2 process that will automatically restart itself as changes are detected*

As changes are saved to this project's files, subsequent calls to PM2's `list` command will indicate how many times PM2 has restarted the application, as seen in a previous example.

Monitoring Logs

Refer back to Listing 3-2 and note this application's use of `morgan`, a module for logging incoming HTTP requests. In this example, `morgan` is configured to print such information to the console. We can see the result by running our application directly via the `node` executable, as shown in Figure 3-7.

```
Tims-MacBook-Pro:my-app tim$ node index.js
App is listening on port: 8000
::1 - - [27/Jul/2015:13:17:09 +0000] "GET / HTTP/1.1" 200 14 "-" "Mozilla/5.0 (Macintosh; Intel Mac OS X 10_10_4) AppleWebKit
/537.36 (KHTML, like Gecko) Chrome/44.0.2403.107 Safari/537.36"
::1 - - [27/Jul/2015:13:17:09 +0000] "GET /favicon.ico HTTP/1.1" 404 24 "http://localhost:8000/" "Mozilla/5.0 (Macintosh; Int
el Mac OS X 10_10_4) AppleWebKit/537.36 (KHTML, like Gecko) Chrome/44.0.2403.107 Safari/537.36"
::1 - - [27/Jul/2015:13:17:12 +0000] "GET / HTTP/1.1" 304 - "-" "Mozilla/5.0 (Macintosh; Intel Mac OS X 10_10_4) AppleWebKit/
537.36 (KHTML, like Gecko) Chrome/44.0.2403.107 Safari/537.36"
::1 - - [27/Jul/2015:13:17:14 +0000] "GET / HTTP/1.1" 304 - "-" "Mozilla/5.0 (Macintosh; Intel Mac OS X 10_10_4) AppleWebKit/
537.36 (KHTML, like Gecko) Chrome/44.0.2403.107 Safari/537.36"
::1 - - [27/Jul/2015:13:17:16 +0000] "GET / HTTP/1.1" 304 - "-" "Mozilla/5.0 (Macintosh; Intel Mac OS X 10_10_4) AppleWebKit/
537.36 (KHTML, like Gecko) Chrome/44.0.2403.107 Safari/537.36"
::1 - - [27/Jul/2015:13:17:16 +0000] "GET / HTTP/1.1" 304 - "-" "Mozilla/5.0 (Macintosh; Intel Mac OS X 10_10_4) AppleWebKit/
537.36 (KHTML, like Gecko) Chrome/44.0.2403.107 Safari/537.36"
```

Figure 3-7. *Logging incoming requests to Express with* `morgan`

We recently explored how to allow PM2 to manage the execution of this application for us via the `start` command (see Figure 3-1). Doing so provides us with several benefits, but it also causes us to lose immediate insight into the output being generated by our application to the console. Fortunately, PM2 provides us with a simple mechanism for monitoring such output.

In Figure 3-3, we requested information from PM2 regarding a specific process under its control via the `show` command. Contained within the provided information were paths to two log files that PM2 automatically created for this process—one labeled "out log path" and one labeled "error log path"—to which PM2 will save this process's standard output and error messages, respectively. We could view these files directly, but PM2 provides a much more convenient method for interacting with them, as shown in Figure 3-8.

```
● ○ ○                                        Default
Tims-MacBook-Pro:my-app tim$ pm2 logs
[PM2] Starting streaming logs for [all] process
PM2: 2015-07-27 08:19:05: Starting execution sequence in -fork mode- for app name:my-app id:0
PM2: 2015-07-27 08:19:05: App name:my-app id:0 online
my-app-0 (out): App is listening on port: 8000
my-app-0 (out): ::1 - - [27/Jul/2015:13:05:01 +0000] "GET / HTTP/1.1" 200 14 "-" "curl/7.37.1"
my-app-0 (out): App is listening on port: 8000
my-app-0 (out): App is listening on port: 8000
my-app-0 (out): ::1 - - [27/Jul/2015:13:19:17 +0000] "GET / HTTP/1.1" 304 - "-" "Mozilla/5.0 (Macintosh; Intel Mac OS X 10_10
_4) AppleWebKit/537.36 (KHTML, like Gecko) Chrome/44.0.2403.107 Safari/537.36"
my-app-0 (out): ::1 - - [27/Jul/2015:13:19:19 +0000] "GET / HTTP/1.1" 304 - "-" "Mozilla/5.0 (Macintosh; Intel Mac OS X 10_10
_4) AppleWebKit/537.36 (KHTML, like Gecko) Chrome/44.0.2403.107 Safari/537.36"
my-app-0 (out): ::1 - - [27/Jul/2015:13:19:21 +0000] "GET / HTTP/1.1" 304 - "-" "Mozilla/5.0 (Macintosh; Intel Mac OS X 10_10
_4) AppleWebKit/537.36 (KHTML, like Gecko) Chrome/44.0.2403.107 Safari/537.36"
```

Figure 3-8. *Monitoring the output from processes under PM2's control*

Here we see how the output from processes under PM2's control can be monitored as needed via the `logs` command. In this example, we monitor the output from *all* processes under PM2's control. Notice how PM2 helpfully prefixes each entry with information regarding the process from which each line of output originated. This information is particularly useful when using PM2 to manage multiple processes, which we will begin doing in the upcoming section. Alternatively, we can also monitor the output from a specific process by passing the name (or ID) for that process to the `logs` command (see Figure 3-9).

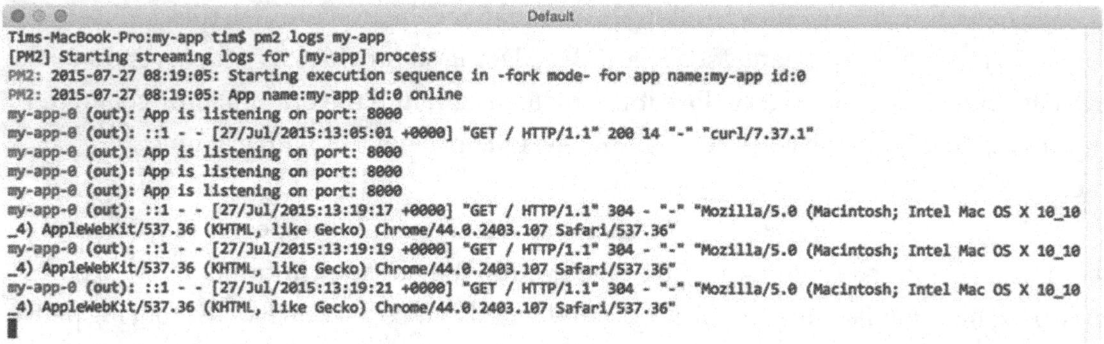

Figure 3-9. *Monitoring the output from a specific process under PM2's control*

Should you wish to clear out the content of log files generated by PM2 at any point, you can quickly do so by calling PM2's `flush` command. The behavior of the utility's `logs` command can also be tweaked slightly with the use of two optional arguments, which are listed in Table 3-3.

Table 3-3. *Arguments Accepted by PM2's* `logs` *Command*

Argument	Description
-raw	Displays the raw content of log files, stripping prefixed process identifiers in the process
-lines <N>	Instructs PM2 to display the last *N* lines, instead of the default of 20

Monitoring Resource Usage

In the previous section, you learned how PM2 can assist you in monitoring the standard output and errors being generated by processes under its control. In much the same way, PM2 also provides easy-to-use tools for monitoring the health of those processes, as well as for monitoring the overall health of the server on which they are running.

Monitoring Local Resources

Figure 3-10 demonstrates the output that is generated when PM2's `monit` command is called. Here we see a continuously updated view that allows us to track the amount of CPU processing power as well as the amount of RAM consumed by each process being managed by PM2.

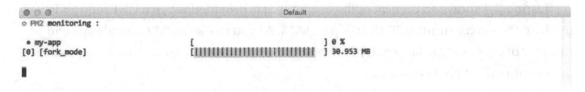

Figure 3-10. *Monitoring CPU and memory usage via PM2's* monit *command*

Monitoring Remote Resources

The information provided by PM2's monit command provides us with a quick and easy method for monitoring the health of its processes. This functionality is particularly helpful during development, when our primary focus is on the resources being consumed within our own environment. It's less helpful, however, as an application moves into a remote, production environment that could easily consist of *multiple* servers, each running its own instance of PM2.

PM2 takes this into account by also providing a built-in JSON API that can be accessed over the Web on port 9615. Disabled by default, the process for enabling it is shown in Figure 3-11.

```
Tims-MacBook-Pro:my-app tim$ pm2 web
Launching web interface on port 9615
[PM2] Process /Users/tim/.nvm/versions/node/v0.12.4/lib/node_modules/pm2/lib/HttpInterface.js launched
[PM2] Process launched

| App name          | id | mode | pid   | status | restart | uptime | memory    | watching |
|-------------------|----|------|-------|--------|---------|--------|-----------|----------|
| my-app            | 0  | fork | 58211 | online | 0       | 7m     | 30.953 MB | disabled |
| pm2-http-interface| 1  | fork | 58769 | online | 0       | 0s     | 21.926 MB | disabled |

 Use `pm2 show <id|name>` to get more details about an app
Tims-MacBook-Pro:my-app tim$
```

Figure 3-11. *Enabling PM2's JSON web API*

In this example, we enable PM2's web-accessible JSON API by calling the utility's web command. PM2 implements this functionality as part of a separate application that runs independently of PM2 itself. As a result, we can see that a new process, pm2-http-interface, is now under PM2's control. Should we ever wish to disable PM2's JSON API, we can do so by removing this process as we would any other, by passing its name (or ID) to the delete (or stop) commands.

Listing 3-4 shows an excerpt of the output that is provided when a GET request is made to the server running PM2 over port 9615. As you can see, PM2 provides us with a number of details regarding each of the processes currently under its control, as well as the system on which it is running.

Listing 3-4. Excerpt of the Information Provided by PM2's JSON API

```
{
    "system_info": {
        "hostname": "iMac.local",
        "uptime": 2186
    },
    "monit": {
        "loadavg": [1.39794921875],
        "total_mem": 8589934592,
        "free_mem": 2832281600,
        "cpu": [{
            "model": "Intel(R) Core(TM) i5-4590 CPU @ 3.30GHz",
            "speed": 3300,
            "times": {
                "user": 121680,
                "nice": 0,
                "sys": 176220,
                "idle": 1888430,
                "irq": 0
            }
        }],
        "interfaces": {
            "lo0": [{
                "address": "::1",
                "netmask": "ffff:ffff:ffff:ffff:ffff:ffff:ffff:ffff",
                "family": "IPv6",
                "mac": "00:00:00:00:00:00",
                "scopeid": 0,
                "internal": true
            }],
```

```
        "en0": [{
            "address": "10.0.1.49",
            "netmask": "255.255.255.0",
            "family": "IPv4",
            "mac": "ac:87:a3:35:9c:72",
            "internal": false
        }]
    }
},
"processes": [{
    "pid": 1163,
    "name": "my-app",
    "pm2_env": {
        "name": "my-app",
        "vizion": true,
        "autorestart": true,
        "exec_mode": "fork_mode",
        "exec_interpreter": "node",
        "pm_exec_path": "/opt/my-app/index.js",
        "env": {
            "_": "/usr/local/opt/nvm/versions/node/v0.12.4/bin/pm2",
            "NVM_IOJS_ORG_MIRROR": "https://iojs.org/dist",
            "NVM_BIN": "/usr/local/opt/nvm/versions/node/v0.12.4/bin",
            "LOGNAME": "user",
            "ITERM_SESSION_ID": "w0t0p0",
            "HOME": "/Users/user",
            "COLORFGBG": "7;0",
            "SHLVL": "1",
            "XPC_SERVICE_NAME": "0",
            "XPC_FLAGS": "0x0",
            "ITERM_PROFILE": "Default",
            "LANG": "en_US.UTF-8",
            "PWD": "/opt/my-app",
            "NVM_NODEJS_ORG_MIRROR": "https://nodejs.org/dist",
```

```
                "PATH": "/usr/local/opt/nvm/versions/node/v0.12.4/bin",
                "__CF_USER_TEXT_ENCODING": "0x1F5:0x0:0x0",
                "SSH_AUTH_SOCK": "/private/tmp/com.apple.launchd.
                  kEqu8iouDS/Listeners",
                "USER": "user",
                "NVM_DIR": "/usr/local/opt/nvm",
                "NVM_PATH": "/usr/local/opt/nvm/versions/node/v0.12.4/lib/node",
                "TMPDIR": "/var/folders/y3/2fphz1fd6rg9l4cg2t8t7g840000gn/T/",
                "TERM": "xterm",
                "SHELL": "/bin/bash",
                "TERM_PROGRAM": "iTerm.app",
                "NVM_IOJS_ORG_VERSION_LISTING": "https://iojs.org/dist/
                  index.tab",
                "pm_cwd": "/opt/my-app"
            },
            "versioning": {
                "type": "git",
                "url": "git@github.com:tkambler/pro-javascript-frameworks.git",
                "revision": "18104d13d14673652ee7a522095fc06dcf87f8ba",
                "update_time": "2015-05-25T20:53:50.000Z",
                "comment": "Merge pull request #28 from tkambler/ordered-build",
                "unstaged": true,
                "branch": "pm2",
                "remotes": ["origin"],
                "remote": "origin",
                "branch_exists_on_remote": false,
                "ahead": false,
                "next_rev": null,
                "prev_rev": "b0e486adab79821d3093c6522eb8a24455bfb051",
                "repo_path": "/Users/user/repos/pro-javascript-frameworks"
            }
        },
```

```
        "pm_id": 0,
        "monit": {
            "memory": 32141312,
            "cpu": 0
        }
    }]
}
```

Advanced Process Management

Most of this chapter's focus so far has revolved around interactions with PM2 that occur primarily via the command line. On their own, commands such as start, stop, restart, and delete provide us with simple mechanisms for managing processes in a quick, one-off fashion. But what about more complex scenarios? Perhaps an application requires that additional parameters be specified at runtime, or perhaps it expects that one or more environment variables be set.

JSON Application Declarations

To meet these needs, additional configuration is needed, and the best way to accomplish this is with the help of what PM2 refers to as "JSON application configuration" files. An example configuration file that demonstrates most of the various options that are available is shown in Listing 3-5.

Listing 3-5. Sample of the Various Options Available Within a JSON Application Configuration File

```
{
    "name"              : "my-app",
    "cwd"               : "/opt/my-app",
    "args"              : ["--argument1=value", "--flag", "value"],
    "script"            : "index.js",
    "node_args"         : ["--harmony"],
    "log_date_format"   : "YYYY-MM-DD HH:mm Z",
    "error_file"        : "/var/log/my-app/err.log",
    "out_file"          : "/var/log/my-app/out.log",
```

```
    "pid_file"             : "pids/my-app.pid",
    "instances"            : 1, // or 0 => 'max'
    "max_restarts"         : 10, // defaults to 15
    "max_memory_restart": "1M", // 1 megabytes, e.g.: "2G", "10M", "100K"
    "cron_restart"         : "1 0 * * *",
    "watch"                : false,
    "ignore_watch"         : ["node_modules"],
    "merge_logs"           : true,
    "exec_mode"            : "fork",
    "autorestart"          : false,
    "env": {
        "NODE_ENV": "production"
    }
}
```

JSON application configuration files provide us with a standard format for passing advanced settings to PM2 in a way that is easily repeatable and that can be shared with others. Several of the options that you see here should be familiar, based on previous examples (e.g., name, out_file, error_file, watch, etc.). Others will be touched on later in the chapter. Descriptions for each are provided in Table 3-4.

Table 3-4. *Descriptions of the Various Configuration Settings Shown in Listing 3-5*

Setting	Description
name	Name of the application.
cwd	Directory from which the application will be launched.
args	Command-line arguments to be passed to the application.
script	Path to the script with which PM2 will launch the application (relative to cwd).
node_args	Command-line arguments to be passed to the node executable.
log_date_format	Format with which log timestamps will be generated.
error_file	Path to which standard error messages will be logged.
out_file	Path to which standout output messages will be logged.
pid_file	Path to which the application's PID (process identifier) will be logged.
instances	The number of instances of the application to launch. Discussed in further detail in the next section.
max_restarts	The maximum number of times PM2 will attempt to restart (consecutively) a failed application before giving up.
max_memory_restart	PM2 will automatically restart the application if the amount of memory it consumes crosses this threshold.
cron_restart	PM2 will automatically restart the application on a specified schedule.
watch	Whether or not PM2 should automatically restart the application as changes to its file structure are detected. Defaults to false.
ignore_watch	An array of locations for which PM2 should ignore file changes, if watching is enabled.
merge_logs	If multiple instances of a single application are created, PM2 should use a single output and error log file for all of them.
exec_mode	Method of execution. Defaults to fork. Discussed in further detail in the next section.
autorestart	Automatically restarts a crashed or exited application. Defaults to true.
vizon	If enabled, PM2 will attempt to read metadata from the application's version control files, if they exist. Defaults to true.
env	Object containing environment variable keys/values to pass to the application.

Included with this chapter is a `microservices` project that provides a working demonstration of JSON configuration files in action. Contained within this project are two applications: a `weather` application with an API that returns random temperature information for a specified postal code and a `main` application that generates a request to the API every 2 seconds and prints the result to the console. The main script for each of these applications is shown in Listing 3-6.

Listing 3-6. Source Code for the `main` and `weather` Applications

```
// microservices/main/index.js

var request = require('request');

if (!process.env.WEATHER_API_URL) {
    throw new Error('The `WEATHER_API_URL` environment variable must be set.');
}

setInterval(function() {

    request({
        'url': process.env.WEATHER_API_URL + '/api/weather/37204',
        'json': true,
        'method': 'GET'
    }, function(err, res, result) {
        if (err) throw new Error(err);
        console.log('The temperature is: %s', result.temperature.fahrenheit);
    });

}, 2000);


// microservices/weather/index.js

if (!process.env.PORT) {
    throw new Error('The `PORT` environment variable must be set.');
}

var express = require('express');
var morgan = require('morgan');
var app = express();
app.use(morgan('combined'));
```

```
var random = function(min, max) {
    return Math.floor(Math.random() * (max - min + 1) + min);
};

app.get('/api/weather/:postal_code', function(req, res, next) {
    var fahr = random(70, 110);
    res.send({
        'temperature': {
            'fahrenheit': fahr,
            'celsius': (fahr - 32) * (5/9)
        }
    });
});

app.listen(process.env.PORT);
```

A single JSON application configuration file is also included with the microservices project, the content of which is shown in Listing 3-7.

Listing 3-7. JSON Application Configuration File for This Chapter's microservices Projectmicroservices/pm2/development.json

```
[
    {
        "name"                : "main",
        "cwd"                 : "../microservices",
        "script"              : "main/index.js",
        "max_memory_restart": "60M",
        "watch"               : true,
        "env": {
            "NODE_ENV": "development",
            "WEATHER_API_URL": "http://localhost:7010"
        }
    },
    {
        "name"                : "weather-api",
        "cwd"                 : "../microservices",
        "script"              : "weather/index.js",
```

```
        "max_memory_restart": "60M",
        "watch"              : true,
        "env": {
            "NODE_ENV": "development",
            "PORT": 7010
        }
    }
]
```

The application configuration file shown here provides PM2 with instructions on how to launch each of the applications included within this project. In this example, PM2 is instructed to restart each application if changes are detected to either's file structure, or if they begin to consume more than 60MB of memory. The file also provides PM2 with separate environment variables to be passed to each process.

Note   Before running this example, you will need to adjust the values for the cwd settings within this file so that they reference the absolute path to the microservices folder on your computer. After making the appropriate adjustments, launch both applications with a single call to PM2, as shown in Figure 3-12.

```
Tims-MacBook-Pro:microservices tim$ pm2 start ./pm2/development.json
[PM2] Spawning PM2 daemon
[PM2] PM2 Successfully daemonized
[PM2] Process launched
[PM2] Process launched
```

App name	id	mode	pid	status	restart	uptime	memory	watching
main	0	fork	58873	online	0	0s	27.242 MB	enabled
weather-api	1	fork	58874	online	0	0s	20.875 MB	enabled

```
Use `pm2 show <id|name>` to get more details about an app
Tims-MacBook-Pro:microservices tim$
```

Figure 3-12. Launching the main and weather-api applications with PM2

As expected, PM2 has created two instances for us, one for each of the applications referenced within our configuration file. As in previous examples, we can monitor the output that is generated with the help of PM2's logs command (see Figure 3-13).

```
● ○ ○                                    Default
Tims-MacBook-Pro:microservices tim$ pm2 logs
[PM2] Starting streaming logs for [all] process
main-0 (out): The temperature is: 84
weather-api-1 (out): ::ffff:127.0.0.1 - - [27/Jul/2015:13:29:15 +0000] "GET /api/weather/37204 HTTP/1.1" 200 61 "-" "-"
weather-api-1 (out): ::ffff:127.0.0.1 - - [27/Jul/2015:13:29:17 +0000] "GET /api/weather/37204 HTTP/1.1" 200 46 "-" "-"
main-0 (out): The temperature is: 77
weather-api-1 (out): ::ffff:127.0.0.1 - - [27/Jul/2015:13:29:19 +0000] "GET /api/weather/37204 HTTP/1.1" 200 61 "-" "-"
main-0 (out): The temperature is: 73
weather-api-1 (out): ::ffff:127.0.0.1 - - [27/Jul/2015:13:29:21 +0000] "GET /api/weather/37204 HTTP/1.1" 200 62 "-" "-"
main-0 (out): The temperature is: 78
weather-api-1 (out): ::ffff:127.0.0.1 - - [27/Jul/2015:13:29:23 +0000] "GET /api/weather/37204 HTTP/1.1" 200 61 "-" "-"
main-0 (out): The temperature is: 70
weather-api-1 (out): ::ffff:127.0.0.1 - - [27/Jul/2015:13:29:25 +0000] "GET /api/weather/37204 HTTP/1.1" 200 61 "-" "-"
main-0 (out): The temperature is: 91
▋
```

Figure 3-13. *Excerpt of the output generated by PM2's* logs *command*

Load Balancing Across Multiple Processors

The single-threaded, nonblocking nature of Node's I/O model makes it possible for developers to create applications capable of handling thousands of concurrent connections with relative ease. While impressive, the efficiency with which Node is capable of processing incoming requests comes with one major expense: an inability to spread computation across multiple CPUs. Thankfully, Node's core cluster module provides a method for addressing this limitation. With it, developers can write applications capable of creating their own child processes—each running on a separate processor, and each capable of sharing the use of ports with other child processes and the parent process that launched it.

Before we close out this chapter, let's take a look at a convenient abstraction of Node's cluster module that is provided by PM2. With this functionality, applications that were not originally written to take advantage of Node's cluster module can be launched in a way that allows them to take full advantage of multiprocessor environments. As a result, developers can quickly scale up their applications to meet increasing demand without immediately being forced to bring additional servers to bear.

Listing 3-8 shows the source code for a simple Express application that we will be scaling across multiple processors with the help of PM2, while Listing 3-9 shows the accompanying JSON application configuration file.

Listing 3-8. Express Application to Be Scaled Across Multiple CPUs

```
// multicore/index.js

if (!process.env.port) throw new Error('The port environment variable must
be set');

var express = require('express');
var morgan = require('morgan');
var app = express();
app.use(morgan('combined'));

app.route('/')
    .get(function(req, res, next) {
        res.send('Hello, world.');
    });

app.listen(process.env.port);
```

Listing 3-9. JSON Application Configuration File with Which Our Application
Will Be Launched

```
// multicore/pm2/development.json

{
    "name": "multicore",
    "cwd": "../multicore",
    "max_memory_restart": "60M",
    "watch": false,
    "script": "index.js",
    "instances": 0, // max
    "exec_mode": "cluster",
    "autorestart": true,
    "merge_logs": true,
    "env": {
        "port": 9000
    }
}
```

The application configuration file shown in Listing 3-9 contains two key items of interest. The first is the `instances` property. In this example, we specify a value of 0, which instructs PM2 to launch a separate process for every CPU that it finds. The second is the `exec_mode` property. By specifying a value of `cluster`, we instruct PM2 to launch its own parent process, which will in turn launch separate child processes for our application with the help of Node's `cluster` module.

In Figure 3-14, we launch the application by passing the path to our application configuration file to PM2's `start` command. Afterward, PM2 displays a listing of every known process, as in previous examples. In this instance, we see that PM2 has launched a separate process for each of the eight CPUs available within our environment. We can verify this by monitoring CPU usage for each of these new processes using the `monit` command, as shown in Figure 3-15.

```
Tims-MacBook-Pro:multicore tim$ pm2 start ./pm2/development.json
[PM2] Spawning PM2 daemon
[PM2] PM2 Successfully daemonized
[PM2] Process launched

| App name  | id | mode    | pid   | status | restart | uptime | memory    | watching |
|-----------|----|---------|-------|--------|---------|--------|-----------|----------|
| multicore | 0  | cluster | 59154 | online | 0       | 0s     | 34.715 MB | disabled |
| multicore | 1  | cluster | 59155 | online | 0       | 0s     | 34.613 MB | disabled |
| multicore | 2  | cluster | 59164 | online | 0       | 0s     | 34.996 MB | disabled |
| multicore | 3  | cluster | 59181 | online | 0       | 0s     | 35.098 MB | disabled |
| multicore | 4  | cluster | 59196 | online | 0       | 0s     | 35.023 MB | disabled |
| multicore | 5  | cluster | 59211 | online | 0       | 0s     | 35.020 MB | disabled |
| multicore | 6  | cluster | 59226 | online | 0       | 0s     | 34.801 MB | disabled |
| multicore | 7  | cluster | 59240 | online | 0       | 0s     | 32.617 MB | disabled |

Use `pm2 show <id|name>` to get more details about an app
Tims-MacBook-Pro:multicore tim$
```

Figure 3-14. *Launching the application on cluster mode with PM2*

Note   When launching applications in cluster mode, PM2 will print a message to the console warning that this functionality is still a beta feature. According to the lead developer of PM2, however, this functionality is stable enough for production environments, so long as Node v0.12.0 or higher is being used.

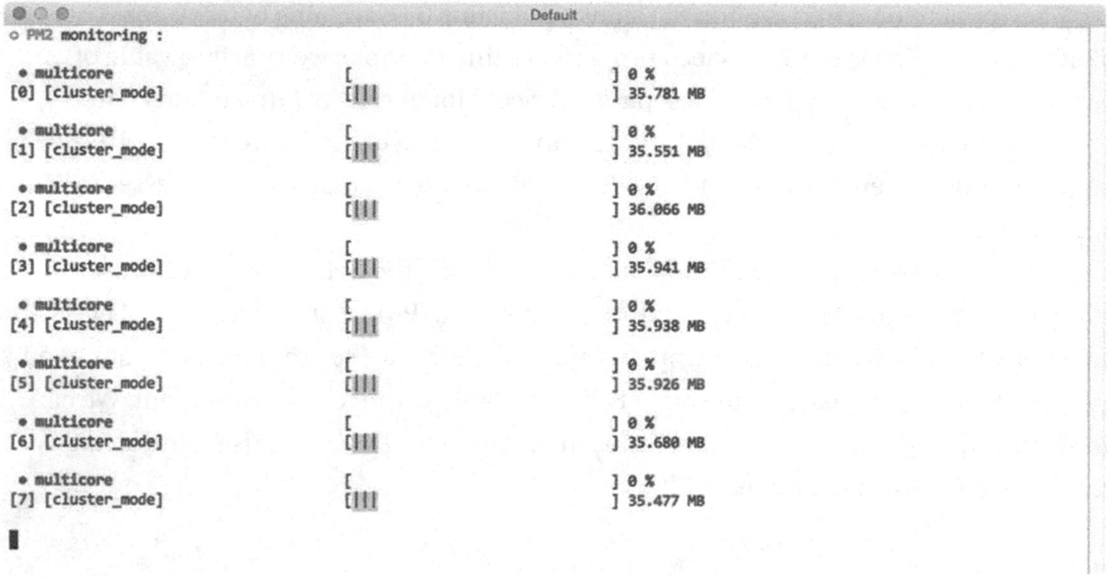

Figure 3-15. *Monitoring CPU usage with PM2's* `monit` *command*

Before you continue, you can quickly remove each of the eight processes launched by this example by running $ `pm2 delete multicore`.

Zero Downtime Deployments

After launching an application in cluster mode, PM2 will begin forwarding incoming requests in a round-robin fashion to each of the eight processes under its control—providing us with an enormous increase in performance. As an added benefit, having our application distributed across multiple processors also allows us to release updates without incurring any downtime, as we will see in a moment.

Imagine a scenario in which an application under PM2's control is running on one or more servers. As updates to this application become available, releasing them to the public will involve two critical steps:

- Copying the updated source code to the appropriate server(s)

- Restarting each of the processes under PM2's control

As these steps take place, a brief period of downtime will be introduced, during which incoming requests to the application will be rejected—unless special precautions are taken. Fortunately, launching applications with PM2 in cluster mode provides us with the tools we need to take those precautions.

To avoid any downtime when relaunching the application we previously saw in Listing 3-8, we will first need to make a minor adjustment to our application's source code and application configuration files. The updated versions are shown in Listing 3-10.

Listing 3-10. Application Designed to Take Advantage of PM2's `gracefulReload` Command

```
// graceful/index.js

if (!process.env.port) throw new Error('The port environment variable must
be set');

var server;
var express = require('express');
var morgan = require('morgan');
var app = express();
app.use(morgan('combined'));

app.route('/')
    .get(function(req, res, next) {
        res.send('Hello, world.');
    });

process.on('message', function(msg) {
    switch (msg) {
        case 'shutdown':
            server.close();
        break;
    }
});

server = app.listen(process.env.port, function() {
    console.log('App is listening on port: %s', process.env.port);
});

// graceful/pm2/production.json

{
    "name": "graceful",
    "cwd": "../graceful",
```

```
    "max_memory_restart": "60M",
    "watch": false,
    "script": "index.js",
    "instances": 0, // max
    "exec_mode": "cluster",
    "autorestart": true,
    "merge_logs": false,
    "env": {
        "port": 9000,
        "PM2_GRACEFUL_TIMEOUT": 10000
    }
}
```

Previous examples have demonstrated the use of PM2's restart command, which immediately stops and starts a specified process. While this behavior is typically not a problem within nonproduction environments, issues begin to surface when we consider the impact it would have on any active requests that our application may be processing at the moment this command is issued. When stability is of the utmost importance, PM2's gracefulReload command serves as a more appropriate alternative.

When called, gracefulReload first sends a shutdown message to each of the processes under its control, providing them with the opportunity to take any necessary precautions to ensure that any active connections are not disturbed. Only after a configurable period of time has passed (specified via the PM2_GRACEFUL_TIMEOUT environment variable) will PM2 then move forward with restarting the process.

In this example, after receiving the shutdown message, our application responds by calling the close() method on the HTTP server that was created for us by Express. This method instructs our server to stop accepting *new* connections, but allows those that have already been established to complete. Only after 10 seconds have passed (as specified via PM2_GRACEFUL_TIMEOUT) will PM2 restart the process, at which point any connections managed by this process should already have been completed.

Figure 3-16 demonstrates the process by which this application can be started and subsequently restarted through the use of the gracefulReload command. By doing so, we are able to release updates without interrupting our application's users.

```
● ○ ○                                    Default
Tims-MacBook-Pro:graceful tim$ pm2 start ./pm2/production.json
[PM2] Spawning PM2 daemon
[PM2] PM2 Successfully daemonized
[PM2] Process launched
┌──────────┬────┬─────────┬───────┬────────┬─────────┬────────┬───────────┬──────────┐
│ App name │ id │ mode    │ pid   │ status │ restart │ uptime │ memory    │ watching │
├──────────┼────┼─────────┼───────┼────────┼─────────┼────────┼───────────┼──────────┤
│ graceful │ 0  │ cluster │ 60536 │ online │ 0       │ 0s     │ 34.563 MB │ disabled │
│ graceful │ 1  │ cluster │ 60537 │ online │ 0       │ 0s     │ 34.922 MB │ disabled │
│ graceful │ 2  │ cluster │ 60544 │ online │ 0       │ 0s     │ 35.074 MB │ disabled │
│ graceful │ 3  │ cluster │ 60563 │ online │ 0       │ 0s     │ 34.953 MB │ disabled │
│ graceful │ 4  │ cluster │ 60578 │ online │ 0       │ 0s     │ 34.781 MB │ disabled │
│ graceful │ 5  │ cluster │ 60593 │ online │ 0       │ 0s     │ 35.012 MB │ disabled │
│ graceful │ 6  │ cluster │ 60608 │ online │ 0       │ 0s     │ 34.801 MB │ disabled │
│ graceful │ 7  │ cluster │ 60623 │ online │ 0       │ 0s     │ 32.781 MB │ disabled │
└──────────┴────┴─────────┴───────┴────────┴─────────┴────────┴───────────┴──────────┘
 Use `pm2 show <id|name>` to get more details about an app
Tims-MacBook-Pro:graceful tim$ pm2 gracefulReload all
[PM2] Process graceful succesfully reloaded
[PM2] Process graceful succesfully reloaded
[PM2] Process graceful succesfully reloaded
[PM2] Process graceful succesfully reloaded
[PM2] Process graceful succesfully reloaded
[PM2] Process graceful succesfully reloaded
[PM2] Process graceful succesfully reloaded
[PM2] Process graceful succesfully reloaded
┌──────────┬────┬─────────┬───────┬────────┬─────────┬────────┬───────────┬──────────┐
│ App name │ id │ mode    │ pid   │ status │ restart │ uptime │ memory    │ watching │
├──────────┼────┼─────────┼───────┼────────┼─────────┼────────┼───────────┼──────────┤
│ graceful │ 0  │ cluster │ 60674 │ online │ 1       │ 67s    │ 34.078 MB │ disabled │
│ graceful │ 1  │ cluster │ 60694 │ online │ 1       │ 58s    │ 34.633 MB │ disabled │
│ graceful │ 2  │ cluster │ 60713 │ online │ 1       │ 50s    │ 34.430 MB │ disabled │
│ graceful │ 3  │ cluster │ 60865 │ online │ 1       │ 42s    │ 34.652 MB │ disabled │
│ graceful │ 4  │ cluster │ 60887 │ online │ 1       │ 33s    │ 34.520 MB │ disabled │
│ graceful │ 5  │ cluster │ 60906 │ online │ 1       │ 25s    │ 34.602 MB │ disabled │
│ graceful │ 6  │ cluster │ 60925 │ online │ 1       │ 16s    │ 34.711 MB │ disabled │
│ graceful │ 7  │ cluster │ 61078 │ online │ 1       │ 8s     │ 34.668 MB │ disabled │
└──────────┴────┴─────────┴───────┴────────┴─────────┴────────┴───────────┴──────────┘
 Use `pm2 show <id|name>` to get more details about an app
Tims-MacBook-Pro:graceful tim$ ▮
```

Figure 3-16. *Gracefully reloading each of the processes under PM2's control*

Summary

PM2 provides developers with a powerful utility for managing Node applications that is equally at home in both production and nonproduction environments. Simple aspects, such as the utility's ability to automatically restart processes under its control as source code changes occur, serve as convenient timesavers during development. More advanced features, such as the ability to load balance applications across multiple processors and to *gracefully* restart those applications in a way that does not negatively impact users, also provide critical functionality for using Node in a significant capacity.

Related Resources

- PM2: https://github.com/Unitech/pm2

- PM2 Home: http://pm2.keymetrics.io/

PART II

Module Loaders

CHAPTER 4

RequireJS

It is more productive to think about what is within my control than to worry and fret about things that are outside of my control. Worrying is not a form of thinking.

—Peter Saint-Andre

While JavaScript now plays a far more significant role in web applications, the HTML5 specification (and therefore modern browsers) does not specify a means to detect dependency relationships among scripts or how to load script dependencies in a particular order. In the simplest scenario, scripts are typically referenced in page markup with simple `<script>` tags. These tags are evaluated, loaded, and executed in order, which means that common libraries or modules are typically included first, then application scripts follow. (For example, a page might load jQuery and then load an application script that uses jQuery to manipulate the Document Object Model [DOM].) Simple web pages with easily traceable dependency hierarchies fit well into this model, but as the complexity of a web application increases, the number of application scripts will grow and the Web of dependencies may become difficult, if not impossible, to manage.

The whole process is made even messier by asynchronous scripts. If a `<script>` tag possesses an `async` attribute, the script content will be loaded over HTTP in the background and executed as soon as it becomes available. While the script is loading, the remainder of the page, *including any subsequent script tags*, will continue to load. Large dependencies (or dependencies delivered by slow sources) that are loaded asynchronously may not be available when application scripts are evaluated and executed. Even if application `<script>` tags possess `async` attributes as well, a developer has no means of controlling the order in which all asynchronous scripts are loaded, and therefore no way to ensure that the dependency hierarchy is respected.

Tip   The HTML5 `<script>` tag attribute `defer` is similar to `async` but delays script execution until page parsing has finished. Both of these attributes reduce page rendering delays, thereby improving user experience and page performance. This is especially important for mobile devices.

RequireJS was created to address this dependency orchestration problem by giving developers a standard way to write JavaScript modules ("scripts") that declare their own dependencies before any module execution occurs. By declaring all dependencies up front, RequireJS can ensure that the overall dependency hierarchy is loaded asynchronously while executing modules in the correct order. This pattern, known as Asynchronous Module Definition (AMD), stands in contrast to the CommonJS module-loading pattern adopted by Node.js and the Browserify module-loading library. While there are certainly strong points to be made for using both patterns in a variety of use cases, RequireJS and AMD were developed to address issues specific to web browsers and DOM shortcomings. In reality, the concessions that RequireJS and Browserify make in their implementations are usually mitigated by workflow and community plugins.

For example, RequireJS can create dynamic shims for non-AMD dependencies that it must load (usually remote libraries on content delivery networks or legacy code). This is important because RequireJS assumes that scripts in a web application may come from multiple sources and will not all directly be under a developer's control. By default, RequireJS does not concatenate all application scripts ("packing") into a single file, opting instead to issue HTTP requests for every script it loads. The RequireJS tool r.js, discussed later, produces packed bundles for production environments, but can still load remote, shimmed scripts from other locations. Browserify, on the other hand, takes a "pack-first" approach. It assumes that all internal scripts and dependencies *will* be packed into a single file and that other remote scripts will be loaded separately. This places remote scripts beyond the control of Browserify, but plugins like `bromote` work within the CommonJS model to load remote scripts during the packing process. For both approaches, the end result is the same: a remote resource is made available to the application at runtime.

Running the Examples

This chapter contains a variety of examples that may be run in a modern web browser. Node.js is necessary to install code dependencies and to run all web server scripts.

To install the example code dependencies, open the code/requirejs directory in a terminal and execute the command npm install. This command will read the package.json file and download the few packages necessary to run each example.

Example code blocks throughout the chapter contain a comment at the top to indicate in which file the source code may be found. The fictitious index.html file in Listing 4-1, for example, would be found in the example-000/public directory. (This directory does not really exist, so don't worry if you can't find it.)

Listing 4-1. An Exciting HTML File

```
<!-- example-000/public/index.html -->
<html>
  <head></head>
  <body><h1>Hello world!</h1></body>
</html>
```

Unless otherwise specified, assume that all example code directories contain an index.js file that launches a very basic web server. Listing 4-2 shows how Node.js would be used in a terminal to run the fictitious web server script example-000/index.js.

Listing 4-2. Launching an Exciting Web Server

```
example-000$ node index.js
>> mach web server started on node 0.12.0
>> Listening on :::8080, use CTRL+C to stop
```

The command output shows that the web server is listening at http://localhost:8080. In a web browser, navigating to http://localhost:8080/index.html would render the HTML snippet in Listing 4-1.

Working with RequireJS

The workflow for using RequireJS in a web application typically includes some common steps. First, RequireJS must be loaded in an HTML file with a `<script>` tag. RequireJS may be referenced as a stand-alone script on a web server or CDN, or it may also be installed with package managers like Bower and npm, then served from a local web server. Next, RequireJS must be configured so that it knows where scripts and modules live, how to shim scripts that are not AMD compliant, which plugins to load, and so on. Once configuration is complete, RequireJS will load a primary application module that is responsible for loading the major page components, essentially "kicking off" the page's application code. At this point RequireJS evaluates the dependency tree created by modules and begins asynchronously loading dependency scripts in the background. Once all modules are loaded, the application code proceeds to do whatever is within its purview.

Each step in this process is given detailed consideration in the following sections. The example code used in each section represents the evolution of a simple application that will show inspirational and humorous quotes by (semi-)famous persons.

Installation

The RequireJS script may be downloaded directly from `http://requirejs.org`. It comes in a few distinct flavors: a vanilla RequireJS script, a vanilla RequireJS script prebundled with jQuery, and a Node.js package that includes both RequireJS and its packing utility, r.js. For most examples in this chapter, the vanilla script is used. The prebundled jQuery script is merely offered as a convenience for developers. If you wish to add RequireJS to a project that is already using jQuery, the vanilla RequireJS script can accommodate the existing jQuery installation with no issues, though older versions of jQuery may need to be shimmed. (Shimmed scripts will be covered later.)

If you are working with CoffeeScript, RequireJS also comes with a plugin for CS integration. Internationalization plugin is also available and can be downloaded directly from `https://requirejs.org`.

Once acquired, the RequireJS script is referenced in the web application with a `<script>` tag. Because RequireJS is a module loader, it bears the responsibility of loading all other JavaScript files and modules that an application may need. It is therefore very likely that the RequireJS `<script>` tag will be the *only* `<script>` tag that occupies a web page. A simplified example is given in Listing 4-3.

Listing 4-3. Including the RequireJS Script on a Web Page

```
<!-- example-001/public/index.html -->
<body>
  <header>
    <h1>Ponderings</h1>
  </header
  <script src="/scripts/require.js"></script>
</body>
```

Configuration

After the RequireJS script is loaded on a page, it looks for a configuration which will primarily tell RequireJS where script and modules live. Configuration options can be provided in one of three ways.

First, a global `require` object may be created *before* the RequireJS script is loaded. This object may contain all of the RequireJS configuration options as well as a "kickoff" callback that will be executed once RequireJS has finished loading all application modules.

The script block in Listing 4-4 shows a newly minted RequireJS configuration object stored in the global `require` variable.

Listing 4-4. Configuring RequireJS with a Global `require` Object

```
<!-- example-001/public/config01.html -->
<body>
  <header>
    <h1>Ponderings</h1>
  </header>
  <section id="quotes"></section>
  <script>
  /*
   * Will be automatically attached to the
   * global window object as window.require.
   */
  var require = {
```

95

```
    // configuration
    baseUrl: '/scripts',
    // kickoff
    deps: ['quotes-view'],
    callback: function (quotesView) {
      quotesView.addQuote('Lorem ipsum dolor sit amet, consectetur adipiscing
      elit.');
      quotesView.addQuote('Nunc non purus faucibus justo tristique porta.');
    }
  };
  </script>
  <script src="/scripts/require.js"></script>
</body>
```

The most important configuration property on this object, `baseUrl`, identifies a path relative to the application root where RequireJS should begin to resolve module dependencies. The `deps` array specifies modules that should be loaded immediately after configuration, and the `callback` function exists to receive these modules once they are loaded. This example loads a single module, `quotes-view`. Once the callback is invoked, it may access the properties and methods on this module.

The directory tree in Listing 4-5 shows the position of the `quotes-view.js` file relative to both `config01.html` (the page being viewed) and `require.js`.

Listing 4-5. Application File Locations

```
├── config01.html
├── scripts
│   ├── quotes-view.js
│   └── require.js
└── styles
    └── app.css
```

Notice that the absolute path and file extension for the `quotes-view` module is omitted in the `deps` array. By default, RequireJS assumes that any given module is located relative to the *page* being viewed and that it is contained within a single JavaScript file with the appropriate file extension. In this case the latter assumption is true but the first is not, which is why specifying a `baseUrl` property is necessary. When RequireJS attempts to resolve any module, it will combine any configured `baseUrl` value and the module name, then append the `.js` file extension to produce a full path relative to the application root.

When the `config01.html` page loads, the strings passed to the `quotesView.addQuote()` method will be displayed on the page.

The second configuration method is similar to the first but uses the RequireJS API to perform configuration *after* the RequireJS script is loaded, as demonstrated in Listing 4-6.

Listing 4-6. Configuration with the RequireJS API

```
<!-- example-001/public/config02.html -->
<body>
  <header>
    <h1>Ponderings</h1>
  </header>
  <section id="quotes"></section>
  <script src="/scripts/require.js"></script>
  <script>
  // configuration
  requirejs.config({
    baseUrl: '/scripts'
  });
  // kickoff
  requirejs(['quotes-view'], function (quotesView) {
    quotesView.addQuote('Lorem ipsum dolor sit amet, consectetur adipiscing
    elit.');
    quotesView.addQuote('Nunc non purus faucibus justo tristique porta.');
  });
  </script>
</body>
```

In this example a `<script>` block first uses the global `requirejs` object, created by the `require.js` script, to configure RequireJS by invoking its `config()` method. It then invokes `requirejs` to kick off the application. The object passed to the `config()` method resembles the global `require` object from Listing 4-4, but lacks its `deps` and `callback` properties. The `requirejs` function accepts an array of application dependencies and a callback function instead, a pattern that will become very familiar when module design is covered later.

The net effect is the same: RequireJS uses its configuration to load the `quotes-view` module, and once loaded, the callback function interacts with it to affect the page.

The third configuration method uses the syntax of the second, but moves the configuration and kickoff code into its own script. The RequireJS `<script>` tag in Listing 4-7 uses the `data-main` attribute to tell RequireJS where its configuration and kickoff module live.

Listing 4-7. Configuring RequireJS with an External Script

```
<!-- example-001/public/config03.html -->
<body>
  <header>
    <h1>Ponderings</h1>
  </header>
  <section id="quotes"></section>
  <script src="/scripts/require.js" data-main="/scripts/main.js"></script>
</body>
```

Once RequireJS has loaded, it will look for the `data-main` attribute and, if found, asynchronously load the script specified in the attribute. Listing 4-8 shows the content of `main.js`, which is identical to the `<script>` block in Listing 4-6.

Listing 4-8. The RequireJS Main Module

```
// example-001/public/scripts/main.js
// configuration
requirejs.config({
  baseUrl: '/scripts'
});
```

```
// kickoff
requirejs(['quotes-view'], function (quotesView) {
  quotesView.addQuote('Lorem ipsum dolor sit amet, consectetur adipiscing elit.');
  quotesView.addQuote('Nunc non purus faucibus justo tristique porta.');
});
```

> **Tip** Because the `data-main` script is loaded asynchronously, scripts or
> `<script>` blocks included immediately *after* RequireJS will likely be run first. If
> RequireJS manages *all* scripts in an application, or if scripts loaded after RequireJS
> have no bearing on the application itself (such as advertiser scripts), there will be
> no conflicts.

Application Modules and Dependencies

RequireJS modules are defined by three things:

1. A module name

2. A list of dependencies (modules)

3. A module closure that will accept the output from each
    dependency module as function arguments, set up module code,
    and potentially return something that other modules can use

Listing 4-9 shows each of these points in a fake module definition. Modules are
created when the global `define()` function is invoked. This function takes three
arguments, corresponding to the three points earlier.

Listing 4-9. Module Anatomy

```
define(/*#1*/'m1', /*#2*/['d1', 'd2'], /*#3*/function (d1, d2) {
  /*
   * Variables declared within the module closure
   * are private to the module, and will not be
   * exposed to other modules
   */
  var privateModuleVariable = "can't touch this";
```

99

```
  /*
   * The returned value (if any) will now be available
   * to any other module if they specify m1 as a
   * dependency.
   */
  return {
    getPrivateModuleVariable: function () {
      return privateModuleVariable;
    }
  };
})
```

A module's name is key. In Listing 4-9 a module name, m1, is explicitly declared. If a module name is omitted (leaving the dependencies and module closure as the only arguments passed to define()), then RequireJS will assume that the name of the module is the file name containing the module script, without its .js extension. This is fairly common in practice, but the module name is shown here for clarity.

Tip   Giving modules specific names can introduce unwanted complexity, as RequireJS depends on script URL paths for loading modules. If a module is explicitly named and the *file name does not match the module name*, then a module alias *that maps the module name to an actual JavaScript file* needs to be defined in the RequireJS configuration. This is covered in the next section.

The dependency list in Listing 4-9 identifies two other modules that RequireJS should load. The values d1 and d2 are the names of these modules, located in script files d1.js and d2.js. These scripts look similar to the module definition in Listing 4-9, but they will load their own dependencies.

Finally, the module closure accepts the output from each dependency module as function arguments. This output is any value returned from each dependency module's closure function. The closure in Listing 4-9 returns its own value, and if another module were to declare m1 as a dependency, it is this returned value that would be passed to that module's closure.

If a module has no dependencies, its dependency array will be empty and it will receive no arguments to its closure.

Once a module is loaded, it exists in memory until the application is terminated. If multiple modules declare the same dependency, that dependency is loaded only once. Whatever value it returns from its closure will be passed to both modules by reference. The state of a given module, then, is shared among all other modules that use it.

A module may return any valid JavaScript value, or none at all if the module exists only to manipulate other modules or simply produce side effects in the application.

Listing 4-10 shows the structure of the example-002/public directory. This looks similar to example-001 but a few additional modules have been added, namely, data/quotes.js (a module for fetching quote data) and util/dom.js (a module that wraps the global window object for other modules so that they do not need to access window directly).

Listing 4-10. Public Directory Structure for example-002

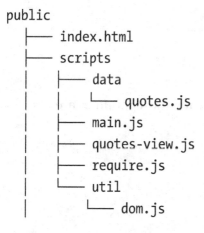

```
public
    ├── index.html
    ├── scripts
    │   ├── data
    │   │   └── quotes.js
    │   ├── main.js
    │   ├── quotes-view.js
    │   ├── require.js
    │   └── util
    │       └── dom.js
```

Recall that a module's dependencies exist relative to the RequireJS baseUrl value. When a module specifies dependency paths, it does so *relative to the* baseUrl *path*. In Listing 4-11 the main.js file depends on the data/quotes module (public/scripts/data/quotes.js), while the quotes-view.js module depends on util/dom (public/scripts/util/dom.js).

Listing 4-11. Module Dependency Paths

```
// example-002/public/scripts/main.js
requirejs(['data/quotes', 'quotes-view'], function (quoteData, quotesView) {
  // ...
});

// example-002/public/scripts/data/quotes.js
define([/*no dependencies*/], function () {
  // ...
});

// example-002/public/scripts/quotes-view.js
define(['util/dom'], function (dom) {
  // ...
});

// example-002/public/scripts/util/dom.js
define([/*no dependencies*/], function () {
    // ...
});
```

Figure 4-1 shows the logical dependency tree created when these modules are loaded.

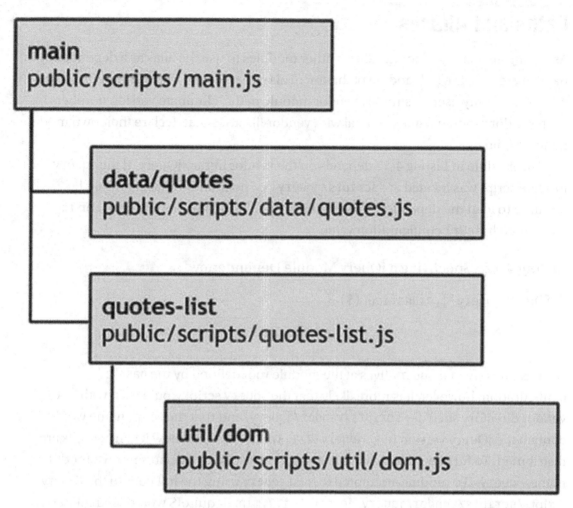

Figure 4-1. *RequireJS dependency tree*

As application dependencies multiply, module pathing can become tedious, but there are two ways to mitigate this.

First, a module may use leading dot notation to specify dependencies relative to itself. For example, a module with the declared dependency `./foo` would load `foo.js` as a sibling file, located on the same URL segment as itself, whereas a module with the dependency `../bar` would load `bar.js` one URL segment "up" from itself. This greatly reduces dependency verbosity.

Second, modules may be named with path aliases, defined in the RequireJS configuration, as described in the next section.

Paths and Aliases

Assigning an alias to a module allows other modules to use the alias as a dependency name instead of the full module pathname. This can be useful for a variety of reasons but is commonly used to simplify vendor module paths, eliminate version numbers from vendor module names, or deal with vendor libraries that declare their own module names explicitly.

The module in Listing 4-12 depends on the vendor library jQuery. If the `jquery` module script was located at `/scripts/jquery.js`, no module aliasing would be required to load the dependency; RequireJS would locate the module based on the configured `baseUrl` configuration value.

Listing 4-12. Specifying a jQuery Module Dependency

```
define(['jquery'], function ($) {
  // ...
});
```

It is unlikely that `jquery` lives at the module root defined by the `baseUrl` configuration, however. It is more likely that the `jquery` script would exist within a vendor directory such as `/scripts/vendor/jquery`, and that the script name would contain the jQuery version (e.g., `jquery-2.1.3.min`), as this is how jQuery scripts are distributed. To further complicate matters, jQuery explicitly declares its own module name, `jquery`. If a module attempted to load `jquery` using the full path to the jQuery script, `/scripts/vendor/jquery/jquery-2.1.3.min`, RequireJS would load the script over HTTP and then fail to import the module because its declared name is `jquery`, not `jquery-2.1.3.min`.

Tip   Explicitly naming modules is considered bad practice because application modules *must* use a module's declared name, and the script file that contains the module must either share its name or be aliased in the RequireJS configuration. A special concession is made for jQuery because it is a fairly ubiquitous library.

Aliases are specified in the RequireJS configuration hash under the `paths` property. In Listing 4-13 the alias `jquery` is assigned to `vendor/jquery/jquery-2.1.3.min`, a path which is relative to the `baseUrl`.

Listing 4-13. Configuration Module Path Aliases

```
requirejs.config({
  baseUrl: '/scripts',
  // ... other options ...
  paths: {
    'jquery': 'vendor/jquery/jquery-2.1.3.min'
  }
});
```

In the `paths` object, aliases are keys and the scripts to which they are mapped are values. Once a module alias is defined, it may be used in any other module's dependency list. Listing 4-14 shows the `jquery` alias in use.

Listing 4-14. Using a Module Alias in a Dependency List

```
// jquery alias points to vendor/jquery/jquery-2.1.3.min
define(['jquery'], function ($) {
    // ...
});
```

Because module aliases take precedence over actual module locations, RequireJS will resolve the location of the jQuery script before attempting to locate it at `/scripts/jquery.js`.

Note   Anonymous modules (that do not declare their own module names) may be aliased with any module name, but if named modules are aliased (like `jquery`), they *must* be aliased with their declared module names.

Loading Plugins with Proxy Modules

Libraries such as jQuery, Underscore, Lodash, Handlebars, and so forth all have plugin systems that let developers extend the functionality of each. Strategic use of module aliases can actually help developers load extensions for these libraries all at once, without having to specify such extensions in every module that makes use of them.

In Listing 4-15 the jQuery script location is aliased with the name jquery, and a custom module, util/jquery-all, is aliased with the name jquery-all for brevity. All application modules will load jQuery by specifying jquery-all as a dependency. The jquery-all module, in turn, loads the normal jquery module and then attaches custom plugins to it.

Listing 4-15. Using Module Aliases to Load jQuery Plugins

```
requirejs.config({
  baseUrl: '/scripts',
  // ... other options ...
  paths: {
    // vendor script
    'jquery': 'vendor/jquery/jquery-2.1.3.min',
    // custom extensions
    'jquery-all': 'util/jquery-all'
  }
});

// example-003/public/scripts/util/jquery-all
define(['jquery'], function ($) {

  $.fn.addQuotes = function () {/*...*/};

  return $;
  // or
  //return $.noConflict(true);
});
```

The jquery-all proxy module returns the jQuery object itself, which allows modules that depend on jquery-all to access jquery with the loaded custom extensions. By default, jQuery registers itself with the global window object, even when it is used as an AMD module. If all application modules are accessing jQuery through the jquery-all module (or even the plain jquery module, as most vendor libraries do), then there is no need for the jQuery global. It may be removed by invoking $.noConflict(true). This will return the jquery object and is the alternate return value for the jquery-all module in Listing 4-15.

Because jQuery is now part of the example application, the quotes-view module, responsible for rendering quote data in the DOM, need no longer rely on the util/dom module. It can specify jquery-all as a dependency and load jquery and the custom addQuotes() plugin method all at once. Listing 4-16 shows the changes made to the quotes-view module.

Listing 4-16. Loading jQuery and Custom Plugins in the quotes-view Module

```
// example-003/public/scripts/quotes-view.js
define(['jquery-all'], function ($) {
  var $quotes = $('#quotes');

  return {
    render: function (groupedQuotes) {
      for (var attribution in groupedQuotes) {
        if (!groupedQuotes.hasOwnProperty(attribution)) continue;
        $quotes.addQuotes(attribution, groupedQuotes[attribution]);
      }
    }
  };
});
```

The advantage to using a module proxy to load jquery is that it eliminates the need to specify both jquery and custom plugin modules in other modules that depend on both. Without this technique, for example, application modules would all have multiple dependencies to ensure that the appropriate jQuery plugins are loaded when needed, as shown in Listing 4-17.

Listing 4-17. Loading Plugins Without a Proxy Module

```
// scripts/util/jquery-plugin-1.js
define(['jquery'], function ($) {
    $.fn.customPlugin1 = function () {/*...*/};
});

// scripts/util/jquery-plugin-2.js
define(['jquery'], function ($) {
    $.fn.customPlugin2 = function () {/*...*/};
});
```

107

```
// scripts/*/module-that-uses-jquery.js
define(['jquery', 'util/jquery-plugins-1', 'util/jquery-plugins-2'],
function ($) {
  // ...
});
```

In this case, even though `jquery-plugin-1` and `jquery-plugin-2` do not return values, they must still be added as dependencies so that their side effects—adding plugins to the `jquery` module—still occur.

Shims

Libraries that support the AMD module format are straightforward to use with RequireJS. Non-AMD libraries may still be used by configuring RequireJS shims or by creating shimmed modules manually.

The `data/quotes` module in `example-003` exposes a `groupByAttribution()` method that iterates over the collection of quotes. It creates a hash where keys are the names of people and values are arrays of quotes attributed to them. This grouping functionality would likely be useful for other collections as well.

Fortunately, a vendor library, *undrln*, can provide a generalized version of this functionality, but it is not AMD compatible. A shim would be necessary for other AMD modules to use undrln as a dependency. Undrln is written as a standard JavaScript module within a function closure, shown in Listing 4-18. It assigns itself to the global `window` object, where it may be accessed by other scripts on a page.

Note   The `undrln.js` script blatantly mimics a subset of the Lodash API *without* AMD module compatibility, exclusively for this chapter's examples.

Listing 4-18. The Completely Original Undrln Library

```
// example-004/public/scripts/vendor/undrln/undrln.js
/**
 * undrln (c) 2015 l33th@x0r
 * MIT license.
 * v0.0.0.0.1-alpha-DEV-theta-r2
 */
```

```
(function () {

  var undrln = window._ = {};

  undrln.groupBy = function (collection, key) {
    // ...
  };

}());
```

Several things must be added to the RequireJS configuration to create a shim. First, a module alias must be created under paths so that RequireJS knows where the shimmed module lives. Second, a shim configuration entry must be added to the shim section. Both are added to the RequireJS configuration in Listing 4-19.

Listing 4-19. Configuration of a Module Shim

```
// example-004/public/scripts/main.js
requirejs.config({
  baseUrl: '/scripts',
  paths: {
    jquery: 'vendor/jquery/jquery-2.1.3.min',
    'jquery-all': 'util/jquery-all',
    // giving undrln a module alias
    undrln: 'vendor/undrln/undrln'
  },
  shim: {
    // defining a shim for undrln
    undrln: {
      exports: '_'
    }
  }
});
```

Each key under the shim section identifies the module alias (or name) to be shimmed, and the objects assigned to those keys specify details about how the shim works. Under the hood, RequireJS creates a shim by defining an empty AMD module that returns the *global* object created by a script or library. Undrln creates the global window._ object, and so the name _ is specified in the shim configuration as undrln's *export*. The final, generated RequireJS shim will look something like the module in Listing 4-20. Note that these shims are created dynamically as modules are loaded and do not actually exist as "files" on the web server. (One exception to this rule is the r.js packing utility, discussed later, which writes generated shim output to a bundle file as an optimization measure.)

Listing 4-20. Example RequireJS Shim Module

```
define('undrln', [], function () {
  return window._;
});
```

The quotes module in Listing 4-21 may now use the undrln shim as a dependency.

Listing 4-21. Using the Undrln Shim As a Dependency

```
// example-004/public/scripts/data/quotes.js
define(['undrln'], function (_) {
  //...
  return {
    groupByAttribution: function () {
      return _.groupBy(quoteData, 'attribution');
    },
    //...
  }
});
```

By shimming non-AMD scripts, RequireJS can use its asynchronous module-loading capabilities behind the scenes to load non-AMD scripts when they are dependencies of other AMD modules. Without this capability these scripts would need to be included on every page with a standard <script> tag and loaded synchronously to ensure availability.

Running the web application in `example-004` and then browsing to `http://localhost:8080/index.html` will display a list of quotes. Figure 4-2 shows the rendered page and Chrome's Network panel in which all loaded JavaScript modules are listed. Note that the Initiator column clearly shows that RequireJS is responsible for loading all modules and that even `undrln.js`, a non-AMD module, is included in the list.

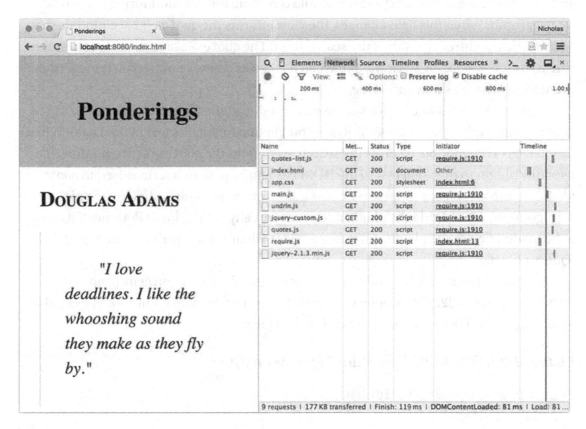

Figure 4-2.   *RequireJS modules shown loaded in Chrome*

Shim Dependencies

It is reasonable to expect shimmed scripts to have dependencies, likely objects in the global scope. When AMD modules specify dependencies, RequireJS ensures that the dependencies are loaded first, before the module code is executed. Dependencies for shimmed scripts are specified in a similar manner within the shim configuration. A shimmed script may depend on other shimmed scripts, or even AMD modules if those modules make content available in the global scope (usually a bad idea, but sometimes necessary).

111

To enhance the example application, a search field has been added to the quote page in example-005. Terms entered into the search field appear highlighted in the text of any quote in which they are found. Up to this point, all examples have used a single view, quotes-view, to display the rendered markup. Because the application features are growing, two new modules will be introduced to help manage features: search-view and quotes-state. The search-view module is responsible for monitoring a text field for user input. When this field changes, the view informs the quotes-state module that a search has occurred, passing it the search term. The quotes-state module acts as the single source of state for all views, and when it receives a new search term, it triggers an event to which views may subscribe.

Digging through some legacy source code produced the file public/scripts/util/jquery.highlight.js, a non-AMD jQuery plugin that highlights text in the DOM. When the quotes-view module receives the search event from the quotes-state module, it uses this plugin to highlight text in the DOM based on the search term stored in quotes-state. To use this legacy script, a path and a shim entry are both added to the main.js configuration. The highlight plugin doesn't export any values, but it does need jQuery to be loaded first or the plugin will throw an error when it attempts to access the global jQuery object.

Dependencies have been added to the highlight shim with the deps property, shown in Listing 4-22. This property contains an array of module names (or aliases) that should be loaded *before* the shim—in this case jQuery.

Listing 4-22. The highlight Shim Depends on jQuery

```
// example-005/public/scripts/main.js
requirejs.config({
  baseUrl: '/scripts',
  paths: {
    jquery: 'vendor/jquery/jquery-2.1.3.min',
    'jquery-all': 'util/jquery-all',
    undrln: 'vendor/undrln/undrln',
    ventage: 'vendor/ventage/ventage',
    highlight: 'util/jquery.highlight'
  },
```

```
shim: {
  undrln: {
    exports: '_'
  },
  highlight: {
    deps: ['jquery']
  }
}
});
```

Once the highlight plugin has been shimmed, it may be loaded as a dependency of another module. Since the jquery-all module is responsible for loading custom plugins anyway, making the highlight module one of its dependencies in Listing 4-23 seems sensible.

Shimmed scripts should only have two kinds of dependencies:

- Other shimmed scripts that execute immediately and potentially create one or more reusable variables or namespaces in the global scope

- AMD modules that also create reusable variables or namespaces in the global scope (such as window.jQuery) as a side effect

Because AMD modules *typically* don't meddle with the global scope at all, it is practically useless to use them as dependencies for a shimmed script because there is no way for the shimmed script to access an AMD module's API. If an AMD module adds nothing to the global scope, it is useless to shimmed scripts. Also, AMD modules are loaded asynchronously, and their closures are executed in a particular order (discussed in the next section), whereas shimmed scripts will be run as soon as they are loaded. (Remember: Shimmed scripts are *normal* scripts that run once they've been introduced into the DOM. A generated shim module simply delivers the global export created by a non-AMD script to other AMD modules as a dependency.) Even if a shimmed script *could* access an AMD module's API, there is no guarantee that the module would be available when the shimmed script actually runs.

Listing 4-23. Loading the `highlight` Module As a Dependency of Another Module

```
// example-005/public/scripts/util/jquery-all.js
define(['jquery', 'highlight'], function ($) {

  $.fn.addQuotes = function (attribution, quotes) {
    // ...
  };

  return $;
});
```

With this arrangement, there are likely two questions that spring to mind immediately:

1. Since both the `highlight` and `jquery-all` modules declare `jquery` as a dependency, when is jQuery actually loaded?

2. Why isn't a second `highlight` parameter specified in the `jquery-all` module closure function?

First, when RequireJS evaluates dependencies among modules, it creates an internal dependency tree based on module hierarchy. By doing this it can determine the optimal time to load any particular module, starting from the leaves and moving toward the trunk. In this case the "trunk" is the `jquery-all` module, and the furthest leaf is the `jquery` module on which `highlight` depends. RequireJS will execute module closures in the following order: `jquery`, `highlight`, `jquery-all`. Because `jquery` is also a dependency of `jquery-all`, RequireJS will simply deliver the same `jquery` instance created for the `highlight` module.

Second, the `highlight` module returns no value and is used merely for side effects— for adding a plugin to the jQuery object. No parameter is passed to the `jquery-all` module because `highlight` returns none. Dependencies that are used only for side effects should always be placed at the end of a module's dependency list for this reason.

Loader Plugins

There are several RequireJS loader plugins that are so useful, they find a home in most projects. A loader plugin is an external script that is used to conveniently load, and sometimes parse, specific kinds of resources that may then be imported as standard AMD dependencies, even though the resources themselves may not be actual AMD modules.

text.js

The RequireJS `text` plugin can load a plain text resource over HTTP, serialize it as a string, and deliver it to an AMD module as a dependency. This is commonly used to load HTML templates or even raw JSON data from HTTP endpoints. To install the plugin, the `text.js` script must be copied from the project repository and, by convention, placed in the same directory as the `main.js` configuration file. (Alternative installation methods are listed in the plugin project's README.)

The `quotes-view` module in the example application uses a jQuery plugin to build up the list of quotes, one DOM element at a time. This is not very efficient and could easily be replaced by a templating solution. The AMD-compatible Handlebars templating library is a popular choice for such tasks. In Listing 4-24 the library has been added to the `vendor` directory in `example-006`, and a convenient module alias has been created in the `main.js` configuration.

Listing 4-24. Handlebars Module Alias

```
// example-006/public/scripts/main.js
requirejs.config({
  baseUrl: '/scripts',
  paths: {
    //...
    Handlebars: 'vendor/handlebars/handlebars-v3.0.3'
  },
  //...
});
```

When the `quotes-view` module renders itself, it uses quote data in an object hash where the keys are attributions (i.e., the person credited with each quote) and the values are arrays of quotes for each. (A given attribution may be associated with one or more quotes.) Listing 4-25 shows the template that will be bound to this data structure, located in the `public/scripts/templates/quotes.hbs` file.

Listing 4-25. The `quotes-view` Handlebars Template

```
<!-- example-006/public/scripts/templates/quotes.hbs -->
{{#each this as |quotes attribution|}}
<section class="multiquote">
```

115

```
<h2 class="attribution">{{attribution}}</h2>
{{#each quotes}}
<blockquote class="quote">
{{#explode text delim="\n"}}
  <p>{{this}}</p>
{{/explode}}
</blockquote>
{{/each}}
</section>
{{/each}}
```

It is not necessary to be completely familiar with Handlebars syntax to understand that this template iterates over the data object, pulling out each attribution and its associated quotes. It creates an <h2> element for the attribution, then for each quote builds a <blockquote> element to hold the quote text. A special block helper, #explode, breaks the quote text apart at the new line (\n) delimiter and then wraps each segment of the quote text in a <p> tag.

The #explode helper is significant because it is not native to Handlebars. It is defined and registered as a Handlebars helper in the file public/scripts/util/handlebars-all.js, as shown in Listing 4-26.

Listing 4-26. #explode Handlebars Helper

```
// example-006/public/scripts/util/handlebars-all.js
define(['Handlebars'], function (Handlebars) {
  Handlebars.registerHelper('explode', function (context, options) {
    var delimiter = options.hash.delim || ";
    var parts = context.split(delimiter);
    var processed = ";
    while (parts.length) {
      processed += options.fn(parts.shift().trim());
    }
    return processed;
  });
  return Handlebars;
});
```

Because this module adds helpers and then returns the Handlebars object, the quotes-view module will import it as a dependency instead of the vanilla Handlebars module, in much the same way as the jquery-all module is used in lieu of jquery. The appropriate module alias has been added to the configuration in Listing 4-27.

Listing 4-27. handlebars-all Module Alias

```
// example-006/public/scripts/main.js
requirejs.config({
  baseUrl: '/scripts',
  paths: {
    //...
    Handlebars: 'vendor/handlebars/handlebars-v3.0.3',
    'handlebars-all': 'util/handlebars-all'
  },
  //...
});
```

In Listing 4-28, the quotes-view module has been modified to import both handlebars-all and the quotes.hbs template. The module name for the text template is very specific: it must begin with the prefix text! followed by the path to the template file relative to the baseUrl path defined in main.js.

Listing 4-28. The quotes.hbs Template Imported As a Module Dependency

```
// example-006/public/scripts/quotes-view.js
define([
  'jquery-all',
  'quotes-state',
  'handlebars-all',
  'text!templates/quote.hbs'
],
function ($, quotesState, Handlebars, quotesTemplate) {

  var bindTemplate = Handlebars.compile(quotesTemplate);
```

```
var view = {
  // ...
  render: function () {
    view.$el.empty();
    var groupedQuotes = quotesState.quotes;
    view.$el.html(bindTemplate(groupedQuotes));
  },
  // ...
};

// ...
});
```

When RequireJS encounters a dependency name with the `text!` prefix, it automatically attempts to load the `text.js` plugin script, which will then load and serialize the specified file content as a string. The `quotesTemplate` function argument in the `quotes-view` closure will contain the serialized content of the `quotes.hbs` file, which is then compiled by Handlebars and used to render the module in the DOM.

Page Load

When a web page has fully loaded, it triggers a `DOMContentLoaded` event (in modern browsers). Scripts that are loaded before the browser has finished building the DOM often listen for this event to know when it is safe to begin manipulating page elements. If scripts are loaded just before the ending `</body>` tag, they may assume that the bulk of the DOM has already been loaded and that they need not listen for this event. Scripts anywhere else in the `<body>` element, or more commonly the `<head>` element, have no such luxury, however.

Even though RequireJS is loaded before the closing `</body>` tag in the application example, the `main.js` file (configuration omitted) in Listing 4-29 still passes a function to jQuery that will be executed once the `DOMContentLoaded` has fired. If the RequireJS `<script>` tag were moved into the document `<head>`, nothing would break.

Listing 4-29. Using jQuery to Determine If the DOM Is Fully Loaded

```
// example-006/public/scripts/main.js
// ...

requirejs(['jquery-all', 'quotes-view', 'search-view'],
  function ($, quotesView) {
  $(function () {
    quotesView.ready();
  });
});
```

The domReady plugin is a peculiar kind of "loader" in that it simply stalls the invocation of a module's closure until the DOM is completely ready. Like the text plugin, the domReady.js file must be accessible to RequireJS within the baseUrl path defined in the main.js configuration. By convention it is typically a sibling of main.js.

Listing 4-30 shows a modified version of main.js (configuration omitted) in which the jquery dependency has been removed and the domReady! plugin has been appended to the dependency list. The trailing exclamation mark tells RequireJS that this module acts as a loader plugin rather than a standard module. Unlike the text plugin, domReady actually loads nothing, so no additional information is required after the exclamation mark.

Listing 4-30. Using the domReady Plugin to Determine If the DOM Is Fully Loaded

```
// example-007/public/scripts/main.js
// ...

requirejs(['quotes-view', 'search-view', 'domReady!'],
  function (quotesView) {
    quotesView.ready();
});
```

i18n

RequireJS supports internationalization via the i18n loader plugin. (i18n is a numeronym, which means that the number "18" represents the 18 characters between "i" and "n" in the word "internationalization".) Internationalization is the act of writing a web application such that it can adapt its content to a user's language and locale (also known as National Language Support, or NLS). The i18n plugin is primarily used for translating text in a web site's controls and "chrome": button labels, headers, hyperlink text, fieldset legends, and so forth. To demonstrate this plugin's capabilities, two new templates have been added to the example application, one for the page title in the header and one for the search field with placeholder text. The actual quote data will not be translated because, presumably, it comes from an application server that would be responsible for rendering the appropriate translation. In this application, though, the data is hard-coded in the data/quotes module for simplicity and will always appear in English.

The search.hbs template in Listing 4-31 has also been extracted from the index. html file and now accepts placeholder text for the search field as its only input. The search-view module has been adapted to use this template when it renders content in the DOM.

Listing 4-31. The search.hbs Template Will Display the Placeholder Translation

```
<!-- example-008/public/scripts/templates/search.hbs -->
<form>
  <fieldset>
    <input type="text" name="search" placeholder="{{searchPlaceholder}}" />
  </fieldset>
</form>
```

Listing 4-32 shows the new header.hbs template that will be rendered by the new header-view module. The template accepts a single input, the page title.

Listing 4-32. The header.hbs Template Will Display the Page Title Translation

```
<!-- example-008/public/scripts/templates/header.hbs -->
<h1>{{pageTitle}}</h1>
```

The header-view module in Listing 4-33 demonstrates not only how the template dependency is imported with the text plugin but also how a language module dependency is imported with the i18n plugin. The familiar loader syntax looks nearly identical: the plugin name followed by an exclamation mark and a module path relative to the configured baseUrl, in this case nls/lang. When a template is loaded, its serialized string content is passed to a module's closure, but the i18n plugin loads a language module that contains translated text data and passes that module's object to the closure. In Listing 4-33 this object will be accessible through the lang parameter.

Listing 4-33. The header-view Module Depends on the i18n Language Object

```
// example-008/public/scripts/header-view.js
define([
  'quotes-state',
  'jquery-all',
  'handlebars-all',
  'text!templates/header.hbs',
  'i18n!nls/lang'
], function (quotesState, $, Handlebars, headerTemplate, lang) {
  // ...
});
```

The language module is a regular AMD module, but instead of passing a list of dependencies and a closure to define(), a simple object literal is used. This object literal follows a very specific syntax, shown in Listing 4-34.

Listing 4-34. Default English Language Module

```
// example-008/public/scripts/nls/lang.js
define({
  root: {
    pageTitle: 'Ponderings',
    searchPlaceholder: 'search'
  },
  de: true
});
```

121

First, a `root` property holds the key/value pairs that will be used to fetch translated data when the plugin resolves the language translations. The keys in this object are simply keys by which the translated text may be accessed programmatically. In the `search` template, for example, `{{searchPlaceholder}}` will be replaced with the string value at the language object's key `searchPlaceholder` when the template is bound to it.

Second, siblings to the `root` property are the various IETF language tags for active and inactive translations that should be resolved based on a browser's language setting. In this example, the German `de` language tag is assigned the value `true`. If a Spanish translation was made available, an `es-es` property with the value `true` could be added. And for a French translation, an `fr-fr` property could be added, and so forth for other languages.

When a new language tag is enabled in the default language module, a directory corresponding to the language code must be made as a sibling to the module file. The `nls/de` directory can be seen in Listing 4-35.

Listing 4-35. Directory Structure for NLS Modules

```
├── nls
│    ├── de
│    │    └── lang.js
│    └── lang.js
```

Once the language-specific directory has been created, a language module file *of the same name as the default language module file* must be created within. This new language module will contain the translated content of the `root` property in the default language module *only*. Listing 4-36 shows the German (`de`) translation of the `pageTitle` and `searchPlaceholder` properties.

Listing 4-36. German (`de`) Translation Module

```
// example-008/public/scripts/nls/de/lang.js
define({
  pageTitle: 'Grübeleien',
  searchPlaceholder: 'suche'
});
```

When the default language module is loaded with the i18n plugin, it examines the browser's `window.navigator.language` property to determine what locale and language translation should be used. If the default language module specifies a compatible, enabled locale, the i18n plugin loads the locale-specific module and then merges it with the default language module's `root` object. Missing translations in the locale-specific module will be filled with values from the default language module.

Figure 4-3 shows how the quotes page looks when a Google Chrome browser's language has been set to German.

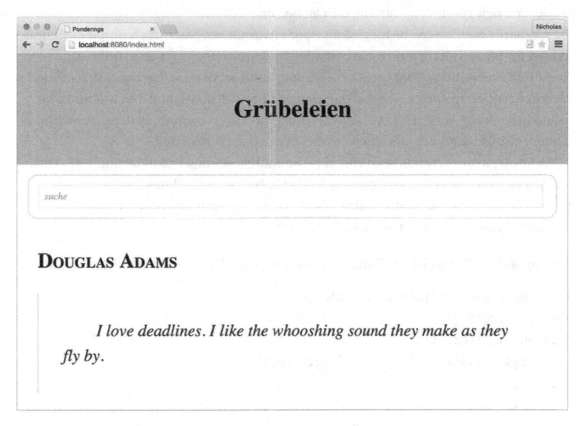

Figure 4-3. *Switching the browser language loads the German translation.*

Note   The `window.navigator.language` property is affected by different settings in different browsers. For example, in Google Chrome it only reflects the user's language setting, whereas in Mozilla Firefox it can be affected by an `Accept-Language` header in a page's HTTP response as well.

Cache Busting

Application servers often cache resources like script files, images, stylesheets, and so on to eliminate unnecessary disk access when serving a resource that has not changed since it was last read. Cached resources are often stored in memory and associated with some key, usually the URL of the resource. When multiple requests for a given URL occur within a specified cache period, the resource is fetched from memory using the key (URL). This can have significant performance benefits in a production environment, but invalidating cache in development or testing environments every time a code change is made, or a new resource is introduced, can become tedious.

Certainly caching can be toggled on a per-environment basis, but a simpler solution, at least for JavaScript (or any resource loaded by RequireJS), might be to utilize the RequireJS cache-busting feature. *Cache busting* is the act of mutating the URL for every resource request in such a way that the resource may still be fetched, but will never be found in cache because its "key" is always different. This is commonly done by including a query string parameter that changes whenever a page is reloaded.

A `urlArgs` property has been added to the configuration script in Listing 4-37. This will append the query string parameter `bust={timestamp}` to all requests generated by RequireJS. The time stamp is recalculated for each page load to ensure that the parameter value changes, making URLs unique.

Listing 4-37. The `urlArgs` Configuration Property Can Be Used to Bust Cache

```
// example-009/public/scripts/main.js
requirejs.config({
  baseUrl: '/scripts',
  urlArgs: 'bust=' + (new Date().getTime()),
  paths: {
    // ...
  },
  shim: {
    // ...
  }
});
```

Figure 4-4 shows that the `bust` parameter is indeed applied to each request initiated by RequireJS, even XHR requests for text resources like `header.hbs`.

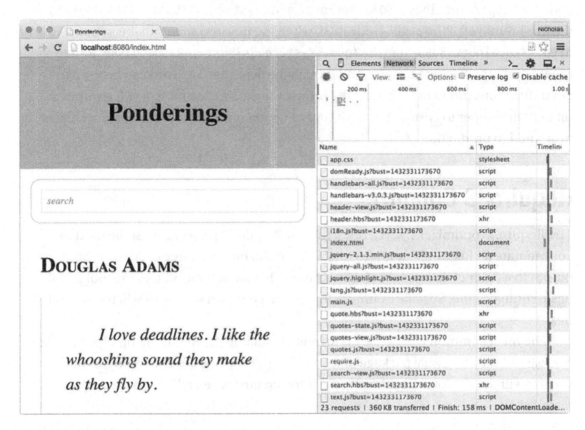

Figure 4-4. *The* `bust` *parameter is appended to each RequireJS request*

While the usefulness of this feature is evident, it can also create a few problems.

First, RequireJS respects HTTP cache headers, so even if `urlArgs` is used as a cache-busting mechanism, RequireJS may still request (and receive) a cached version of a resource, depending on how cache is implemented. If possible, always serve the appropriate cache headers in each environment.

Second, be aware that some proxy servers drop query string parameters. If a development or staging environment includes proxies to mimic a production environment, a cache-busting query string parameter may be ineffective. Some developers use `urlArgs` to specify particular resource versions in a production environment (e.g., `version=v2`), but this is generally discouraged for this very reason. It is an unreliable versioning technique, at best.

Finally, some browsers treat resources with different URLs as distinct, debuggable entities. In Chrome and Firefox, for example, if a debug breakpoint is set in the source code for `http://localhost:8080/scripts/quotes-state.js?bust=1432504595280`, it will be removed if the page is refreshed, when the new resource URL becomes `http://localhost:8080/scripts/quotes-state.js?bust=1432504694566`. Resetting breakpoints can become tedious, and though the `debugger` keyword can be used to circumvent this problem by forcing the browser to pause execution, it still requires a diligent developer to ensure that all `debugger` breakpoints are removed before code is promoted to production.

RequireJS Optimizer

The RequireJS optimizer, r.js, is a build tool for RequireJS projects. It can be used to concatenate all RequireJS modules into a single file, minify source code, copy build output to a distinct directory, and much more. This section introduces the tool and its basic configuration. Specific examples for several common scenarios will be covered next.

The most common way to use r.js involves installing the RequireJS npm package for Node.js, either as a global package or as a local project package. The examples in this section will use the local RequireJS installation created when all npm modules were installed.

Configuring r.js

A wide array of parameters may be passed as arguments to the r.js tool to control its behavior. Fortunately these parameters can also be passed to r.js in a regular JavaScript configuration file, which makes the terminal command significantly shorter. For nontrivial projects, this is the preferred configuration method and will be the only one covered in this chapter.

The code files in the `example-010` directory have been moved into a standard `src` directory, and a new file, `rjs-config.js`, has been placed in the directory root. This file, unsurprisingly, contains the r.js configuration. Its contents are shown in Listing 4-38.

Listing 4-38. `r.js` Configuration

```
// example-010/rjs-config.js
({
  // build input directory for application code
  appDir: './src',
  // build output directory for application code
  dir: './build',
  // path relative to build input directory where scripts live
  baseUrl: 'public/scripts',
  // predefined configuration file used to resolve dependencies
  mainConfigFile: './src/public/scripts/main.js',
  // include all text! references as inline modules
  inlineText: true,
  // do not copy files that were combined in build output
  removeCombined: true,

  // specific modules to be built
  modules: [
    {
      name: 'main'
    }
  ],

  // uglify the output
  optimize: 'uglify'
})
```

Developers who are familiar with build tools will immediately recognize the input/output pattern present in the configuration.

The `appDir` property specifies the project "input" directory, relative to the configuration file, where uncompiled source code lives.

The `dir` property specifies the project "output" directory, relative to the configuration file, where compiled and minified output will be written when the r.js tool runs.

The `baseUrl` property tells r.js where the project scripts are located *relative to the appDir property*. This should not be confused with the `baseUrl` property in the `main.js` file, which tells RequireJS where modules are located relative to the web application root.

127

The `mainConfigFile` property points to the actual RequireJS (not r.js) configuration. This helps r.js understand how modules are related to each other, and what module aliases and shims exist, if any. It is possible to omit this property and specify all of these paths in the r.js configuration, though that is beyond the scope of this example.

Setting the `inlineText` property to `true` ensures that all text files referenced with the text plugin prefix `text!` will be compiled with RequireJS modules in the final build output. This option is enabled by default but is explicitly set in this project for clarity.

By default, r.js will minify and copy *all* scripts (packed and unpacked) to the output directory. The `removeCombined` property toggles this behavior. In this case only the packed, compiled script(s) *and any other scripts that could not be included in the packed output* will be copied to the output directory.

The `modules` array lists all of the top-level modules to be compiled. Because this is a single-page application, only the actual `main` module needs to be compiled.

Finally, the `optimize` property instructs r.js to apply an uglify transform to all scripts, minimizing all JavaScript code.

Running the r.js Command

Building the project is simply a matter of running the `r.js` command in a terminal, passing it the path to the configuration file via its `-o` flag as shown in Listing 4-39.

Listing 4-39. Running the r.js Command

```
example-010$ ../node_modules/.bin/r.js -o rjs-config.js
```

Terminal output shows which files are compiled and copied by r.js during the build. Examining the build output files in Listing 4-40 shows what, exactly, r.js optimized and copied.

Listing 4-40. Build Directory Content

```
example-010/build$ tree
.
├── build.txt
├── index.js
└── public
```

```
├── index.html
├── scripts
│   ├── main.js
│   ├── nls
│   │   └── de
│   │       └── lang.js
│   ├── require.js
│   ├── templates
│   │   ├── header.hbs
│   │   ├── quote.hbs
│   │   └── search.hbs
│   └── vendor
│       └── ventage
│           ├── LICENSE
│           ├── README.md
│           ├── bower.json
│           ├── package.json
│           └── test
│               ├── index.html
│               ├── main.js
│               ├── ventage.clear.js
│               ├── ventage.create.js
│               ├── ventage.ctor.js
│               ├── ventage.off.js
│               ├── ventage.on.js
│               ├── ventage.pipe.js
│               ├── ventage.trigger.js
│               └── ventage.triggerAsync.js
└── styles
    └── app.css

9 directories, 24 files
```

Several things immediately stand out in the `public/scripts` directory.

First, the `require.js` and `main.js` scripts are both present. Since these scripts are the only files referenced in `index.html`, their presence here is expected. Other scripts such as the `quotes-view.js` and `quotes-state.js` scripts are noticeably absent, but examining the content of `main.js` reveals why: they have been packed and minified according to the r.js build settings.

Second, the localization file `nls/lang.js` is now missing because it has been included as part of `main.js`. The `nls/de/lang.js` script still remains as part of the build output, though its contents have been minified. Any user browsing the example web page in the default locale will receive an optimized experience, as RequireJS will not have to make an external AJAX call to load the default language translations. Users from Germany will incur the additional HTTP request because the German localization file has not been included in the packed output. This is a limitation of the localization plugin that r.js must respect.

Third, the Handlebars templates, though compiled as part of the build output in `main.js`, have also been copied to the `public/scripts/templates` directory. This happens because RequireJS plugins currently *have no visibility into the build process* and therefore no method of honoring the `removeCombined` option in the r.js configuration file. Fortunately, because these templates have been wrapped in AMD modules and concatenated with `main.js`, RequireJS will *not* attempt to load them with AJAX requests. If deployment size is an issue for this project, a post-build script or task can be created to remove the `templates` directory if needed.

Fourth, the `vendor/ventage` directory has been copied to the `build` directory even though its core module, `ventage.js`, has been concatenated with `main.js`. While RequireJS can automatically remove individual module files (like `ventage.js`) after compilation, it will not clean up other files associated with a module (in this case, unit tests and package definition files like `package.json` and `bower.json`), so they must be removed manually or as part of a post-build process.

Summary

RequireJS is a very pragmatic JavaScript module loader that works well in a browser environment. Its ability to load and resolve modules asynchronously means that it does not rely solely on bundling or packing scripts for performance benefits. For further optimization, though, the r.js optimization tool may be used to combine RequireJS modules into a single, minified script to minimize the number of HTTP requests necessary to load modules and other resources.

Though RequireJS modules must be defined in AMD format, RequireJS can shim non-AMD scripts so that legacy code may be imported by AMD modules where necessary. Shimmed modules may also have dependencies that can automatically be loaded by RequireJS.

The `text` plugin lets modules import external text file dependencies (such as templates) as strings. These text files are loaded like any other module dependency and may even be inlined in build output by the r.js optimizer.

Localization is supported by the `i18n` module loader, which can dynamically load text translation modules based on a browser's locale settings. While the primary locale translation module can be optimized and concatenated with r.js, additional locale translation modules will always be loaded with HTTP requests.

Module execution can be deferred by the `pageLoad` plugin, which prevents a module's closure from executing until the DOM has been fully rendered. This can be an effective way to eliminate repeat calls to jQuery's `ready()` function, or fumbling through the cross-browser code necessary to subscribe to the `DOMContentLoaded` event manually.

Finally, the RequireJS configuration can automatically append query string parameters to all RequireJS HTTP requests, providing a cheap but effective cache-busting feature for development environments.

CHAPTER 5

Browserify

Less is more.

—Ludwig Mies van der Rohe

Browserify is a JavaScript module loader that works around the language's current lack of support for importing modules within the browser by serving as a "pre-processor" for your code. In much the same way that CSS extensions such as SASS and LESS have brought enhanced syntax support to stylesheets, Browserify enhances client-side JavaScript applications by recursively scanning their source code for calls to a global `require()` function. When Browserify finds such calls, it immediately loads the referenced modules (using the same `require()` function that is available within Node.js) and combines them into a single, minified file—a "bundle"—that can then be loaded within the browser.

This simple but elegant approach brings the power and convenience of CommonJS (the method by which modules are loaded within Node.js) to the browser while also doing away with the additional complexity and boilerplate code required by Asynchronous Module Definition (AMD) loaders such as RequireJS (described in Chapter 4).

In this chapter, you will learn how to

- Distinguish between AMD and CommonJS module loaders

- Create modular front-end JavaScript applications that follow the simple patterns for module management popularized by tools such as Node.js

- Visualize a project's dependency tree

- Compile your application as quickly as possible—as changes are made—using Browserify's sister application, Watchify

- Use third-party Browserify plugins ("transforms") to extend the tool beyond its core functionality

© Sufyan bin Uzayr, Nicholas Cloud, Tim Ambler 2019
S. bin Uzayr et al., *JavaScript Frameworks for Modern Web Development*,
https://doi.org/10.1007/978-1-4842-4995-6_5

Note   Portions of this chapter discuss concepts already covered in this book's previous chapters.

The AMD API vs. CommonJS

The Asynchronous Module Definition API, covered in Chapter 4, serves as a clever workaround to JavaScript's current lack of support for loading external modules inline. Often referred to as a "browser-first" approach, the AMD API accomplishes its goal of bringing modules to the browser by requiring that developers wrap each of their modules within a callback function, which can then be loaded asynchronously (i.e., "lazy loaded") as needed. This process is demonstrated by the modules shown in Listing 5-1.

Listing 5-1. Defining and Requiring an AMD Module

```
// requirejs-example/public/app/weather.js

define([], function() {
    return {
        'getForecast': function() {
            document.getElementById('forecast').innerHTML = 'Partly cloudy.';
        }
    };
});

// requirejs-example/public/app/index.js

define(['weather'], function(weather) {
    weather.getForecast();
});
```

The AMD API is both clever and effective, but many developers also find it to be a bit clumsy and verbose. Ideally, JavaScript applications should be capable of referencing external modules without the added complexity and boilerplate code that the AMD API requires. Fortunately, a popular alternative known as CommonJS exists that addresses this concern.

While most people tend to associate JavaScript with web browsers, the truth is that JavaScript has found widespread use in a number of other environments for quite some time—well before Node.js came on the scene. Examples of such environments include Rhino, a server-side runtime environment created by Mozilla, and ActionScript, a derivative used by Adobe's once-popular Flash platform that has fallen out of favor in recent years. Each of these platforms works around JavaScript's lack of built-in module support by creating its own approach.

Sensing a need for a standard solution to this problem, a group of developers got together and proposed what became known as CommonJS, a standardized approach to defining and using JavaScript modules. Node.js follows a similar approach, as does the next major update to JavaScript (ECMAScript 6, a.k.a. ES6 Harmony). This approach can also be used to write modular JavaScript applications that work in all web browsers in use today, although not without the help of additional tools such as Browserify, the subject of this chapter.

Installing Browserify

Before going any further, you should ensure that you have installed Browserify's command-line utility. Available as an npm package, the installation process is shown in Listing 5-2.

Listing 5-2. Installing the browserify Command-Line Utility via npm

```
$ npm install -g browserify
$ browserify --version
16.2.3
```

Note Node's package manager (npm) allows users to install packages in one of two contexts: locally or globally. In this example, browserify is installed within the global context, which is typically reserved for command-line utilities.

Creating Your First Bundle

Much of Browserify's appeal lies in its simplicity; JavaScript developers familiar with CommonJS and Node will find themselves immediately at home. By way of an example, consider Listing 5-3, which shows the CommonJS-based equivalent of the simple RequireJS-based application we saw in Listing 5-1.

Listing 5-3. Front-End Application That Requires Modules via CommonJS

```
// simple/public/app/index.js

var weather = require('./weather');
weather.getForecast();

// simple/public/app/weather.js

module.exports = {
    'getForecast': function() {
        document.getElementById('forecast').innerHTML = 'Partly cloudy.';
    }
};
```

Unlike our RequireJS-based example, this application *cannot* be run directly within the browser because the browser lacks a built-in mechanism for loading modules via require(). Before the browser can understand this application, we must first compile it into a bundle with the help of the browserify command-line utility or via Browserify's API.

The command for compiling this application using Browserify's command-line utility is as follows:

```
$ browserify app/index.js -o public/dist/app.js
```

Here we pass the browserify utility the path to our application's main file, public/app/index.js, and specify that the compiled output should be saved to public/dist/app.js, the script referenced within the project's HTML (see Listing 5-4).

Listing 5-4. HTML File Referencing Our Compiled Browserify Bundle

```
// simple/public/index.html

<!DOCTYPE html>
<html>
<head>
    <meta charset="utf-8">
    <meta http-equiv="X-UA-Compatible" content="IE=edge">
    <meta name="viewport" content="width=device-width, initial-scale=1">
    <title>Browserify - Simple Example</title>
</head>
<body>
    <div id="forecast"></div>
    <script src="/dist/app.js"></script>
</body>
</html>
```

In addition to using Browserify's command-line utility, we also have the option of compiling this application programmatically via Browserify's API. Doing so will allow us to easily incorporate this step into a larger build process (developed with tools such as Grunt). Listing 5-5 shows this project's browserify Grunt task.

Listing 5-5. Grunt Task That Compiles the Application via Browserify's API

```
// simple/tasks/browserify.js

module.exports = function(grunt) {

    grunt.registerTask('browserify', function() {
        var done = this.async();
        var path = require('path');
        var fs = require('fs');
        var src = path.join('public', 'app', 'index.js');
        var target = path.join('public', 'dist', 'app.js');
        var browserify = require('browserify')([src]);
        browserify.bundle(function(err, data) {
            if (err) return grunt.fail.fatal(err);
            grunt.file.mkdir(path.join('public', 'dist'));
```

```
        fs.writeFileSync(target, data);
        done();
    });
  });

};
```

Visualizing the Dependency Tree

If you happen to be more of a visual learner, the chart shown in Figure 5-1 may go a long way toward conveying what occurs during Browserify's compilation process. Here we see a visualization of the various dependencies encountered by Browserify as it compiled this chapter's advanced project.

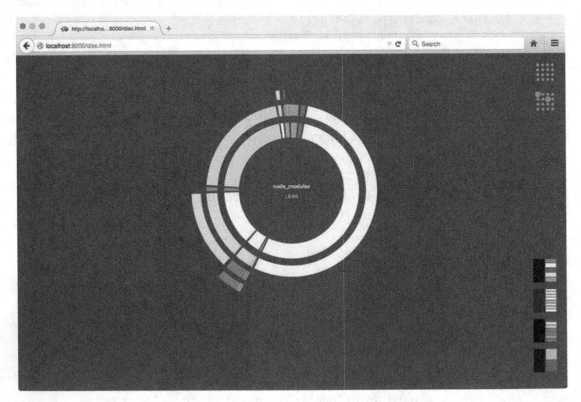

Figure 5-1. *Visualizing the advanced project's dependency tree*

Viewing this chart as a static rendering on a page really does not do it justice. For the full effect, you should compile the project and view the chart within your browser by running `npm start` from within the project's folder. Doing so will allow you to hover your mouse over the various segments of the chart, each of which represents a dependency encountered by Browserify during its compilation process. While it is not evident in Figure 5-1, an in-depth analysis of the chart indicates that our application's custom code accounts for only a tiny sliver (9.7kB) of the total size of the bundle generated by Browserify. The vast majority of this project's nearly 2MB of code consists of third-party dependencies (e.g., Angular, jQuery, Lodash, etc.), an important fact that will be referenced again later in the chapter.

Note   You may also be interested in investigating the `browserify-graph` and `colony` command-line utilities (also available via npm), which you can use to generate additional visualizations of a project's dependency tree.

Creating New Bundles As Changes Occur

Projects that take advantage of Browserify cannot be run directly within the browser—they must first be compiled. In order to make the most efficient use of the tool, it is important that projects be set up in such a way as to *automatically* trigger this step as changes occur within their source code. Let's take a look at two methods by which this can be achieved.

Watching for File Changes with Grunt

In Chapter 1 on Grunt, you discovered how plugins such as `grunt-contrib-watch` allow developers to trigger build steps as changes are made within an application's source code. It's easy to see how such tools could be applied to projects using Browserify, triggering the creation of new bundles as changes are detected. An example of this process in action can be seen by running the default Grunt task for this chapter's `simple` project, as shown in Listing 5-6.

Listing 5-6. Triggering the Creation of New Browserify Builds with Grunt

```
$ grunt
Running "browserify" task

Running "concurrent:serve" (concurrent) task
    Running "watch" task
    Waiting...
    Running "server" task
    App is now available at: http://localhost:7000
    >> File "app/index.js" changed.
    Running "browserify" task

    Done, without errors.
    Completed in 0.615s at Fri Jun 26 2015 08:31:25 GMT-0500 (CDT) - Waiting...
```

In this example, running the default Grunt task triggered three steps:

- A Browserify bundle was immediately created.

- A web server was launched to host the project.

- A watch script was executed that triggers the creation of new Browserify bundles as source code changes are detected.

This simple approach typically serves most small projects quite well; however, as small projects gradually evolve into large projects, developers often grow frustrated, understandably, with the ever-increasing build times that accompany it. Having to wait several seconds before you can try out each of your updates can quickly destroy any sense of "flow" that you might hope to achieve. Fortunately, Browserify's sister application, Watchify, can help us in these situations.

Watching for File Changes with Watchify

If Browserify (which compiles applications in their entirety) can be thought of as a meat cleaver, Watchify can be thought of as a paring knife. When invoked, Watchify initially compiles a specified application in its entirety; however, rather than exiting once this process has completed, Watchify continues to run, watching for changes to a project's source code. As changes are detected, Watchify recompiles *only those files that have changed*, resulting in drastically faster build times. Watchify accomplishes this by maintaining its own internal caching mechanism throughout each build.

As with Browserify, Watchify can be invoked via either the command line or a provided API. In Listing 5-7, this chapter's simple project is compiled with the help of Watchify's command-line utility. In this example, the -v argument is passed to specify that Watchify should run in verbose mode. As a result, Watchify notifies us as changes are detected.

Listing 5-7. Installing Watchify via npm and Running It Against This Chapter's simple Project

```
$ npm install -g watchify
$ watchify public/app/index.js -o public/dist/app.js -v
778 bytes written to public/dist/app.js (0.03 seconds)
786 bytes written to public/dist/app.js (0.01 seconds)
```

As with Browserify, Watchify provides a convenient API that allows us to integrate it into a larger build process (see Listing 5-8). We can do so with just a few small tweaks to the Browserify task previously shown in Listing 5-7.

Listing 5-8. Grunt Task Demonstrating the Use of Watchify's API

```
// simple/tasks/watchify.js

module.exports = function(grunt) {

    grunt.registerTask('watchify', function() {
        var done = this.async();
        var browserify = require('browserify');
        var watchify = require('watchify');
        var fs = require('fs');
        var path = require('path');
        var src = path.join('public', 'app', 'index.js');
        var target = path.join('public', 'dist', 'app.js');
        var targetDir = path.join('public', 'dist');

        var browserify = browserify({
            'cache': {},
            'packageCache': {}
        });
```

```
    browserify = watchify(browserify);
    browserify.add(src);

    var compile = function(err, data) {
        if (err) return grunt.log.error(err);
        if (!data) return grunt.log.error('No data');
        grunt.file.mkdir(targetDir);
        fs.writeFileSync(target, data);
    };

    browserify.bundle(compile);

    browserify.on('update', function() {
        browserify.bundle(compile);
    });

    browserify.on('log', function(msg) {
        grunt.log.oklns(msg);
    });

  });

};
```

In this example, we wrap our browserify instance with watchify. Afterward, we recompile the project as needed by subscribing to the update event emitted by our wrapped instance.

Using Multiple Bundles

In the earlier section "Visualizing the Dependency Tree," we looked at an interactive chart that allowed us to visualize the various dependencies encountered by Browserify as it compiled this chapter's advanced project (see Figure 5-1). One of the most important facts that we can take away from this chart is that the project's custom code (found in /app) accounts for only a tiny portion (9.7kB) of the bundle's total size of 1.8MB. In other words, the vast majority of this project's code consists of third-party libraries (e.g., Angular, jQuery, Lodash, etc.) that are unlikely to frequently change. Let's take a look at how we can use this knowledge to our advantage.

This chapter's extracted project is identical to the advanced project in every way, with one exception: instead of compiling a single Browserify bundle, the extracted project's build process creates two separate bundles:

- /dist/vendor.js: Third-party dependencies

- /dist/app.js: Custom application code

By taking this approach, browsers can more efficiently access project updates as they are released. In other words, as changes occur within the project's custom code, browsers only need to redownload /dist/app.js. Contrast this approach with that of the advanced project, in which each update (no matter how small) forces clients to redownload the project's nearly 2MB bundle.

Listing 5-9 shows the HTML file for the extracted project. As you can see, here we reference two separate bundles, /dist/vendor.js and /dist/app.js.

Listing 5-9. HTML for This Chapter's extracted Project

```
// extracted/public/index.html

<!DOCTYPE html>
<html ng-app="app">
<head>
    <meta charset="utf-8">
    <meta http-equiv="X-UA-Compatible" content="IE=edge">
    <meta name="viewport" content="width=device-width, initial-scale=1">
    <title>Browserify - Advanced Example</title>
    <link rel="stylesheet" href="/css/style.css">
</head>
<body class="container">
    <navbar ng-if="user_id"></navbar>

    <div ng-view></div>

    <footer><a href="/disc.html">View this project's dependency tree</a></footer>

    <script src="/dist/vendor.js"></script>
    <script src="/dist/app.js"></script>
</body>
</html>
```

Listing 5-10 shows the `extracted` project's Gruntfile. Take note of a special configuration value (`browserify.vendor_modules`) that is being set.

Listing 5-10. Gruntfile for This Chapter's `extracted` Project

```
// extracted/Gruntfile.js

module.exports = function(grunt) {

    grunt.initConfig({
        'browserify': {
            'vendor_modules': [
                'angular',
                'bootstrap-sass',
                'jquery',
                'angular-route',
                'angular-sanitize',
                'restangular',
                'jquery.cookie',
                'lodash',
                'underscore.string',
                'lodash-deep'
            ]
        }
    });

    grunt.loadTasks('tasks');

    grunt.registerTask('default', ['compass', 'browserify', 'browserify-
    vendor', 'init-db', 'concurrent']);

};
```

Listing 5-11 shows the contents of the `extracted` project's `browserify` Grunt task. This task largely mimics the corresponding task in the `advanced` project, with one major exception. In this task, we iterate through the third-party modules that we defined in the project's Gruntfile, and for each entry, we instruct Browserify to exclude the referenced module from the compiled bundle.

Listing 5-11. The extracted Project's browserify Grunt Task

```
// extracted/tasks/browserify.js

module.exports = function(grunt) {

    grunt.registerTask('browserify', function() {

        var done = this.async();
        var path = require('path');
        var fs = require('fs');
        var target = path.join('public', 'dist', 'app.js');
        var vendorModules = grunt.config.get('browserify.vendor_modules') || [];

        var browserify = require('browserify')([
            path.join('app', 'index.js')
        ], {
            'paths': ['app'],
            'fullPaths': true,
            'bundleExternal': true
        });

        vendorModules.forEach(function(vm) {
            grunt.log.writelns('Excluding module from application bundle:
            %s', vm);
            browserify.exclude(vm);
        });

        browserify.bundle(function(err, data) {
            if (err) return grunt.fail.fatal(err);
            grunt.file.mkdir(path.join('public', 'dist'));
            fs.writeFileSync(target, data);
            grunt.task.run('disc');
            done();
        });

    });

};
```

Finally, Listing 5-12 shows the contents of the extracted project's browserify-vendor Grunt task. When run, this task will create a separate Browserify bundle consisting solely of the third-party modules that we defined in Listing 5-10.

Listing 5-12. The extracted Project's browserify-vendor Grunt Task

```
// extracted/tasks/browserify-vendor.js

module.exports = function(grunt) {

    grunt.registerTask('browserify-vendor', function() {

        var done = this.async();
        var path = require('path');
        var fs = require('fs');
        var target = path.join('public', 'dist', 'vendor.js');
        var vendorModules = grunt.config.get('browserify.vendor_modules') || [];

        var browserify = require('browserify')({
            'paths': [
                'app'
            ],
            'fullPaths': true
        });

        vendorModules.forEach(function(vm) {
            browserify.require(vm);
        });

        browserify.bundle(function(err, data) {
            if (err) return grunt.fail.fatal(err);
            grunt.file.mkdir(path.join('public', 'dist'));
            fs.writeFileSync(target, data);
            done();
        });

    });

};
```

To see this process in action, navigate to the `extracted` project in your terminal and run $ `npm start`. Any missing npm modules will be installed, and the project's default Grunt task will be run. As this process occurs, two separate bundles will be created. The bundle containing the project's custom code, `/dist/app.js`, comes in at only 14kB in size.

The Node Way

As mentioned in this chapter's introduction, Browserify compiles a project by recursively scanning its source code in search of calls to a global `require()` function. As these calls are found, Browserify loads the modules they reference via the same `require()` function used by Node. Afterward, Browserify merges them into a single bundle that browsers are capable of understanding.

In this regard, projects that use Browserify are best thought of as client-side Node applications. Many aspects of Browserify that tend to confuse newcomers are more readily understood when this concept—along with everything that it entails—is kept in mind. Let's take a look at two such aspects now: module resolution and dependency management.

Module Resolution and the NODE_PATH Environment Variable

Node applications have the ability to reference modules in a number of ways. For example, here we see a simple Node application that requires a module by providing a relative path to its location:

```
var animals = require('./lib/animals');
```

In a similar manner, this example could also have provided the full, absolute path to this module. Either way, the location at which Node is expected to find this module is rather obvious. Now consider the following example, in which a module is referenced solely by name:

```
var animals = require('animals');
```

In situations such as this, Node will first attempt to locate the referenced module within its core library. This process can be seen in action when loading modules such as fs, Node's file system module. If no match is found, Node will then proceed to search for folders named node_modules, starting with the location of the module that called require() and working its way upward through the file system. As these folders are encountered, Node will check to see if they contain a module (or package) matching that which was requested. This process will continue until a match is found, and if none is found, an exception is thrown.

This simple yet powerful method by which module resolution occurs within Node revolves almost exclusively around the node_modules folder. However, Node provides an often-overlooked method that allows developers to augment this behavior by defining *additional* folders within which Node should be allowed to search for modules, should the previous steps turn up empty-handed. Let's take a look at this chapter's path-env project, which demonstrates how this can be accomplished.

Listing 5-13 shows an excerpt from this project's package.json file. Of particular importance is the start script that has been defined. Based on the settings shown here, when $ npm start is run within this project, the NODE_PATH environment variable will be updated to include a reference to this project's /lib folder before the application is run. As a result, Node will add this folder to those it uses to resolve the location of named modules.

Listing 5-13. This Project's npm start Script Updates the NODE_PATH Environment Variable

```
// path-env/package.json

{
    "name": "path-env",
    "version": "1.0.0",
    "main": "./bin/index.js",
    "scripts": {
            "start": "export NODE_PATH=$NODE_PATH:./lib && node ./bin/
            index.js"
    }
}
```

Note   On OS X and Linux, environment variables are set from the terminal by running export `ENVIRONMENT_VARIABLE=value`. The command to be used within the Windows command line is `set ENVIRONMENT_VARIABLE=value`.

The significance of setting the `NODE_PATH` environment variable may not be obvious at first glance; however, doing so can have a dramatically positive impact on the cleanliness and maintainability of complex projects. Why? Because when this approach is used, it essentially allows developers to create a namespace through which an application's modules (those that do not exist as independent npm packages) can be referenced by name, rather than by lengthy relative paths. Listing 5-14 shows a simple example of what this looks like in practice.

Listing 5-14. Several of the Modules Contained Within the `path-env` Project

```
// path-env/bin/index.js

var api = require('app/api');

// path-env/lib/app/api/index.js

var express = require('express');
var path = require('path');
var app = express();
var animals = require('app/models/animal');
app.use('/', express.static(path.join(__dirname, '..', '..', '..', 'public')));
app.get('/animals', function(req, res, next) {
    res.send(animals);
});
app.listen(7000, function() {
    console.log('App is now available at: http://localhost:7000');
});
module.exports = app;

// path-env/lib/app/models/animal/index.js

module.exports = [
    'Aardvarks', 'Cats', 'Dogs', 'Lemurs', 'Three-Toed Sloths', 'Zebras'
];
```

Take note of this example's lack of relative module references. For example, notice how this project's main script, `bin/index.js`, is able to load a custom module responsible for initializing Express via `require('app/api');`. The alternative would be to use a relative path: `require('../lib/app/api');`. Anyone who has worked within complex Node applications and encountered module references along the line of `require('../../../../models/animal');` will quickly come to appreciate the increase in code clarity that this approach affords.

Note   It is important to bear in mind that the use of the NODE_PATH environment variable only makes sense within the context of a Node (or Browserify) application—*not* a package. When creating a reusable package that is intended to be shared with others, you should rely solely on Node's default module resolution behavior.

Taking Advantage of NODE_PATH Within Browserify

Thus far, we have focused on how the NODE_PATH environment variable can have a positive impact on server-side Node applications. Now that we have laid that groundwork, let's see how this concept can be applied within the context of client-side, browser-based applications compiled with Browserify.

Listing 5-15 shows the `browserify` Grunt task for this chapter's `advanced` project, which is responsible for compiling the application via Browserify's API. Of particular importance is the use of the `paths` option, which allows us to provide Browserify with an array of paths that should be appended to the NODE_PATH environment variable before compilation begins. It is this setting that allows us to easily take advantage of the same benefits demonstrated in this section's previous examples.

Listing 5-15. The `browserify` Grunt Task for This Chapter's `advanced` Project

```
// advanced/tasks/browserify.js

module.exports = function(grunt) {

    grunt.registerTask('browserify', function() {
        var done = this.async();
        var path = require('path');
        var fs = require('fs');
```

```
    var target = path.join('public', 'dist', 'app.js');
    var browserify = require('browserify')([
        path.join('app', 'index.js')
    ], {
        'paths': [
            'app'
        ],
        'fullPaths': true
    });
    browserify.bundle(function(err, data) {
        if (err) return grunt.fail.fatal(err);
        grunt.file.mkdir(path.join('public', 'dist'));
        fs.writeFileSync(target, data);
        grunt.task.run('disc');
        done();
    });
  });
};
```

For a simple demonstration of how this approach has positively impacted this project, consider Listing 5-16. Here we see a small module that is responsible for loading lodash and integrating two third-party utilities, underscore.string and lodash-deep. The final, exported value is a single object containing the combined functionality of all three modules.

Listing 5-16. Module Responsible for Loading Lodash and Integrating Various Third-Party Plugins

```
// advanced/app/utils/index.js

var _ = require('lodash');
_.mixin(require('underscore.string'));
_.mixin(require('lodash-deep'));
module.exports = _;
```

As a result of the paths value that was provided to Browserify, our application can now reference this module from any location by simply calling require('app/utils');.

Dependency Management

Up until quite recently, the notion of "dependency management" has (for the most part) been a foreign concept within the context of client-side, browser-based projects. The tide has swiftly turned, however, thanks in large part to the rapidly increasing popularity of Node, along with additional utilities built on top of it—a few of which this book has already covered (e.g., Grunt and Yeoman). These utilities have helped to bring desperately needed tooling and guidance to the untamed, "Wild West" that once was (and largely still is) client-side development.

In regard to dependency management, Bower has helped address this need by providing client-side developers with an easy-to-use mechanism for managing the various third-party libraries that applications rely on. For developers who are new to this concept and are not using client-side compilers such as Browserify, Bower has always been and continues to be a viable option for managing a project's dependencies; however, as developers begin to see the advantages afforded by tools such as Browserify, Bower has begun to show signs of age. Furthermore, Bower is now almost defunct and is no longer under rapid development. As such, more and more developers are migrating away from Bower and turning toward alternative solutions, Browserify being one. Of course, Bower can still be used and is being used by many JS projects, but relying heavily on Bower is not something that is recommended.

At the beginning of this section, we mentioned that projects using Browserify are best thought of as client-side Node applications. In regard to dependency management, this statement is particularly important. Recall that during Browserify's compile process, a project's source code is scanned for calls to a global `require()` function. When found, these calls are executed within Node, and the returned value is subsequently made available to the client-side application. The important implication here is that when using Browserify, dependency management is significantly simplified when developers rely solely on npm, Node's package manager. While technically, yes, it is possible to instruct Browserify on how to load packages installed by Bower, more often than not, it's simply more trouble than it's worth.

Defining Browser-Specific Modules

Consider a scenario in which you would like to create a new module, which you intend to publish and share via npm. You want this module to work both within Node and within the browser (via Browserify). To facilitate this, Browserify supports the use of a `browser` configuration setting within a project's `package.json` file. When defined, this setting allows developers to override the location used to locate a particular module. To better understand how this works, let's take a look at two brief examples.

Listing 5-17 shows the contents of a simple package. Within this package, two modules exist, `lib/node.js` and `lib/browser.js`. According to this package's `package.json` file, the `main` module for this package is `lib/node.js`. In other words, when this package is referenced by name within a Node application, this is the module Node will load. Notice, however, that an additional configuration setting has been defined: `"browser": "./lib/browser.js"`. As a result of this setting, Browserify will load this module rather than the one specified by `main`.

Listing 5-17. Module Exposing Two Distinct Entry Points: One for Node, the Other for Browserify

```
// browser1/package.json

{
  "name": "browser1",
  "version": "1.0.0",
  "main": "./lib/node.js",
  "browser": "./lib/browser.js"
}

// browser1/lib/browser.js

module.exports = {
    'run': function() {
        console.log('I am running within a browser.');
    }
};
```

```
// browser1/lib/node.js

module.exports = {
    'run': function() {
        console.log('I am running within Node.');
    }
};
```

As you will see in a moment, Browserify's `browser` configuration setting need not be limited to simply overriding the location of a package's `main` module. It can also be used to override the location of *multiple* modules within a package. By way of an example, consider Listing 5-18. In this instance, instead of providing a string for our `package.json` file's `browser` setting, we provide an object, allowing us to specify *multiple*, browser-specific overrides.

Listing 5-18. Module Exposing Multiple, Distinct Modules for Node and Browserify

```
// browser2/package.json

{
  "name": "browser2",
  "version": "1.0.0",
  "main": "./lib/node.js",
  "browser": {
    "./lib/node.js": "./lib/browser.js",
    "./lib/extra.js": "./lib/extra-browser.js"
  }
}
```

As in Listing 5-17, a module that implements this pattern will expose distinct entry points into itself: one for Node and a separate one for applications compiled via Browserify. This example takes this concept a step further, however. As this module is compiled, should it ever attempt to load the module located at `lib/extra.js`, the module located at `lib/extra-browser` will be substituted instead. In this way, the `browser` setting allows us to create modules with behavior that can vary greatly depending on whether those modules are run within Node or within the browser.

Extending Browserify with Transforms

Developers can build upon Browserify's core functionality by creating plugins, called *transforms*, that tap into the compilation process that occurs as new bundles are created. Such transforms are installed via npm and are enabled once their names are included within the `browserify.transform` array in an application's `package.json` file. Let's take a look at a few useful examples.

brfs

The `brfs` transform simplifies the process of loading file contents inline. It extends Browserify's compilation process to search for calls to the `fs.readFileSync()` method. When found, the contents of the referenced file are immediately loaded and returned.

Listing 5-19 shows an excerpt from the `package.json` file for this chapter's `transforms-brfs` project. In this example, the `brfs` module has been installed and included within the `browserify.transform` configuration setting.

Listing 5-19. Excerpt from the `package.json` File for This Chapter's `transforms-brfs` Project

```
// transforms-brfs/package.json

{
  "name": "transforms-brfs",
  "dependencies": {
    "browserify": "^10.2.4",
    "brfs": "^1.4.0"
  },
  "browserify": {
    "transform": [
        "brfs"
    ]
  }
}
```

Listing 5-20 shows the contents of this project's `/app/index.js` module. In this example, the `brfs` transform will load the contents of `/app/templates/lorem.html`, which is subsequently assigned to the `tpl` variable.

Listing 5-20. Loading a Template via `fs.readFileSync()`

```
// transforms-brfs/app/index.js

var fs = require('fs');
var $ = require('jquery');
var tpl = fs.readFileSync(__dirname + '/templates/lorem.html', 'utf8');
$('#container').html(tpl);
```

folderify

Much like the `brfs` transform, the `folderify` transform allows you to load the contents of files inline. Rather than operating on a single file at a time, however, `folderify` allows you to quickly load the contents of *multiple* files. By way of an example, consider Listing 5-21, which shows the contents of this chapter's `transforms-folderify` application.

Listing 5-21. Loading the Contents of Multiple Files with `folderify`

```
// transforms-folderify/app/index.js

var $ = require('jquery');
var includeFolder = require('include-folder');
var folder = includeFolder(__dirname + '/templates');

for (var k in folder) {
    $('#container').append('<p>' + k + ': ' + folder[k] + '</p>');
}
```

As in the previous example, the `package.json` file for this project has been modified to include `folderify` within its `browserify.transform` array. When compiled, Browserify will search for references to the `include-folder` module. When the function it returns is called, Browserify will load the contents of each file it finds within the specified folder and return them in the form of an object.

bulkify

With the bulkify transform, developers can import multiple modules with a single call. To better understand how this works, see Listing 5 22, which shows an excerpt of the contents of the main application file for this chapter's transforms-bulkify project.

Listing 5-22. Main Application File for This Chapter's transforms-bulkify Project

```
// transforms-bulkify/app/index.js

var bulk = require('bulk-require');

var app = angular.module('app', [
    'ngRoute'
]);

var routes = bulk(__dirname, [
    'routes/**/route.js'
]).routes;

app.config(function($routeProvider) {

    var defaultRoute = 'dashboard';

    _.each(routes, function(route, route_name) {
        route = route.route;
        route.config.resolve = route.config.resolve || {};
        $routeProvider.when(route.route, route.config);
    });

    $routeProvider.otherwise({
        'redirectTo': defaultRoute
    });

});
```

This particular example demonstrates the use of Browserify within the context of an Angular application. If you are unfamiliar with Angular (covered in Chapter 7), don't worry—the important aspect of this example is the manner in which the bulk() method allows us to require() multiple modules matching one or more specified patterns (in this case, routes/**/route.js).

Figure 5-2 shows the file structure for this project. As you can see, the app/routes module contains three folders, each representing a route within our Angular application. The bulkify transform has allowed us to quickly require() each of these modules with a single call to bulk(). Afterward, we are able to iterate over the resulting object and pass each route to Angular.

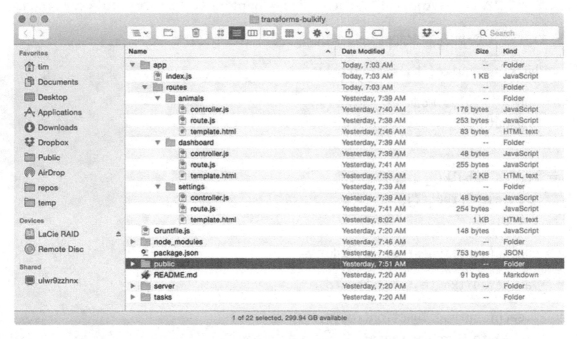

Figure 5-2. *File structure for this chapter's* `transforms-bulkify` *project*

Browserify-Shim

Developers using Browserify will occasionally find themselves needing to import modules that do not conform to the CommonJS way of doing things. Consider a third-party Foo library that, once loaded, assigns itself to the global window.Foo variable (see Listing 5-23). Such libraries can be imported with the help of the browserify-shim transform.

Listing 5-23. Third-Party Foo Library That Assigns Itself to the Global Foo Variable

```
// transforms-shim/app/vendor/foo.js

function Foo() {
    console.log('Bar');
}
```

After installing the browserify-shim module locally via npm, enable it by adding its name to the list of enabled transforms within a project's package.json file, as shown previously in Listing 5-19. Next, create a browserify-shim object at the root level of your application's package.json file, which will serve as the configuration object for this transform (see Listing 5-24). In this example, each key within this object represents the path to an improperly exposed module, while the corresponding value specifies the global variable to which the module has assigned itself.

Listing 5-24. Configuring browserify-shim Within a Project's package.json File

```
// transforms-shim/package.json

{
  "name": "transforms-shim",
  "version": "1.0.0",
  "main": "server.js",
  "browserify": {
    "transform": [
      "browserify-shim"
    ]
  },
  "browserify-shim": {
    "./app/vendor/foo.js": "Foo"
  }
}
```

With the browserify-shim transform installed and configured, the module located at app/vendor/foo.js can now be properly imported via require().

Summary

Browserify is a powerful utility that extends the intuitive process by which modules are created and imported within Node to the browser. With its help, browser-based JavaScript applications can be organized as a series of small, easy-to-understand, and tightly focused modules that work together to form a larger and more complicated whole. What's more, there is nothing preventing applications that currently have no module management system in place from putting Browserify to use right away. The process of refactoring a monolithic application down into smaller components is not an overnight process and is best taken one step at a time. With the help of Browserify, you can do just that—as time and resources allow.

Related Resources

- Browserify: `http://browserify.org`
- Browserify transforms: `https://github.com/substack/node-browserify/wiki/list-of-transforms`
- brfs: `https://github.com/substack/brfs`
- Watchify: `https://github.com/substack/watchify`

PART III

Client-Side Frameworks

CHAPTER 6

Knockout

Complex systems are characterized by simple elements, acting on local knowledge with local rules, giving rise to complicated, patterned behavior.

—David West

Knockout is a JavaScript library concerned with binding HTML markup to JavaScript objects. It is not a full framework. It has no state router, HTTP AJAX capability, internal message bus, or module loader. Instead, it focuses on two-way data binding between JavaScript objects and the DOM. When the data in a JavaScript application changes, HTML elements bound to Knockout views receive automatic updates. Likewise, when DOM input occurs—through form field manipulation, for example—Knockout captures the input changes and updates the application state accordingly.

In place of low-level, imperative HTML element manipulation, Knockout uses specialized objects called *observables* and a custom binding syntax to express how application data relates to markup. The internal mechanics are fully customizable so developers can extend Knockout's capabilities with custom binding syntax and behaviors.

As an independent JavaScript library, Knockout has no dependencies. The presence of other libraries is often required to fulfill the application functions that Knockout does not perform, however, so it plays well with many other common libraries like jQuery, Underscore, Q, and so on. The Knockout API represents data binding operations at a much higher level than strict DOM manipulation, and so places Knockout closer to Backbone or Angular in terms of abstraction, but its slim, view-oriented feature set means it has a far smaller footprint.

Knockout is fully functional in all modern browsers and, as of this writing, extends back to cover Firefox 3.5+, Internet Explorer 6+, and Safari 6+. Its backward compatibility is especially impressive in light of its newest feature, HTML5-compatible components

163

© Sufyan bin Uzayr, Nicholas Cloud, Tim Ambler 2019
S. bin Uzayr et al., *JavaScript Frameworks for Modern Web Development*,
https://doi.org/10.1007/978-1-4842-4995-6_6

with custom markup tags. The Knockout team has taken pains to make the Knockout development experience seamless in a variety of browser environments.

This chapter explores Knockout's features and API through an example application that manages kitchen recipes. All chapter code examples will be prefixed with a comment to indicate in which file the example code actually resides. For example, in Listing 6-1, the `index.js` file would be found in the `knockout/example-000` directory distributed with this book's source code.

Listing 6-1. Not a Real Example

```
// example-000/index.js
console.log('this is not a real example');
```

To run examples, first install Node.js (refer to the Node.js documentation for your system) and then run `npm install` in the `knockout` directory to install all example code dependencies. Each example directory will contain an `index.js` file that runs a simple Node.js web server. To run each example, it will be necessary to launch this server and then navigate to a specified URL in a web browser. For example, to run the `index.js` file in Listing 6-1, navigate to the `knockout/example-000` directory at a terminal prompt and run `node index.js`.

All example pages include the core Knockout script in a `<script>` tag reference. You can download this script from `http://knockoutjs.com` or from one of a number of reputable content delivery networks. Knockout can also be installed as a Bower package or npm module and is both AMD and CommonJS compatible. The Knockout documentation contains detailed instructions for all of these installation methods.

Views, Models, and View Models

Knockout distinguishes between two sources of information in an application's user interface: the *data model*, which represents the state of the application, and the *view model*, which represents how that state is displayed or communicated to the user. Both of these models are created in an application as JavaScript objects. Knockout bridges them by giving view models a way to represent a data model in a view (HTML) friendly way while establishing bidirectional communication between views and data models so that input affects application state, and application state affects how a view represents data.

Since HTML is the technology that represents data in a web browser, Knockout view models can either bind directly to preexisting HTML document elements or create new elements with HTML templates. Knockout can even create complete reusable HTML components (custom HTML tags with their own attributes and behaviors).

The example application included with this chapter, *Omnom Recipes*, displays recipe data ("data model") in a browsable master/detail user interface. Both parts of this interface—the list of recipes and the details presented for each—are logical components situated ideally for Knockout view models. Each will have its own view model, and the application will coordinate the interactions between them. Eventually users will want to add or edit recipes, so additional HTML markup and view models will be introduced for that purpose.

Figure 6-1 shows the example application structure in the `example-001` directory as output of the `tree` command.

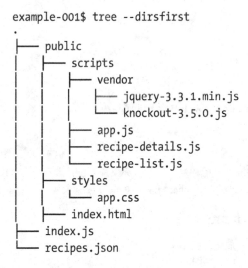

```
example-001$ tree --dirsfirst
.
├── public
│   ├── scripts
│   │   ├── vendor
│   │   │   ├── jquery-3.3.1.min.js
│   │   │   └── knockout-3.5.0.js
│   │   ├── app.js
│   │   ├── recipe-details.js
│   │   └── recipe-list.js
│   ├── styles
│   │   └── app.css
│   ├── index.html
├── index.js
└── recipes.json
```

Figure 6-1. *Example application structure*

The `index.js` file is responsible for launching a web server that will service requests for files in the `public` directory. When the application's web page makes an AJAX request for recipe data, the web server will serialize the data in `recipes.json` and return it to the client.

In the `public` directory, the `index.html` file will be served up by default when a user visits `http://localhost:8080`. This file contains application markup augmented with Knockout attributes. The `index.html` file also references the `app.css` stylesheet in public/styles, the two vendor scripts in public/scripts/vendor, and the three application scripts in public/scripts.

A Knockout view model can be applied to an entire page or scoped to specific elements on a page. For nontrivial applications, it is advisable to use multiple view models to maintain modularity. In the *Omnom Recipes* application, the user interface exists as two logical "components": a list of recipes and a detailed view of a selected recipe. Instead of using a monolithic view model for the entire page, the application divides Knockout logic into two JavaScript modules in public/scripts: recipe-list.js and recipe-details.js. The app.js module consumes both of these view models and coordinates their activities on the page.

Figure 6-2 shows a screenshot of the rendered application, the recipe list clearly visible on the left and the recipe details on the right.

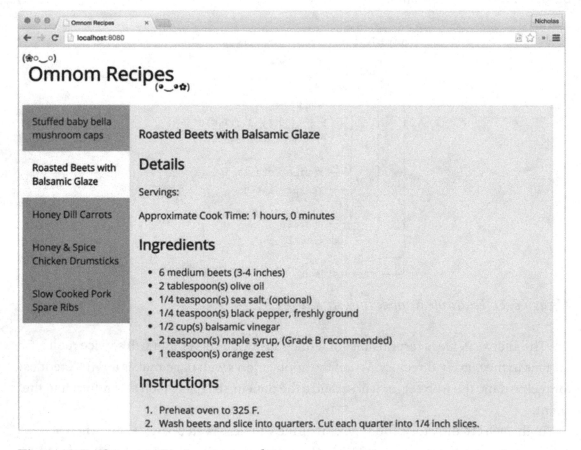

Figure 6-2. *Omnom Recipes screenshot*

Note   To avoid confusion the example application makes use of simple JavaScript closures instead of client-side frameworks or module-oriented build tools to organize modules. These closures often assign a single object to a property on the global `window` object that will be consumed by other scripts. For example, the `recipe-list.js` file creates a global object, `window.RecipeList`, to be used in the `app.js` file. While completely valid, this architectural decision should be viewed in light of the example application's simplistic requirements.

The Recipe List

The `index.html` file, which contains the full page markup and Knockout templates, is divided into three key top-level elements:

- The `<header>` element, which contains static HTML content that will not be manipulated by Knockout

- The `<nav id="recipe-list">` element, which contains an unordered list of recipes and *will* be manipulated by Knockout

- The `<section id="recipe-details">` element, which displays recipe information and *will also* be manipulated by Knockout

Although the recipe list element is small, it contains a number of different Knockout-specific bindings. The view model for this bit of HTML will be bound to the `<nav>` element. With that in mind, there are a number of things that may be inferred about how Knockout bindings work strictly from examining the markup in Listing 6-2.

Listing 6-2. Recipe List Markup and Bindings

```
<!-- example-001/public/index.html -->

<nav id="recipe-list">
  <ul data-bind="foreach: recipes">
    <li data-bind="text: title,
       click: $parent.selectRecipe.bind($parent),
       css: {selected: $parent.isSelected($data)}"></li>
  </ul>
</nav>
```

First, it is apparent that Knockout bindings are applied to HTML elements with the `data-bind` attribute. This is not the sole binding method but it is the most common. Both the `<ul>` element and the `<li>` element have bindings in the form `binding-name: binding-value`.

Second, multiple bindings may be applied to an element as a comma-delimited list, demonstrated by the `<li>` element, which has bindings for `text`, `click`, and `css`.

Third, bindings with more complex values, such as the `css` binding on the `<li>` element, use key/value hashes (`{key: value, ... }`) to define specific binding options.

Finally, binding *values* may refer to JavaScript primitives, view model properties, view model methods, or any valid JavaScript expression.

The recipe list Knockout bindings reveal certain things about the Knockout view model that will be bound to the `<nav>` element. Developers will immediately recognize the `foreach` flow control statement and correctly infer that `recipes` will be some collection exposed by the view model over which `foreach` will loop.

The `<li>` element within the unordered list has no HTML content of its own, so it may also be inferred that this element serves as a kind of *template* element that will be bound and rendered for each item in the `recipes` collection. As with most `foreach` loops, it is reasonable to expect the object *within* the loop (the loop's "context") to be an element of the collection. The list item's `text` binding references the `title` property of the recipe object for the current iteration and will be injected as the text content of the `<li>` element when rendered.

The `click` and `css` bindings both reference the special `$parent` object, which tells Knockout that the binding values should target the view model bound with `foreach` and not the current recipe object. (The view model is the "parent" context and the recipe is its "child.")

The `click` binding invokes the `selectRecipe()` method on the view model whenever the list item's `click` event is triggered. It binds the method to the view model specifically, by passing the `$parent` reference to the method's `bind()` function. This ensures that the value of `this` within the `selectRecipe()` method does not refer to the DOM element on which the handler is attached when it executes (the DOM's default behavior).

In contrast, the `isSelected()` method on the `$parent` (view model) object is invoked by the `css` binding, but Knockout, not the DOM, manages the invocation, ensuring the value of `this` within the method refers to the view model and not a DOM element.

The css binding instructs Knockout to apply specific CSS classes to a DOM element whenever specific criteria are met. The css binding value is a hash of selector/function pairs that Knockout evaluates whenever the DOM element is rendered. If the isSelected() method returns true, the selected CSS class will be added to the list item element. Another special variable, $data, is passed to isSelected(). The $data variable always refers to the *current* object context in which Knockout is working, in this case an individual recipe object. Some Knockout bindings, like text, operate on the current object context by default; others, like foreach, cause a context switch as a side effect.

In Listing 6-3, the context objects and values of each special variable are shown in HTML comments. Bindings have been abbreviated for clarity.

Listing 6-3. Changing Contexts with Knockout Bindings

```html
<!-- example-001/public/index.html -->

<nav id="recipe-list">
  <!-- context: viewmodel -->
  <!-- $parent === undefined -->
  <!-- $data === viewmodel -->
  <ul data-bind="foreach: ...">
    <!-- context: recipe -->
    <!-- $parent === viewmodel -->
    <!-- $data === recipe -->
    <li data-bind="text: ..."></li>
  </ul>
</nav>
```

The recipe list module in Listing 6-4 creates the view model object that Knockout will bind to the recipe list markup when the page is rendered. The module's create() method accepts a list of recipe objects—JSON data loaded from the server—and returns a view model object with data properties and methods. Nearly all Knockout view models will need to access helper functions on the global window.ko object, so it is passed to the module's closure function as an argument.

Listing 6-4. Recipe List View Model

```
// example-001/public/scripts/recipe-list.js
'use strict';
window.RecipeList = (function (ko) {

  return {
    create: function (recipes) {
      var viewmodel = {};

      // properties
      viewmodel.recipes = recipes;
      viewmodel.selectedRecipe = ko.observable(recipes[0]);

      // methods
      viewmodel.selectRecipe = function (recipe) {
        this.selectedRecipe(recipe);
      };

      viewmodel.isSelected = function (recipe) {
        return this.selectedRecipe() === recipe;
      };

      return viewmodel;
    }
  };

}(window.ko));
```

Note   The view model object itself may be created in any manner a developer chooses. In the example code, each view model is a simple object literal created by a factory method. It is common to see the JavaScript constructor function pattern used to create view models in the wild, but view models are merely objects and may be constructed as a developer sees fit.

Other than the `selectedRecipe` property, the recipe list view model is wholly unremarkable. The template's `foreach` binding is applied to the `recipes` property (an array of plain JavaScript objects), the `click` binding on each list item invokes

170

the `selectRecipe()` method (passing it a specific recipe), and when each list item is rendered, the `isSelected()` method is called to determine if the recipe being evaluated has been assigned to the `selectedRecipe` property or not. Actually, that is not entirely correct. The value of `selectedRecipe` is not actually a recipe object, but a function—a Knockout *observable*.

An observable is a special kind of function that holds a value and can notify potential subscribers whenever that value changes. Bindings between HTML elements and observables automatically create subscriptions that Knockout manages in the background. Observables are created with special factory functions on the global ko object. The `selectedRecipe` observable in Listing 6-5 is created when `ko.observable(recipes[0])` is called. Its initial value is the first element in the `recipes` array. When `selectedRecipe()` is invoked with no argument, it returns the value it contains (in this case, the object in `recipes[0]`). Any value passed to `selectedRecipe()` will become its new value. Although the `selectedRecipe()` property is not bound to any element in the recipe list template, it *is* manipulated when the user interacts with the recipe list via the view model's methods. The changing value of this element will be used as input for the next page component: recipe details.

Recipe Details

When a recipe is clicked in the recipe list, the recipe details are displayed in the right pane (refer to Figure 6-2). The markup in Listing 6-5 shows the HTML elements and Knockout bindings used to render the recipe details view model in the DOM.

Listing 6-5. Recipe Details Markup and Bindings

```
<!-- example-001/public/index.html -->
<section id="recipe-details">
  <h1 data-bind="text: title"></h1>

  <h2>Details</h2>
  <p>Servings: <span data-bind="text: servings"></span></p>
  <p>Approximate Cook Time: <span data-bind="text: cookingTime"></span></p>

  <h2>Ingredients</h2>

  <ul data-bind="foreach: ingredients">
    <li data-bind="text: $data"></li>
  </ul>
```

```
<h2>Instructions</h2>

<ol data-bind="foreach: instructions">
  <li data-bind="text: $data"></li>
</ol>

<a data-bind="visible: hasCitation,
  attr: {href: citation, title: title}"
  target="_blank">Source</a>
```

```
</section>
```

Some bindings, like the `<h1>` `text` binding, read a value from a view model property and inject its string value into the HTML element.

Because the paragraphs under the "Details" heading have static content (the text "Servings:" and "Approximate Cook Time:"), `<span>` tags are used to anchor the Knockout bindings for the `servings` and `cookingTimes` properties at the end of each paragraph.

The ingredients list iterates over a collection of strings with the `foreach` binding, so the context object within each loop is a string represented by the `$data` variable. Each string becomes the text content of a list item.

The `<a>` tag at the bottom links to the recipe's web site of origin as a citation. If the recipe has no citation, the anchor will not be displayed. The element's `visible` binding examines the view model's `hasCitation` observable and, if the value is empty, hides the anchor element. Like the `css` binding used in the recipe list, the `attr` binding takes a key/value hash as its binding value. Hash keys (`href` and `title`) are the element attributes to be set on the anchor, and values are properties on the view model that will be bound to each attribute.

The recipe details view model has many more members than the recipe list view model. Listing 6-6 shows that the recipe details view model is created in a similar fashion, by invoking the `RecipeDetails.create()` function with a specific recipe object that will be used to add data to the view model. This module uses several functions on the global `ko` object, and so, like the recipe list, it is passed as an argument to the module closure.

Listing 6-6.   Recipe Details View Model

```
// example-001/public/scripts/recipe-details.js
'use strict';
window.RecipeDetails = (function (ko) {

  return {
    create: function (recipe) {
      var viewmodel = {};
      // add properties and methods...
      return viewmodel;
    }
  };

}(window.ko));
```

For each property on the recipe object, the recipe details view model has a corresponding observable property, shown in Listing 6-7. Observables are really only useful if the value they contain is expected to *change*. If values are expected to be static, plain JavaScript properties and values may be used instead. Observables are used in the recipe details view model because there will only be one instance of the view model bound to the page. When a new recipe is selected in the recipe list, the recipe details view model will be updated with the new recipe's values. Because its properties are observables, the page's markup will change immediately.

Listing 6-7.   Recipe Details View Model Properties

```
// example-001/public/scripts/recipe-details.js
// properties
viewmodel.title = ko.observable(recipe.title);
viewmodel.servings = ko.observable(recipe.servings);
viewmodel.hours = ko.observable(recipe.cookingTime.hours);
viewmodel.minutes = ko.observable(recipe.cookingTime.minutes);
viewmodel.ingredients = ko.observableArray(recipe.ingredients);
viewmodel.instructions = ko.observableArray(recipe.instructions);
viewmodel.citation = ko.observable(recipe.citation);
```

```
viewmodel.cookingTime = ko.computed(function () {
  return '$1 hours, $2 minutes'
    .replace('$1', this.hours())
    .replace('$2', this.minutes());
}, viewmodel);
```

Listing 6-8 shows two new types of observables: `ko.observableArray()` and `ko.computed()`.

Observable arrays monitor their values (normal JavaScript arrays) for additions, deletions, and index changes, so that if the array mutates, any subscriber to the observable array is notified. While the ingredients and instructions do not change in this example, code will be introduced later to manipulate the collections and show the observable array's automatic binding updates in action.

Computed observables *generate* or *compute* a value based on other values exposed by observables on the view model. The `ko.computed()` function accepts callback that will be invoked to generate the value of the computed observable and optionally a context object that acts as the value of `this` within the callback. When referenced by a template binding, a computed observable's value will be whatever its callback returns. The `cookingTime` property in Listing 6-8 creates a formatted string interpolated with the values from the `hours` and `minutes` observables. If either `hours` or `minutes` changes, the `cookingTime` computed observable will also update its subscribers.

Note   Because `hours` and `minutes` are really *functions* (though they are treated as properties in Knockout binding expressions), each must be invoked in the body of the computed observable in order to retrieve its value.

The recipe details view model methods in Listing 6-8 are fairly straightforward. The `hasCitation()` method tests the `citation` property for a nonempty value, while the `update()` method accepts a recipe and updates observable properties on the view model with new values. This method is not bound to the view, but will be used when a recipe in the recipe list view model is selected.

Listing 6-8. Recipe Details View Model Methods

```
// example-001/public/scripts/recipe-details.js
// methods
viewmodel.hasCitation = function () {
  return this.citation() !== ";
};

viewmodel.update = function (recipe) {
  this.title(recipe.title);
  this.servings(recipe.servings);
  this.hours(recipe.cookingTime.hours);
  this.minutes(recipe.cookingTime.minutes);
  this.ingredients(recipe.ingredients);
  this.instructions(recipe.instructions);
  this.citation(recipe.citation);
};
```

Binding View Models to the DOM

Both view model factories are attached to the global window object and can be used to create individual view model instances that will be bound to the page. The app.js file, shown in Listing 6-9, is the main script that ties both recipe view models together.

Listing 6-9. Binding View Models to the DOM

```
// example-001/public/scripts/app.js
(function app ($, ko, RecipeList, RecipeDetails) {
  // #1
  var getRecipes = $.get('/recipes');

  // #2
  $(function () {
    // #3
    getRecipes.then(function (recipes) {
      // #4
      var list = RecipeList.create(recipes);
```

```
  // #5
  var details = RecipeDetails.create(list.selectedRecipe());
  // #6
  list.selectedRecipe.subscribe(function (recipe) {
    details.update(recipe);
  });
  // #7
  ko.applyBindings(list, document.querySelector('#recipe-list'));
  ko.applyBindings(details, document.querySelector('#recipe-details'));

}).fail(function () {
  alert('No recipes for you!');
});
});

}(window.jQuery, window.ko, window.RecipeList, window.RecipeDetails));
```

The app module is responsible for loading an initial set of recipe data from the server, waiting for the DOM to enter a ready state, and then instantiating view model instances and binding each to the appropriate elements. The following list describes each step comment (e.g., // #1) shown in Listing 6-10.

1. A jQuery promise is created that will resolve at some point in the future, when the data obtained from the GET /recipes request becomes available.

2. The function passed to $() will be triggered when the DOM has been completely initialized to ensure that all Knockout template elements will be present before any binding attempts.

3. When the jQuery promise resolves, it passes the list of recipes to its resolution handler. If the promise fails, an alert is shown to the user indicating that a problem occurred.

4. Once the recipe data has been loaded, the list view model is created. The recipe array is passed as an argument to RecipeList.create(). The return value is the actual recipe list view model object.

5. The recipe details view model is created in a similar fashion. Its factory function accepts a single recipe, and so the selectedRecipe property on the recipe list is queried for a value. (The recipe list view model chooses the very first recipe in its data array for this value, by default.)

6. After the recipe details view model has been created, it subscribes to change notifications on the recipe list's selectedRecipe observable. This is the manual equivalent of a DOM subscription created by Knockout when an observable is bound to an HTML element. The function provided to the subscribe() method will be invoked whenever selectedRecipe changes, receiving the new value as an argument. When the callback fires, the recipe details view model uses any newly selected recipe to update itself, thereby changing the values of its own observable properties.

7. Finally, view models are bound to the DOM when the global ko.applyBindings() function is invoked. In Listing 6 9 this function receives two arguments: the view model to be bound and the DOM element to which the view model will be bound. Any binding attribute Knockout encounters on this element or its descendants will be applied to the specified view model. If no DOM element is specified, Knockout assumes that the view model applies to the entire page. For simplistic pages this might be appropriate, but for more complex scenarios, using multiple view models that encapsulate their own data and behavior is the better option.

View Models and Forms

Knockout view model properties may be bound to form controls. Many controls, such as the <input> elements, share standard bindings like value; but others like <select> have element-specific bindings. For example, the options binding controls the creation of <option> elements within a <select> tag. In general, form field bindings behave much like bindings seen in example code up to this point, but complex forms can be tricky beasts and sometimes require more creative binding strategies.

The examples in this section build on the recipe details template and view model. Specifically, an "edit" mode is introduced whereby a user viewing a particular recipe can choose to alter its details through form fields. The same view model is used, but new form field elements have been added to the recipe details template, adding additional complexity to both.

Switching to "Edit" Mode

Three buttons have been added to the top and bottom of the recipe details markup. Figures 6-3 and 6-4 show how the buttons appear when rendered.

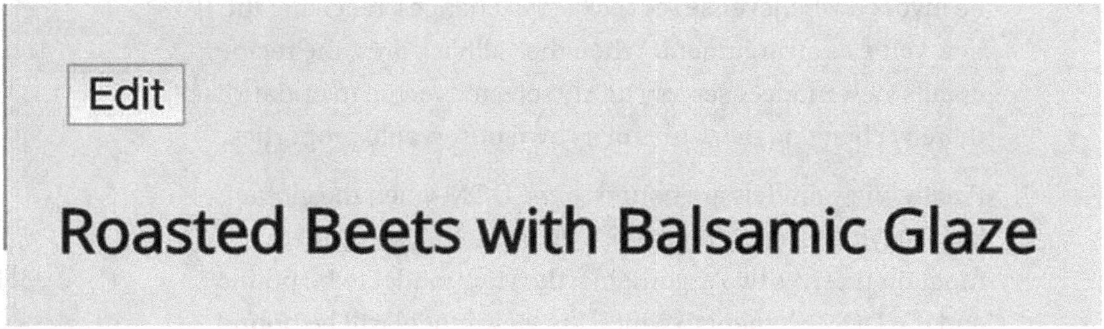

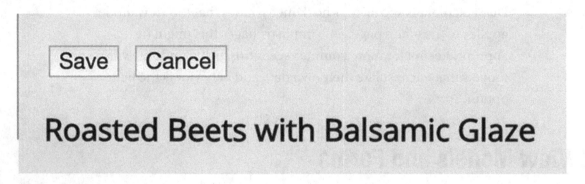

Figure 6-3. *In "view" mode, the Edit button is visible*

Figure 6-4. *In "edit" mode, the Save and Cancel buttons are visible*

The Edit button switches the page from viewing mode to edit mode (and shows the appropriate form fields for each part of the recipe being viewed). While in edit mode, the Edit button itself is hidden, but two other buttons, Save and Cancel, become visible.

If the user clicks the Save button, any changes made to the recipe will be persisted; in contrast, if the user clicks the Cancel button, the edit session will be aborted and the recipe details will revert to their original states.

The Knockout bindings for each button, shown in Listing 6-10, vary slightly from the bindings discussed so far.

Listing 6-10. Editing Button Markup

```
<!-- example-002/public/index.html -->
<div>
  <!-- in read-only view -->
  <button data-bind="click: edit, visible: !isEditing()">Edit</button>
  <!-- in edit view -->
  <button data-bind="click: save, visible: isEditing">Save</button>
  <button data-bind="click: cancelEdit, visible: isEditing">Cancel</button>
</div>
```

First, each button has a click event handler that calls a method on the view model: edit(), save(), and cancelEdit(). But unlike previous examples, these methods do not use the bind() function to ensure the value of this within the view model. Instead, all occurrences of the keyword this *within the view* model have been replaced with a reference to the object literal viewmodel, shown in Listing 6-11. The new properties and methods for these buttons have also been added to the recipe details view model. For brevity, Listing 6-11 omits the portions of recipe-list.js that have not changed.

Listing 6-11. Methods Reference the viewmodel Object, Not this

```
// example-002/public/scripts/recipe-details.js
// properties
viewmodel.previousState = null;
viewmodel.isEditing = ko.observable(false);

// methods
viewmodel.edit = function () {
  viewmodel.previousState = ko.mapping.toJS(viewmodel);
  viewmodel.isEditing(true);
};
```

```
viewmodel.save = function () {
  // TODO save recipe
  viewmodel.isEditing(false);
};

viewmodel.cancelEdit = function () {
  viewmodel.isEditing(false);
  ko.mapping.fromJS(viewmodel.previousState, {}, viewmodel);
};
```

Because the view model itself is assigned to a variable within the `RecipeDetails.` `create()` closure, its methods may reference it by name. By avoiding `this` altogether, event bindings are simplified and potential bugs are avoided.

Second, each button has a `visible` binding attached to the view model's `isEditing` observable, but only the Edit button invokes the method directly as a function. It also possesses the only binding that uses a negation (!) operator, which turns the binding value into an *expression*. Any observable evaluated within an expression must be invoked as a function to retrieve its value. If an observable is itself used as the binding value, as is the case with `visible` bindings for the Save and Cancel buttons, it will be invoked automatically when Knockout evaluates the binding.

All three methods, `edit()`, `save()`, and `cancelEdit()`, manipulate the value of the `isEditing` observable, which determines which button or buttons are displayed on the form (and, as shall be demonstrated shortly, which form fields are displayed as well). Editing begins when the `edit()` method is called and ends when the user either saves the recipe or cancels the editing session.

To ensure that changes to the recipe are discarded when a user cancels the edit session, the view model serializes its state when the editing session begins in anticipation of possible reversion. If the editing session is canceled, the previous state is deserialized and the value of each observable property is effectively reset.

The Knockout mapping plugin is used to serialize and deserialize the view model's state in the `edit()` and `cancelEdit()` methods:

```
// serializing the view model
viewmodel.previousState = ko.mapping.toJS(viewmodel);
// deserializing the view model
ko.mapping.fromJS(viewmodel.previousState, {}, viewmodel);
```

Tip   Knockout's mapping plugin is distributed separately from the core Knockout library. The current version may be downloaded from `http://knockoutjs.com/documentation/plugins-mapping.html`. To install the plugin, simply add a `<script>` tag reference to the plugin script *after* the core Knockout `<script>` tag on an HTML page. It will automatically create the `ko.mapping` namespace property on the global `ko` object.

The mapping plugin serializes/deserializes objects that possess observable properties, reading their values during serialization and setting their values during deserialization. When the `edit()` method calls `ko.mapping.toJS(viewmodel)`, it receives a plain JavaScript object literal whose property names are identical to those of the view model, but contain plain JavaScript data instead of observable functions. To push these values back into the view model's own observables when the edit session is cancelled, the `cancelEdit()` method invokes `ko.mapping.fromJS()` with three arguments:

- The plain JavaScript object literal that contains the data to be written to the view model's observable properties

- An object literal that maps properties on the plain JavaScript state object to observable properties on the view model (if this object is empty, it is assumed that the properties for both share the same names)

- The view model that will receive the object literal's data

Note   The Knockout mapper plugin can serialize/deserialize view models as plain JavaScript object literals with its `toJS()` and `fromJS()` functions, or as JSON strings with its `toJSON()` and `fromJSON()` functions. These functions can be particularly useful for CRUD (create + read + update + delete) view models that bind JSON data to simple forms.

Although the Save button is present on the form, its method has only been stubbed in the view model. Its functionality will be added in a later example.

Changing the Recipe Title

The recipe title is visible regardless of whether the recipe details view is in edit mode or read-only mode. When the user clicks the Edit button, a label and input field become visible beneath the `<h1>` tag so the user may update the recipe title if necessary. A `visible` binding on the containing `<div>` element controls shows and hides this field by subscribing to the `isEditing` observable on the view model. The value of the input field is bound to the view model's `title` observable via the `value` binding. By default, the `value` binding will only refresh data in an observable when the field to which the observable is bound loses focus. When the title input in Listing 6-12 loses focus, the `<h1>` tag's content will be instantly updated with the new title value because both are bound to the `title` observable. The rendered field is shown in Figure 6-5.

Listing 6-12. Recipe Title Markup

```
<!-- example-002/public/index.html -->
<h1 data-bind="text: title"></h1>
<!-- in edit view -->
<div data-bind="visible: isEditing" class="edit-field">
  <label for="recipe-title">Title:</label>
  <input data-bind="value: title" name="title" id="recipe-title"
type="text" />
</div>
```

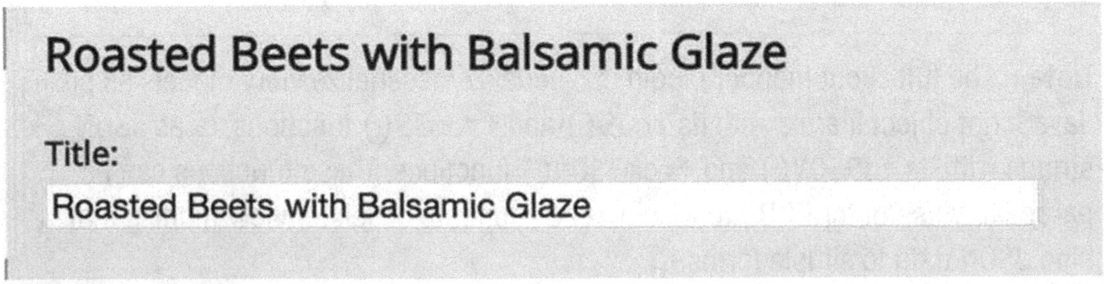

Roasted Beets with Balsamic Glaze

Title:

Roasted Beets with Balsamic Glaze

Figure 6-5. *Editing the recipe title*

Updating Recipe Servings and Cooking Time

In Listing 6-13 the recipe's read-only serving size <p> element is hidden when the form enters edit mode. In its place a <select> element is displayed with a number of serving size options from which the user may select. Once again, the isEditing observable is used to determine which elements are displayed.

Listing 6-13. Serving Size Markup

```
<!-- example-002/public/index.html -->
<h2>Details</h2>
<!-- in read-only view -->
<p data-bind="visible: !isEditing()">
  Servings: <span data-bind="text: servings"></span>
</p>
<!-- in edit view -->
<div data-bind="visible: isEditing" class="edit-field">
  <label for="recipe-servings">Servings:</label>
  <select data-bind="options: servingSizes,
          optionsText: 'text',
          optionsValue: 'numeral',
          value: servings,
          optionsCaption: 'Choose...'"
          name="recipeServings"
          id="recipe-servings">
  </select>
</div>
```

New, element-specific Knockout bindings are declared for the <select> tag in Listing 6-14 to control the manner in which it uses view model data. The options binding tells Knockout which property on the view model holds the data set that will be used to create <option> elements within the tag. The binding value is the name of the property (in this case servingSizes), a plain array of read-only reference data.

For primitive values, like strings or numbers, the options binding assumes that each primitive should be both the text and value of its <option> element. For complex objects, the optionsText and optionsValue bindings tell Knockout which properties on each object in the array will be used to generate the text and value of each <option> element instead. The serving size objects are defined in Listing 6-14. Notice that the text value is the name of each number, while the numeral value is a corresponding digit. When a serving size is selected by the user, the numeral value will be assigned to `viewmodel. servings()`.

Listing 6-14. Recipe Serving Size Data in the View Model

```
// example-002/public/scripts/recipe-details.js
// properties
viewmodel.servings = ko.observable(recipe.servings);
viewmodel.servingSizes = [
  {text: 'one', numeral: 1},
  {text: 'two', numeral: 2},
  {text: 'three', numeral: 3},
  {text: 'four', numeral: 4},
  {text: 'five', numeral: 5},
  {text: 'six', numeral: 6},
  {text: 'seven', numeral: 7},
  {text: 'eight', numeral: 8},
  {text: 'nine', numeral: 9},
  {text: 'ten', numeral: 10}
];
```

The `<select>` tag's `value` binding ties the selected value of the drop-down to an observable on the view model. When the `<select>` tag is rendered, this value will be automatically selected for the user in the DOM; when the user chooses a new value, the bound observable will be updated.

Finally, the `optionsCaption` binding creates a special `<option>` element in the DOM that appears at the top of the drop-down options list, but will never be set as the selected value on the view model. It is a mere cosmetic enhancement that gives some instruction to the user about how the drop-down is to be used.

Figures 6-6 and 6-7 show a collapsed and expanded serving size drop-down.

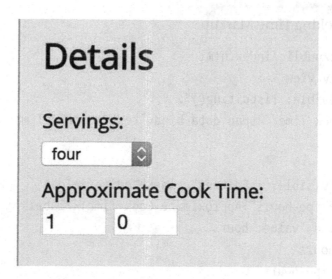

Figure 6-6. *Servings drop-down with a preselected value*

Figure 6-7. *Choosing a new value from the Servings drop-down*

The cooking time fields, also shown in Figure 6-5, contain no special bindings. Both input fields (hours and minutes) shown in Listing 6-15 are number fields that use simple `value` bindings to update observables on the view model. They are shown and hidden by the same visibility mechanism discussed earlier.

Listing 6-15. Cooking Time Markup

```
<!-- example-002/public/index.html -->
<!-- in read-only view -->
<p data-bind="visible: !isEditing()">
  Approximate Cook Time: <span data-bind="text: cookingTime"></span>
</p>
<!-- in edit view -->
<div data-bind="visible: isEditing" class="edit-field">
  <label for="recipe-hours">Approximate Cook Time:</label>
  <input data-bind="value: hours"
         name="hours"
         id="recipe-hours"
         type="number" />
  <input data-bind="value: minutes"
         name="minutes"
         id="recipe-minutes"
         type="number" />
</div>
```

Recall that when cooking time is displayed to the user in read-only mode, the cookingTime computed observable in Listing 6-16 is used, not the hours and minutes observables. When the values of these observables change based on the input bindings in Listing 6-16, the computed observable regenerates the formatted string for the view. Also notice that the computed observable no longer has a context argument, because inside the observable the view model variable is referenced by name instead of being resolved with the this keyword.

Listing 6-16. View Model Hours, Minutes, and Computed Cooking Time

```
// example-002/public/scripts/recipe-details.js
// properties
viewmodel.hours = ko.observable(recipe.cookingTime.hours);
viewmodel.minutes = ko.observable(recipe.cookingTime.minutes);
viewmodel.cookingTime = ko.computed(function () {
```

```
return '$1 hours, $2 minutes'
    .replace('$1', viewmodel.hours())
    .replace('$2', viewmodel.minutes());
});
```

Adding and Removing Ingredients

In read-only mode, recipe ingredients are rendered as an unordered list. To maintain form, when the recipe details view enters edit mode, an input is generated for each item in the list, shown in Figure 6-8. A minus button next to each ingredient allows the user to remove any or all ingredients, while an empty input field and a plus button below the input list may be used to add a new ingredient. Text changes made within any ingredient input will update the values in the view model's ingredients array.

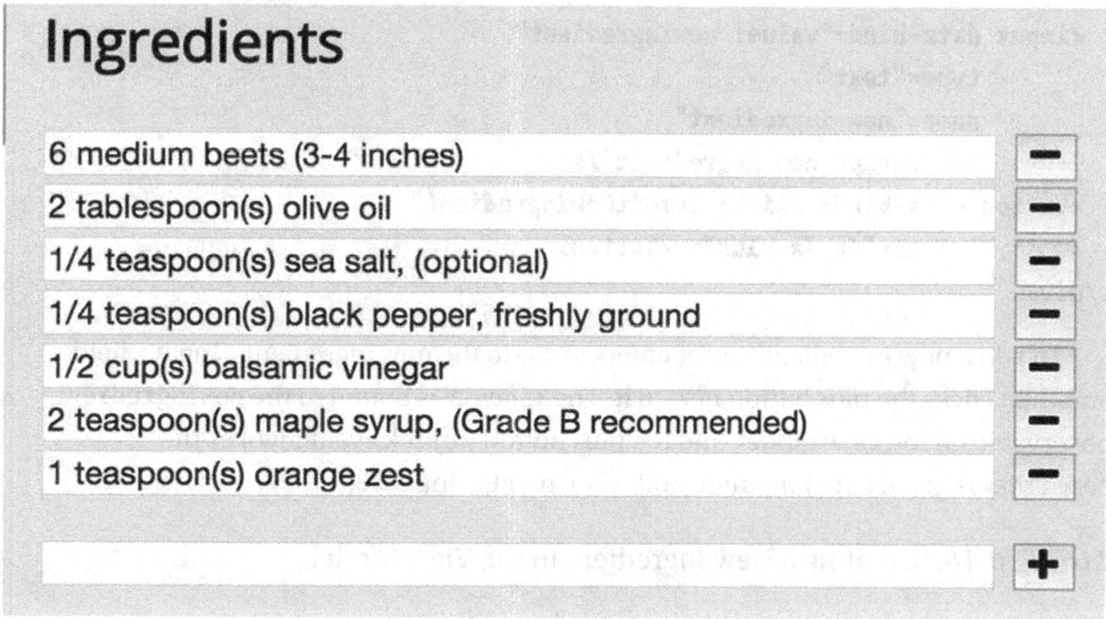

Ingredients

6 medium beets (3-4 inches)   —

2 tablespoon(s) olive oil   —

1/4 teaspoon(s) sea salt, (optional)   —

1/4 teaspoon(s) black pepper, freshly ground   —

1/2 cup(s) balsamic vinegar   —

2 teaspoon(s) maple syrup, (Grade B recommended)   —

1 teaspoon(s) orange zest   —

                                                              +

Figure 6-8. *Creating and editing recipe ingredients*

Adding a new ingredient is more straightforward than editing existing ingredients in place. The markup in Listing 6-17 shows *part* of the changes to the Ingredients section of the form. The read-only unordered list is present, and below it is a <div> element that contains all the new form fields. A comment block indicates where the <input> elements

187

for *existing* ingredients will go (discussed in a moment), but the new Ingredients fields are shown below it.

Listing 6-17. New Ingredients Markup

```
<!-- example-002/public/index.html -->
<h2>Ingredients</h2>
<!-- in read-only view -->
<ul data-bind="foreach: ingredients, visible: !isEditing()">
  <li data-bind="text: $data"></li>
</ul>
<!-- in edit view -->
<div data-bind="visible: isEditing" class="edit-field">

  <!-- ingredient list inputs here... -->

  <input data-bind="value: newIngredient"
       type="text"
       name="new-ingredient"
       id="recipe-new-ingredient"/>
  <button data-bind="click: commitNewIngredient"
         class="fa fa-plus"></button>
</div>
```

To add a new ingredient, a user enters text into the new ingredient `<input>` field and then clicks the plus button next to it. The `<input>` is bound to the `newIngredient` observable on the view model, and the plus button's `click` event invokes the `commitNewIngredient()` method, both shown in Listing 6-18.

Listing 6-18. Creating a New Ingredient in the View Model

```
// example-002/public/scripts/recipe-details.js
// properties
viewmodel.ingredients = ko.observableArray(recipe.ingredients);
viewmodel.newIngredient = ko.observable(");

// methods
viewmodel.commitNewIngredient = function () {
```

```
  var ingredient = viewmodel.newIngredient();
  if (ingredient === '') return;
  viewmodel.ingredients.push(ingredient);
  viewmodel.newIngredient('');
};
```

The `commitNewIngredient()` method evaluates the content of the `newIngredient` observable to determine if it is empty or not. If it is, the user has entered no text into the `<input>`, and so the method returns prematurely. If not, the value of `newIngredient` is pushed into the `ingredients` observable array and the `newIngredient` observable is cleared.

Tip   Observable arrays share a nearly identical API with normal JavaScript arrays. Most array operations, such as `push()`, `pop()`, `slice()`, `splice()`, and so on, are available on observable arrays and will trigger update notifications to the observable array's subscribers when called.

When the new ingredient is appended to `ingredients`, Knockout updates the DOM to reflect the change. The read-only list, hidden while in edit mode, silently acquires a new list item element, and the editable list of existing `<input>` elements, shown in Listing 6-19, gains a new entry as well.

Listing 6-19. Ingredients Markup

```
<!-- example-002/public/index.html -->
<h2>Ingredients</h2>
<!-- in read-only view -->
<ul data-bind="foreach: ingredients, visible: !isEditing()">
  <li data-bind="text: $data"></li>
</ul>
<!-- in edit view -->
<div data-bind="visible: isEditing" class="edit-field">
  <ul data-bind="foreach: ingredients" class="listless">
    <li>
      <input data-bind="value: $data,
              valueUpdate: 'input',
```

```
                attr: {name: 'ingredient-' + $index()},
                event: {input: $parent.changeIngredient.bind($parent, $index())}"
                type="text" />
        <button data-bind="click: $parent.removeIngredient.bind($parent,
        $index())"
                class="fa fa-minus"></button>
    </li>
  </ul>

  <!-- new ingredient input here... -->
</div>
```

For each ingredient in the `ingredients` observable array, an input is rendered above the new ingredient field. These inputs are nested within an unordered list, and their values are all bound to specific ingredients in the array, denoted by the `$data` variable within the `foreach` loop. The `attr` binding is used to give a name to each `<input>` element by concatenating the string "ingredient-" with the current index of the loop, exposed by the special `$index` observable. Like any observable used in a binding *expression*, `$index` must be invoked to retrieve its value.

It cannot be emphasized enough that the bindings exposed by observable arrays apply only to the arrays themselves and *not* to the elements they contain. When each ingredient is bound to a DOM `<input>` element, it is wrapped in the `$data` observable, but there is no communication between this observable and the containing observable array. If the value within `$data` changes because of input, the array will be oblivious and still contain its own copy of the unchanged data. This is a source of consternation, but there are several coping strategies that make it bearable.

First, the observable `ingredients` array could be filled with objects that each expose the ingredient text as an observable property (something like `{ ingredient: ko.observable('20 mushrooms') }`). The `value` binding of each `<input>` would then use each object's `$data.ingredient` property to establish a two-way binding. The observable array still remains ignorant of changes to its members, but because each element is an object that tracks its own data through an observable, this becomes a moot point.

The second approach, taken in Listing 6-19, is to listen for change events on each `<input>` element through the `valueUpdate` and `event` bindings and then tell the *view model* to replace specific ingredient values in the `ingredients` observable array as they change. Neither way is "right"—both merely have their own advantages and disadvantages.

The `valueUpdate` binding first instructs Knockout to change the value of `$data` each time the DOM `input` event fires on each `<input>` element. (Remember: Knockout normally updates `$data` once an element loses focus, not when it receives input.) Second, a Knockout event binding is added that invokes the `changeIngredient()` method on the view model every time the DOM `input` event fires as well. By default Knockout submits the current value of `$data` to `changeIngredient()`, but since the new value will replace the old, the view model must know which index in the `ingredients` array is being targeted. Using `bind()`, the value of `$index` is bound to the method as the first argument ensuring that the value of `$data` will be the second.

The code in Listing 6-20 shows that the `changeIngredient()` method accesses the actual *underlying* array within the `ingredients` observable array in order to replace a value at a given index.

Listing 6-20. Changing a Recipe Ingredient in the View Model

```
// example-002/public/scripts/recipe-details.js
// properties
viewmodel.ingredients = ko.observableArray(recipe.ingredients);

// methods
viewmodel.changeIngredient = function (index, newValue) {
  viewmodel.ingredients()[index] = newValue;
};
```

Unfortunately, when an observable array's underlying array structure is changed, the observable array will not automatically notify any subscribers, which means that other DOM elements, such as the read-only unordered list that displays the ingredients, will remain unchanged. To mitigate this, the view model listens to its own `isEditing` observable, shown in Listing 6-21. When the value passed to the observable is `false` (meaning that the user has either saved changes to the recipe or canceled the editing session), the view model forcibly notifies any subscribers to the `ingredients` observable array by calling its `valueHasMutated()` method. This ensures that the read-only unordered list displayed in "view" mode will accurately reflect any changed values in the `ingredients` array.

Listing 6-21. Forcing Observable Arrays to Notify Their Subscribers of Underlying Changes

```
// example-002/public/scripts/recipe-details.js
// properties
viewmodel.isEditing = ko.observable(false);
viewmodel.isEditing.subscribe(function (isEditing) {
  if (isEditing) return;
  // force refresh
  //
  viewmodel.ingredients.valueHasMutated();
});
```

Next to each recipe `<input>` is a minus button used to remove a given ingredient from the `ingredients` observable array. Its click event is bound to the `removeIngredient()` method which, like `changeIngredient()`, must also receive the value of `$index` so that the view model knows which element to remove. Observable arrays expose a `splice()` method, shown in Listing 6-22, that may be used to remove an element at a specific index. Using this method instead of manipulating the underlying array directly ensures that subscribers to the `ingredients` observable array are notified of the change immediately.

Listing 6-22. Removing a Recipe Ingredient

```
// example-002/public/scripts/recipe-details.js
// properties
viewmodel.ingredients = ko.observableArray(recipe.ingredients);

// methods
viewmodel.removeIngredient = function (index) {
  viewmodel.ingredients.splice(index, 1);
};
```

Instructions

Recipe instructions are very similar to recipe ingredients but differ in two notable ways. First, instructions are rendered in an *ordered list* because instructions must be followed step by step. And second, instructions may be promoted or demoted within the list. Figure 6-9 shows a screenshot of the ordered Instructions fields and the buttons associated with each.

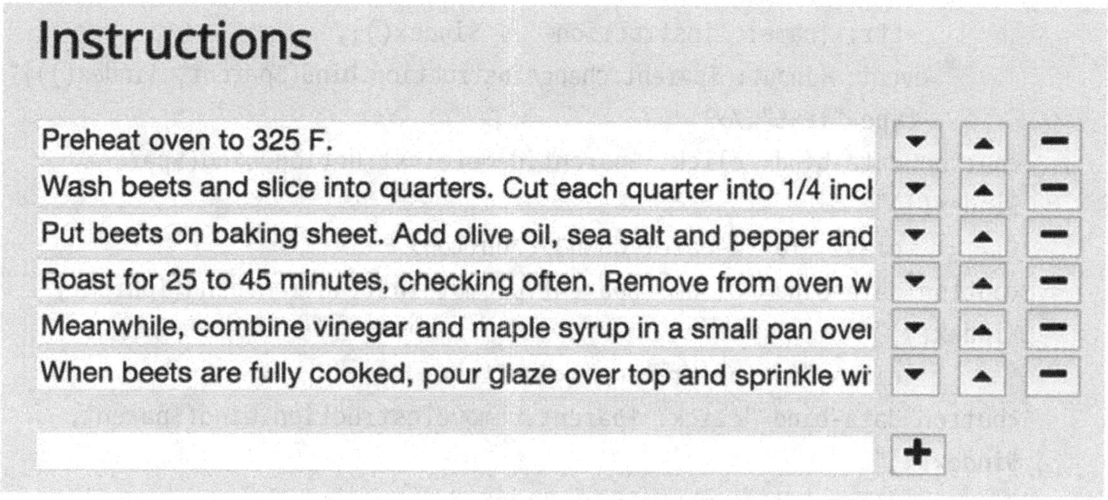

Figure 6-9. *Creating and editing recipe instructions*

The recipe instruction use cases that overlap with ingredient use cases (creating an instruction, removing an instruction, updating an existing instruction) will not be discussed, as the markup, Knockout bindings, and view model structure of both are essentially the same, but operate on the instructions observable array instead. Instruction demotion and promotion within the array are new features, however, represented by the addition of up and down <button> tags in Listing 6-23.

Listing 6-23. Instructions Markup

```
<!-- example-002/public/index.html -->
<h2>Instructions</h2>
<!-- in read-only view -->
<ol data-bind="foreach: instructions, visible: !isEditing()">
  <li data-bind="text: $data"></li>
</ol>
```

```
<!-- in edit view -->
<div data-bind="visible: isEditing" class="edit-field">
  <!-- existing instructions -->
  <ul data-bind="foreach: instructions" class="listless">
    <li>
      <input data-bind="value: $data,
              valueUpdate: 'input',
              attr: {name: 'instruction-' + $index()},
             event: {input: $parent.changeInstruction.bind($parent, $index())}"
             type="text" />
      <button data-bind="click: $parent.demoteInstruction.bind($parent,
      $index())"
              class="fa fa-caret-down"></button>
      <button data-bind="click: $parent.promoteInstruction.bind($parent,
      $index())"
              class="fa fa-caret-up"></button>
      <button data-bind="click: $parent.removeInstruction.bind($parent,
      $index())"
              class="fa fa-minus"></button>
    </li>
  </ul>

  <!-- new instruction input here... -->
</div>
```

Like the minus button, both up and down buttons use Knockout click bindings
to invoke methods on the view model, passing the associated item index as an argument
to each.

Listing 6-24 shows how both methods manipulate the instructions observable array.
The promoteInstruction() method evaluates the index and, if it is zero, exits early (the
first instruction cannot be promoted). It then plucks the instruction at the given index
from the observable array using its splice() method, calculates the new index for the
instruction by subtracting one (e.g., going from index 2 to 1 would be a promotion in
the list), and then splices the instruction back into the observable array at its new index.
The demoteInstruction() method does the opposite. It prevents the instruction at the
"end" of the list from being demoted further; otherwise it moves instructions down the

list by resplicing the observable array. In both cases any DOM elements bound to the `instructions` property are notified of changes automatically.

Listing 6-24. Promoting and Demoting Recipe Instructions in the View Model

```
// example-002/public/scripts/recipe-details.js
// properties
viewmodel.instructions = ko.observableArray(recipe.instructions);

viewmodel.promoteInstruction = function (index) {
  if (index === 0) return;
  var instruction = viewmodel.instructions.splice(index, 1);
  var newIndex = index - 1;
  viewmodel.instructions.splice(newIndex, 0, instruction);
};

viewmodel.demoteInstruction = function (index) {
  var lastIndex = (viewmodel.instructions.length - 1);
  if (index === lastIndex) return;
  var instruction = viewmodel.instructions.splice(index, 1);
  var newIndex = index + 1;
  viewmodel.instructions.splice(newIndex, 0, instruction);
};
```

Citation

The Citation field addition is a fairly vanilla affair considering the complexities involved with instructions and ingredients. A single text `<input>` uses the `value` binding to update the view model's `citation` observable. The rendered field is shown in Figure 6-9.

Citation:
http://www.paleoplan.com/2011/06-09/roasted-beets-with-balsa

Figure 6-10. *Updating a recipe's citation*

The `visible` binding on the citation hyperlink has been changed to a compound expression. Now, the hyperlink in Listing 6-25 will only be displayed if the recipe details view is in read-only mode (`!isEditing()`) *and* the recipe actually has a citation.

Listing 6-25. Citation Field Markup

```
<!-- example-002/public/index.html -->
<a data-bind="visible: hasCitation() && !isEditing(),
  attr: {href: citation, title: title}"
  target="_blank">Source</a>
<div data-bind="visible: isEditing" class="edit-field">
  <label>Citation:</label>
  <input name="citation" type="text" data-bind="value: citation" />
</div>
```

Custom Components

With inspiration from the popular webcomponents.js polyfill (`http://webcomponents.org`), Knockout provides a custom component system that produces reusable HTML elements with custom tag names, markup, and behavior.

In the *Omnom Recipes* application, the recipe details view contains two editable lists, Ingredients and Instructions, that share many similar characteristics, both in terms of markup and view model properties and methods. A custom component can, with a little effort, replace both of these lists in the application. The goal is to reduce the complex markup and binding expressions in the DOM to new, custom elements, envisioned in Listing 6-26.

Listing 6-26. Input List Element

```
<!-- example-003/public/index.html -->
<!-- editable ingredients list -->
<input-list params="items: ingredients,
         isOrdered: false"></input-list>

<!-- ... -->
```

```
<!-- editable instructions list -->
<input-list params="items: instructions,
            isOrdered: true"></input-list>
```

Knockout components are the intersection of several things:

- A factory function that creates a view model for each instance of the custom component on a page

- An HTML template with its own Knockout bindings that will be injected wherever the component is used

- A custom tag registration that tells Knockout where to find the template and how to instantiate its view model when it encounters component tags on a page

The Input List View Model

The recipe details view model already possesses the properties and methods used to manipulate its `ingredients` and `instructions` arrays, but it is necessary to abstract this code and move it into its own module, `input-list.js`, so that Knockout can use it exclusively for the new input list component.

Listing 6-27 shows an abbreviated version of the input list module. It is structured in the same manner as the other view model factory modules, exposing a `create()` method on the global `InputList` object. This factory method accepts a `params` parameter that will be used to pass the input list component a reference to an observable array (`params.items`) and a host of optional settings that will determine how the input list will behave when bound to the rendered template: `params.isOrdered`, `params.enableAdd`, `params.enableUpdate`, and `params.enableRemove`.

The `defaultTo()` function exists as a simple utility function that returns default values for missing properties on the `params` object.

Listing 6-27. Input List View Model

```
// example-003/public/scripts/input-list.js
'use strict';
window.InputList = (function (ko) {

  function defaultTo(object, property, defaultValue) {/*...*/}
```

```
  return {
    create: function (params) {
      var viewmodel = {};

      // properties
      viewmodel.items = params.items; // the collection
      viewmodel.newItem = ko.observable("");

      viewmodel.isOrdered = defaultTo(params, 'isOrdered', false);
      viewmodel.enableAdd = defaultTo(params, 'enableAdd', true);
      viewmodel.enableUpdate = defaultTo(params, 'enableUpdate', true);
      viewmodel.enableRemove = defaultTo(params, 'enableRemove', true);

      // methods
      viewmodel.commitNewItem = function () {/*...*/};
      viewmodel.changeItem = function (index, newValue) {/*...*/};
      viewmodel.removeItem = function (index) {/*...*/};
      viewmodel.promoteItem = function (index) {/*...*/};
      viewmodel.demoteItem = function (index) {/*...*/};

      return viewmodel;
    }
  };

}(window.ko));
```

The `params.items` and `params.isOrdered` properties correspond to the binding attributes in Listing 6-26. When a component is used on a page, the values of its binding attributes are passed, by reference, to the component's view model via the `params` object. In this scenario, input list components will be given access to the `ingredients` and `instructions` observable arrays on the recipe details view model.

Input list methods have been redacted in Listing 6-27 because they are nearly identical to their counterparts in Listing 6-24. Instead of referencing ingredients or instructions, however, these methods reference the abstracted `items` observable array. The component populates this array with data it receives from `params.items`. The `newItem` observable holds the value of the new item input, in exactly the same manner as the `newIngredient` and `newInstruction` observables behaved in the `recipe-details.js` module. It is not shared with the recipe details view model, however, as it only has relevance within the input list.

Since the input list component will now handle the manipulation of the Ingredients and Instructions lists on the page, the properties and methods in the recipe details view model that previously performed these manipulations have been removed.

The Input List Template

A reusable component needs an abstracted, reusable template, so the markup associated with editing instructions and ingredients has also been collected into a single HTML template. Each time an instance of the input list component is created on the page, Knockout will inject the template into the DOM, then bind a new instance of the input list view model to it.

Since the input list component can accommodate both ordered and unordered lists, the template must use Knockout bindings to intelligently decide which kind of list to display. Only ordered lists will have promotion and demotion buttons, while items can be added and removed from both kinds of lists. Since the input list view model exposes boolean properties it receives from its `params` object, the template can alter its behavior based on the values of those properties. For example, if the view model property `isOrdered` is `true`, the template will show an ordered list; otherwise it will show an unordered list. Likewise the fields and buttons associated with adding new items or removing existing items are toggled by the `enableAdd` and `enableRemove` properties, respectively.

Template markup is typically added to the DOM in nonparsed elements like `<template>` or the `<script type="text/html">` element. In Listing 6-28, the full component markup and all bindings are shown within a `<template>` tag. The element's `id` will be used by Knockout to find the template content within the DOM when the component is registered with the framework.

Listing 6-28. Input List Component Template

```
<!-- example-003/public/index.html -->
<template id="item-list-template">
  <!-- ko if: isOrdered -->
  <!-- #1 THE ORDERED LIST -->
  <ol data-bind="foreach: items" class="listless">
    <li>
      <input data-bind="value: $data,
```

```
                        valueUpdate: 'input',
                        attr: {name: 'item-' + $index()},
                        event: {input: $parent.changeItem.bind($parent, $index())}"
                type="text" />
        <button data-bind="click: $parent.demoteItem.bind($parent, $index())"
                class="fa fa-caret-down"></button>
        <button data-bind="click: $parent.promoteItem.bind($parent, $index())"
                class="fa fa-caret-up"></button>
        <button data-bind="click: $parent.removeItem.bind($parent, $index()),
                visible: $parent.enableRemove"
                class="fa fa-minus"></button>
    </li>
</ol>
<!-- /ko -->

<!-- ko ifnot: isOrdered -->
<!-- #2 THE UN-ORDERED LIST -->
<ul data-bind="foreach: items" class="listless">
    <li>
        <input data-bind="value: $data,
                    valueUpdate: 'input',
                    attr: {name: 'item-' + $index()},
                    event: {input: $parent.changeItem.bind($parent,
                    $index())}"
                type="text" />
        <button data-bind="click: $parent.removeItem.bind($parent, $index()),
                visible: $parent.enableRemove"
                class="fa fa-minus"></button>
    </li>
</ul>
<!-- /ko -->

<!-- ko if: enableAdd -->
<!-- #3 THE NEW ITEM FIELD -->
<input data-bind="value: newItem"
        type="text"
```

```
        name="new-item" />
  <button data-bind="click: commitNewItem"
          class="fa fa-plus"></button>
  <!-- /ko -->
</template>
```

There is a lot of markup to digest in the input list template, but it is really just the combination of both the unordered Ingredients list and the ordered Instructions list, with a shared new item field.

Special binding comments—the `ko if` and `ko ifnot` comment blocks—wrap portions of the template to determine if the elements within the comment blocks should be added to the page. These comment blocks evaluate properties on the view model and alter the template processing control flow accordingly. This differs from the `visible` element bindings, which merely hide elements that already exist in the DOM.

Tip   The syntax used within ko comment block bindings is known as *containerless control flow syntax*.

All fields and buttons in the input list template are bound to properties and methods on the input list view model. If a demote button is clicked, for example, the input list view model will manipulate its internal `items` collection, which is really a reference to the `instructions` observable array in the recipe details view model, shared via the `items` binding. The template determines which type of list to display based on the `isOrdered` property, while the add and remove controls are toggled based on the `enableAdd` and `enableRemove` properties. Because these properties are read from the `params` object in the view model, any of them may be added to the `<input-list>` component tag as a binding attribute. In this way the component abstracts and encapsulates all operations made against any collection that can be represented as a list of inputs.

Registering the Input List Tag

Once a component view model and template have been defined, the component itself must be registered with Knockout. This tells Knockout how to resolve component instances when it encounters the component's custom tag in the DOM and also what template and view model to use when rendering the component's contents.

The `app.js` script has been updated in Listing 6-29 to register the input list component immediately after the DOM becomes ready, but before any Knockout bindings are applied to the page (with `ko.applyBindings()`). This ensures that Knockout has time to render the component's markup in the DOM so before any view model is bound to it.

Listing 6-29. Registering the Input List Component

```
// example-003/public/scripts/app.js
(function app ($, ko, InputList /*...*/) {
  // ...

  $(function () {
    // register the custom component tag before
    // Knockout bindings are applied to the page
    ko.components.register('input-list', {
      template: {
        element: 'item-list-template'
      },
      viewModel: InputList.create
    });

    // ...
  });

}(window.jQuery, window.ko, window.InputList /*...*/));
```

In Listing 6-29, the `ko.components.register()` function receives two arguments: the name of the new component's custom tag, `input-list`, and an options hash that provides Knockout with the information it needs to construct the component.

Knockout uses the custom tag name to identify the `<input-list>` element in the DOM and replace it with the template content specified in the options hash.

Since markup for the input list element has been defined in a `<template>` element, the Knockout component system only needs to know what element ID it should use to find that element in the DOM. The `template` object in the options hash contains this ID in its `element` property. For smaller components, the entire HTML template could be assigned, as a string, to the `template` property directly.

To construct a view model for the component, a factory function is assigned to the
viewModel property of the options hash. This property can also reference a regular
constructor function, but using factory functions sidesteps potential problems that
arise when event bindings reassign the this keyword within view models. Regardless of
approach, the view model function will receive a params object populated with values
from the template's binding declarations.

Tip   Knockout can load component templates and view model functions via
RequireJS automatically. Consult the Knockout component documentation for more
details. The RequireJS module loader is covered in Chapter 5.

Now that the input list component is registered with Knockout, the complicated
markup for the editable Ingredients and Instructions lists can be replaced with simple
instances of <input-list>. Listing 6-30 shows the resulting lighter, cleaner page markup.

Listing 6-30. Editing Instructions and Ingredients with the Input List Component

```
<!-- example-003/public/index.html -->

<h2>Ingredients</h2>
<!-- in read-only view -->
<ul data-bind="foreach: ingredients, visible: !isEditing()">
  <li data-bind="text: $data"></li>
</ul>
<!-- in edit view -->
<div data-bind="visible: isEditing" class="edit-field">
  <input-list params="items: ingredients,
             isOrdered: false"></input-list>
</div>

<h2>Instructions</h2>
<!-- in read-only view -->
<ol data-bind="foreach: instructions, visible: !isEditing()">
  <li data-bind="text: $data"></li>
</ol>
<!-- in edit view -->
```

```
<div data-bind="visible: isEditing" class="edit-field">
  <input-list params="items: instructions,
              isOrdered: true"></input-list>
</div>
```

Not only are the complexities of the input list obscured behind the new `<input-list>` tag, but aspects of the list, such as the ability to add and remove items, are controlled through bound attributes. This promotes both flexibility and maintainability as common behaviors are bundled into a single element.

Subscribables: Cheap Messaging

At this point the recipe details view model manipulates the recipe data but does nothing to persist changes. It also fails to communicate recipe changes to the recipe list, so even if a user modifies a recipe's title, the recipe list continues to display the recipe's original title. From a use case perspective, the recipe list should only be updated if the recipe details are sent to the server and successfully persisted. A more sophisticated mechanism is needed to facilitate this workflow.

Knockout observables implement the behavior of a Knockout *subscribable*, a more abstract object that does not hold a value but acts as a kind of eventing mechanism to which other objects may subscribe. Observables take advantage of the subscribable interface by publishing their own changes through subscribables, to which DOM bindings (and perhaps even other view models) listen.

Subscribables may be directly attached to view models as properties or passed around by reference to any object interested in their events. In Listing 6-31 a subscribable is constructed in the app.js file and passed as an argument to both the recipe list and recipe details modules. Note that, unlike an observable, subscribables must be instantiated with the new keyword.

Listing 6-31. Knockout Subscribable Acting As a Primitive Message Bus

```
// example-004/public/scripts/app.js
var bus = new ko.subscribable();
var list = RecipeList.create(recipes, bus);
var details = RecipeDetails.create(list.selectedRecipe(), bus);
```

To effectively publish an updated recipe to the subscribable, the recipe details view model has been modified in several ways.

First, the subscribable is passed to the recipe details factory function as an argument named bus (shorthand for "poor developer's message bus"). The recipe details module will use this subscribable to raise events when recipe details change.

Second, the view model now tracks the recipe's ID since this value will be used to update recipe data on the server. The recipe list will also use the ID to replace stale recipe data after changes have been saved.

Finally, the save() method has been updated to trigger the recipe.saved event on the bus subscribable, passing the modified recipe data as an argument that will be delivered to any subscribers. The modified save() method is shown in Listing 6-32.

Listing 6-32. Recipe Details View Model Saving a Modified Recipe

```
// example-004/public/scripts/recipe-details.js
viewmodel.save = function () {
  var savedRecipe = {
    id: viewmodel.id,
    title: viewmodel.title(),
    ingredients: viewmodel.ingredients(),
    instructions: viewmodel.instructions(),
    cookingTime: {
      hours: viewmodel.hours(),
      minutes: viewmodel.minutes()
    },
    servings: viewmodel.servings(),
    citation: viewmodel.citation()
  };
  bus.notifySubscribers(savedRecipe, 'recipe.saved');
  viewmodel.isEditing(false);
};
```

The notifySubscribers() method on a subscribable accepts two arguments—the data object subscribers will receive and the name of the event being raised. The app. js module subscribes to the recipe.saved event on the subscribable bus, shown in Listing 6-33, and initiates an AJAX request to send the modified recipe data to the server. Because the recipe details view model and the app.js module share a reference to the bus object, any events triggered by the recipe details view model can be handled in the app.js module.

Listing 6-33. Saved Recipe Is Persisted to the Server

```
// example-004/public/scripts/app.js
var bus = new ko.subscribable();

bus.subscribe(function (updatedRecipe) {
  $.ajax({
    method: 'PUT',
    url: '/recipes/' + updatedRecipe.id,
    data: updatedRecipe
  }).then(function () {
    bus.notifySubscribers(updatedRecipe, 'recipe.persisted');
  })
}, null, 'recipe.saved');
```

The subscribable's subscribe() method accepts three arguments:

- The callback function to be executed when the specified event is triggered on the subscribable

- The context object that will be bound to the this keyword within the callback function (or null, if the this keyword is never used within the callback)

- The name of the event to which the callback is subscribed (e.g., recipe.saved)

If the AJAX update succeeds, the app.js module triggers a recipe.persisted event on the subscribable to notify listeners. A reference to the bus subscribable has also been passed to the recipe list view model, which actively listens for the recipe.persisted event. When the event fires, the recipe list receives the saved data in Listing 6-34 and updates its internal recipes collection and selected recipe based on the persisted recipe's ID.

Listing 6-34. Updating the Recipe List with a Persisted Recipe

```javascript
// example-004/public/scripts/recipe-list.js
window.RecipeList = (function (ko) {

  return {
    create: function (recipes, bus) {
      var viewmodel = {};

      // properties
      viewmodel.recipes = ko.observableArray(recipes);
      viewmodel.selectedRecipe = ko.observable(recipes[0]);

      // ...
      bus.subscribe(function (updatedRecipe) {

        var recipes = viewmodel.recipes();
        var i = 0,
          count = recipes.length;
        while (i < count) {
          if (recipes[i].id !== updatedRecipe.id) {
            i += 1;
            continue;
          }
          recipes[i] = updatedRecipe;
          viewmodel.recipes(recipes);
          viewmodel.selectRecipe(recipes[i]);
          break;
        }

      }, null, 'recipe.persisted');
      // ...
    }
  };

}(window.ko));
```

Though subscribables aren't the only way to raise events in an application, they can be effective for straightforward use cases, creating a decoupled communication chain between modules.

Summary

Many front-end frameworks offer suites of compelling features and plugins, but Knockout really focuses on the interaction between the HTML view and data model in an application. Knockout's observables alleviate the pain of manually pulling data from, and pushing data to, HTML DOM elements. Developers can add `data-bind` attributes to any element on a page, gluing the markup to one or more view models through two-way bindings.

While form data can be directly bound to view model properties, DOM event bindings can also invoke methods on Knockout view models as well. Any changes these methods make to view model observable properties are immediately reflected in the DOM. Bindings like `visible` and `css` determine how an element is displayed to the user, while bindings like `text` and `value` determine an element's content.

Observables are special objects that hold view model data values. When their values change, observables notify any interested subscribers, including bound DOM elements. Primitive observables hold single values, while observable arrays hold collections. Mutations that happen on observable arrays can be tracked and mirrored by HTML elements that are bound to the collection. The `foreach` binding is especially useful when iterating over an observable array's elements, though special considerations must be taken if individual members of an observable array are changed or replaced.

Knockout templates and view models can be abstracted into reusable components with unique HTML tags. These components can be added to a page and bound to other view model properties, just as any standard HTML elements would be bound. Encapsulating state and behavior in a component reduces the total markup on a page and also guarantees that similar portions of an application (e.g., a list of inputs bound to a collection) behave the same wherever used.

Finally, subscribable objects—the basic building blocks behind observables—can be used as primitive message busses, notifying subscribers of published events and potentially delivering payloads of data where needed.

Resources

- Knockout web site: `http://knockoutjs.com/`
- GitHub: `https://github.com/knockout/knockout/`

CHAPTER 7

Angular

In this chapter, we will be turning our attention toward a very popular framework, that is, Angular. It is one of the world's most popular frameworks and is a leading name in the field of JavaScript and web development. In fact, if you have had even a basic amount of introduction to web development, you might have already heard of Angular as well as AngularJS.

Basically, Angular is a front-end web application development framework that is maintained and developed by the Angular Team at Google. Yes, it is backed by the likes of Google and has a very thriving and active community around the world.

In this chapter, we will be learning about installation, setup, Dependency Injection, as well as how to get the most out of this web application framework. But before going any further, we need to understand one key difference.

Did you notice we mentioned Angular and AngularJS separately? Yes, both are two different frameworks built atop two different, albeit rather closely related, platforms. Therefore, it is a good idea to first familiarize ourselves with the basic differences between the two. Web developers of all levels of ability are interested in learning Angular, especially those working on web apps.

Differences Between Angular and AngularJS

If we are to speak purely of JavaScript frameworks when comparing Angular with AngularJS, the latter is the answer. This is because Angular is written in TypeScript, which happens to be a superscript of JavaScript.

With that out of the way, the differences do not stop there. At the beginning, AngularJS was the only framework with no existence of Angular. AngularJS was developed by the team at Google, along with a large community of volunteers, to address the challenges associated with dynamic app development for the Web, such as Single Page Apps.

209

S. bin Uzayr et al., *JavaScript Frameworks for Modern Web Development*,
https://doi.org/10.1007/978-1-4842-4995-6_7

Figure 7-1. *Angular is a popular web framework that is used to build progressive web apps*

In September 2016, AngularJS 2.0 was released, and this is where the stark difference began. The name was now just "Angular," (see Figure 7-1) to reflect the steering toward TypeScript as opposed to JavaScript. Angular in itself is a complete rewrite of AngularJS.

Going forward, all future releases of Angular began to be named just "Angular," with Angular 7 being the latest one. Angular 8, however, is likely to be released soon.

To sum it up:

> AngularJS is the original release, and it can also be called Angular 1.0. This particular version of the framework is based on pure JavaScript.

> Angular 2.0 and its subsequent versions are based on TypeScript and do not follow the same nomenclature as version 1.0 (no "JS").

But this is not where the differences end.

Angular makes use of Components as the basic building blocks of its projects or apps. AngularJS, on the other hand, relied on Scope or Controllers. Furthermore, Angular has a module-based approach and makes good leverage of TypeScript features. As such, Angular can boast of the following aspects:

- Support for object-oriented programming

- Static types

- Lambdas and iterators

- For loops

- Dynamic loading

- A custom set of UI components

- Python-style generators

Much of the preceding features are made possible due to the fact that Angular is based on TypeScript. Having said that, whatever happened to AngularJS? Well, it is still under active development, albeit under Long Term Support mode (means it receives only vital and essential updates). The reason is simple—a good number of agencies, developers, and organizations have long relied on the popular JavaScript framework that is AngularJS. Migrating away from AngularJS entirely toward Angular requires a good deal of time and efforts and possibly invites code and compatibility issues.

As such, both AngularJS and Angular continue to be under development, and each has its own share of community and user base. Considering the fact that Angular is the newer variant and comes loaded with additional features, it is only natural that more and more new developers are keen on learning Angular as opposed to AngularJS. In this chapter, as a result, we will be focusing on Angular.

However, it should also be pointed out that since AngularJS is still being used in the industry in a large number of enterprise-level projects, it is far from obsolete, and at times, many developers choose to learn both the frameworks in order to improve their job prospects. Nevertheless, even the AngularJS web site has a call to action button that takes visitors to Angular—the new version is the future of this framework.

You can learn more about AngularJS here: `https://angularjs.org/`

Getting Started with Angular

Now that we have learned what the major differences are between AngularJS and Angular, we can safely focus on getting things rolling with Angular development.

The first step, obviously, is to install Angular on our development environment.

Installation

Angular requires Node.js version 8.x or higher to function. This means if our system does not already have the latest version of Node.js, we need to first install it.

Thankfully, installing Node.js is no rocket science. We can simply head to the Node.js official web site (see Figure 7-2) and then grab the installer depending on the operating system and architecture that we are using.

Figure 7-2. *Node.js supports multiple operating systems and can be installed on Windows, Mac, as well as Linux*

Node.js comes with multiple installers, each suited to a particular family of operating systems. For Windows users, for instance, the installer is a simple executable file. Similarly, there are relevant versions available for Linux and Mac users as well. All of these versions as well as the older and other releases of Node.js are available on the download page.[1]

Learn more about Node.js here: `https://nodejs.org/en/`

Once we have Node.js installed and set up on our system, we are ready to begin Angular installation. It is noteworthy that npm, the Node Package Manager, will automatically be installed when we install Node.js

---

[1]Node.js download page: `https://nodejs.org/en/download/`

As such, we can simply run the relevant npm command to do the needful. As first step it is recommended to install the Angular CLI, which will enable us to create projects and generate and execute apps in Angular right from the command line. Angular CLI can perform a multitude of tasks related to testing, building, and deployment of Angular apps.

In order to install the Angular CLI via npm, we need to run the following command:

```
npm install -g @angular/cli
```

That is all. If all goes right, Angular CLI will shortly be installed on our system, and we can get things rolling with Angular app development (see Figure 7-3).

```
sufyan@sufyan-Aspire-3:~$ sudo su
[sudo] password for sufyan:
root@sufyan-Aspire-3:/home/sufyan# npm install -g @angular/cli
/ |----------------------------------------------------------------------------------
WARN engine @angular/cli@7.3.6: wanted: {"node":">= 8.9.0","npm":">= 5.5.1"} (current: {"node":"8.10.0","npm":"3.5.2"})
loadDep:symbol-observable / |########################------------------------------------------------------
loadDep:symbol-observable \ |########################------------------------------------------------------
loadDep:symbol-observable | |########################------------------------------------------------------
loadDep:symbol-observable | |########################------------------------------------------------------
WARN engine @schematics/angular@7.3.6: wanted: {"node":">= 8.9.0","npm":">= 5.5.1"} (current: {"node":"8.10.0","npm":"3.5.2"})
loadDep:typescript -> net \ |################################------------------------------------------
█
```

Figure 7-3. *Installing Angular CLI using npm*

It is very important to ensure that Node.js and npm versions are latest. As can be seen in the preceding example, npm version is less than the recommended one, and as such, the engine throws a warning.

Creating a Workspace in Angular

Now that we have installed Angular CLI, we can start by creating an Angular workspace.

But wait, what exactly is meant by an Angular workspace? Here is how the official Angular glossary defines a workspace[2]:

> In Angular, a folder that contains projects (i.e., apps and libraries). The CLI ng new command creates a workspace to contain projects. Commands that create or operate on apps and libraries (such as add and generate) must be executed from within a workspace folder.

---

[2]https://angular.io/guide/glossary#workspace

213

In simpler words, all applications in Angular are made up of files. Now, these files are contained within a given project, thereby implying that a project will contain files that are related to a particular app or library.

Now, a workspace is an entity that contains files for one or more project. As such, we first need to create a workspace, and then build our app, and then modify or tweak or code its files to suit our purpose. Furthermore, in Angular, a "project" refers to a collection of set files and libraries that are related to a specific purpose or app.

Therefore, our first step is to create a workspace and an initial project to work with. To do so, the following command is what we need:

```
ng new my-first-app
```

The preceding command creates an app project with the name my-first-app. We will be prompted with a series of questions about the project—we can customize the answers or just accept the initial prompt (see Figure 7-4).

```
sufyan@sufyan-Aspire-3:~$ ng new my-first-app
? Would you like to add Angular routing? Yes
? Which stylesheet format would you like to use? CSS
CREATE my-first-app/README.md (1027 bytes)
CREATE my-first-app/.editorconfig (246 bytes)
CREATE my-first-app/.gitignore (629 bytes)
CREATE my-first-app/angular.json (3861 bytes)
CREATE my-first-app/package.json (1311 bytes)
CREATE my-first-app/tsconfig.json (435 bytes)
CREATE my-first-app/tslint.json (1621 bytes)
CREATE my-first-app/src/favicon.ico (5430 bytes)
CREATE my-first-app/src/index.html (297 bytes)
CREATE my-first-app/src/main.ts (372 bytes)
CREATE my-first-app/src/polyfills.ts (2841 bytes)
CREATE my-first-app/src/styles.css (80 bytes)
CREATE my-first-app/src/test.ts (642 bytes)
CREATE my-first-app/src/browserslist (388 bytes)
CREATE my-first-app/src/karma.conf.js (1025 bytes)
CREATE my-first-app/src/tsconfig.app.json (166 bytes)
CREATE my-first-app/src/tsconfig.spec.json (256 bytes)
CREATE my-first-app/src/tslint.json (244 bytes)
CREATE my-first-app/src/assets/.gitkeep (0 bytes)
CREATE my-first-app/src/environments/environment.prod.ts (51 bytes)
CREATE my-first-app/src/environments/environment.ts (662 bytes)
CREATE my-first-app/src/app/app-routing.module.ts (245 bytes)
CREATE my-first-app/src/app/app.module.ts (393 bytes)
CREATE my-first-app/src/app/app.component.css (0 bytes)
CREATE my-first-app/src/app/app.component.html (1152 bytes)
CREATE my-first-app/src/app/app.component.spec.ts (1113 bytes)
CREATE my-first-app/src/app/app.component.ts (216 bytes)
CREATE my-first-app/e2e/protractor.conf.js (752 bytes)
CREATE my-first-app/e2e/tsconfig.e2e.json (213 bytes)
CREATE my-first-app/e2e/src/app.e2e-spec.ts (641 bytes)
```

Figure 7-4. *Creating our first app in Angular*

Following that, Angular will install the required dependencies and project files.

Directory Structure

Once our workspace and project have been set up, we can navigate to the concerned directory. We will find that the workspace has a root folder named after our app, that is, my-first-app which contains the files and data related to the project.

The src subdirectory too will have a my-first-app directory, but this is where our skeleton app project resides. The end-to-end test files will be in the e2e folder.

Here is what a sample Angular app's directory structure looks like (Figure 7-5), complete with the various configuration files for the app.

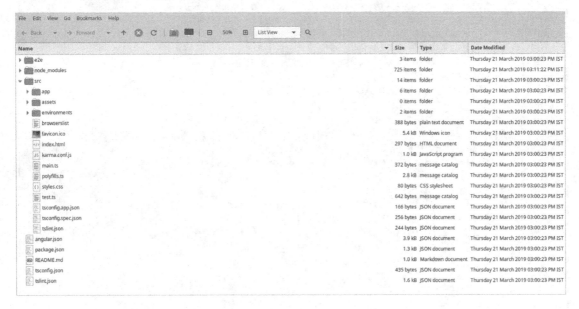

Figure 7-5. *Directory structure of an Angular project by default*

Serving the App

The app project that we just built contains a sample welcome app. It might be a good idea to try running it locally first.

To do so, we first need to navigate to the concerned directory:

```
cd my-first-app
```

And then serve the app locally:

```
ng serve --open
```

In the preceding example, the ng serve command will launch the server and serve our app and also keep track of any live changes in real time. So if we make changes to the app files, the output will automatically be updated (Figure 7-6).

```
sufyan@sufyan-Aspire-3:~$ cd my-first-app
sufyan@sufyan-Aspire-3:~/my-first-app$ ng serve --open
** Angular Live Development Server is listening on localhost:4200, open your browser on http://localhost:4200/ **

Date: 2019-03-21T09:43:05.441Z
Hash: ea1dd2820f9f776221be
Time: 8852ms
chunk {es2015-polyfills} es2015-polyfills.js, es2015-polyfills.js.map (es2015-polyfills) 284 kB [initial] [rendered]
chunk {main} main.js, main.js.map (main) 11.5 kB [initial] [rendered]
chunk {polyfills} polyfills.js, polyfills.js.map (polyfills) 236 kB [initial] [rendered]
chunk {runtime} runtime.js, runtime.js.map (runtime) 6.08 kB [entry] [rendered]
chunk {styles} styles.js, styles.js.map (styles) 16.3 kB [initial] [rendered]
chunk {vendor} vendor.js, vendor.js.map (vendor) 3.76 MB [initial] [rendered]
i ｢wdm｣: Compiled successfully.
```

Figure 7-6. *Launching our Angular app using ng serve command*

The --open append will automatically launch the app. If we so desire, we can omit it and then manually navigate to localhost:4200 in a web browser.

Figure 7-7 is what the sample Angular app looks like.

```
Date: 2019-03-21T09:47:10.664Z - Hash: 6c24f915deabd533ba95 - Time: 2742ms
5 unchanged chunks
chunk {main} main.js, main.js.map (main) 11.5 kB [initial] [rendered]
i ｢wdm｣: Compiled successfully.
i ｢wdm｣: Compiling...
i ｢wdm｣: wait until bundle finished: /

Date: 2019-03-21T09:47:11.062Z - Hash: 6c24f915deabd533ba95 - Time: 165ms
6 unchanged chunks
i ｢wdm｣: Compiled successfully.
i ｢wdm｣: Compiling...

Date: 2019-03-21T09:51:53.784Z - Hash: d3bc1052f925487142d9 - Time: 184ms
5 unchanged chunks
chunk {main} main.js, main.js.map (main) 11.8 kB [initial] [rendered]
i ｢wdm｣: Compiled successfully.
```

Figure 7-7. *Angular application running at localhost:4200—any changes will automatically be reflected upon save*

Customizing the App

When we built our first Angular app using the CLI, we also created our first Angular component.

In Angular, "components" are the fundamental building blocks of apps. Again, to quote the glossary[3]:

---

[3]https://angular.io/guide/glossary#component

An Angular component class is responsible for exposing data and handling most of the view's display and user-interaction logic through data binding.

In other words, Angular components are what we use to display data on screen, seek input from the user, and so on.

In general, most Angular apps have a root component named app-root. In our sample app, it is the file named app.component.ts in the directory /src/app.

Let us look at the contents of the file in Figure 7-8.

```ts
1   import { Component } from '@angular/core';
2
3   @Component({
4     selector: 'app-root',
5     templateUrl: './app.component.html',
6     styleUrls: ['./app.component.css']
7   })
8   export class AppComponent {
9     title = 'my-first-app';
10  }
```

Figure 7-8. Contents of the App components file

Changing the title here will reflect on the locally served app too. First, in the terminal as seen in Figure 7-9.

```
sufyan@sufyan-Aspire-3:~/my-first-app$ ng serve --open
** Angular Live Development Server is listening on localhost:4200, open your browser on http://localhost:4200/ **

Date: 2019-03-21T09:43:05.441Z
Hash: ea1dd2820f9f776221be
Time: 8852ms
chunk {es2015-polyfills} es2015-polyfills.js, es2015-polyfills.js.map (es2015-polyfills) 204 kB [initial] [rendered]
chunk {main} main.js, main.js.map (main) 11.5 kB [initial] [rendered]
chunk {polyfills} polyfills.js, polyfills.js.map (polyfills) 236 kB [initial] [rendered]
chunk {runtime} runtime.js, runtime.js.map (runtime) 6.08 kB [entry] [rendered]
chunk {styles} styles.js, styles.js.map (styles) 16.3 kB [initial] [rendered]
chunk {vendor} vendor.js, vendor.js.map (vendor) 3.76 MB [initial] [rendered]
i ｢wdm｣: Compiled successfully.
i ｢wdm｣: Compiling...

Date: 2019-03-21T09:47:10.664Z - Hash: 6c24f915deabd533ba95 - Time: 2742ms
5 unchanged chunks
chunk {main} main.js, main.js.map (main) 11.5 kB [initial] [rendered]
i ｢wdm｣: Compiled successfully.
i ｢wdm｣: Compiling...
i ｢wdm｣: wait until bundle finished: /

Date: 2019-03-21T09:47:11.062Z - Hash: 6c24f915deabd533ba95 - Time: 165ms
6 unchanged chunks
i ｢wdm｣: Compiled successfully.
```

Figure 7-9. *The server automatically updates the output as per the changes*

And then in the browser too as seen in Figure 7-10.

Welcome to I have updated my title!

Here are some links to help you start:

- **Tour of Heroes**
- **CLI Documentation**
- **Angular blog**

Figure 7-10. *The new title is shown in the browser*

219

Furthermore, we can see that the app.component.css file is responsible for CSS styles for our app.

Modifying the app.component.css with some CSS will change the appearance of our app too. Let us add some sample CSS in Figure 7-11.

```
# app.component.css  ●
1    h1 {
2        color:  ☐#006400;
3        font-family: Arial, Helvetica, sans-serif;
4        font-size: 250%;
5    }
6    |
```

Figure 7-11. *Adding CSS to modify the app heading appearance*

Again, the server responds in the terminal as seen in Figure 7-12.

Figure 7-12. *Recompiling to reflect the latest saved changes*

And then, the browser output is also modified. Note in Figure 7-13 that we have added green color for the heading.

Welcome to I have updated my title!

Here are some links to help you start:

- Tour of Heroes
- CLI Documentation
- Angular blog

Figure 7-13. *CSS changes reflected in output of Angular app*

At this point, we have learned how to build and serve a basic app in Angular. Obviously, this is not all that Angular can do. However, from here, we can focus on more complex app development and dig deeper to see if Angular suits our workflow needs.

Dependency Injection in Angular

One of the key features of Angular, especially its latest versions, is the fact that it has its own Dependency Injection framework. As an application design pattern, Dependency Injection in Angular is used by several apps to implement a modular design workflow.

In web development, we define "dependencies" as simple entities (such as classes, objects, or actions) that a class needs in order to perform its role. In other words, if all the dependencies are not met, the class cannot function properly.

In Angular, Dependency Injection framework ensures that all the dependencies are available when the class is first initiated. This makes it easy to develop flexible and faster apps, as we do not really need to create bulky and bloated code.

Creating and Registering an Injection Service

The first step, obviously, is to generate a new service class that is injectable. The Angular CLI can do it for us:

```
ng generate service example/exam
```

Now, let us analyze the following sample code, which is basically defining an injectable service for us:

```
import { Injectable } from '@angular/core';
@Injectable()
export class falsService {
  constructor() {
    console.log("Ok, now this has been injected!");
  }
  falsPoster(qty) {
    console.log(qty, "Alright, all done!");
  }
}
```

What does the preceding code do? It simply defines an injectable service for us. Now, let us inject this service into a Component:

```
import { Component } from '@angular/core';
import { falsService } from './some.path';
@Component({
  selector: 'app-root',
  templateUrl: './app.component.html',
  styleUrls: ['./app.component.css'],
  providers: [falsService]
})
export class AppComponent {
  constructor(private fals: falsService) {}
  funcDemo(qty) {
    this.fals.falsPoster(qty);
  }
}
```

In the preceding code, we are calling the `falsPoster()` method.

Now, we can make use of our `funcDemo()` method and use the DI framework within the injected service.

Conclusion

In this chapter, we familiarized ourselves with Angular at a basic level. We learned what this particular TypeScript framework is, how it differs from its other variant, and how to get started with Angular. Furthermore, we also learned how to install Angular and build as well as serve a sample app. Finally, we looked at Dependency Injection, one of the key features of Angular.

At this point, the next step should ideally be to turn toward more complex projects and delve deeper into Angular. It is, however, noteworthy that Angular, as a framework, has a very large community and user base. In fact, it is one of the most popular web frameworks when it comes to building web apps. Naturally, the job market as well as industry scope is stellar as well.

As a result, it might be a good idea to learn Angular at a more minute scale. The official documentation is surely a good place to start, but Apress also has a praiseworthy list of Angular-specific titles that you can make use of to learn more about Angular.

- Angular Homepage: `https://angular.io/`

- Angular Documentation: `https://angular.io/docs`

- Progressive Web Apps with Angular: `www.apress.com/in/book/9781484244470`

- Pro Angular 6: `www.apress.com/in/book/9781484236482`

PART IV

Server-Side Frameworks

CHAPTER 8

Kraken

An organization's ability to learn, and translate that learning into action rapidly, is the ultimate competitive advantage.

—Jack Welch

As development platforms go, Node is no longer the new kid on the block. But as many well-known and respected organizations will attest, the benefits afforded by JavaScript as a server-side language have already had a tremendous impact on the manner in which they develop and deploy software. Among the many accolades for Node, Michael Yormark, Project Manager at Dow Jones, has proclaimed "The simple truth is Node has reinvented the way we create websites. Developers build critical functionality in days, not weeks." (`www.joyent.com/blog/the-node-firm-and-joyent-offer-node-js-training`)

Kiran Prasad, Director of Mobile Engineering at LinkedIn, has stated "On the server side, our entire mobile software stack is completely built in Node. One reason was scale. The second is Node showed us huge performance gains."

(`https://nodejs.org/download/docs/v0.6.7/`)

Node is certainly generating some rather large waves in the development community. All that said, however, let's be clear: the platform is far from perfect. JavaScript is beautifully expressive and flexible, but it's also flexible in a way that is easily abused. While Node-based projects enjoy rapid development cycles and impressive performance gains, they frequently suffer at the hands of an overall lack of convention both within the language itself and throughout the development

© Sufyan bin Uzayr, Nicholas Cloud, Tim Ambler 2019
S. bin Uzayr et al., *JavaScript Frameworks for Modern Web Development*,
https://doi.org/10.1007/978-1-4842-4995-6_8

community as a whole. While this problem may not be obvious within small, centralized development teams, it can quickly rear its head as teams grow in size and distribution—just ask Jeff Harrell, Director of Engineering at PayPal (`www.paypal-engineering.com/2013/11/`):

> *We especially liked the ubiquity of Express, but found it didn't scale well in multiple development teams. Express is non-prescriptive and allows you to set up a server in whatever way you see fit. This is great for flexibility, but bad for consistency in large teams... Over time we saw patterns emerge as more teams picked up node.js and turned those into Kraken.js; it's not a framework in itself, but a convention layer on top of express that allows it to scale to larger development organizations. We wanted our engineers to focus on building their applications and not just focus on setting up their environments.*

This chapter will introduce you to Kraken, a secure and scalable layer for Express-based applications brought to you by the developers at PayPal. Topics covered within this chapter include

- Environment-aware configuration

- Configuration-based middleware registration

- Structured route registration

- The Dust template engine

- Internationalization and localization

- Enhanced security techniques

Note   Kraken builds on the already firm foundation of Express, the minimalist web framework for Node whose API has become the de facto standard for frameworks in this category. As a result, this chapter assumes the reader already has a basic, working familiarity with Express. Portions of this chapter also discuss concepts covered in this book's chapters on Grunt, Yeoman, and Knex/Bookshelf. If you are unfamiliar with these subjects, you may wish to read those chapters before you continue.

Environment-Aware Configuration

As applications are developed, tested, staged, and deployed, they naturally progress through a series of corresponding environments, each requiring its own unique set of configuration rules. For example, consider Figure 8-1, which illustrates the process by which an application moves through a continuous integration and delivery deployment pipeline.

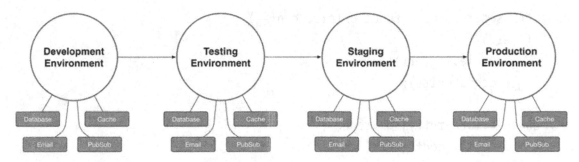

Figure 8-1. *Application that requires unique settings based on its environment*

As the application in Figure 8-1 progresses through each environment, the settings that tell it how to connect to the various external services on which it relies must change accordingly. Kraken's `confit` library provides developers with a standard convention for accomplishing this goal by offering a simple, environment-aware configuration layer for Node applications.

Confit operates by loading a default JSON configuration file (typically named `config.json`). Confit then attempts to load an additional configuration file based on the value of the `NODE_ENV` environment variable. If an environment-specific configuration file is found, any settings it specifies are recursively merged with those defined within the default configuration.

This chapter's `confit-simple` project provides a simple application that relies on `confit` for determining its configuration. Listing 8-1 demonstrates the process by which `confit` is initialized, while Listing 8-2 shows the contents of the project's `/config` folder, from which `confit` is instructed to search for configuration files.

Listing 8-1. Initializing Confit

```
// confit-simple/index.js

var confit = require('confit');
var prettyjson = require('prettyjson');
var path = require('path');
var basedir = path.join(__dirname, 'config');

confit(basedir).create(function(err, config) {
    if (err) {
        console.log(err);
        process.exit();
    }
    console.log(prettyjson.render({
        'email': config.get('email'),
        'cache': config.get('cache'),
        'database': config.get('database')
    }));
});
```

Listing 8-2. Contents of the /config Folder

```
// Default configuration
// confit-simple/config/config.json

{
    // SMTP server settings
    "email": {
        "hostname": "email.mydomain.com",
        "username": "user",
        "password": "pass",
        "from": "My Application <noreply@myapp.com>"
    },
    "cache": {
        "redis": {
            "hostname": "cache.mydomain.com",
            "password": "redis"
```

```
        }
      }
    }

// Development configuration
// confit-simple/config/development.json

{
    "database": {
        "postgresql": {
            "hostname": "localhost",
            "username": "postgres",
            "password": "postgres",
            "database": "myapp"
        }
    },
    "cache": {
        "redis": {
            "hostname": "localhost",
            "password": "redis"
        }
    }
}

// Production configuration
// confit-simple/config/production.json

{
    "database": {
        "postgresql": {
            "hostname": "db.myapp.com",
            "username": "postgres",
            "password": "super-secret-password",
            "database": "myapp"
        }
    },
```

```
    "cache": {
        "redis": {
            "hostname": "redis.myapp.com",
            "password": "redis"
        }
    }
}
```

Before continuing, notice that our project's default configuration file provides connection settings for an e-mail server under the email property, while neither of the project's environment-specific configuration files provides such information. In contrast, the default configuration provides connection settings for a Redis cache server under the nested cache:redis property, while both of the environment-specific configurations provide overriding information for this property.

Notice also that the default configuration file includes a comment above the email property. Comments, which are *not* part of the JSON specification, would normally result in an error being thrown if we attempted to use Node's require() method to parse the contents of this file. Confit, however, will strip out such comments before attempting to parse the file, allowing us to embed comments within our configuration as needed.

Listing 8-3 shows the output that is logged to the console when the project is run with the NODE_ENV environment variable set to development.

Listing 8-3. Running the confit-simple Project in development Mode

```
$ export NODE_ENV=development && node index

email:
  hostname: email.mydomain.com
  username: user
  password: pass
  from:     My Application noreply@myapp.com
cache:
  redis:
    hostname: localhost
    password: redis
```

```
database:
  postgresql:
    hostname: localhost
    username: postgres
    password: postgres
    database: myapp
```

Note   In Listing 8-3, `$ export NODE_ENV=development` is run from the terminal to set the value of the NODE_ENV environment variable. This command applies only to Unix and Unix-like systems (including OS X). Windows users will instead need to run `$ set NODE_ENV=development`. It's also important to remember that if the NODE_ENV environment variable is not set, `confit` will assume the application is running in the `development` environment.

As you can see in Listing 8-3, `confit` compiled our project's configuration object by merging the contents of the `config/development.json` environment configuration file with the default `config/config.json` file, giving priority to any settings specified in `development.json`. As a result, our configuration object inherited the `email` settings that only exist in `config.json`, along with the `cache` and `database` settings defined within the configuration file for the development environment. In Listing 8-1, these settings are accessed through the use of the configuration object's `get()` method.

Note   In addition to accessing top-level configuration settings (e.g., `database`, as shown in Listing 8-1), our configuration object's `get()` method can also be used to access deeply nested configuration settings using `:` as a delimiter. For example, we could have referenced the project's `postgresql` settings directly with `config.get('database:postgresql')`.

In Listing 8-4, we run the `confit-simple` project again, only this time we set the NODE_ENV environment variable with a value of `production`. As expected, the output shows that our configuration object inherited the `email` property from `config.json` while also inheriting the `cache` and `database` properties from `production.json`.

Listing 8-4. Running the `confit-simple` Project in `production` Mode

```
$ export NODE_ENV=production && node index
email:
  hostname: email.mydomain.com
  username: user
  password: pass
  from:     My Application noreply@myapp.com
cache:
  redis:
    hostname: redis.myapp.com
    password: redis
database:
  postgresql:
    hostname: db.myapp.com
    username: postgres
    password: super-secret-password
    database: myapp
```

Shortstop Handlers

Confit is designed for processing JSON configuration files, as previous examples have shown. As a configuration format, JSON is easy to work with, but it can occasionally leave a bit to be desired in terms of flexibility. Confit helpfully makes up for this shortcoming with support for plugins that it refers to as "shortstop handlers." By way of an example, consider Listing 8-5, in which the two shortstop handlers included within `confit`'s core library, `import` and `config`, are used.

Listing 8-5. Demonstrating the Use of the `import` and `config` Shortstop Handlers

```
// confit-shortstop/config/config.json

{
    // The `import` handler allows us to set a property's value to the contents
    // of the specified JSON configuration file.
    "app": "import:./app",
    // The `config` handler allows us to set a property's value to that of the
```

```
    // referenced property. Note the use of the `.` character as a delimiter,
    // in this instance.
    "something_else": "config:app.base_url"
}

// confit-shortstop/config/app.json

{

    // The title of the application
    "title": "My Demo Application",
    // The base URL at which the web client can be reached
    "base_url": "https://myapp.com",
    // The base URL at which the API can be reached
    "base_api_url": https://api.myapp.com
}
```

Listing 8-6 shows the output that is printed to the console when this chapter's confit-shortstop project is run. In this example, the import shortstop handler has allowed us to populate the app property with the contents of a separate JSON file, making it possible for us to break down particularly large configuration files into smaller and more easily manageable components. The config handler has allowed us to set a configuration value by referencing a preexisting value in another section.

Listing 8-6. Output of This Chapter's confit-shortstop Project

```
$ node index.js

app:
  title:        My Demo Application
  base_url:     https://myapp.com
  base_api_url: https://api.myapp.com
something_else: https://myapp.com
```

While confit itself only includes support for the two shortstop handlers that we've just covered (import and config), several additional handlers that are quite useful can be found in the shortstop-handlers module. Let's take a look at four examples.

The main script (index.js) from this chapter's confit-shortstop-extras project is shown in Listing 8-7. This script largely mirrors the one we've already seen in Listing 8-1, with a few minor differences. In this example, additional handlers are imported from the shortstop-handlers module. Also, instead of instantiating confit by passing the path to our project's config folder (basedir), we pass an object of options. Within this object, we continue to specify a value for basedir, but we also pass a protocols object, providing confit with references to the additional shortstop handlers we'd like to use.

Listing 8-7. index.js Script from the confit-shortstop-extras Project

```
// confit-shortstop-extras/index.js

var confit = require('confit');
var handlers = require('shortstop-handlers');
var path = require('path');
var basedir = path.join(__dirname, 'config');
var prettyjson = require('prettyjson');

confit({
    'basedir': basedir,
    'protocols': {
        // The `file` handler allows us to set a property's value to the contents
        // of an external (non-JSON) file. By default, the contents of the file
        // will be loaded as a Buffer.
        'file': handlers.file(basedir /* Folder from which paths should be
        resolved */, {
            'encoding': 'utf8' // Convert Buffers to UTF-8 strings
        }),
        // The `require` handler allows us to set a property's value to that
        // exported from a module.
        'require': handlers.require(basedir),
        // The `glob` handler allows us to set a property's value to an array
        // containing files whose names match a specified pattern
        'glob': handlers.glob(basedir),
    // The path handler allows us to resolve relative file paths
    'path': handlers.path(basedir)
    }
```

```
}).create(function(err, config) {
    if (err) {
        console.log(err);
        process.exit();
    }
    console.log(prettyjson.render({
        'app': config.get('app'),
        'something_else': config.get('something_else'),
        'ssl': config.get('ssl'),
        'email': config.get('email'),
        'images': config.get('images')
    }));
});
```

In this example, four additional shortstop handlers (imported from the shortstop-handlers module) are used:

- file: Sets a property using the contents of a specified file

- require: Sets a property using the exported value of a Node module (particularly useful for dynamic values that can only be determined at runtime)

- glob: Sets a property to an array containing files whose names match a specified pattern

- path: Sets a property to the absolute path of a referenced file

Listing 8-8 shows the default configuration file for this project. Finally, Listing 8-9 shows the output that is printed to the console when this project is run.

Listing 8-8. Default Configuration File for the confit-shortstop-extras Project

```
// confit-shortstop-extras/config/config.json

{
    "app": "import:./app",
    "something_else": "config:app.base_url",
    "ssl": {
        "certificate": "file:./certificates/server.crt",
```

```
    "certificate_path": "path:./certificates/server.crt"
  },
  "email": "require:./email",
  "images": "glob:../public/images/**/*.jpg"
}
```

Listing 8-9. Output from the `confit-shortstop-extras` Project

```
$ export NODE_ENV=development && node index

app:
  title:        My Demo Application
  base_url:     https://myapp.com
  base_api_url: https://api.myapp.com
something_else: https://myapp.com
ssl:
  certificate_path: /opt/confit-shortstop-extras/config/certificates/
  server.crt
  certificate:
    """
```

```
      -----BEGIN CERTIFICATE-----
      MIIDnjCCAoYCCQDy8G1RKCEz4jANBgkqhkiG9w0BAQUFADCBkDELMAkGA1UEBhMC
      VVMxEjAQBgNVBAgTCVRlbm5lc3NlZTESMBAGA1UEBxMJTmFzaHZpbGxlMSEwHwYD
      VQQKExhJbnRlcm5ldCBXaWRnaXRzIFB0eSBMdGQxFDASBgNVBAMUCyoubXlhcHAu
      Y29tMSAwHgYJKoZIhvcNAQkBFhFzdXBwb3J0QG15YXBwLmNvbTAeFw0xNTA0MTkw
      MDA4MzRaFw0xNjA0MTgwMDA4MzRaMIGQMQswCQYDVQQGEwJVUzESMBAGA1UECBMJ
      VGVubmVzc2VlMRIwEAYDVQQHEwlOYXNodmlsbGUxITAfBgNVBAoTGEludGVybmVo
      IFdpZGdpdHMgUHR5IExoZDEUMBIGA1UEAxQLKi5teWFwcC5jb20xIDAeBgkqhkiG
      9w0BCQEWEXN1cHBvcnRAbXlhcHAuY29tMIIBIjANBgkqhkiG9w0BAQEFAAOCAQ8A
      MIIBCgKCAQEAyBFxMVlMjP7VCU5w70okfJX/oEytrQIl1ZOAXnErryQQWwZpHOlu
      ZhTuZ8sBJmMBH3jju+rx4C2dFlXxWDRp8nYt+qfd1aiBKjYxMda2QMwXviToTd9b
      kPFBCaPQpMrzexwTwK/edoaxzqs/IxMs+n1PfvpuwOuPk6UbwFwWc8UQSWrmbGJw
      UEfs1X9kOSvt85IdrdQ1hQP2fBhHvt/xVVPfi1ZW1yBrWscVHBOJO4RyZSGclayg
      7LP+VHMvkvNm0au/cmCWThHtRt3aXhxAztgkI9IT2G4B9R+7ni8eXw5TLl65bhr1
      Gt7fMK2HnXclPtd3+vy9EnM+XqYXahXFGwIDAQABMA0GCSqGSIb3DQEBBQUAA4IB
      AQDH+QmuWk0Bx1kqUoL1Qxtqgf7s81eKoW5X3Tr4ePFXQbwmCZKHEudC98XckI2j
      qGA/SViBr+nbofq6ptnBhAoYV0IQd4YT3qvO+m3otGQ7NQkO2HwD3OUG9khHe2mG
```

k8Z7pFOpwu3lbTGKadiJsJSsS1fJGs9hy2vSzRulgOZozT3HJ+2SJpiwy7QAROaF
jqMC+HcP38zZkTWj1sO45HRCU1HdPjrOU3oJtupiU+HAmNpf+vdQnxS6aM5nzc7G
tZq74ketSxEYXTU8gjfMlR4gBewfPmu2KGuHNV51GAjWgm9wLfPFvMMYjcIEPB3k
Mla9+pYx1YvXiyJmOnUwsaop
-----END CERTIFICATE-----

```
    """

email:
  hostname: smtp.myapp.com
  username: user
  password: pass
  from:      My Application noreply@myapp.com
images:
  - /opt/confit-shortstop-extras/public/images/cat1.jpg
  - /opt/confit-shortstop-extras/public/images/cat2.jpg
  - /opt/confit-shortstop-extras/public/images/cat3.jpg
```

Configuration-Based Middleware Registration

Express processes incoming HTTP requests by pushing them through a series of configurable "middleware" functions, as shown in Figure 8-2.

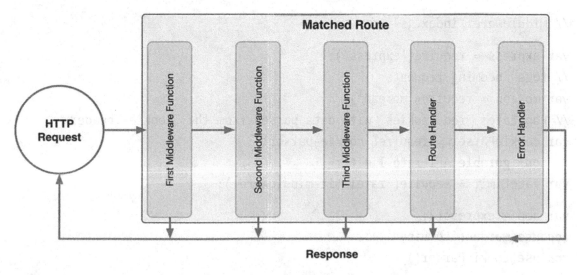

Figure 8-2. *Series of Express middleware calls*

At each step of this process, the active middleware function has the ability to

- Modify the incoming request object

- Modify the outgoing response object

- Execute additional code

- Close the request-response cycle

- Call the next middleware function in the series

By way of an example, consider Listing 8-10, which shows a simple Express application that relies on three middleware modules: `morgan`, `cookie-parser`, and `ratelimit-middleware`. As this application processes incoming HTTP requests, the following steps occur:

1. The `morgan` module logs the request to the console.

2. The `cookie-parser` module parses data from the request's `Cookie` header and assigns it to the request object's `cookies` property.

3. The `ratelimit-middleware` module rate-limits clients that attempt to access the application too frequently.

4. Finally, the appropriate route handler is called.

Listing 8-10. Express Application That Relies on Three Middleware Modules

```
// middleware1/index.js

var express = require('express');
// Logs incoming requests
var morgan = require('morgan');
// Populates `req.cookies` with data parsed from the `Cookie` header
var cookieParser = require('cookie-parser');
// Configurable API rate-limiter
var rateLimit = require('ratelimit-middleware');

var app = express();
app.use(morgan('combined'));
app.use(cookieParser());
```

```
app.use(rateLimit({
    'burst': 10,
    'rate': 0.5,
    'ip': true
}));

app.get('/animals', function(req, res, next) {
    res.send(['squirrels', 'aardvarks', 'zebras', 'emus']);
});

app.listen(7000);
```

This approach provides developers with a considerable degree of flexibility, allowing them to execute their own logic at any point during the request-response cycle. It also allows Express to maintain a relatively small footprint by delegating responsibility for performing nonessential tasks to third-party middleware modules. But as flexible as this approach is, it can also prove troublesome to manage as applications and the teams that develop them grow in size and complexity.

Kraken's `meddleware` module simplifies middleware management by providing a configuration-based middleware registration process for Express applications. In doing so, it provides developers with a standardized approach for specifying which middleware modules an Express application should rely on, in what order they should be loaded, and the options that should be passed to each. Listing 8-11 shows an updated version of the previous example, in which the `meddleware` module manages the registration of all middleware functions.

Listing 8-11. Configuration-Based Middleware Registration with the `meddleware` Module

```
// middleware2/index.js

var express = require('express');
var confit = require('confit');
var meddleware = require('meddleware');
var app = express();
var path = require('path');
```

```
confit(path.join(__dirname, 'config')).create(function(err, config) {
    app.use(meddleware(config.get('middleware')));
    app.get('/animals', function(req, res, next) {
        res.send(['squirrels', 'aardvarks', 'zebras', 'emus']);
    });
    app.listen(7000);
});

// middleware2/config/config.json

{
    "middleware": {
        "morgan": {
            // Toggles the middleware module on / off
            "enabled": true,
            // Specifies the order in which middleware should be registered
            "priority": 10,
            "module": {
                // The name of an installed module (or path to a module file)
                "name": "morgan",
                // Arguments to be passed to the module's factory function
                "arguments": ["combined"]
            }
        },
        "cookieParser": {
            "enabled": true,
            "priority": 20,
            "module": {
                "name": "cookie-parser"
            }
        },
        "rateLimit": {
            "enabled": true,
            "priority": 30,
            "module": {
                "name": "ratelimit-middleware",
```

```
            "arguments": [{
                "burst": 10,
                "rate": 0.5,
                "ip": true
            }]
        }
    }
  }
}
```

With the help of Kraken's `meddleware` module, all aspects of third-party middleware management within this application have been moved from code to standardized configuration files. The result is an application that is not only more organized but also easier to understand and modify.

Event Notifications

As middleware functions are registered with Express via the `meddleware` module, corresponding events are emitted by the application, providing developers with an easy method for determining what middleware functions are being loaded and in what order (see Listing 8-12).

Listing 8-12. Events Are Emitted As Middleware Registered via the `meddleware` Module

```
var express = require('express');
var confit = require('confit');
var meddleware = require('meddleware');
var app = express();
var path = require('path');

confit(path.join(__dirname, 'config')).create(function(err, config) {

    // Listening to all middleware registrations
    app.on('middleware:before', function(data) {
        console.log('Registering middleware: %s', data.config.name);
    });
```

```
// Listening for a specific middleware registration event
app.on('middleware:before:cookieParser', function(data) {
    console.log('Registering middleware: %s', data.config.name);
});

app.on('middleware:after', function(data) {
    console.log('Registered middleware: %s', data.config.name);
});

app.on('middleware:after:cookieParser', function(data) {
    console.log('Registered middleware: %s', data.config.name);
});

app.use(meddleware(config.get('middleware')));

app.get('/animals', function(req, res, next) {
    res.send(['squirrels', 'aardvarks', 'zebras', 'emus']);
});

app.listen(7000);
});
```

Structured Route Registration

In the previous section, you learned how Kraken's meddleware module can simplify
middleware function registration by moving the logic required for loading and
configuring those functions into standardized JSON configuration files. In much the
same way, Kraken's enrouten module applies the same concept to bring structure where
there often is none to be found—Express routes.

Simple Express applications with a small number of routes can often make do with
a single module in which every available route is defined. However, as applications
gradually grow in depth and complexity, such an organizational structure (or lack
thereof) can quickly become unwieldy. Enrouten solves this problem by providing three
approaches with which Express routes can be defined in a consistent, structured fashion.

Index Configuration

Using enrouten's `index` configuration option, the path to a single module can be specified. This module will then be loaded and passed an Express Router instance that has been mounted to the root path. This option provides developers with the simplest method for defining routes, as it does not enforce any specific type of organizational structure. While this option provides a good starting point for new applications, care must be taken not to abuse it. This option is often used in combination with enrouten's `directory` and `routes` configuration options, which we will cover shortly.

Listing 8-13 shows a simple Express application whose routes are configured with the help of `confit`, `meddleware`, and `enrouten`, along with the accompanying `confit` configuration file. Listing 8-14 shows the contents of the module that is passed to enrouten's index option. Subsequent examples within this section will build on this example.

Listing 8-13. Express Application Configured with confit, meddleware, and enrouten

```
// enrouten-index/index.js

var express = require('express');
var confit = require('confit');
var handlers = require('shortstop-handlers');
var meddleware = require('meddleware');
var path = require('path');
var configDir = path.join(__dirname, 'config');
var app = express();

confit({
    'basedir': configDir,
    'protocols': {
        'path': handlers.path(configDir),
        'require': handlers.require(configDir)
    }
}).create(function(err, config) {
    app.use(meddleware(config.get('middleware')));
    app.listen(7000);
    console.log('App is available at: http://localhost:7000');
});
```

```
// enrouten-index/config/config.json

{
    "middleware": {
        "morgan": {
            "enabled": true,
            "priority": 10,
            "module": {
                "name": "morgan",
                "arguments": ["combined"]
            }
        },
        "enrouten": {
            "enabled": true,
            "priority": 30,
            "module": {
                "name": "express-enrouten",
                "arguments": [
                    {
                        "index": "path:../routes/index"
                    }
                ]
            }
        }
    }
}
```

Listing 8-14. Contents of the Module Passed to Enrouten's index Option

```
// enrouten-index/routes/index.js

module.exports = function(router) {

    router.route('/')
    .get(function(req, res, next) {
        res.send('Hello, world.');
    });
```

```
router.route('/api/v1/colors')
.get(function(req, res, next) {
    res.send([
    'blue', 'green', 'red', 'orange', 'white'
    ]);
});

};
```

Directory Configuration

Listing 8-15 demonstrates the use of enrouten's `directory` configuration option. When set, enrouten will recursively scan the contents of the specified folder, searching for modules that export a function accepting a single argument. For each module it finds, enrouten will pass an Express Router instance that has been mounted to a path predetermined by that module's location within the directory structure—a "convention over configuration" approach.

Listing 8-15. Setting Enrouten's `directory` Configuration Option

```
// enrouten-directory/config/config.json

{
    "middleware": {
        "enrouten": {
            "enabled": true,
            "priority": 10,
            "module": {
                "name": "express-enrouten",
                "arguments": [{ "directory": "path:../routes" }]
            }
        }
    }
}
```

Figure 8-3 shows the structure of this project's /routes folder, while Listing 8-16 shows the contents of the /routes/api/v1/accounts/index.js module. Based on this module's location within the /routes folder, the URLs for each route that it defines will be prefixed with /api/v1/accounts.

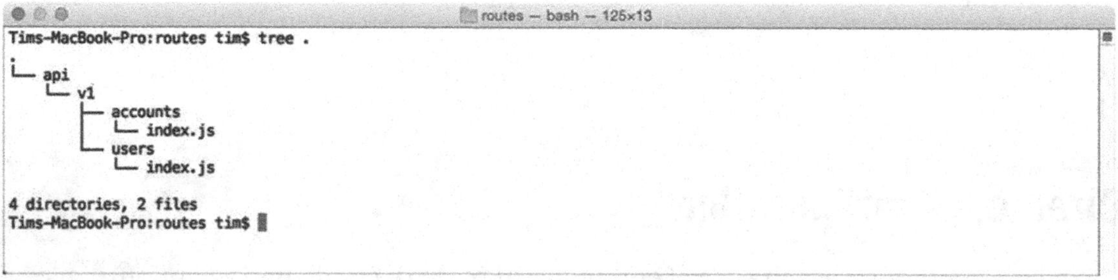

```
●  ●  ●                          routes — bash — 125×13
Tims-MacBook-Pro:routes tim$ tree .
.
└── api
    └── v1
        ├── accounts
        │   └── index.js
        └── users
            └── index.js

4 directories, 2 files
Tims-MacBook-Pro:routes tim$ ▊
```

Figure 8-3. *Structure of this project's /routes folder*

Listing 8-16. The /api/v1/accounts Controller

```
// enrouten-directory/routes/api/v1/accounts/index.js

var _ = require('lodash');
var path = require('path');

module.exports = function(router) {

    var accounts = require(path.join(APPROOT, 'models', 'accounts'));

    /**
     * @route /api/v1/accounts
     */
    router.route('/')
        .get(function(req, res, next) {
            res.send(accounts);
        });

    /**
     * @route /api/v1/accounts/:account_id
     */
    router.route('/:account_id')
        .get(function(req, res, next) {
        var account = _.findWhere(accounts, {
```

```
        'id': parseInt(req.params.account_id, 10)
    });
    if (!account) return next(new Error('Account not found'));
        res.send(account);
    });

};
```

Routes Configuration

Enrouten's `directory` configuration option provides an approach that favors "convention over configuration" by automatically determining the structure of an application's API based on the layout of a specified folder. This approach provides a quick and easy method for structuring Express routes in an organized and consistent way. However, complex applications may eventually come to find this approach to be rather confining.

Applications with APIs that feature a number of complex, deeply nested routes will likely find greater benefit from enrouten's `routes` configuration option, which allows developers to create completely separate modules for *each* of the application's routes. API endpoints, methods, handlers, and route-specific middleware are then specified within configuration files—an organized approach that allows for the greatest degree of flexibility, at the expense of being slightly more verbose.

Listing 8-17 shows an excerpt from the configuration file for this chapter's enrouten-routes project. Here we pass an array of objects to enrouten's `routes` configuration option, the entries of which describe the various routes to be made available by Express. Note that in addition to specifying a route, HTTP method, and handler, each entry also has the option of specifying an array of route-specific middleware functions. As a result, this application is able to apply a middleware function responsible for authorizing incoming requests on a route-by-route basis. As shown in Listing 8-17, the `auth` middleware function is *not* applied to the route at which users initially sign in, allowing them to sign in before making subsequent requests.

Listing 8-17. Specifying Individual Routes via Enrouten's `routes` Configuration Option

```
// enrouten-routes/config/config.json (excerpt)

"arguments": [{
    "index": "path:../routes",
    "routes": [
        {
            "path": "/api/v1/session",
            "method": "POST",
            "handler": "require:../routes/api/v1/session/create"
        },
        {
            "path": "/api/v1/session",
            "method": "DELETE",
            "handler": "require:../routes/api/v1/session/delete",
            "middleware": [
                "require:../middleware/auth"
            ]
        },
        {
            "path": "/api/v1/users",
            "method": "GET",
            "handler": "require:../routes/api/v1/users/list",
            "middleware": [
                "require:../middleware/auth"
            ]
        },
        // ...
    ]
}]
```

Listing 8-18 shows the contents of the module responsible for handling incoming GET requests to this application's /api/v1/users route. The module exports a single function, which accepts the standard req, res, next Express route handler signature.

Listing 8-18. The `/routes/api/v1/users/list` Route Handler

```
var models = require('../../../../lib/models');

module.exports = function(req, res, next) {

    models.User.fetchAll()
        .then(function(users) {
            res.send(users);
        })
        .catch(next);

};
```

Dust Templates

Many popular JavaScript template engines (e.g., Mustache and Handlebars) tout
themselves as being "logic-less"—an attribute that describes their ability to help developers
maintain a clear separation of concerns between an application's business logic and
its presentation layer. When properly maintained, this separation makes it possible for
significant changes to occur within the interface that users are presented with while
requiring minimal (if any) accompanying changes behind the scenes (and vice versa).

So-called "logic-less" template engines accomplish this goal by enforcing a strict
set of rules that prevents developers from creating what is often referred to as "spaghetti
code," a tangled mess that combines code with presentation in a way that is hard to
grasp and even harder to unravel. Anyone who has ever had to deal with a PHP script
resembling that shown in Listing 8-19 will immediately grasp the importance of
maintaining a layer of separation between these two concerns.

Listing 8-19. Spaghetti Code, an Unmaintainable Mess

```php
<?php

print "<!DOCTYPE html><head><title>";
$result = mysql_query("SELECT * FROM settings") or die(mysql_error());
print $result[0]["title"] . "</title></head><body><table>";
print "<thead><tr><th>First Name</th><th>Last Name</th></tr></thead><tbody>";
```

```
$users = mysql_query("SELECT * FROM users") or die(mysql_error());
while ($row = mysql_fetch_assoc($users)) {
    print "<tr><td>" . $row["first_name"] . "</td><td>" . $row["last_name"]
. "</td></tr>";
}
print "</tbody></table></body></html>";

?>
```

Logic-less template engines attempt to prevent developers from creating spaghetti code by banning the use of logic within an application's views. Such templates are typically capable of referencing values within a provided payload of information, iterating through arrays, and toggling specific portions of their content on and off based on simple boolean logic.

Unfortunately, this rather heavy-handed approach often brings about the very problems it hoped to prevent, albeit in an unexpected way. Although logic-less template engines such as Handlebars prevent the use of logic within templates themselves, they do not negate the need for that logic to exist in the first place. The logic required for preparing data for template use must exist *somewhere*, and more often than not, the use of logic-less template engines results in presentation-related logic spilling over into the business layer.

Dust, which is the JavaScript template engine favored by Kraken, seeks to solve this problem by taking an approach that is better thought of as "less-logic" rather than strictly "logic-less." By allowing developers to embed slightly more advanced logic within their templates in the form of "helpers," Dust allows presentation logic to remain where it belongs, in the *presentation* layer, rather than the *business* layer.

Context and References

When using Dust templates, two primary components come into play: the template itself and an (optional) object literal containing any data to be referenced from within the template. In Listing 8-20, this process is demonstrated by an Express application that has specified Dust as its rendering engine. Note the use of the adaro module in this example. The adaro module serves as a convenient wrapper for Dust, abstracting away some additional setup that would otherwise be necessary to integrate Dust with Express. It also includes some convenient helper functions by default that we will be covering later in the chapter.

Listing 8-20. Express Application Using Dust As Its Rendering Engine

```
// dust-simple/index.js

var express = require('express');
var adaro = require('adaro');
var app = express();

/**
 * By default, Dust will cache the contents of an application's templates
   as they are
 * loaded. In a production environment, this is usually the preferred behavior.
 * This behavior will be disabled in this chapter's examples, allowing you
   to modify
 * templates and see the result without having to restart Express.
 */
app.engine('dust', adaro.dust({
    'cache': false
}));

app.set('view engine', 'dust');
app.use('/', express.static('./public'));

var data = {
    'report_name': 'North American Countries',
    'languages': ['English', 'Spanish'],
    'misc': {
        'total_population': 565000000
    },
    'countries': [
        {
            'name': 'United States',
            'population': 319999999,
            'english': true,
            'capital': { 'name': 'Washington D.C.', 'population': 660000 }
        },
```

```
        {
            'name': 'Mexico',
            'population': 118000000,
            'english': false,
            'capital': { 'name': 'Mexico City', 'population': 9000000 }
        },
        {
            'name': 'Canada',
            'population': 35000000,
            'english': true,
            'capital': { 'name': 'Ottawa', 'population': 880000 }
        }
    ]
};

app.get('/', function(req, res, next) {
    res.render('main', data);
});

app.listen(8000);
```

In Listing 8-20, an object literal containing an array of North American countries (referred to by Dust as a "context") is passed to a Dust template, the content of which is shown in Listing 8-21. Within this template, data is referenced by wrapping the desired key within a single pair of curly brackets. Nested properties can also be referenced through the use of dot notation ({misc.total_population}).

Listing 8-21. Accompanying main Dust Template

```
// dust-simple/views/main.dust

<!DOCTYPE html>
<html lang="en">
<head>
    <meta charset="utf-8">
    <meta http-equiv="X-UA-Compatible" content="IE=edge">
    <meta name="viewport" content="width=device-width, initial-scale=1">
    <title>App</title>
    <link href="/css/style.css" rel="stylesheet">
```

```
</head>
<body>
    {! Dust comments are created using this format. Data is referenced by
    wrapping the
    desired key within a single pair of curly brackets, as shown below. !}
    <h1>{report_name}</h1>
    <table>
        <thead>
            <tr>
                <th>Name</th>
                <th>Population</th>
                <th>Speaks English</th>
                <th>Capital</th>
                <th>Population of Capital</th>
            </tr>
        </thead>
        <tbody>
            {! Templates can loop through iterable objects !}
            {#countries}
            <tr>
                <td>{name}</td>
                <td>{population}</td>
                <td>{?english}Yes{:else}No{/english}</td>
                {#capital}
                    <td>{name}</td>
                    <td>{population}</td>
                {/capital}
            </tr>
            {/countries}
        </tbody>
    </table>
    <h2>Languages</h2>
    <ul>
        {#languages}
        <li>{.}</li>
        {/languages}
```

```
    </ul>
    <h2>Total Population: {misc.total_population}</h2>
</body>
</html>
```

Sections

As Dust goes about its rendering process, it fetches referenced data by applying one or more "contexts" to the template in question. The simplest templates have a single context that references the outermost level of the JSON object that was passed. For example, consider the template shown in Listing 8-21, in which two references are used, {report_name} and {misc.total_population}. Dust processes these references by searching for matching properties (starting at the outermost level) within the object shown in Listing 8-20.

Dust sections provide a convenient method by which additional contexts can be created, allowing a template to access nested properties without requiring references that start at the outermost level. For example, consider Listing 8-22, in which a new context, {#misc}...{/misc}, is created, allowing nested properties to be accessed using a shorter syntax.

Listing 8-22. Creating a New Dust Section

```
// Template
<h1>{report_name}</h1>
{#misc}
<p>Total Population: {total_population}</p>
{/misc}

// Rendered Output
<h1>Information About North America</h1>
<p>Total Population: 565000000</p>
```

Iteration

In the previous example, a new Dust section (and corresponding context) was created. As a result, the contents of the new section received direct access to the properties of the object literal that was referenced. In much the same way, Dust sections can also be used to iterate through the entries of an array. Listing 8-23 demonstrates this process by creating a new section that references the countries array. Unlike the section from the previous example, which was applied only once, the {#countries} ... {/countries} section will be applied multiple times, once for each entry within the array that it references.

Listing 8-23. Iterating Through an Array with Sections

```
// Template
{#countries}
{! The current position within the iteration can be referenced at `$idx` !}
{! The size of the object through which we are looping can be referenced at
`$len` !}
<tr>
    <td>{name}</td>
    <td>{population}</td>
    <td>{capital.name}</td>
    <td>{capital.population}</td>
</tr>
{/countries}

// Rendered Output
<tr>
    <td>United States</td>
    <td>319999999</td>
    <td>Washington D.C.</td>
    <td>660000</td>
</tr>
<tr>
    <td>Mexico</td>
    <td>118000000</td>
    <td>Mexico City</td>
    <td>9000000</td>
</tr>
```

```
<tr>
    <td>Canada</td>
    <td>35000000</td>
    <td>Ottawa</td>
    <td>880000</td>
</tr>
```

Listing 8-24 demonstrates the process by which a template can loop through an array whose entries are primitive data types (i.e., not objects). For each iteration, the value itself can be directly referenced via the {.} syntax.

Listing 8-24. Iterating Through an Array Containing Primitive Data Types

```
// Template
<ul>
    {#languages}<li>{.}</li>{/languages}
</ul>

// Rendered Output
<ul>
    <li>English</li>
    <li>Spanish</li>
</ul>
```

Conditionality

Dust provides built-in support for *conditionally* rendering content, based on whether a simple truth test is passed. The template shown in Listing 8-25 demonstrates this concept by rendering the text "Yes" or "No" based on whether each country's english property references a "truthy" value.

Listing 8-25. Applying Conditionality Within a Dust Template

```
// Template
{#countries}
<tr>
    <td>{name}</td>
    <td>{?english}Yes{:else}No{/english}</td>
```

```
    {!
        The opposite logic can be applied as shown below:
        <td>{^english}No{:else}Yes{/english}</td>
    !}
</tr>
{/countries}

// Rendered Output
<tr>
    <td>United States</td>
    <td>Yes</td>
</tr>
<tr>
    <td>Mexico</td>
    <td>No</td>
</tr>
<tr>
    <td>Canada</td>
    <td>Yes</td>
</tr>
```

Note   When applying conditionality within a template, it is important to understand the rules that Dust will apply as it determines the "truthiness" of a property. Empty strings, boolean false, empty arrays, null, and undefined are all considered to be false. The number 0, empty objects, and string-based representations for "0," "null," "undefined," and "false" are all considered to be true.

Partials

One of Dust's most powerful features, partials, allows developers to include templates *within* other templates. As a result, complex documents can be broken down into smaller components (i.e., "partials") that are easier to manage and reuse. A simple example that demonstrates this process is shown in Listing 8-26.

Listing 8-26. Dust Template That References an External Template (i.e., "Partial")

```
// Main Template
<h1>{report_name}</h1>
<p>Total Population: {misc.total_population}</p>
{>"countries"/}
{!
    In this example, an external template - `countries` - is included by a
    parent
    template which references it by name (using a string literal that is
    specified
    within the template itself). Alternatively, the name of the external
    template
    could have been derived from a value held within the template's
    context, using
    Dust's support for "dynamic" partials. To do so, we would have wrapped the
    `countries` string in a pair of curly brackets, as shown here:
    {>"{countries}"/}
!}

// "countries" template
{#countries}
<tr>
    <td>{name}</td>
    <td>{population}</td>
    <td>{capital.name}</td>
    <td>{capital.population}</td>
</tr>
{/countries}

// Rendered Output
<h1>Information About North America</h1>
<p>Total Population: 565000000</p>
<tr>
    <td>United States</td>
    <td>Yes</td>
</tr>
```

```
<tr>
    <td>Mexico</td>
    <td>No</td>
</tr>
<tr>
    <td>Canada</td>
    <td>Yes</td>
</tr>
```

Blocks

Consider a commonly encountered scenario in which a complex web application consisting of multiple pages is created. Each of these pages displays a unique set of content while at the same time sharing common elements, such as headers and footers, with the other pages. With the help of Dust blocks, developers can define these shared elements in a single location. Afterward, templates that wish to inherit from them can, while also retaining the ability to overwrite their content when necessary.

Let's take a look at an example that should help to clarify this point. Listing 8-27 shows the content of a Dust template that defines the overall layout of a site. In this instance, a default page title is specified, {+title}App{/title}, along with an empty placeholder for body content.

Listing 8-27. Dust Block from Which Other Templates Can Inherit

```
// dust-blocks/views/shared/base.dust

<!DOCTYPE html>
<html lang="en">
<head>
    <meta charset="utf-8">
    <meta http-equiv="X-UA-Compatible" content="IE=edge">
    <meta name="viewport" content="width=device-width, initial-scale=1">
    <title>{+title}App{/title}</title>
    <link href="/css/style.css" rel="stylesheet">
</head>
```

```
<body>
    {+bodyContent/}
</body>
</html>
```

Listing 8-28 shows the content of a Dust template that inherits from the example presented in Listing 8-27. It does so by first embedding the parent template within itself as a partial ({>"shared/base"/}). Next, it injects content into the {+bodyContent/} placeholder that was defined, {<bodyContent}...{/bodyContent}. In this instance, our template chooses *not* to overwrite the default page title that was specified in our parent template.

Listing 8-28. Dust Template Inheriting from a Block

```
 // dust-blocks/views/main.dust

{>"shared/base"/}

{<bodyContent}
    <p>Hello, world!</p>
{/bodyContent}
```

Filters

Dust includes several built-in filters that allow a template to modify a value before it is rendered. By way of an example, consider the fact that Dust will automatically HTML escape any values referenced within a template. In other words, if a context were to contain a content key with a value matching that shown here:

```
<script>doBadThings();</script>
```

Dust would automatically render this value as

```
<script>doBadThings()</script>
```

While the behavior that we see here is typically desired, it is not uncommon to run into situations in which this behavior needs to be disabled. This can be accomplished through the use of a filter:

```
{content|s}
```

In this example, the |s filter disables auto-escaping for the referenced value. Table 8-1 contains a list of the built-in filters provided by Dust.

Table 8-1. *List of Built-in Filters Provided by Dust*

Filter	Description
s	Disables HTML escaping
h	Forces HTML escaping
j	Forces JavaScript escaping
u	Encodes with encodeURI()
uc	Encodes with encodeURIComponent()
js	Stringifies a JSON literal
jp	Parses a JSON string

Creating Custom Filters

In addition to providing several core filters, Dust also makes it easy for developers to extend this behavior by creating their own custom filters, such as that shown in Listing 8-29. In this example, a custom formatTS filter is created. When applied, this filter will convert a referenced timestamp to a human-readable format (e.g., Jul. 4, 1776).

Listing 8-29. Defining a Custom Dust Filter

```
// dust-filters/index.js

var express = require('express');
var adaro = require('adaro');
var app = express();
var moment = require('moment');

app.engine('dust', adaro.dust({
    'cache': false,
    'helpers': [
        function(dust) {
            dust.filters.formatTS = function(ts) {
```

263

```
                    return moment(ts, 'X').format('MMM. D, YYYY');
                };
            }
        ]
    }));

app.set('view engine', 'dust');
app.use('/', express.static('./public'));

app.get('/', function(req, res, next) {
    res.render('main', {
        'events': [
            { 'label': 'Moon Landing', 'ts': -14558400 },
            { 'label': 'Fall of Berlin Wall', 'ts': 626616000 },
            { 'label': 'First Episode of Who\'s the Boss', 'ts': 464529600
}
        ]
    });
});

// dust-filters/views/main.dist (excerpt)

<tbody>
    {#events}
    <tr>
        <td>{label}</td>
        <td>{ts|formatTS}</td>
    </tr>
    {/events}
</tbody>
```

Context Helpers

In addition to storing data, Dust contexts are also capable of storing functions (referred
to as "context helpers"), the output of which can later be referenced by the templates
to which they are passed. In this way, a Dust context can be thought of as more than a
simple payload of raw information, but rather as a *view model*, a mediator between an

application's business logic and its views, capable of formatting information in the most appropriate manner along the way.

This feature is demonstrated by the example shown in Listing 8-30, in which an application presents the user with a table of servers. Each entry displays a name, along with a message indicating whether each server is online. A header displays the overall health of the system, which is generated by the systemStatus() context helper. Note that the template is able to reference our context helper just as it would any other type of value (e.g., object literals, arrays, numbers, strings).

Listing 8-30. Dust Context Helper

```
// dust-context-helpers1/index.js (excerpt)

app.all('/', function(req, res, next) {
    res.render('main', {
        'servers': [
            { 'name': 'Web Server', 'online': true },
            { 'name': 'Database Server', 'online': true },
            { 'name': 'Email Server', 'online': false }
        ],
        'systemStatus': function(chunk, context, bodies, params) {
            var offlineServers = _.filter(this.servers, { 'online': false });
            return offlineServers.length ? 'Bad' : 'Good';
        }
    });
});

// dust-context-helpers1/views/main.dust (excerpt)

<h1>System Status: {systemStatus}</h1>
<table>
    <thead><tr><th>Server</th><th>Online</th></tr></thead>
    <tbody>
        {#servers}
            <tr>
                <td>{name}</td>
                <td>{?online}Yes{:else}No{/online}</td>
            </tr>
```

```
        {/servers}
    </tbody>
</table>
```

As shown in this example, every Dust context helper receives four arguments: chunk, context, bodies, and params. Let's take a look at a few examples that demonstrate their usage.

chunk

A context helper's chunk argument provides it with access to the current portion of the template being rendered—referred to by Dust as a "chunk." By way of an example, consider Listing 8-31, in which a context helper is paired with default content that is defined within the template. In this example, the systemStatus() context helper can choose to override the chunk's default content, "Unknown," with its own value by calling the chunk.write() method. The helper can indicate that it has chosen to do so by returning chunk as its value.

Listing 8-31. Dust Context Helper Paired with Default Content

```
// dust-context-helpers2/index.js (excerpt)

app.all('/', function(req, res, next) {
    res.render('main', {
        'servers': [
            { 'name': 'Web Server', 'online': true },
            { 'name': 'Database Server', 'online': true },
            { 'name': 'Email Server', 'online': false }
        ],
        'systemStatus': function(chunk, context, bodies, params) {
            if (!this.servers.length) return;
            if (_.filter(this.servers, { 'online': false }).length) {
                return chunk.write('Bad');
            } else {
                return chunk.write('Good');
            }
        }
    });
```

```
});

// dust-context-helpers2/views/main.dust (excerpt)

<h1>System Status: {#systemStatus}Unknown{/systemStatus}</h1>
```

context

The context argument provides context helpers with convenient access to the *active* section of the context, as determined by the template. The template shown in Listing 8-32 demonstrates this by referencing the isOnline() context helper once for every server it has been passed. Each time, the isOnline() helper fetches the value of the active section's online property via context.get().

Listing 8-32. The context Argument Provides Context Helpers with Access to the Active Section

```
// dust-context-helpers3/index.js (excerpt)

app.all('/', function(req, res, next) {
    res.render('main', {
        'servers': [
            { 'name': 'Web Server', 'online': true },
            { 'name': 'Database Server', 'online': true },
            { 'name': 'Email Server', 'online': false }
        ],
        'systemStatus': function(chunk, context, bodies, params) {
            return _.filter(this.servers, { 'online': false }).length ?
            'Bad': 'Good';
        },
        'isOnline': function(chunk, context, bodies, params) {
            return context.get('online') ? 'Yes' : 'No';
        }
    });
});

// dust-context-helpers3/views/main.dust (excerpt)

<h1>System Status: {systemStatus}</h1>
```

267

```
<table>
    <thead><tr><th>Server</th><th>Online</th></tr></thead>
    <tbody>
        {#servers}
            <tr>
                <td>{name}</td>
                <td>{isOnline}</td>
            </tr>
        {/servers}
    </tbody>
</table>
```

bodies

Imagine a scenario in which large portions of a template's content are determined
by one or more context helpers. Instead of forcing developers to concatenate strings
in an unwieldy fashion, Dust allows such content to remain where it belongs—in the
template—available as options from which a context helper can choose to render.

Listing 8-33 demonstrates this by passing four different bodies of content to the
description() context helper. The helper's bodies argument provides it with references
to this content, which it can then choose to render by passing the appropriate value to
chunk.render().

Listing 8-33. Selectively Rendering Portions of a Template via the bodies
Argument

```
// dust-context-helpers4/index.js (excerpt)

app.all('/', function(req, res, next) {
    res.render('main', {
        'servers': [
            { 'name': 'Web Server', 'online': true },
            { 'name': 'Database Server', 'online': true },
            { 'name': 'Email Server', 'online': false },
            { 'name': 'IRC Server', 'online': true }
        ],
        'systemStatus': function(chunk, context, bodies, params) {
```

```
            return _.filter(this.servers, { 'online': false }).length ?
            'Bad': 'Good';
        },
        'isOnline': function(chunk, context, bodies, params) {
            return context.get('online') ? 'Yes' : 'No';
        },
        'description': function(chunk, context, bodies, params) {
            switch (context.get('name')) {
                case 'Web Server':
                    return chunk.render(bodies.web, context);
                break;
                case 'Database Server':
                    return chunk.render(bodies.database, context);
                break;
                case 'Email Server':
                    return chunk.render(bodies.email, context);
                break;
            }
        }
    });
});

// dust-context-helpers4/index.js (excerpt)

<h1>System Status: {systemStatus}</h1>
<table>

<thead><tr><th>Server</th><th>Online</th><th>Description</th></tr></thead>
    <tbody>
        {#servers}
            <tr>
                <td>{name}</td>
                <td>{isOnline}</td>
                <td>
                    {#description}
                        {:web}
                            A web server serves content over HTTP.
```

```
                            {:database}
                                A database server fetches remotely stored
                                information.
                            {:email}
                                An email server sends and receives messages.
                            {:else}
                                -
                        {/description}
                    </td>
                </tr>
            {/servers}
        </tbody>
</table>
```

params

In addition to referencing properties of the context in which it is called (via context.
get()), a context helper can also access parameters that have been passed to it by a
template. The example shown in Listing 8-34 demonstrates this by passing each server's
uptime property to the formatUptime() context helper. In this example, the helper
converts the provided value, params.value, into a more easily readable form before
writing it out to the chunk.

Listing 8-34. Context Helpers Can Receive Parameters via the params Argument

```
// dust-context-helpers5/index.js (excerpt)

app.all('/', function(req, res, next) {
    res.render('main', {
        'servers': [
            { 'name': 'Web Server', 'online': true, 'uptime': 722383 },
            { 'name': 'Database Server', 'online': true, 'uptime': 9571 },
            { 'name': 'Email Server', 'online': false, 'uptime': null }
        ],
        'systemStatus': function(chunk, context, bodies, params) {
            return _.filter(this.servers, { 'online': false }).length ?
            'Bad': 'Good';
```

```
    },
    'formatUptime': function(chunk, context, bodies, params) {
        if (!params.value) return chunk.write('-');
        chunk.write(moment.duration(params.value, 'seconds').humanize());
    }
  });
});
```

```
// dust-context-helpers5/views/main.dust (excerpt)

{#servers}
    <tr>
        <td>{name}</td>
        <td>{?online}Yes{:else}No{/online}</td>
        <td>{#formatUptime value=uptime /}</td>
    </tr>
{/servers}
```

In Listing 8-35, we see a slightly more complex demonstration of context helper parameters at work. In this example, the parseLocation() helper receives a string in which context properties are referenced: value="{name} lives in {location}". In order for these references to be correctly interpreted, the parameter must first be evaluated with the help of Dust's helpers.tap() method.

Listing 8-35. Parameters That Reference Context Properties Must Be Evaluated

```
// dust-context-helpers6/index.js

var express = require('express');
var adaro = require('adaro');
var app = express();
var morgan = require('morgan');
app.use(morgan('combined'));
var engine = adaro.dust();
var dust = engine.dust;

app.engine('dust', engine);

app.set('view engine', 'dust');
app.use('/', express.static('./public'));
```

```
app.all('/', function(req, res, next) {
    res.render('main', {
        'people': [
            { 'name': 'Joe', 'location': 'Chicago' },
            { 'name': 'Mary', 'location': 'Denver' },
            { 'name': 'Steve', 'location': 'Oahu' },
            { 'name': 'Laura', 'location': 'Nashville' }
        ],
        'parseLocation': function(chunk, context, bodies, params) {
            var content = dust.helpers.tap(params.value, chunk, context);
            return chunk.write(content.toUpperCase());
        }
    });
});

app.listen(8000);

// dust-context-helpers6/views/main.dust

{#people}
    <li>{#parseLocation value="{name} lives in {location}" /}</li>
{/people}
```

Asynchronous Context Helpers

Helper functions provide Dust with much of its power and flexibility. They allow a context object to serve as a view model—an intelligent bridge between an application's business logic and its user interface, capable of fetching information and formatting it appropriately for a specific use case before passing it along to one or more views for rendering. But as useful as this is, we've really only begun to scratch the surface in terms of how these helper functions can be applied to powerful effect.

In addition to returning data directly, Dust helper functions are also capable of returning data *asynchronously*, a process that is demonstrated by the example shown in Listing 8-36. Here we create two context helpers, cars() and trucks(). The former returns an array, while the latter returns a promise that *resolves* to an array. From the template's perspective, both of these functions are consumed identically.

Listing 8-36. Helper Functions Can Return Promises

```
// dust-promise1/index.js (excerpt)

app.get('/', function(req, res, next) {
    res.render('main', {
        'cars': function(chunk, context, bodies, params) {
            return ['Nissan Maxima', 'Toyota Corolla', 'Volkswagen Jetta'];
        },
        'trucks': function(chunk, context, bodies, params) {
            return new Promise(function(resolve, reject) {
                resolve(['Chevrolet Colorado', 'GMC Canyon', 'Toyota Tacoma']);
            });
        }
    });
});

// dust-promise1/views/main.dust (excerpt)

<h1>Cars</h1>
<ul>{#cars}<li>{.}</li>{/cars}</ul>
<h2>Trucks</h1>
<ul>{#trucks}<li>{.}</li>{/trucks}</ul>
```

Dust also provides a convenient method for conditionally displaying content, in the event that a promise is rejected. This process is demonstrated by Listing 8-37.

Listing 8-37. Handling Rejected Promises

```
// dust-promise2/index.js (excerpt)

app.get('/', function(req, res, next) {
    res.render('main', {
        'cars': function(chunk, context, bodies, params) {
            return ['Nissan Maxima', 'Toyota Corolla', 'Volkswagen Jetta'];
        },
```

```
        'trucks': function(chunk, context, bodies, params) {
            return new Promise(function(resolve, reject) {
                reject('Unable to fetch trucks.');
            });
        }
    });
});
```

```
// dust-promise2/views/main.dust (excerpt)
```

```
<h1>Cars</h1>
<ul>{#cars}<li>{.}</li>{/cars}</ul>
<h2>Trucks</h1>
<ul>{#trucks}
    <li>{.}</li>
    {:error}
    An error occurred. We were unable to get a list of trucks.
{/trucks}</ul>
```

Having the ability to feed information to a template in the form of promises is useful for a number of reasons, but things begin to get much more interesting when this functionality is paired with Dust's streaming interface. To better understand this, consider Listing 8-38, which largely mirrors our previous example. In this instance, however, we take advantage of Dust's streaming interface to push portions of our template down to the client *as they are rendered*, rather than waiting for the entire process to complete.

Listing 8-38. Streaming a Template to the Client As Data Becomes Available

```
// dust-promise2/index.js
```

```
var Promise = require('bluebird');
var express = require('express');
var adaro = require('adaro');
var app = express();
var engine = adaro.dust();
var dust = engine.dust;
app.engine('dust', engine);
```

```
app.set('view engine', 'dust');
app.use('/', express.static('./public'));

app.get('/', function(req, res, next) {
    dust.stream('views/main', {
        'cars': ['Nissan Maxima', 'Toyota Corolla', 'Volkswagen Jetta'],
        'trucks': function(chunk, context, bodies, params) {
            return new Promise(function(resolve, reject) {
                setTimeout(function() {
                    resolve(['Chevrolet Colorado', 'GMC Canyon', 'Toyota
                    Tacoma']);
                }, 4000);
            });
        }
    }).pipe(res);
});

app.listen(8000);
```

Depending on the complexity of the template in question, the impact this approach can have on user experience can often be dramatic. Rather than forcing users to wait for an entire page to load before they can proceed, this approach allows us to push content down to the client as it becomes available. As a result, the delay that users perceive when accessing an application can often be reduced significantly.

Dust Helpers

In the previous section, we explored how context objects can be extended to include logic that is relevant to a specific view through the use of context helpers. In a similar manner, Dust allows helper functions to be defined at a global level, making them available to all templates without being explicitly defined within their contexts. Dust comes packaged with a number of such helpers. By taking advantage of them, developers can more easily solve many of the challenges that are often encountered when working with stricter, logic-less template solutions.

Listing 8-39 shows an excerpt of the JSON data that will be referenced by the rest of this section's examples.

Listing 8-39. Excerpt of the JSON Data Passed to a Dust Template

```
// dust-logic1/people.json (excerpt)

[{
    "name": "Joe", "location": "Chicago", "age": 27,
    "education": "high_school", "employed": false, "job_title": null
}, {
    "name": "Mary", "location": "Denver", "age": 35,
    "education": "college", "employed": true, "job_title": "Chef"
}]
```

Logic Helpers

Listing 8-40 demonstrates the usage of a Dust logic helper, @eq, with which we can perform a strict comparison between two specified values, key and value. In this example, the first value, job_title, references a property within the current context. The second value, "Chef", is defined as a literal value from within the template.

Listing 8-40. Using a Dust Logic Helper to Conditionally Display Content

```
// dust-logic1/views/main.dust (excerpt)

{#people}
    {@eq key=job_title value="Chef"}
        <p>{name} is a chef. This person definitely knows how to cook.</p>
        {:else}
        <p>{name} is not a chef. This person may or may not know how to
        cook.</p>
    {/eq}
{/people}
```

Knowing this, imagine a scenario in which we want to perform a strict equality check between two numbers, one of which is referenced as a context property, while the other is specified as a literal from within the template. In order to do so, we must *cast* our literal value to the appropriate type, as shown in Listing 8-41.

Listing 8-41. Casting a Literal Value to the Desired Type

```
{#people}
    {@eq key=age value="27" type="number"}
        <p>{name} is 27 years old.</p>
    {/eq}
{/people}
```

Dust provides a number of logic helpers with which simple comparisons can be made. Their names and descriptions are listed in Table 8-2.

Table 8-2. *Logic Helpers Provided by Dust*

Logic Helper	Description
@eq	Strictly equal to
@ne	Not strictly equal to
@gt	Greater than
@lt	Less than
@gte	Greater than or equal to
@lte	Less than or equal to

Switch Statements

The frequently used @select helper provides a method by which we can mimic switch (...) statements, making it possible for a template to specify *multiple* variations of content based on a specified value (see Listing 8-42).

Listing 8-42. Mimicking a switch Statement with the @select Helper

```
{@gte key=age value=retirement_age}
    <p>{name} has reached retirement age.</p>
    {:else}
        <p>
        {@select key=job_title}
            {@eq value="Chef"}Probably went to culinary school, too.{/eq}
```

```
            {@eq value="Professor"}Smarty pants.{/eq}
            {@eq value="Accountant"}Good with numbers.{/eq}
            {@eq value="Astronaut"}Not afraid of heights.{/eq}
            {@eq value="Pilot"}Travels frequently.{/eq}
            {@eq value="Stunt Double"}Fearless.{/eq}
            {! @none serves as a `default` case !}
            {@none}Not sure what I think.{/none}
        {/select}
        </p>
{/gte}
```

Iteration Helpers

Dust provides three useful helpers for tackling problems that are frequently encountered when dealing with iteration. For example, Listing 8-43 demonstrates the use of the @sep helper, with which we can define content that will be rendered for every iteration *except* the last.

Listing 8-43. Ignoring Content During a Loop's Last Iteration with @sep

```
// dust-logic1/views/main.dust (excerpt)
{#people}{name}{@sep}, {/sep}{/people}

// output
Joe, Mary, Wilson, Steve, Laura, Tim, Katie, Craig, Ryan
```

Dust provides a total of three helpers for tackling iteration challenges. These are listed in Table 8-3.

Table 8-3. *Iteration Helpers*

Iteration Helper	Description
@sep	Renders content for every iteration, except the last
@first	Renders content only for the first iteration
@last	Renders content only for the last iteration

Mathematical Expressions

Using Dust's @math helper, templates can adjust their content based on the result of a mathematical expression. Such adjustments can take place in one of two ways. The first is demonstrated in Listing 8-44, in which the result of a mathematical expression is referenced directly within a template. The second is demonstrated in Listing 8-45, in which content is conditionally rendered based on the result of a call to the @math helper.

Listing 8-44. Directly Referencing the Result of a Mathematical Expression

```
// dust-logic1/views/main.dust (excerpt)

{#people}
    {@lt key=age value=retirement_age}
        <p>{name} will have reached retirement age in
        {@math key=retirement_age method="subtract" operand=age /}
        year(s).</p>
    {/lt}
{/people}
```

Listing 8-45. Conditionally Rendering Content Based on the Result of a Call to the @math Helper

```
// dust-logic1/views/main.dust (excerpt)

{#people}
    {@lt key=age value=retirement_age}
        {@math key=retirement_age method="subtract" operand=age}
            {@lte value=10}{name} will reach retirement age fairly soon.{/lte}
            {@lte value=20}{name} has quite a ways to go before they can
            retire.{/lte}
            {@default}{name} shouldn't even think about retiring.{/default}
        {/math}
    {/lt}
{/people}
```

The various "methods" supported by Dust's @math helper include add, subtract, multiply, divide, mod, abs, floor, and ceil.

Context Dump

Useful during development, Dust's @contextDump helper allows you to quickly render the current context object (in JSON format), providing insight into the values Dust sees within the section in which it is called. An example of its usage is shown here:

```
{#people}<pre>{@contextDump /}</pre>{/people}
```

Custom Helpers

Earlier in the chapter, you learned how to create context helpers with which context objects can be extended to include custom functionality. In the same way, custom Dust helpers can also be created at the global level. Listing 8-46 provides a demonstration of how this can be applied.

Listing 8-46. Creating and Using a Custom Dust Helper

```
// dust-logic1/index.js (excerpt)

dust.helpers.inRange = function(chunk, context, bodies, params) {
    if (params.key >= params.lower && params.key <= params.upper) {
        return chunk.render(bodies.block, context);
    } else {
        return chunk;
    }
}

// dust-logic1/views/main.dust (excerpt)

{#people}
    {@gte key=age value=20}
        {@lte key=age value=29}<p>This person is in their 20's.</p>{/lte}
    {/gte}
    {@inRange key=age lower=20 upper=29}<p>This person is in their 20's.
    </p>{/inRange}
{/people}
```

In this example's template, a loop is created in which we iterate through each person defined within the context. For each person, a message is displayed if they happen to fall within the 20-something age bracket. First, this message is displayed using a combination of preexisting logic helpers, @gte and @lt. Next, the message is displayed again, using a custom @inRange helper that has been defined at the global level.

Now that you are familiar with many of the fundamental components that Kraken relies on, let's move forward with creating our first real Kraken application.

Let's Get Kraken

In this book's first section on development tools, we covered four useful utilities that help manage many of the tasks associated with web development—among them: Bower, Grunt, and Yeoman. Kraken relies on each of these tools, along with a Yeoman generator that will assist us in building out the initial structure of our project. If you have not already done so, you should install these modules globally via npm, as shown here:

```
$ npm install -g yo generator-kraken bower grunt-cli
```

Creating a new Kraken project with Yeoman is an interactive process. In this example, we pass the generator a name for our new project (app), at which point it begins to prompt us with questions. Figure 8-4 shows the steps that were taken to create this chapter's app project.

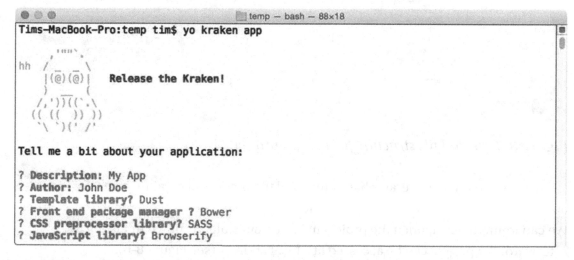

Figure 8-4. *Creating a Kraken application using the Yeoman generator*

Once you have answered these questions, the generator will create the project's initial file structure and begin installing the necessary dependencies. Afterward, you should find a new app folder containing the contents of the project, which should resemble that shown in Figure 8-5.

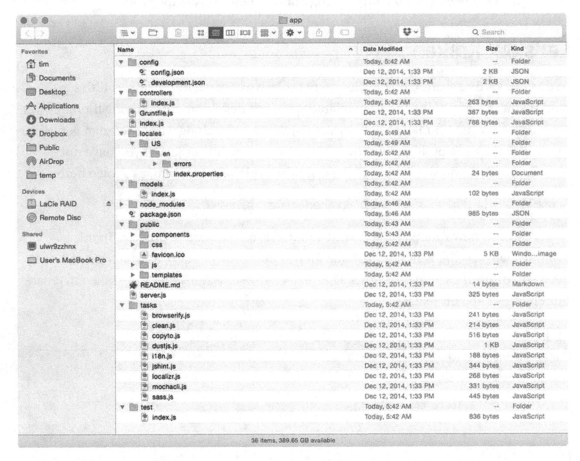

Figure 8-5. *Initial file structure for the* app *project*

Kraken's Yeoman generator has automated the process of creating a new Express application that is organized using modules that were previously covered in this chapter. We can immediately launch the project in its current state as shown in Listing 8-47. Afterward, the project can be accessed at a local address (see Figure 8-6).

Listing 8-47. Launching the Project for the First Time

```
$ npm start

> app@0.1.0 start /Users/tim/temp/app
> node server.js

Server listening on http://localhost:8000
Application ready to serve requests.
Environment: development
```

Hello, index!

Figure 8-6. *Viewing the project in the browser for the first time*

As you can see, our project has been preconfigured (with the help of confit and meddleware) to use a number of helpful middleware modules (e.g., cookieParser, session, etc.). For some additional insight into how all of this comes together, Listing 8-48 shows the contents of the project's index.js script.

Listing 8-48. Contents of Our New Project's index.js Script

```
// app/index.js

var express = require('express');
var kraken = require('kraken-js');

var options, app;

/*
 * Create and configure application. Also exports application instance for
   use by tests.
 * See https://github.com/krakenjs/kraken-js#options for additional
   configuration options.
 */
options = {
```

```
    onconfig: function (config, next) {
        /*
         * Add any additional config setup or overrides here. `config` is
           an initialized
         * `confit` (https://github.com/krakenjs/confit/) configuration object.
         */
        next(null, config);
    }
};

app = module.exports = express();

app.use(kraken(options));
app.on('start', function () {
    console.log('Application ready to serve requests.');
    console.log('Environment: %s', app.kraken.get('env:env'));
});
```

The kraken-js module, which we see here, is nothing more than a standard Express middleware library. However, instead of simply augmenting Express with some small bit of additional functionality, Kraken takes responsibility for configuring a complete Express application. It will do so with the help of many other modules, including those that have already been covered in this chapter: confit, meddleware, enrouten, and adaro.

As shown in Listing 8-48, Kraken is passed a configuration object containing an onconfig() callback function, which will be called after Kraken has taken care of initializing confit for us. Here we can provide any last-minute overrides that we may not want to define directly within the project's JSON configuration files. In this example, no such overrides are made.

Controllers, Models, and Tests

In this chapter's "*Structured Route Registration*" section, we discovered how enrouten can help bring order to the often haphazard manner in which Express routes are defined. By default, a new Kraken project is set up to use enrouten's directory configuration option, allowing it to recursively scan the contents of a specified folder, searching for modules that export a function accepting a single argument (i.e., router). For each module it finds (referred to as a "controller"), enrouten will pass an Express Router instance that has been mounted to a path predetermined by that module's location within the directory structure. We can see this process in action by looking at the default controller that Kraken has created for our project, shown in Listing 8-49.

Listing 8-49. Our Project's Default Controller

```
// app/controllers/index.js

var IndexModel = require('../models/index');

module.exports = function (router) {

    var model = new IndexModel();

    /**
     * The default route served for us when we access the app at: http://
       localhost:8000
     */
    router.get('/', function (req, res) {
        res.render('index', model);
    });

};
```

In addition to creating a default controller for our project, Kraken has also taken care of creating a corresponding model, IndexModel, which you can see referenced in Listing 8-49. We will discuss Kraken's relationship with models shortly, but first, let's walk through the process of creating a new controller of our own.

Chapter 2, which covered Yeoman, demonstrated that generators have the ability to provide subcommands capable of providing developers with functionality whose usefulness extends well beyond the initial creation of a project. Kraken's Yeoman generator takes advantage of this by providing a controller subcommand, with which new controllers can quickly be created. By way of an example, let's create a new controller that will be responsible for managing a collection of RSS feeds:

```
$ yo kraken:controller feeds
```

After specifying our desired path, `feeds`, to the generator's `controller` subcommand, five new files are automatically created for us:

- `controllers/feeds.js`: Controller
- `models/feeds.js`: Model
- `test/feeds.js`: Test suite
- `public/templates/feeds.dust`: Dust template
- `locales/US/en/feeds.properties`: Internationalization settings

For the moment, let's place our focus on the first three files listed here, starting with the model. We'll take a look at the accompanying Dust template and internalization settings file in the next section.

The Model

Listing 8-50 shows the initial state of our project's new `feeds` model. If you were expecting something sophisticated, you will likely be disappointed. As you can see, this file serves as little more than a generic stub that we are expected to replace with our own persistence layer.

Listing 8-50. Initial Contents of the `feeds` Model

```
// models/feeds.js

module.exports = function FeedsModel() {
    return {
        name: 'feeds'
    };
};
```

Unlike many other "full-stack" frameworks that attempt to provide developers with tools that address every conceivable need (including data persistence), Kraken takes a minimalistic approach that does not attempt to reinvent the wheel. This approach recognizes that developers already have access to a wide variety of well-supported libraries for managing data persistence, two of which are covered by this book: Knex/Bookshelf and Mongoose.

By way of an example, let's update this module so that it exports a Bookshelf model capable of fetching and storing information within a feeds table stored in a SQLite database. Listing 8-51 shows the updated contents of the feeds model.

Listing 8-51. Updated feeds Model That Uses Knex/Bookshelf

```
// models/feeds.js

var bookshelf = require('../lib/bookshelf');
var Promise = require('bluebird');
var feedRead = require('feed-read');

var Feed = bookshelf.Model.extend({
    'tableName': 'feeds',
    'getArticles': function() {
        var self = this;
        return Promise.fromNode(function(callback) {
            feedRead(self.get('url'), callback);
        });
    }
});

module.exports = Feed;
```

Note   The updated model shown in Listing 8-51 assumes that you are already familiar with the Knex and Bookshelf libraries, along with the steps necessary to configure them. If that is not the case, you may want to read Chapter 10. Regardless, this chapter's app project provides a fully functioning demonstration of the code shown here.

The Controller

Listing 8-52 shows the initial contents of our project's new feeds controller. As with the original controller that accompanied our project, this controller references a corresponding model that Kraken has conveniently created for us, which we have already seen.

Listing 8-52. Initial Contents of the feeds Controller

```
// controllers/feeds.js

var FeedsModel = require('../models/feeds');

/**
 * @url http://localhost:8000/feeds
 */
module.exports = function (router) {
    var model = new FeedsModel();
    router.get('/', function (req, res) {
    });
};
```

In its default state, the feeds controller accomplishes very little. Let's update this controller to include a few additional routes that will allow clients to interact with our application's Feed model. The updated version of the feeds controller is shown in Listing 8-53.

Listing 8-53. Updated feeds Controller

```
var Feed = require('../models/feeds');

module.exports = function(router) {

    router.param('feed_id', function(req, res, next, id) {
        Feed.where({
            'id': id
        }).fetch({
            'require': true
        }).then(function(feed) {
            req.feed = feed;
            next();
        }).catch(next);
    });

    /**
     * @url http://localhost:8000/feeds
     */
```

```
router.route('/')
    .get(function(req, res, next) {
        return Feed.where({})
            .fetchAll()
            .then(function(feeds) {
                if (req.accepts('html')) {
                    return res.render('feeds', {
                        'feeds': feeds.toJSON()
                    });
                } else if (req.accepts('json')) {
                    return res.send(feeds);
                } else {
                    throw new Error('Unknown `Accept` value: ' + req.
                    headers.accept);
                }
            })
            .catch(next);
    });

/**
 * @url http://localhost:8000/feeds/:feed_id
 */
router.route('/:feed_id')
    .get(function(req, res, next) {
        res.send(req.feed);
    });

/**
 * @url http://localhost:8000/feeds/:feed_id/articles
 */
router.route('/:feed_id/articles')
    .get(function(req, res, next) {
        req.feed.getArticles()
            .then(function(articles) {
                res.send(articles);
            })
```

```
                .catch(next);
    });
};
```

With these updates in place, clients now have the ability to

- List feeds

- Fetch information regarding a specific feed

- Fetch articles from a specific feed

In the next section, we will take a look at the test suite that Kraken has created for this portion of our application. With this test suite, we can verify that the routes we have defined work as expected.

The Test Suite

Listing 8-54 shows the initial contents of the test suite that Kraken has created for our new controller. Here we see a single test, which is defined with the help of SuperTest, which is an extension of SuperAgent, a simple library for making HTTP requests.

Listing 8-54. Test Suite for the `feeds` Controller

```
// test/feeds.js

var kraken = require('kraken-js');
var express = require('express');
var request = require('supertest');

describe('/feeds', function() {

    var app, mock;

    beforeEach(function(done) {
        app = express();
        app.on('start', done);
        app.use(kraken({
            'basedir': process.cwd()
        }));
```

```
    mock = app.listen(1337);
});

afterEach(function (done) {
    mock.close(done);
});

it('should say "hello"', function(done) {
    request(mock)
        .get('/feeds')
        .expect(200)
        .expect('Content-Type', /html/)
        .expect(/"name": "index"/)
        .end(function (err, res) {
            done(err);
        });
});
});
});
```

In this example, a GET request is made to our application's /feeds endpoint, and the following assertions are made:

- The server should respond with an HTTP status code of 200.

- The server should respond with a Content-Type header containing the string html.

- The body of the response should contain the string "name": "index".

Given the recent updates that we have made to our new controller, these assertions no longer apply. Let's replace them with a few tests that are relevant. Listing 8-55 shows the updated contents of the test suite.

Listing 8-55. Updated Contents of the feeds Test Suite

```
// test/feeds/index.js

var assert = require('assert');
var kraken = require('kraken-js');
var express = require('express');
```

```
var request = require('supertest');

describe('/feeds', function() {

    var app, mock;

    beforeEach(function(done) {
        app = express();
        app.on('start', done);
        app.use(kraken({'basedir': process.cwd()}));
        mock = app.listen(1337);
    });

    afterEach(function(done) {
        mock.close(done);
    });

    it('should return a collection of feeds', function(done) {
        request(mock)
            .get('/feeds')
            .expect('Content-Type', /json/)
            .expect(200)
            .end(function(err, res) {
                if (err) return done(err);
                assert(res.body instanceof Array, 'Expected an array');
                done();
            });
    });

    it('should return a single feed', function(done) {
        request(mock)
            .get('/feeds/1')
            .expect('Content-Type', /json/)
            .expect(200)
            .end(function(err, res) {
                if (err) return done(err);
                assert.equal(typeof res.body.id, 'number',
                    'Expected a numeric `id` property');
```

```
            done();
        });
    });

    it('should return articles for a specific feed', function(done) {
        request(mock)
            .get('/feeds/1/articles')
            .expect('Content-Type', /json/)
            .expect(200)
            .end(function(err, res) {
                if (err) return done(err);
                assert(res.body instanceof Array, 'Expected an array');
                done();
            });
    });
});

});
```

Our updated test suite now contains three tests designed to verify that each of our new controller's routes are functioning correctly. Consider the first test, for instance, which will make a GET request to our application's /feeds endpoint and make the following assertions:

- The server should respond with an HTTP status code of 200.

- The server should respond with a Content-Type header containing the string json.

- The server should return one or more results in the form of an array.

Note   Recall that our application's Feed model was created with the help of the Knex and Bookshelf libraries. The data that you see referenced in this project originates from a Knex "seed" file (seeds/developments/00-feeds.js) with which we can populate our database with sample data. At any point, this project's SQLite database can be reset to its initial state by running $ grunt reset-db from the command line. If these concepts are unfamiliar to you, you may want to read Chapter 10.

Figure 8-7 shows the output that is printed to the console when our project's `test` Grunt task is called.

```
● ● ●                              📁 app — bash — 108×24
Tims-MacBook-Pro:app tim$ grunt test
Running "jshint:files" (jshint) task
>> 6 files lint free.

Running "mochacli:src" (mochacli) task


  /feeds
127.0.0.1 - - [11/Jun/2015:13:21:28 +0000] "GET /feeds HTTP/1.1" 200 172 "-" "-"
    ✓ should return a collection of feeds (86ms)
127.0.0.1 - - [11/Jun/2015:13:21:28 +0000] "GET /feeds/1 HTTP/1.1" 200 73 "-" "-"
    ✓ should return a single feed
127.0.0.1 - - [11/Jun/2015:13:21:29 +0000] "GET /feeds/1/articles HTTP/1.1" 200 15946 "-" "-"
    ✓ should return articles for a specific feed (244ms)

  /
127.0.0.1 - - [11/Jun/2015:13:21:29 +0000] "GET / HTTP/1.1" 200 244 "-" "-"
    ✓ should say "hello"


  4 passing (1s)

Done, without errors.
```

Figure 8-7. *Running the test suite*

Internationalization and Localization

Kraken provides built-in support for creating applications that are capable of adapting themselves to meet the unique needs of multiple languages and regions, an important requirement for most products that hope to see widespread use across multiple, diverse markets. In this section we'll take a look at the two steps by which this is accomplished, internationalization and localization, and how they can be applied within the context of a Kraken application whose templates are generated on the server.

Internationalization (frequently shortened to i18n) refers to the act of developing applications that are *capable* of supporting multiple regions and dialects. In practice, this is accomplished by avoiding the direct use of locale-specific words, phrases, and symbols (e.g., currency symbols) within an application's templates. Placeholders are instead used, which are later populated at the moment a template is requested, based on the location or settings of the user who is making the request. By way of an example, consider the Dust template that is shown in Listing 8-56, which is responsible for rendering the home page of this chapter's `app` project.

Listing 8-56. Dust Template for the Home Page of app Project

```
// app/public/templates/index.dust

{>"layouts/master" /}

{<body}

    <div class="panel panel-default">
        <div class="panel-heading">
            <h3 class="panel-title">{@pre type="content" key="greeting" /}</h3>
        </div>
        <div class="panel-body">

            <form method="post" action="/sessions">
                <div class="form-group">
                    <label>{@pre type="content" key="email_address" /}
                    </label>
                    <input type="email" name="email" class="form-control">
                </div>
                <div class="form-group">
                    <label>{@pre type="content" key="password" /}</label>
                    <input type="password" name="password" class="form-
                    control">
                </div>
                <button type="submit" class="btn btn-primary">
                    {@pre type="content" key="submit" /}
                </button>
            </form>

        </div>
    </div>

{/body}
```

The basic semantics at work here should be familiar, based on material that was previously covered in this chapter's section on Dust. As you can see, instead of directly embedding content, this template relies on a special Dust helper provided by Kraken, @pre, with which we can reference content that is stored in separate, locale-specific content files. The corresponding content files for this particular template are shown in Listing 8-57.

Listing 8-57. Corresponding Content Files for the Dust Template Shown in Listing 8-56

```
// app/locales/US/en/index.properties
# Comments are supported
greeting=Welcome to Feed Reader
submit=Submit
email_address=Email Address
password=Password

// app/locales/ES/es/index.properties
greeting=Bienvenida al Feed Reader
submit=Presentar
email_address=Correo Electrónico
password=Contraseña
```

Note   Take note of the location of this example's template, `public/templates/index.dust`, and the location of its corresponding content property files, `locales/US/en/index.properties` and `locales/ES/es/index.properties`. Kraken is configured to pair Dust templates with content property files such as these on a one-to-one basis, by matching them based on their paths and file names.

In contrast to internationalization (i18n), which is primarily concerned with the creation of applications that are *capable* of supporting the injection of localized content, localization (l10n) refers to the process by which locale- and dialect-specific content files, such as those shown in this example, are created. The controller shown in Listing 8-58 demonstrates how Kraken helps developers bring these concepts together to provide users with content that is tailored to meet their specific needs.

Listing 8-58. Serving a Locale-Specific Version of the Home Page

```
// app/controllers/index.js

module.exports = function (router) {

    /**
     * The default route served for us when we access the app
     * at http://localhost:8000
     */
    router.get('/', function (req, res) {
        res.locals.context = { 'locality': { 'language': 'es', 'country':
        'ES' } };
        res.render('index');
    });

};
```

This example is an updated version of the controller that we originally saw in Listing 8-49, which is responsible for rendering our application's home page. Here we specify the country and language to be used for locating content files by assigning them to the locals.context property of the incoming Express response object. If no such value is specified, Kraken's default behavior is to use US English. The English and Spanish versions of the rendered template are shown in Figure 8-8 and Figure 8-9, respectively.

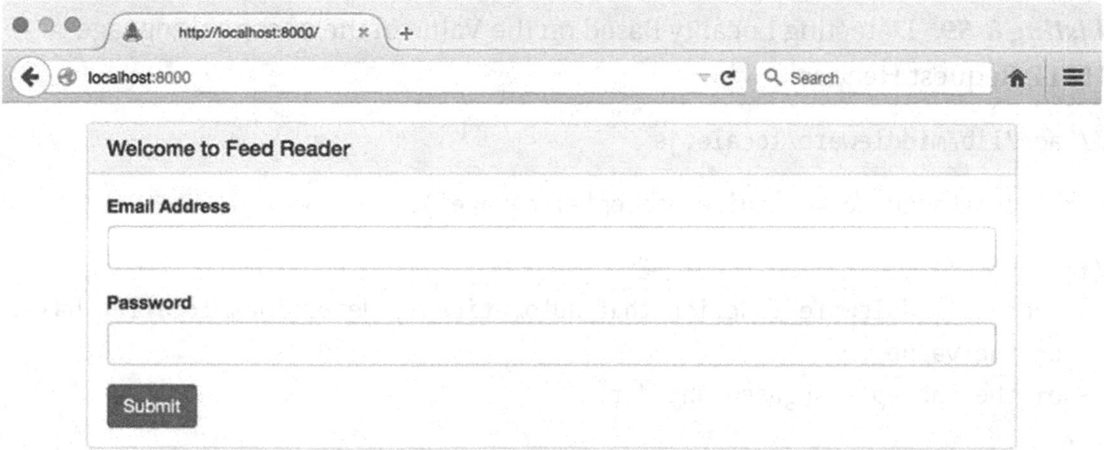

Figure 8-8. *English version of the application's home page*

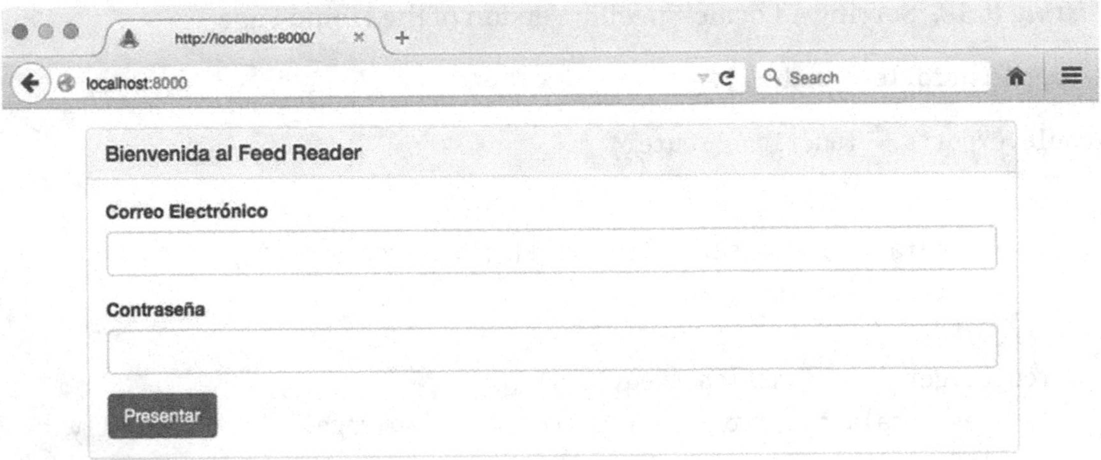

Figure 8-9. *Spanish version of the application's home page*

Detecting Locality

The example shown in Listing 8-58 demonstrates the process by which specific regional settings can be manually assigned to an incoming request. What it does *not* demonstrate, however, is the process by which a user's desired localization settings can be *automatically* detected.

Listing 8-59 demonstrates a simple method for determining locality based on the value of the accept-language HTTP request header. In this example, we have removed the logic for determining a user's locality from our route and placed it in a more appropriate location—a middleware function that will be called for *every* incoming request.

Listing 8-59. Detecting Locality Based on the Value of the accept-language HTTP Request Header

```
// app/lib/middleware/locale.js

var acceptLanguage = require('accept-language');

/**
 * Express middleware function that automatically determines locality based
   on the value
 * of the `accept-language` header.
 */
module.exports = function() {
```

```
    return function(req, res, next) {
        var locale = acceptLanguage.parse(req.headers['accept-language']);
        res.locals.context = {
            'locality': { 'language': locale[0].language, 'country':
                locale[0].region }
        };
        next();
    };

};

// app/config/config.json (excerpt)

"middleware":{
    "locale": {
        "module": {
         "name": "path:./lib/middleware/locale"
        },
        "enabled": true
    }

}
```

Note   While helpful, the accept-language HTTP request header does not always reflect the desired localization settings of the user making the request. Always be sure to provide users with a method for manually specifying such settings on their own (e.g., as part of a "Settings" page).

Security

Given Kraken's origins at PayPal, a worldwide online payments processor, it should come as no surprise that the framework focuses heavily on security. Kraken does so with the help of Lusca, a library that extends Express with a number of enhanced security techniques, as suggested by the Open Web Application Security Project (OWASP). These extensions are provided in the form of multiple, independently configurable middleware modules. In this section, we will briefly examine two ways in which Kraken can help secure Express against commonly encountered attacks.

Note   This material should by no means be considered exhaustive. It is merely intended to serve as a starting point for implementing security within the context of a Kraken/Express application. Readers with a hand in implementing security on the Web are highly encouraged to delve further into this topic by reading a few of the many great books that are devoted entirely to this subject.

Defending Against Cross-Site Request Forgery Attacks

To understand the basic premise behind cross-site request forgery (CSRF) attacks, it is important to understand the method by which most web applications authenticate their users: cookie-based authentication. This process is illustrated in Figure 8-10.

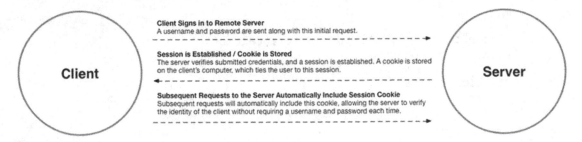

Figure 8-10.   *Cookie-based authentication*

In a typical scenario, a user will submit their credentials to a web application, which will then compare them with those it has on file. Assuming the credentials are valid, the server will then create a new session—essentially, a record representing the user's successful sign-in attempt. A unique identifier belonging to this session is then transmitted to the user in the form of a cookie, which is automatically stored by the user's browser. Subsequent requests to the application made by the browser will automatically attach the information stored in this cookie, allowing the application to look up the matching session record. As a result, the application has the ability to verify the user's identity without requiring the user to resubmit their username and password along with every request.

A CSRF attack takes advantage of the trusted relationship (i.e., session) that exists between an application and a user's browser, by tricking that user into submitting an unintended request to the application. Let's take a look at an example that should help explain how this works. Figure 8-11 illustrates the process by which a user signs into a trusted application—in this case, the `csrf-server` project that is included with this chapter's source code.

Figure 8-11. *Signing into a trusted application*

Figure 8-12 shows the welcome screen that the user is presented with after successfully signing into the application. Here we see some basic information about the user, including their name and when their account was created.

Figure 8-12. *Successful sign-in attempt*

At this point, imagine a scenario in which the user leaves the application (without signing out) and visits another site, which, unbeknownst to the user, has malicious intent (see Figure 8-13). A copy of this malicious site can be found in this chapter's csrf-attack project. In this example, the malicious site lures the user into clicking a button with the tempting promise of free candy and butterflies.

Figure 8-13. *Malicious web site attempting to convince the user to click a button*

Listing 8-60 shows an excerpt from the HTML for this malicious site, which should help explain what is going to happen when the user clicks this button. As you can see, clicking the button will trigger the creation of a POST request to the original application's /transfer-funds route.

Listing 8-60. Malicious Web Form

```
// csrf-attack/views/index.dust (excerpt)

<form method="post" action="http://localhost:7000/transfer-funds">
    <button type="submit" class="btn btn-primary">
        Click Here for Free Candy and Butterflies
    </button>
</form>
```

After clicking the button, instead of receiving the free candy and butterflies that they were promised, the user is greeted with a message indicating that all of the funds have been transferred out of their account, as shown in Figure 8-14.

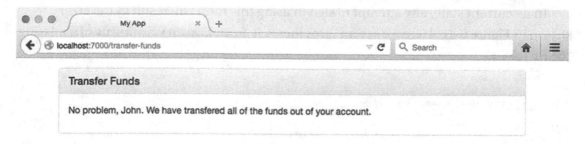

Figure 8-14. *Successful CSRF attack*

Several different steps can be taken to defend against attacks of this nature. The method by which Kraken defends against them is referred to as the "synchronizer token pattern." In this approach, a random string is generated for each incoming request, which the client can subsequently access as part of a template's context or via a response header. Importantly, this string is *not* stored as a cookie. The next POST, PUT, PATCH, or DELETE request made by the client must include this string, which the server will then compare with the one it previously generated. The request will only be allowed to proceed if a match is made.

Let's take a look at how this works in practice. Figure 8-15 shows the sign-in page for this chapter's app project. Refer back to Listing 8-56 to see the underlying HTML for this page.

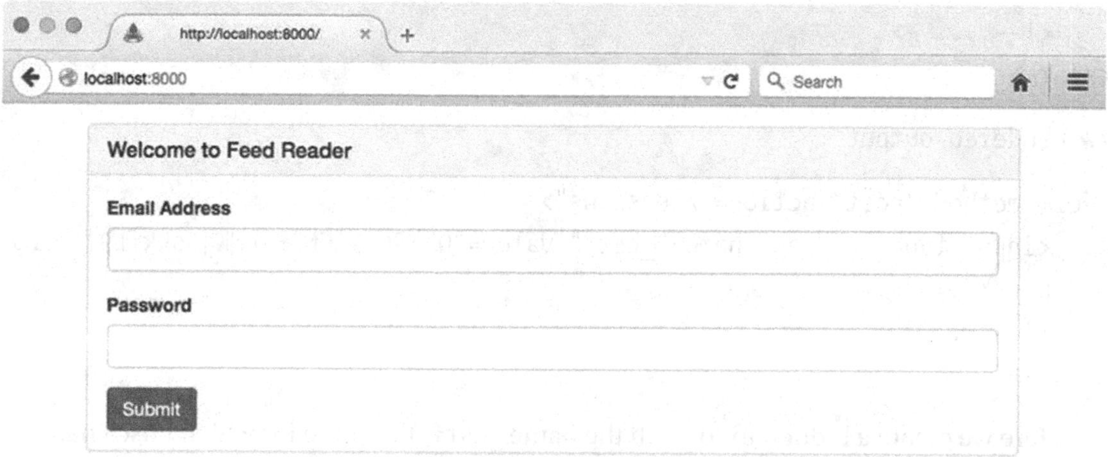

Figure 8-15. *Sign-in page for this chapter's app project*

In its current state, any attempt to sign in using this form will result in the error shown in Figure 8-16. Here we see an error message from Kraken warning us of a missing "CSRF token."

Internal server error

The URL `/sessions` had the following error `Error: CSRF token missing`.

Figure 8-16. *Kraken's "CSRF token missing" error*

This error can be resolved with the addition of a single, hidden input to our application's login form. Listing 8-61 shows an excerpt from our application's updated Dust template, along with an excerpt from the rendered output.

Listing 8-61. Inserting a Hidden _csrf Field into the Sign-In Form

```
// app/public/templates/index.dust (excerpt)

<form method="post" action="/sessions">
    <input type="hidden" name="_csrf" value="{_csrf}">
    <!-- ... ->
</form>

// Rendered output

<form method="post" action="/sessions">
    <input type="hidden" name="_csrf" value="OERRGi9AGNPEYnNWj8skkfL9fOJIWJ
    p3uKK8g=">
    <!-- ... ->
</form>
```

Here we create a hidden input with the name _csrf, the value for which Lusca has automatically passed to our template's context under a property with the same name. The value that we see rendered in this example, OERRGi9AGNPEYnNWj8skkfL9fOJIWJp3uKK8g=, is a random hash that Lusca has generated for us (i.e., the "synchronizer token"). When we submit this form, Lusca will verify that this value matches the one it previously gave us.

If they match, the request is allowed to proceed. Otherwise, an error is thrown. This approach allows applications to defend against CSRF attacks by requiring additional, identifying information that is *not* stored as part of a cookie, making it much more difficult for attackers to trick users into performing unintended actions.

Configuring Content Security Policy Headers

Lusca provides developers with a convenient mechanism for configuring an application's Content Security Policy (CSP). These rules provide instructions to supporting browsers regarding the locations from which various resources (e.g., scripts, stylesheets, images, etc.) can be loaded. When defined, these rules are conveyed to browsers in the form of the `Content-Security-Policy` response header.

By way of an example, see Listing 8-62, in which Lusca's `csp` middleware module is provided with a configuration object specifying that *only* images may be loaded from any domain. All other resources must originate from the application's domain.

Listing 8-62. Configuring an Application's Content Security Policy

```
app.use(lusca({
    'csp': {
    'default-src': '\'self\",
    'img-src': '*'
    }
});
```

Note   For a full list of the various options that can be configured via the `Content-Security-Policy` header, visit the Open Web Application Security Project (OWASP) at `https://owasp.org`.

Summary

The Node community is heavily influenced by the so-called "Unix philosophy," which promotes (among other things) the creation of small, tightly focused modules that are designed to do one thing well. This approach has allowed Node to thrive as a development platform by fostering a large ecosystem of open source modules. PayPal has taken this philosophy to heart by structuring Kraken not as a single, monolithic framework, but rather as a collection of modules that extends and provides structure to Express-based applications. By taking this approach, PayPal has managed to contribute several modules to the Node ecosystem from which developers can benefit, regardless of whether they choose to use Kraken as a whole.

Related Resources

- Kraken: `http://krakenjs.com/`

- Confit: `https://github.com/krakenjs/confit`

- Meddleware: `https://github.com/krakenjs/meddleware`

- Enrouten: `https://github.com/krakenjs/express-enrouten`

- Dust.js: `www.dustjs.com`

- SuperAgent: `https://github.com/visionmedia/superagent`

- SuperTest: `https://github.com/visionmedia/supertest`

- Mocha: `http://mochajs.org`

- Open Web Application Security Project (OWASP): `https://owasp.org`

- Lusca: `https://github.com/krakenjs/lusca`

PART V

Managing Database Interaction

CHAPTER 9

Mongoose

The human mind gets used to strangeness very quickly if [strangeness] does not exhibit interesting behavior.

—Dan Simmons

MongoDB is a popular cross-platform document database, often lumped into the "NoSQL" classification with other nonrelational data stores such as CouchDB, Cassandra, RavenDB, and so forth. It is a popular choice for data storage among Node.js developers because its "records" are stored as plain JSON objects, and its query interface and stored functions are written in plain JavaScript.

Storing, accessing, and manipulating data in MongoDB are not terribly complex, but Node.js libraries such as Mongoose can help application developers map MongoDB documents onto application objects that have definite schemas, validations, and behavior—all concepts that are not (by design) parts of MongoDB. Mongoose implements the query interface native to MongoDB, but also gives developers a composable, fluent interface that simplifies portions of the query API.

Though MongoDB is not the direct subject of this chapter, it is necessary to establish a few basic concepts about how MongoDB works before delving into Mongoose. If you're familiar with MongoDB already, feel free to skip the next section.

Basic MongoDB Concepts

A relational database server hosts database schemas (sometimes just called databases), which encapsulate related entities like tables, views, stored procedures, functions, and so on. Database tables in turn contain tuples (also known as rows or records). A tuple is composed of a number of fields, each containing a value of a predetermined data type. The tuple is one-dimensional, and its definition (the data types its fields can hold) is

309

S. bin Uzayr et al., *JavaScript Frameworks for Modern Web Development*,
https://doi.org/10.1007/978-1-4842-4995-6_9

determined at the table level. All tuples within a table, then, share the same structure, though their individual field values may differ. The names and data types of a tuple's fields are referred to as the tuple's schema.

MongoDB has a superficially similar data hierarchy, as shown in Table 9-1.

Table 9-1. *Understanding MongoDB by Analogy to Relational Database Systems*

RDBMS	MongoDB
Server	Server
Schema	Database
Table	Collection
Tuple	Document
Field	Property

Table 9-2 defines the key terms that describe Mongoose components and how they relate to each other. The code in Listing 9-1 shows how these terms appear in code. This chapter will cover each in detail, but because many of them are closely related, you might wish to refer back to this section as the chapter progresses.

Table 9-2. *Mongoose Terms and Definitions*

Term	Definition
Schema	Defines the data types, constraints, defaults, validations, and so forth for the properties of a document instance; enforced at the application level
Model	Constructor function that creates or fetches document instances
Document	Instance object created or fetched by a Mongoose model; will have Mongoose-specific properties and methods as well as data properties
JSON object	Plain JavaScript object that contains only the data properties from a document

Listing 9-1. Mongoose Terms and Definitions in Code

```
// albumSchema is a schema
var albumSchema = mongoose.Schema({/*...*/});

// Album is a model
var Album = mongoose.model('Album', albumSchema);

// Album is a model
Album.findById(/*...*/, function (err, album) {
  // album is a document
  console.log(album);
});

// Album is a model
Album.findById(/*...*/)
  .lean(true)
  .exec(function (err, album) {
    // album is a JSON object (because of `lean(true)`)
    console.log(album);
  });

// Album is a model
Album.findById(/*...*/)
  .exec(function (err, album) {
    // album is a document
    // toObject() returns a JSON object
    console.log(album.toObject());
  });
```

Unlike RDBMS tuples, MongoDB documents are *not* one-dimensional. They are complete JSON objects that may contain other objects or arrays. In fact, documents within the same collection need not even have the same properties, because MongoDB collections are actually schemaless. A MongoDB collection can hold document objects of any shape or size (within MongoDB's storage limits). In practice, though, collections tend to hold documents of similar "shape," though some may have optional properties, or may contain properties that represent some arbitrary data. But in general, applications usually assume that data exists in particular "shapes," so although MongoDB does not enforce document schemas, applications often do.

By default, MongoDB documents are automatically assigned a surrogate primary key called _id. This key has a special type (MongoDB's ObjectId type) and is used as MongoDB's primary collection index. MongoDB can use a different field as a primary key if directed. Additional fields can be added to secondary indexes within a collection, either as simple or compound keys.

MongoDB does not support the notion of foreign keys, a strong feature of RDBMS databases. Instead, MongoDB relies on the power of nested documents to store data associations. Consider the classic trinity of all RDBMS examples: customer, postal address, and shopping cart order. In an RDBMS system, there would likely be foreign keys from the postal address to the customer (to identify residency), and from the order to one or more postal addresses (to identify shipping and billing addresses). In a MongoDB customer document, however, it would be sufficient to simply store the postal address as a nested object in the customer document *as well as* the order document. Consider Listing 9-2.

Listing 9-2. Duplication Sometimes Acceptable in MongoDB

```
// customer
{
  "_id": 1001,
  "name": "...",
  "postalAddress" {
    "street": "...",
    "city": "...",
    "state": "...",
    "zip": "..."
  }
}

// order
{
  "_id": 2001,
  "customer": 1001,
  "items": [
    {"sku": 3001, "qty": 2}
  ],
  "shippingAddress" {
```

```
    "street": "...",
    "city": "...",
    "state": "...",
    "zip": "..."
  }
}
```

There are a number of reasons why this "violation" of referential integrity might be acceptable from a business point of view:

- Perhaps orders are never altered. If there is a mistake in an order—for example, the shipping address is wrong—the entire order gets re-created to offset the faulty order. The correct shipping address gets added to the new order.

- If a customer changes a postal address, old orders won't be updated with the new address, so there's no data integrity issue at stake.

- Maybe changing a postal address always happens within the customer domain, never in the order domain.

- Perhaps a customer can override a shipping address with a "temporary" address (shipping a gift) that should *not* be added to the customer record.

- If different postal metrics are derived from orders than from customers (e.g., a C-level executive wants to know how many orders were shipped to Missouri last month regardless of who actually *lives* in Missouri this month), that data is already segregated.

- Maybe disk space is cheap and the velocity gained by not enforcing referential integrity outweighs any potential cost.

While foreign keys and referential integrity are critical to RDBMS databases, strong MongoDB document design can often render the issue moot.

Finally, though MongoDB's query API may look a bit daunting to SQL practitioners, it quickly becomes obvious that, for the most part, looking for data involves the same concepts: selecting (`find`), filtering (`where`), applying compound conditions (`and`, `or`, `in`), aggregating (`group`), paging (`skip`, `limit`), and so on. How queries are composed and executed differs mostly in syntax.

A Simple Mongoose Example

Mongoose is an object modeling library for Node.js applications. To develop with Mongoose (and follow the examples in this chapter), you need to install Node.js and MongoDB on your platform of choice. The default installation procedure and configuration for both should be sufficient to run this chapter's example code.

Note   This chapter assumes that you are familiar with Node.js applications and modules and that you know how to install them with npm. A working knowledge of MongoDB will be very helpful, but it is not required to run the examples of this chapter, since interaction with MongoDB will mostly occur through Mongoose in the chapter examples. Some examples will demonstrate how to query MongoDB directly to verify the results of Mongoose operations. It is noteworthy that you need to have a functional understanding of MongoDB in order to get the most out of Mongoose for production-level environments.

This section demonstrates basic Mongoose concepts that will be explored in detail later in this chapter. This example involves three steps:

1. Create a basic Mongoose schema that reflects the structured data in a JSON file.

2. Read the JSON file and import the data into MongoDB with a Mongoose model.

3. Run a basic web server that will use a Mongoose model to fetch data from MongoDB and deliver it to a web browser.

The first line of each listing that follows will show the file path in which the example code may be found. Subsequent examples will indicate whether a particular example file should be executed with Node.js in a terminal.

Creating a Mongoose Schema for JSON Data

Mongoose documents represent the domain data in an application. For this chapter's example application, a JSON file of music albums defines the initial set of data to be added to MongoDB. Listing 9-3 shows the structure of example-001/albums.json:

an array of album objects, each containing information about the composer, title, publication year, track list, and so forth.

Listing 9-3. Album JSON Data File

```
// example-001/albums.json
[
  {
    "composer": "Kerry Muzzey",
    "title": "Renaissance",
    "price": 4.95,
    "releaseDate": "2014-01-13T06:00:00.000Z",
    "inPublication": true,
    "genre": ["Classical", "Trailer Music", "Soundtrack"],
    "tracks": [
      {
        "title": "The Looking Glass",
        "duration": {
          "m": 3,
          "s": 20
        }
      }
      //additional tracks...
    ]
  }
  //additional albums...
]
```

Mongoose is an object data mapper (ODM), so at the heart of Mongoose data access are model functions that can be used to query the MongoDB collections they represent. A Mongoose model must have a name by which it can be referred and a schema that enforces the shape of the data it will access and manipulate. The code in Listing 9-4 creates an album schema that closely matches the JSON data in `example-001/albums.json`. Schemas will be covered in detail later, but it should be apparent that a schema defines the properties and their data types for a given Mongoose model. Finally, a model function is created by pairing a name ("Album") with a schema. This model function is assigned to `module.exports` in the `example-001/album-model.js` file so that it can be imported into other modules as needed in a Node.js application.

Tip   A Mongoose schema defines the data structure for a model. The model function provides the query interface for working with stored document data. A model must have a name and a schema.

Listing 9-4. Mongoose Album Schema and Model

```
// example-001/album-model.js
'use strict';
var mongoose = require('mongoose');

var albumSchema = mongoose.Schema({
  composer: String,
  title: String,
  price: Number,
  releaseDate: Date,
  inPublication: Boolean,
  genre: [String],
  tracks: [
    {
      title: String,
      duration: {
        m: Number,
        s: Number
      }
    }
  ]
});

var Album = mongoose.model('Album', albumSchema);

module.exports = Album;
```

Importing Data with Mongoose

Now that the Album schema and model are defined, a Node.js script can read the data from albums.json and use the Album model to create documents in MongoDB. The import script needs to do three things:

1. Connect to a running MongoDB server with Mongoose.

2. Read and parse the contents of the albums.json file.

3. Use the Album model to create documents in MongoDB.

Mongoose connects to MongoDB with a URI that identifies the protocol, server, and database that Mongoose will use. In Listing 9-5 the URI simply points to the local MongoDB instance: mongodb://localhost/music. Mongoose will proactively create the database if it does not already exist on the MongoDB instance, so there is no need to do so manually. If the MongoDB connection fails, Mongoose will raise an error event, and if it succeeds, Mongoose will raise an open event. Listing 9-5 demonstrates how both events are handled with callback functions. Once the open event is emitted, the albums.json file is read and parsed, and the array of albums is passed to the Album.create() method of the Album model. This creates the album documents in MongoDB, which may then be queried with the Album model later.

Listing 9-5. Importing Album Data with Mongoose

```
// example-001/import-albums.js
'use strict';
var mongoose = require('mongoose');
var Album = require('./album-model');
var file2json = require('./file2json');
var fs = require('fs');
var path = require('path');

// connect to the "music" database on localhost;
// the database will be automatically created
// if it does not exist
mongoose.connect('mongodb://localhost/music');
var db = mongoose.connection;

db.on('error', function (err) {
  console.error(err);
```

```
  process.exit(1);
});

db.once('open', function importAlbums() {
  var albumsFile = path.join(__dirname, 'albums.json');
  file2json(albumsFile, 'utf8', function (err, albums) {
    if (err) {
      console.error(err);
      return process.exit(1);
    }

    console.log('creating %d albums', albums.length);

    // use the model to create albums in bulk;
    // the collection will be automatically created
    // if it does not exist
    Album.create(albums, function (err) {
      if (err) {
        console.error(err);
        return process.exit(1);
      }
      process.exit(0);
    });
  });
});
```

Before running the script, MongoDB needs to be running locally. Some MongoDB installations will configure MongoDB to start automatically, but others leave that decision to users. To determine if MongoDB is running, simply execute the mongo command in your terminal. You should see output similar to Listing 9-6 if MongoDB is running. You may kill the process at any time by pressing Ctrl+C.

Listing 9-6. MongoDB Terminal Client, mongo

```
$ mongo
MongoDB shell version: 2.6.7
connecting to: test
>
```

If you receive an error, start the MongoDB server manually by executing `mongod -f` followed by the location of the default MongoDB configuration file. The location of this file varies by system, so you may need to consult the MongoDB installation documentation. On OS X systems with a Homebrew MongoDB installation, for example, the configuration file may be found at `/usr/local/etc/mongod.conf`. Listing 9-7 shows how to start the daemon manually with this configuration file path.

Listing 9-7. Starting `mongod` Manually

```
$ mongod -f /usr/local/etc/mongod.conf
```

Once the `mongod` server has been started, you can run the `example-001/import-albums.js` script with Node.js. Listing 9-8 shows the output that will be displayed when the script has imported documents into MongoDB.

Listing 9-8. Running the Import Script

```
example-001$ node import-albums.js
creating 3 albums
```

In Listing 9-9 the `mongo` terminal client is launched, followed by a series of commands (after each > prompt) to verify that the `music` database and `albums` collection have been created. The `show dbs` command displays all databases hosted by the running MongoDB instance. To see the collections in a database, first switch to that database context by issuing the `use <db>` command, where `<db>` is the name of the database you are targeting. Next, execute `show collections` to see a list of collections owned by the database—in this case, `albums` and `system.indexes` (a collection that MongoDB manages).

Listing 9-9. Verifying Album Data Has Been Added to MongoDB

```
$ mongo
MongoDB shell version: 2.6.7
connecting to: test
> show dbs
admin      (empty)
local      0.078GB
music      0.078GB
> use music
```

```
switched to db music
> show collections
albums
system.indexes
>
```

With the `music` database selected, you can issue a few basic queries to see the album data added during the import. Within a database context, the database collections are accessed through the `db` object. Collections exist as properties of the `db` object, and operations performed against collections are methods on each collection object, respectively. To see the number of records within the `albums` collection, for example, the `db.albums.count()` method can be invoked on the collection, as shown in Listing 9-10. Likewise, to query album records, the `db.albums.find()` method can be used with criteria ("where" clause) and projection ("select" clause) arguments to control what data is returned.

Listing 9-10. Querying Album Data in the `albums` Collection

```
> db.albums.count()
3
> db.albums.find({}, {composer: 1})
{ "_id" : ObjectId("54c537ca46a13e0f4cebda82"), "composer" : "Kerry Muzzey" }
{ "_id" : ObjectId("54c537ca46a13e0f4cebda88"), "composer" : "Audiomachine" }
{ "_id" : ObjectId("54c537ca46a13e0f4cebdaa3"), "composer" : "Jessica Curry" }
```

Because the criteria argument (the first object passed to `db.albums.find()`) is empty in Listing 9-10, all records are returned. The projection object, however, specifies a single property to be returned by the query: `composer`. All other properties are excluded except for _id, which is returned by default and will always be included unless the projection parameter specifies otherwise.

Querying Data with Mongoose

Once the album data has been loaded into MongoDB, you can use the same model from Listing 9-4 to query that data.

The code in Listing 9-11 uses the Node.js `http` module to create a rudimentary web server that can receive HTTP requests and return JSON data in response. In this example the web server returns the same response for *any* URL query (to keep things simple).

320

When a request is received, the `Album` Mongoose model is used to query MongoDB for album documents. Its `find()` function is invoked with a criteria argument, a projection argument, and a callback. With the exception of the callback, this syntax is identical to the `db.albums.find()` method used in Listing 9-10 to examine album documents.

Listing 9-11. Querying MongoDB with Mongoose

```
// example-001/http-server.js
'use strict';
var mongoose = require('mongoose');
var Album = require('./album-model');
var http = require('http');
var url = require('url');

/*
 * The http server will handle requests and responses
 */
var server = http.createServer(function (req, res) {
  Album.find({}, {composer: 1}, function (err, albums) {
    var statusCode = err ? 500 : 200;
    var payload = err ? err : albums;
    res.writeHead(statusCode, {'Content-Type': 'application/json'});
    res.write(JSON.stringify(payload, null, '  '));
    res.end();
  });
});

/*
 * Connect to the MongoDB instance and report
 * errors if any occur.
 */
mongoose.connect('mongodb://localhost/music');
var db = mongoose.connection;

db.on('error', function (err) {
  console.error(err);
  process.exit(1);
});
```

```
db.once('open', function () {
  /*
   * The MongoDB connection is open, start
   * listening for HTTP requests.
   */
  server.listen(8080);
  console.log('listening on port 8080');
});
```

In Listing 9-12, the web server is launched from the example-001 directory with the command node http-server.js. Pressing Ctrl+C will stop the server.

Listing 9-12. Running the HTTP Server

```
example-001$ node http-server.js
listening on port 8080
```

The album data fetched from MongoDB may now be viewed in a web browser by navigating to http://localhost:8080 or by issuing the curl terminal command as shown in Listing 9-13.

Listing 9-13. Sending a curl Request to the HTTP Server

```
$ curl -v http://localhost:8080/
* Hostname was NOT found in DNS cache
*   Trying 127.0.0.1...
* Connected to localhost (127.0.0.1) port 8080 (#0)
> GET / HTTP/1.1
> User-Agent: curl/7.37.1
> Host: localhost:8080
> Accept: */*
>
< HTTP/1.1 200 OK
< Content-Type: application/json
< Date: Thu, 29 Jan 2015 01:20:09 GMT
< Connection: keep-alive
< Transfer-Encoding: chunked
<
```

```
[
  {
    "_id": "54c7020c342ee81670b261ef",
    "composer": "Kerry Muzzey"
  },
  {
    "_id": "54c7020c342ee81670b261f5",
    "composer": "Audiomachine"
  },
  {
    "_id": "54c7020c342ee81670b26210",
    "composer": "Jessica Curry"
  }
]
```

The rest of this chapter will build on this Mongoose schema, model, and album data stored in the MongoDB database.

Working with Schemas

Mongoose schemas are simple objects that describe the structure of and data types in a MongoDB document. While MongoDB itself is schemaless, Mongoose enforces schemas for documents at the application level. Schemas are defined by invoking the Mongoose module's Schema() function, passing it an object hash where the keys represent document properties and the values represent the data type for each property. The return value is an object of type Schema with additional helper properties and functions for expanding or augmenting the schema's definition.

Data Types

For scalar properties, Mongoose uses the native JavaScript data types String, Boolean, Number, and Date, shown in Listing 9-14.

Listing 9-14. Primitive Types in a Mongoose Schema

```
// example-001/album-model.js
var albumSchema = mongoose.Schema({
  composer: String,
  title: String,
  price: Number,
  releaseDate: Date,
  inPublication: Boolean
  // other properties...
});
```

Properties that are object literals or arrays use the literal notation for each type ({} and []). Nested object literals are written inline, using the same Mongoose schema types for their own properties. Array types contain only one element, which defines the type of object that will occupy the array. This type can be any valid Mongoose data type, including an object literal defined inline as the first element of the array. In Listing 9-15, genre is declared as an array of strings, while tracks is declared as an array of object literals.

Listing 9-15. Complex Types in a Mongoose Schema

```
// example-001/album-model.js
var albumSchema = mongoose.Schema({
  // ...other properties
  genre: [String],
  tracks: [
    {
      title: String,
      duration: {
        m: Number,
        s: Number
      }
    }
  ]
});
```

Mongoose itself provides two special object types: ObjectId and Mixed.

When a document is created in MongoDB, it is assigned an _id property that serves as a unique identifier for the record. This property uses MongoDB's own `ObjectId` data type. Mongoose exposes this type via `mongoose.Schema.Types.ObjectId`. This type is rarely used directly. When querying a document by ID, for example, the string representation of the identifier is typically used.

Note   When a schema property holds arbitrary data (remember, MongoDB is schemaless), it may be declared with the type `mongoose.Schema.Types.Mixed`. If a property is marked as `Mixed`, Mongoose will not track changes made against it. When Mongoose persists a document, it creates a query internally that only adds or updates properties that have changed, and since a `Mixed` property is not tracked, the application must inform Mongoose when it has changed. Documents created by Mongoose models expose a `markModified(path)` method that will force Mongoose to consider the property identified by the `path` argument as dirty.

Setting a Mongoose schema property to an empty object literal (one with no properties) will cause Mongoose to treat it as `Mixed`.

Finally, because Mongoose is a Node.js library, it takes advantage of Node's `Buffer` type to store large blocks of binary data such as image, audio, or video assets. Because binary data can be quite large, many applications store URL references to binary assets located on a content delivery network such as Amazon's Simple Storage Service (S3) instead of storing binaries in a data store such as MongoDB. Use cases differ across applications, however, and Mongoose schemas are flexible enough to support either approach.

Nested Schemas

Mongoose schemas may be nested; that is, a schema may reference another schema as a property type. This can be particularly useful if larger schemas share common custom data types, such as customer and order schemas sharing a postal address data type. In Listing 9-16 the album track schema is declared independent of the album schema and gets assigned as the data type for the `albumSchema.tracks` property.

Listing 9-16. Nested Mongoose Schemas

```
// breaking apart schemas...
var trackSchema = mongoose.Schema({
  title: String,
  duration: {
    m: Number,
    s: Number
  }
});

var albumSchema = mongoose.Schema({
  // ...
  tracks: [trackSchema]
});
```

Default Property Values

Adding sensible default values to schema properties instructs Mongoose to fill in missing data when a document is created. This is useful for document properties that aren't optional but typically hold some known value.

In Listing 9-17 the m and s properties (minute and second) of the album schema default to 0 because it is entirely possible that a track would be less than 1 minute long or be exactly *X* minutes and 0 seconds. The releaseDate property in the album schema also has a default value: the function Date.now. When a default value is a function, Mongoose will invoke the function, cast its return value to the type of the property, and then assign that value to the property.

Listing 9-17. Default Property Values

```
// adding default property values...
var trackSchema = mongoose.Schema({
  // ...
  duration: {
    m: {type: Number, default: 0},
    s: {type: Number, default: 0}
  }
});
```

```
var albumSchema = mongoose.Schema({
  // ...
  price: {type: Number, default: 0.0},
  releaseDate: {type: Date, default: Date.now},
  // ...
});
```

Adding a default to a property requires that the type assignment look a bit different. Notice that `m: Number` has become `m: {type: Number, default: 0}`. Normally, assigning an object hash to a property would cause the property to have a Mixed or object type, but the presence of the `type` property in the object literal short-circuits that process and tells Mongoose that the other key/value pairs in the hash are property settings.

Required Properties

The `required` attribute may be used on the type definition of nonoptional properties. When a document is saved, any missing property that the document schema requires will raise a validation error, which will be passed to the save operation's callback. Album composers, album titles, track titles, and even track duration objects are all required in Listing 9-18.

Listing 9-18. Required Properties

```
// adding required attributes
var trackSchema = mongoose.Schema({
  title: {type: String, required: true},
  duration: {
    required: true,
    type: {
      m: {type: Number, default: 0},
      s: {type: Number, default: 0}
    }
  }
});
```

```
var albumSchema = mongoose.Schema({
  composer: {type: String, required: true},
  title: {type: String, required: true},
  // ...
});
```

If a string is used in place of a boolean value for a required attribute, the string will be used as the error message if a validation error is raised, as shown in Listing 9-19. (Document validation will be covered shortly.)

Listing 9-19. Custom Error Message for a Required Property

```
var trackSchema = mongoose.Schema({
  title: {type: String, required: 'Missing track title!'},
  // ...
});
```

Secondary Indexes

Mongoose documents automatically acquire an indexed _id property when saved to MongoDB. Secondary indexes can be added to a schema, however, to enhance performance when querying against other fields.

MongoDB supports both simple (single field) and compound (multifield) indexes. In Listing 9-20 the following indexes are added to the track and album schemas:

- Track title (simple)

- Album composer (simple)

- Album title (simple)

- Album title + album composer (compound)

- Album genre (simple)

Listing 9-20. Adding Secondary Indexes to Schemas

```
// adding secondary indexes...
var trackSchema = mongoose.Schema({
  title: {type: String, required: true, index: true},
  // ...
```

```
});
var albumSchema = mongoose.Schema({
  composer: {type: String, required: true, index: true},
  title: {type: String, required: true, index: true},
  // ...
  genre: {type: [String], index: true},
  // ...
});

albumSchema.index({composer: 1, title: 1});
```

Simple indexes are added at the property level by appending an index field to a property type declaration and setting it to true. Compound indexes, on the other hand, must be defined for the schema as a whole using the Schema.index() method. The object passed to index() contains property names that correspond to the schema properties to be indexed and a numeric value that may be either 1 or -1.

MongoDB sorts indexes in either ascending or descending order. Compound indexes are defined with a numeric value instead of a boolean value (like simple indexes) to indicate the order in which each field should be indexed. For simple indexes, the order doesn't matter because MongoDB can search either way. But for compound indexes, the order is very important because it limits the kind of sort operations MongoDB can perform when a query uses a compound index. The MongoDB documentation covers compound indexing strategies in depth.

In Listing 9-20 a compound index for composer and title is added to the album schema in addition to simple indexes for both fields. It is entirely likely that a user will search for an album by composer, title, or both.

Schema Validation

Mongoose will enforce schema validation rules when documents are persisted. A validation rule is a function defined for a particular schema property that evaluates the property's value and returns a boolean value to indicate validity. Listing 9-21 demonstrates how to attach a property validator to a schema object.

Listing 9-21. Validating Schema Properties

```
// adding schema validation...
var trackSchema = mongoose.Schema({/*...*/});

var albumSchema = mongoose.Schema({
  // ...
  tracks: [trackSchema]
});

albumSchema.path('tracks').validate(function (tracks) {
  return tracks.length > 0;
}, 'Album has no tracks.');
```

The schema's path() method returns an instance of SchemaType, an object that encapsulates the definition of a schema's property—in this case, the tracks property, which is an array of track objects for the album. The SchemaType.validate() method attaches a validation function to the schema's property. The first argument is the actual validation function, which receives, as its only argument, the value to be validated. The second argument to validate() is the message that will be used if a validation error is raised.

When an album document is saved, this function will be executed as part of the Mongoose validation process, evaluating the tracks property to ensure that the album has at least one track.

Validation rules may also be attached to schema properties as part of the property definition. The tracks definition in Listing 9-22 includes the validate property. The value of this property is a two-element array (a tuple) where the validation function is element 0 and the error message is element 1.

Listing 9-22. Declaring Property Validators Inline

```
function validateTrackLength (tracks) {
  return tracks.length > 0;
}

var albumSchema = mongoose.Schema({
  // ...
  tracks: {
```

```
    type: [trackSchema],
    validate: [validateTrackLength, 'Album has no tracks.']
  }
});
```

While the Mongoose validation process is itself asynchronous, simple validation functions, like those in Listing 9-22, are synchronous. For most cases synchronous validation is perfectly acceptable, but for other cases asynchronous validators might be required. An asynchronous validation function accepts a second argument—a callback called respond (by convention)—that will be invoked when the asynchronous validation has completed. A true or false value is passed to respond to indicate successful or failed validation, respectively. Listing 9-23 shows how the validation function for album tracks could be made asynchronous.

Listing 9-23. Asynchronous Property Validators

```
albumSchema.path('tracks').validate(function (tracks, respond) {
  process.nextTick(function () {
    respond(tracks.length > 0);
  });
}, 'Album has no tracks.');
```

To see the validation function at work, the tracks for each album in example-002/ albums.json can be removed so that the JSON data resembles Listing 9-24.

Listing 9-24. Albums Without Tracks

```
// example-002/albums.json
[
  {
    "composer": "Kerry Muzzey",
    "title": "Renaissance",
    "price": 4.95,
    "releaseDate": "2014-01-13T06:00:00.000Z",
    "inPublication": true,
    "genre": ["Classical", "Trailer Music", "Soundtrack"],
    "tracks": []
  },
```

```
{
  "composer": "Audiomachine",
  "title": "Tree of Life",
  "price": 9.49,
  "releaseDate": "2013-07-16T05:00:00.000Z",
  "inPublication": true,
  "genre": ["Classical", "Trailer Music"],
  "tracks": []
},
{
  "composer": "Jessica Curry",
  "title": "Dear Esther",
  "price": 6.99,
  "releaseDate": "2012-02-14T06:00:00.000Z",
  "inPublication": true,
  "genre": ["Classical", "Video Game Soundtrack"],
  "tracks": []
}
]
```

Validation occurs whenever documents are persisted; that is, whenever `Model.create()` is called, or the `save()` method is called on a document instance. If validation fails, an error is passed as the first argument to a callback for each of these methods. (Documents will be discussed in detail later.)

If the import process is run again, the validator will trigger in `example-002/import-albums.js` when `Album.create()` is called to create new Mongoose documents from the incomplete JSON data. The console output in Listing 9-25 shows the serialized `ValidationError` that is raised and the `ValidatorError` for the `tracks` property present in its `errors` collection.

Listing 9-25. Console Output when Schema Validation Fails

```
example-002$ node import-albums.js
creating 3 albums
{ [ValidationError: Validation failed]
  message: 'Validation failed',
```

```
name: 'ValidationError',
errors:
 { tracks:
    { [ValidatorError: Album has no tracks.]
      message: 'Album has no tracks.',
      name: 'ValidatorError',
      path: 'tracks',
      type: 'user defined',
      value: [] } } }
```

After breaking apart the album and track schemas and adding default property values, required attributes, secondary indexes, and validation, the album schema has changed quite a bit from the simple schema in example-001. Listing 9-26 shows the more robust version.

Listing 9-26. More Robust Album Schema

```
// example-002/album.js
'use strict';
var mongoose = require('mongoose');

var trackSchema = mongoose.Schema({
  title: {type: String, required: true, index: true},
  duration: {
    required: true,
    type: {
      m: {type: Number, default: 0},
      s: {type: Number, default: 0}
    }
  }
});

var albumSchema = mongoose.Schema({
  composer: {type: String, required: true, index: true},
  title: {type: String, required: true, index: true},
  price: {type: Number, default: 0.0},
  releaseDate: {type: Date, default: Date.now},
```

```
  inPublication: Boolean,
  genre: {type: [String], index: true},
  tracks: [trackSchema]
});

albumSchema.index({composer: 1, title: 1});

albumSchema.path('tracks').validate(function (tracks) {
  return tracks.length > 0;
}, 'Album has no tracks.');

var Album = mongoose.model('Album', albumSchema);

module.exports = Album;
```

Schema References

Though MongoDB is a relationless data store, relationships between documents in collections can be created through informal references that act as foreign keys. The integrity enforcement and resolution of these foreign keys to objects is left entirely to the application, of course. Mongoose builds these informal relationships through population references—links between schemas that enable automatic eager loading (and manual lazy loading) of document graphs. To expand on the music application example, it is very likely that users will create their own personal album libraries. Because album documents can be large, it might be best to avoid duplicating album data in each library document. Instead, references will be created from library documents to individual albums, a kind of many-to-many relationship. When libraries are loaded by Mongoose, these references can be resolved so that full library object graphs are returned populated with album documents.

To keep things simple, a single library is defined in example-003/library.json. This library, shown in Listing 9-27, references albums by composer and title. Each album will need to be dereferenced to a document ID in a corresponding MongoDB album document when the data is imported.

Listing 9-27. Library JSON Data

```
// example-003/library.json
{
  "owner": "Nicholas Cloud",
  "albums": [
    {
      "composer": "Kerry Muzzey",
      "title": "Renaissance"
    },
    {
      "composer": "Audiomachine",
      "title": "Tree of Life"
    },
    {
      "composer": "Jessica Curry",
      "title": "Dear Esther"
    }
  ]
}
```

The library import script is similar to the album import script, as shown in
Listing 9-28, but it performs one additional important step. After the `library.json` file
is read and turned into a plain JavaScript object, the album data is resolved to the actual
album document objects imported in `example-001/import-albums.js`.

Listing 9-28. Importing Library Data into MongoDB

```
// example-003/import-library.js
'use strict';
var mongoose = require('mongoose');
var Album = require('./album-model');
var Library = require('./library-model');
var file2json = require('./file2json');
var fs = require('fs');
var path = require('path');
```

```
function handleError(err) {
  console.error(err);
  process.exit(1);
}

function resolveAlbums(libraryJSON, cb) {
  /*
   * [3] use a compound $or criteria to look up multiple
   * album documents
   */
  var albumCriteria = {
    $or: libraryJSON.albums
  };

  Album.find(albumCriteria, cb);
}

mongoose.connect('mongodb://localhost/music');
var db = mongoose.connection;
db.on('error', handleError);
db.once('open', function importLibrary () {

  /*
   * [1] read the library.json file data and convert it to
   * a normal JS object
   */
  var libraryFile = path.join(__dirname, 'library.json');
  file2json(libraryFile, 'utf8', function (err, libraryJSON) {
    if (err) return handleError(err);

    /*
     * [2] look up album documents that match each composer/title
     * in the library JSON data
     */
    resolveAlbums(libraryJSON, function (err, albumDocuments) {
      if (err) return handleError(err);

      console.log('creating library');
```

```
    /*
     * [4] assign the album documents to the library object
     */
    libraryJSON.albums = albumDocuments;

    /*
     * [5] then create a library document from the JSON data and
     * save the document
     */
    var libraryDocument = new Library(libraryJSON);

    libraryDocument.save(function (err) {
      if (err) return handleError(err);
      process.exit(0);
    });
  });

  });
});
```

Each step in the import flow is annotated in Listing 9-28, but several steps involve concepts that have not yet been introduced.

In step [3] a compound $or criteria object is created to filter MongoDB album documents by composer and title. The $or criteria property is covered later in the chapter, but for now it is sufficient to understand that MongoDB will examine all documents in the albums collection and determine if the document matches *any* of the composer/title pairs in the $or array, shown in Listing 9-29. Since all three albums previously imported match at least one of the pairs in this criteria, they will all be returned as results.

Listing 9-29. Library Import $or Criteria

```
{ $or:
    [ { composer: 'Kerry Muzzey', title: 'Renaissance' },
      { composer: 'Audiomachine', title: 'Tree of Life' },
      { composer: 'Jessica Curry', title: 'Dear Esther' } ] }
```

In step [4] the found album documents are assigned to the `libraryJSON.albums` property, replacing the existing array of composer/title data. When the library document is saved, Mongoose will enforce the library schema in Listing 9-30. Unlike previous property descriptions, the `albums` property is a reference property that will hold an array of `ObjectIds` as defined by the `type` attribute. The `ref` attribute tells Mongoose that this field can also be populated with album documents during a query (if specified) or when a library document is saved.

Listing 9-30. Library Schema

```
// example-003/library-model.js
'use strict';
var mongoose = require('mongoose');

var librarySchema = mongoose.Schema({
  owner: String,
  albums: [{type: mongoose.Schema.Types.ObjectId, ref: 'Album'}]
});

var Library = mongoose.model('Library', librarySchema);

module.exports = Library;
```

Mongoose documents may all be cast to their `ObjectIds`. Mongoose is smart enough to perform this cast automatically, so adding album documents to the `albums` property will pass the schema check. Alternatively, the import script could pluck the `_id` property from each album document and place it into the `albums` array instead. The result would be identical.

Finally, in step [5] an individual document instance is created by invoking the `Library` constructor and passing in the raw JSON data to assign to each document property. Documents may also be created with no constructor argument, assigning data to each property on the instance imperatively, but using the constructor argument shorthand is common. After the document has been created, its `save()` method is invoked with a callback that is passed an error if the persistence process fails. This differs from the album import script in which multiple album documents were created in MongoDB at once by using the model's static `create()` function. Listing 9-31 demonstrates the difference.

Listing 9-31. Creating a Single Document and Multiple Documents

```
// create a single document
var libraryDocument = new Library(plainJSONLibrary);
libraryDocument.save(function (err) {...});

// create multiple documents at once
Albums.create(arrayOfJSONAlbums, function (err) {...});
```

In Listing 9-32, the library import script is run exactly as the album import script was run.

Listing 9-32. Running the Library Import Script

```
example-003$ node import-library.js
creating library
```

Once the import has completed, the library data may be verified with the `mongo` terminal client. The output in Listing 9-33 reveals that Mongoose did indeed satisfy the library schema by casting each album object to its identifier. (The next section, "Working with Models and Documents," will examine how schema reference properties can be used to eagerly load referenced documents.)

Listing 9-33. Verifying the Library Import in MongoDB

```
example-003$ mongo
MongoDB shell version: 2.6.7
connecting to: test

> use music
switched to db music

> db.libraries.find()
{ "_id" : ObjectId("54ed1dfdb11e8ae7252af342"), "owner" : "Nicholas Cloud",
"albums" : [ ObjectId("54ed1dcb6fb525ba25529bd1"), ObjectId("54ed1dcb6fb525
ba25529bd7"), ObjectId("54ed1dcb6fb525ba25529bf2") ], "__v" : 0 }
```

Schema Middleware

Mongoose raises events on a schema object whenever particular MongoDB documents are validated, saved, or removed from a document collection. Events are raised *before* and *after* each one of these operations. Subscriptions to these events are assigned with a schema's pre() and post() methods, respectively. A subscription is simply a function or *middleware* that receives arguments related to each event. Post-event middleware simply observes the document after the event is complete, but pre-event middleware may actually interrupt the document life cycle before an event is completely processed.

In Listing 9-34, a duration object has been added to the library schema, identical to the duration object in each album track. This object, however, will hold the computed total length of the library as a whole. A pre-event middleware function is attached to the library schema for the save event. Before the library is saved, this function will iterate over each album and each track to sum the lengths of all tracks, then assign the calculated values to properties on the duration object. The middleware function receives a single argument, the callback function next(). When the duration summation has completed, next() is invoked to trigger any additional middleware functions attached to the schema.

Listing 9-34. Pre-save Middleware

```
// example-004/library-model.js
'use strict';
var mongoose = require('mongoose');

var librarySchema = mongoose.Schema({
  owner: String,
  albums: [{type: mongoose.Schema.Types.ObjectId, ref: 'Album'}],
  duration: {
    h: {type: Number, default: 0},
    m: {type: Number, default: 0}
  }
});

librarySchema.pre('save', function (next) {
  var hours = 0, mins = 0;
  /*
```

```
 * iterate over all albums and add hours
 * and minutes
 */
this.albums.forEach(function (album) {
  album.tracks.forEach(function (track) {
    hours += track.duration.h;
    mins += track.duration.m;
  });
});
/*
 * divide total mins by 60 seconds and
 * add that to hours, then assign remaining
 * minutes back to mins
 */
hours += (mins / 60);
mins = (mins % 60);
this.duration = {h: hours, m: mins};
next();
});

var Library = mongoose.model('Library', librarySchema);

module.exports = Library;
```

Pre-event middleware can execute in a synchronous or asynchronous manner. The code in Listing 9-34 is synchronous, which means that other middleware functions will be scheduled only after the duration summation has been completed. To change this behavior and schedule them all immediately, one after the next, the schema's pre() method is called with an additional boolean argument that flags the handler function as asynchronous middleware.

The middleware function itself also receives an additional parameter, the done() function callback shown in Listing 9-35. In synchronous middleware, control is passed to the next middleware function when a previous middleware function has finished and invoked next(). This is still the case with asynchronous middleware, but the done()

function must also be invoked when the asynchronous operation has finished during a future event loop turn. The order of execution in Listing 9-35 is

1. Schedule the duration summation process for the next event loop pass.

2. Invoke next() to pass control to the next piece of middleware.

3. At some future point in time, signal that this middleware operation is complete by invoking done().

Listing 9-35. Asynchronous Pre-save Middleware

```
// example-005/library-model.js
// ...
librarySchema.pre('save', true, function (next, done) {

  var hours = 0, mins = 0;
  process.nextTick(function () {                    // #1
    /*
     * iterate over all albums and add hours
     * and minutes
     */
    this.albums.forEach(function (album) {
      album.tracks.forEach(function (track) {
        hours += track.duration.h;
        mins += track.duration.m;
      });
    });
    /*
     * divide total mins by 60 seconds and
     * add that to hours, then assign remaining
     * minutes back to mins
     */
    hours += (mins / 60);
    mins = (mins % 60);
    this.duration = {h: hours, m: mins};
    done();                                          // #3
  });
```

```
  next();                                         // #2
});

var Library = mongoose.model('Library', librarySchema);

module.exports = Library;
```

If an error is raised in a synchronous, pre-event middleware function, it should be passed as the only argument to `next()`. Errors raised during asynchronous functions, however, should be passed to `done()` instead. Any error passed to these callbacks will cause the operation that triggered the event to fail and will be delivered to the final operation callback (e.g., the callback passed to a document's `save()` method).

Post-event middleware functions receive no control flow arguments, but instead receive a copy of the document as it stands after the event's operation has completed.

Working with Models and Documents

A Mongoose model is a constructor function that creates document instances. These instances conform to a Mongoose schema and expose a collection of methods for document persistence. Models are associated with MongoDB collections. In fact, when a Mongoose document is saved, the collection to which it corresponds will be created if it does not already exist. By convention, models are named in the singular form of the noun they represent (e.g., `Album`), but collections are named in the plural form (e.g., `albums`).

A model constructor function is created by invoking `mongoose.model()` with a model name and a model schema. All documents created with this constructor function, either directly in user code or indirectly when Mongoose executes queries and returns document instances, will conform to the model's schema. Listing 9-36 shows the code responsible for creating the `Album` constructor function used by the import scripts to create album documents in MongoDB.

Listing 9-36. Album Model

```
// example-006/album-model.js

//...schema definition...

var Album = mongoose.model('Album', albumSchema);

module.exports = Album;
```

When a Mongoose model is registered with the `mongoose.model()` function, Mongoose can then resolve that model by name when referenced in relationship properties. This technique was used earlier to create a reference between the library schema and the `Album` model, as shown in Listing 9-37.

Listing 9-37. Library Schema References Album Model

```
// example-006/library-model.js

// ...
var librarySchema = mongoose.Schema({
  // ...
  albums: [{type: mongoose.Schema.Types.ObjectId, ref: 'Album'}],
  // ...
});
```

New documents can be created with a model constructor function or fetched from a MongoDB data store with model query methods. Each document can save or remove itself from a MongoDB collection. This is very similar to the ActiveRecord data access pattern commonly used in RDBMS libraries. In Listing 9-38, a new album document instance is created with the `Album` constructor function. Album data is assigned to each property (with the appropriate data types) defined by the album schema. Finally, the `save()` method is called on the document, and its callback is invoked when the associated document has been created in MongoDB.

Listing 9-38. Creating and Saving a New Document Instance

```
// example-006/add-album-instance.js
'use strict';
var mongoose = require('mongoose');
var Album = require('./album-model');

function handleError(err) {
  console.error(err);
  process.exit(1);
}

mongoose.connect('mongodb://localhost/music');
var db = mongoose.connection;
```

```
db.on('error', handleError);
db.once('open', function addAlbumInstance() {

  var album = new Album();
  album.composer = 'nervous_testpilot';
  album.title = 'Frozen Synapse';
  album.price =  8.99;
  album.releaseDate = new Date(2012, 8, 6);
  album.inPublication = true;
  album.genre = ['Dance', 'DJ/Electronica', 'Soundtrack'];
  album.tracks = [
    {
      title: 'Welcome to Markov Geist',
      duration: {m: 1, s: 14}
    },
    // ...additional tracks...
  ];

  album.save(function (err) {
    if (err) return handleError(err);
    console.log('album saved', album);
    process.exit(0);
  });
});
```

The script output shows the document data after the album has been saved:

```
example-006$ node add-album-instance.js
album saved { __v: 0,
  inPublication: true,
  title: 'Frozen Synapse',
  composer: 'nervous_testpilot',
  _id: 54f117e4a27cc5375e156c6d... }
```

MongoDB can be queried to verify that the document was, in fact, created in the albums collection, as shown in Listing 9-39.

Listing 9-39. Verifying the Mongoose Document Has Been Created in MongoDB

```
example-006$ mongo
MongoDB shell version: 2.6.7
connecting to: test
> use music
switched to db music
> db.albums.find({composer: 'nervous_testpilot'}, {_id: 1, composer: 1,
title: 1})
{ "_id" : ObjectId("54f117e4a27cc5375e156c6d"), "title" : "Frozen Synapse",
"composer" : "nervous_testpilot" }
```

Document instance properties may also be set by passing an object hash directly to the model constructor. This can be particularly useful when document data already exists in a plain JavaScript object, such as a deserialized JSON web request body, or JSON data parsed from a flat file. Listing 9-40 adapts the previous example to load the new album data from a JSON file, then uses the Album model constructor to create a document from the new JSON data. Since the JSON data conforms to the album schema (or, in the case of the releaseDate date string, can be converted directly to the property type Date), the album instance will be persisted without errors.

Listing 9-40. Alternative Way to Create a Document with Property Data

```
// example-007/add-album-instance-alt.js
'use strict';
var mongoose = require('mongoose');
var Album = require('./album-model');
var file2json = require('./file2json');
var path = require('path');

function handleError(err) {
  console.error(err);
  process.exit(1);
}

mongoose.connect('mongodb://localhost/music');
var db = mongoose.connection;
```

```
db.on('error', handleError);
db.once('open', function addAlbumInstance() {

  var albumFile = path.join(__dirname, 'album.json');
  file2json(albumFile, 'utf8', function (err, albumJSON) {
    var album = new Album(albumJSON);
    album.save(function (err) {
      if (err) return handleError(err);
      console.log('album saved', album);
      process.exit(0);
    });
  });

});
```

Document Instance Methods

Documents are more than just data: they may also include custom behavior. When document instances are created, Mongoose creates a prototype chain with copies of functions defined on the schema object's `methods` property. Document methods defined in this way may access particular document instances with the `this` keyword.

Listing 9-41 shows two instance methods defined on the album schema: one to find the next album track given the previous track's title and another that will find similar albums based on shared genres. The `findSimilar()` method uses query syntax that will be covered later in the section "Working with Queries," but for now you simply need to know that it effectively finds albums that have genres that overlap with the instance album and that do not share the same `_id` as the instance album (so the instance itself is excluded from the list).

Listing 9-41. Defining Document Instance Methods in a Schema

```
// example-008/album-model.js

// ...
var albumSchema = mongoose.Schema({/*...*/});

albumSchema.methods.nextTrack = function (previousTrackTitle) {
  var i = 0, len = this.tracks.length;
```

```
  for (i; i < len; i += 1) {
    if (this.tracks[i].title !== previousTrackTitle) {
      continue;
    }
    // return the next track, or, if this is the last track,
    // return the first track
    return this.tracks[i + 1] || this.tracks[0];
  }
  throw new Error('unable to find track ' + previousTrackTitle);
};

albumSchema.methods.findSimilar = function (cb) {
  var criteria = {
    _id: {$ne: this._id},
    genre: {$in: this.genre}
  };
  this.model('Album').find(criteria)
    .exec(cb);
};

var Album = mongoose.model('Album', albumSchema);

module.exports = Album;
```

The script in Listing 9-42 loads the album titled *Renaissance,* then calls album.nextTrack() to determine which track follows "Fall from Grace." Then it calls album.findSimilar() to load albums related to *Renaissance* and prints their titles and genres to the terminal. The output reveals that there is, indeed, overlapping genres for each album and that the instance album itself is not included in the results.

Listing 9-42. Using Document Instance Methods

```
// example-008/index01.js
'use strict';
var mongoose = require('mongoose');
var Album = require('./album-model');
```

```
function handleError(err) {
  console.error(err);
  process.exit(1);
}

mongoose.connect('mongodb://localhost/music');
var db = mongoose.connection;
db.on('error', handleError);
db.once('open', function () {
  Album.findOne({title: 'Renaissance'})
    .exec(function (err, album) {
      if (err) return handleError(err);

      var nextTrack = album.nextTrack('Fall from Grace');
      console.log('next track:', nextTrack.title);

      album.findSimilar(function (err, albums) {
        if (err) return handleError(err);
        console.log('this album:', album.title, album.genre);
        albums.forEach(function (album) {
          console.log('similar album:', album.title, album.genre);
        });
        process.exit(0);
      });
    });
});
```

```
example-008$ node index01.js
next track: Fall from Grace (Choir Version)
this album: Renaissance ["Classical","Trailer Music","Soundtrack"]
similar album: Tree of Life ["Classical","Trailer Music"]
similar album: Dear Esther ["Classical","Video Game Soundtrack"]
similar album: Frozen Synapse ["Dance","Electronica","Soundtrack"]
```

Document Virtuals

Like instance methods, virtual getter and setter *properties* can be added to documents via the schema. These virtual properties act like normal data properties but are not persisted when the document is saved. They are useful for computing and returning values based on document data or for parsing data that contains, or can be converted to, values for other document properties.

A virtual getter and setter have been added to the album schema in Listing 9-43 that define a property, `composerInverse`, that will get the inversed version of a composer's name ("last, first") and set the composer's name correctly ("first last") given an inverse form.

Listing 9-43. Virtual Document Properties

```
// example-08/album-model.js

var albumSchema = mongoose.Schema({/*...*/});

// ...
albumSchema.virtual('composerInverse').get(function () {
  var parts = this.composer.split(' '); //first last
  if (parts.length === 1) {
    return this.composer;
  }
  return [parts[1], parts[0]].join(', '); //last, first
});

albumSchema.virtual('composerInverse').set(function (inverse) {
  var parts = inverse.split(', '); //last, first
  if (parts.length === 1) {
    this.composer = inverse;
  }
  this.composer = [parts[1], parts[0]].join(' '); //first last
});
// ...
```

The string argument passed to the `Schema.virtual()` method defines the document path where the property will reside once a document instance is created. Document virtuals may be assigned to subdocuments and nested objects as well by specifying the full path starting at the root document. For example, if the value of the `composer` property was an object with `firstName` and `lastName` properties, the virtual might live at `composer.inverse` instead.

The script and subsequent output in Listing 9-44 shows the `composerInverse` property in action.

Listing 9-44. Getting and Setting a Virtual Property

```
// example-008/index02.js
'use strict';
var mongoose = require('mongoose');
var Album = require('./album-model');

function handleError(err) {
  console.error(err);
  process.exit(1);
}

mongoose.connect('mongodb://localhost/music');
var db = mongoose.connection;
db.on('error', handleError);
db.once('open', function () {
  Album.find({}).exec(function (err, albums) {
    if (err) return handleError(err);

    albums.forEach(function (album) {
      console.log('album.composer:', album.composer);
      var inverse = album.composerInverse;
      console.log('album.composerInverse:', inverse);
      album.composerInverse = inverse;
      console.log('album.composer:', album.composer);
      console.log(/*newline*/);
    });
```

```
      process.exit(0);
  });
});
```

```
example-008$ node index02.js
album.composer: Kerry Muzzey
album.composerInverse: Muzzey, Kerry
album.composer: Kerry Muzzey

album.composer: Audiomachine
album.composerInverse: Audiomachine
album.composer:  Audiomachine

album.composer: Jessica Curry
album.composerInverse: Curry, Jessica
album.composer: Jessica Curry

album.composer: nervous_testpilot
album.composerInverse: nervous_testpilot
album.composer:  nervous_testpilot
```

Static Model Methods

Static methods may also be added to models (not document instances) and are commonly used to encapsulate complicated criteria construction when querying against a collection. The inPriceRange() method in Listing 9-45 is attached to the album schema's statics property. It receives two numeric arguments that represent the lower and upper bounds of a price range and finds albums that are priced within that range, inclusively.

Listing 9-45. Adding a Static Method to a Model

```
// example-009/album-model.js

var albumSchema = mongoose.Schema({/*...*/});

// ...
albumSchema.statics.inPriceRange = function (lower, upper, cb) {
  var criteria = {
    price: {$gte: lower, $lte: upper}
  };
```

```
  this.find(criteria)
    .exec(cb);
};
// ...
```

When the album model is later created from the schema, any method on `statics` will be bound to the model. While the value of `this` in instance methods is the document itself, the value of the `this` keyword in static methods is the model constructor function (e.g., `Album`). Any function that can be called on the model, such as `find()` and `create()`, may be accessed in a static method.

The script in Listing 9-46 receives two prices as command-line arguments and then finds albums within the range of those prices. The `inPriceRange()` method is called on the `Album` model, just as any other static method. Encapsulating queries in this manner can be a good way to maintain separate concerns, as query logic is isolated to models and won't pollute other portions of the application.

Listing 9-46. Using Static Model Methods

```
// example-009/index.js
'use strict';
var mongoose = require('mongoose');
var Album = require('./album-model');

var lower = Number(process.argv[2] || 0);
var upper = Number(process.argv[3] || lower + 1);

console.log('finding albums between $%s and $%s', lower.toFixed(2), upper.
toFixed(2));

function handleError(err) {
  console.error(err);
  process.exit(1);
}

mongoose.connect('mongodb://localhost/music');
var db = mongoose.connection;
db.on('error', handleError);
db.once('open', function () {
  Album.inPriceRange(lower, upper, function (err, albums) {
```

```
    if (err) return handleError(err);
    console.log('found albums:', albums.length);
    albums.forEach(function (album) {
      console.log(album.title, '$' + album.price.toFixed(2));
    });
    process.exit(0);
  });
});
```

```
example-009$ node index.js 5.00 10.00
finding albums between $5.00 and $10.00
found albums: 3
Tree of Life $9.49
Dear Esther $6.99
Frozen Synapse $8.99

example-009$ node index.js 9.00 10.00
finding albums between $9.00 and $10.00
found albums: 1
Tree of Life $9.49

example-009$ node index.js 20.00
finding albums between $20.00 and $21.00
found albums: 0
```

> **Note**   The query examples in the next section do not use static model methods
> for encapsulation. This is done to simplify each example, though in a real
> maintainable application, it might be considered bad practice.

Working with Queries

Mongoose queries are plain objects composed of zero or more properties that specify the parameters of the query. (An empty query object matches everything.) Properties on these criteria objects share MongoDB's native query syntax. Models expose several different query methods that use criteria objects in order to filter and return Mongoose documents.

For the following examples, a web server provides access to MongoDB data via Mongoose models. To start the web server, ensure that your MongoDB instance is running and then execute the command in Listing 9-47 in each example directory. (A comment at the top of each code example reveals which directory it lives in.) The script output will inform you that the web server is running on port 8080. All interactions with the web server will be demonstrated with the cURL terminal utility available for most platforms, though each example could be run with any standard HTTP client.

Listing 9-47. Starting the Web Server in Example 10

```
example-XYZ$ node index.js
listening on port 8080
```

Model.find()

Basic CRUD operations may be conveniently mapped to corresponding Mongoose model functions with very little effort. The route in Listing 9-48, for example, is a general route that uses Album.find() to locate album documents that contain properties matching those in the criteria object. The criteria object gets composer and title parameters from the URL query string if they have been sent as part of the request. If one or both of these parameters are set on the criteria object, Mongoose will return only documents that have matching properties (similar to a where clause in traditional SQL). If no parameters are sent, the criteria object will remain empty and Mongoose will find *all* album documents.

Listing 9-48. Finding Albums That Match a Given Criteria

```
// example-010/album-routes.js

/**
 * GET /album(?composer={string}&title={string})
 * @param req
 * @param cb
 */
routes.GET['^\/album(?:\\?.+)?$'] = function (req, cb) {
  cb = httpd.asJSON(cb);
  var criteria = {};
```

```
  if (req.query.composer) {
    criteria.composer = req.query.composer;
  }
  if (req.query.title) {
    criteria.title = req.query.title;
  }
  Album.find(criteria)
    .sort({composer: 1, title: 1})
    .lean(true)
    .exec(function (err, albums) {
      if (err) return cb(500, err);
      cb(200, albums);
    });
};
```

The `Album.find()` method will return a Mongoose `Query` object that exposes additional methods for manipulating the results of the find operation.

Note   Model methods can be invoked in several ways. The first, shown in Listing 9-48, returns a `Query` object with a fluent interface that allows query options to be chained together until the `Query.exec()` method is called. The second method avoids the `Query` object altogether. If a callback is passed as the last argument to a model's query method (e.g., `find({}, function () {...})`), the underlying query will be executed immediately and the error or result passed to the callback. For simple queries, the second method is more terse.

The first `Query` directive is `Query.sort()`, which accepts an object that uses MongoDB's sorting notation. The properties in this object tell MongoDB which properties in the document should be used for sorts and in which direction each sort should be ordered (`1` for ascending, `-1` for descending). When the results in Listing 9-48 are fetched, they will be ordered first by composer, then by album title.

After `Query.sort()`, the `Query.lean()` method is invoked to instruct Mongoose to deliver plain JSON objects instead of Mongoose documents as results. By default, Mongoose will always fetch documents, which carry Mongoose-specific properties and methods for validating, persisting, and otherwise managing document objects. Since this route (and most routes in this file) simply serializes results and returns them to the client, it is preferable to fetch them as Plain Old JavaScript Objects (or JSON objects) populated only with data.

Once a query has been prepared, its exec() method is passed a callback to receive either an error or data from the Album.find() operation. The results will be an array of album objects that match whatever criteria (if any) was used to perform the query.

Several curl commands are shown in Listing 9-49 with various query string parameters. In each case the output is a serialized JSON array delivered from the web API.

> **Note**   The following examples use MongoDB identifiers that were generated on my computer. These identifiers will differ on your computer. You may use the mongo terminal client to discover the identifiers assigned to your MongoDB documents, as demonstrated in previous examples.

Listing 9-49. Using curl to Find Albums with Various Criteria

```
example-010$ curl -X GET http://localhost:8080/album?composer=Kerry%20Muzzey
[{"_id":"54ed1dcb6fb525ba25529bd1","composer":"Kerry Muzzey","title":"Renai
ssance"... ]

example-010$ curl -X GET http://localhost:8080/album?title=Dear%20Esther
[{"_id":"54ed1dcb6fb525ba25529bf2","composer":"Jessica Curry","title":"Dear
Esther"... ]

example-010$ curl -X GET "http://localhost:8080/album?composer=Audiomachine
&title=Tree%20of%20Life"
[{"_id":"54ed1dcb6fb525ba25529bd7","composer":"Audiomachine","title":"Tree
of Life"... ]
```

Model.findById()

While Album.find() will always fetch an array of documents (even if its criteria specifies a unique identifier), Album.findById() will only find a single document that matches a given identifier, if any exist. The route in Listing 9-50 fetches a single album by

albumID—a parameter passed as the last URL segment instead of the query string. The
lean() method is again invoked on the returned Query to eliminate the unnecessary
properties and methods in a full Mongoose document instance.

Listing 9-50. Finding a Single Album That Matches a Given Criteria

```
// example-010/album-routes.js

/**
 * GET /album/{id}
 * @param req
 * @param cb
 */
routes.GET['^\/album\/([a-z0-9]+)$'] = function (req, cb) {
  cb = httpd.asJSON(cb);
  var albumID = req.params[0];
  Album.findById(albumID)
    .lean(true)
    .exec(function (err, album) {
      if (err) return cb(500, err);
      cb(200, album);
    });
};
```

```
example-010$ curl -X GET http://localhost:8080/
album/54f3a4df056601726f867685
{"_id":"54f3a4df056601726f867685","composer":"nervous_
testpilot","title":"Frozen Synapse"... }
```

Earlier an additional album was created by the import script example-007/add-
album-instance-alt.js, in which a deserialized JSON object was passed to the Album
constructor to create an album instance. Listing 9-51 demonstrates the same process
within an HTTP POST route. The body of the request is serialized album data that is
first converted to a JSON object, then passed to the Album model constructor. Once the
document instance has been created, the save() method validates the data (with rules
defined in the album schema) and creates the new MongoDB document.

Listing 9-51. Creating a New Album Document

```
// example-010/album-routes.js

/**
 * POST /album
 * @param req
 * @param cb
 */
routes.POST['^\/album$'] = function (req, cb) {
  console.log(req.body);
  cb = httpd.asJSON(cb);
  var albumJSON = req.body;
  var album = new Album(albumJSON);
  album.save(function (err) {
    if (err) return cb(500, err);
    cb(201, album.toObject());
  });
};
```

If validation fails, or if the album otherwise cannot be created, an error will be passed to the final callback and delivered to the client as an HTTP 500 Internal Server Error. If the album document is created, the data is passed back to the client as serialized JSON. Unlike previous routes where Query.lean() was used to ensure that only data is serialized, the album document returns its own data in JSON format when its toObject() method is called. This is the manual equivalent of the process that lean() performs in a query chain.

The curl request in Listing 9-52 reads the content of example-010/new-album.json and sets it as the request body. The Content-Type informs the web server to deserialize the payload accordingly.

Listing 9-52. Creating a New Album with a curl Request

```
example-010$ curl -X POST http://localhost:8080/album \
> -d @new-album.json \
> -H "Content-Type: application/json"
{"_id":"54f66ed2fa4af12b43fee49b","composer":"Aphelion","title":
"Memento"... }
```

The album data in example-010/new-album.json lacks a releaseDate property, a condition that did not cause the schema validation to fail on import because releaseDate is not required. Indeed, releaseDate defaults to Date.now and, if queried with the mongo client, will be exactly that. Unfortunately, the album was not, in fact, released today, so it is necessary to create another route to update the newly minted album document.

Model.findByIdAndUpdate()

An album instance may be updated in a number of ways. The Album.findById() method could fetch the document, its properties could be set with updated data, then it could be saved back to the data store. Or the Album.findByIdAndUpdate() method could be used to do all of that at once and return the newly updated album document, the exact approach taken in Listing 9-53.

Listing 9-53. Finding and Updating an Album by ID

```
// example-010/album-routes.js

/**
 * PUT /album/{id}
 * @param req
 * @param cb
 */
routes.PUT['^\/album\/([a-z0-9]+)$'] = function (req, cb) {
  cb = httpd.asJSON(cb);
  var albumID = req.params[0];
  var updatedFields = req.body;
  Album.findByIdAndUpdate(albumID, updatedFields)
    .lean(true)
    .exec(function (err, album) {
      if (err) return cb(500, err);
      cb(200, album);
    });
};
```

Like Listing 9-51, a serialized JSON object is sent in the body of an HTTP request. This request is a PUT request, however, and includes the album identifier in the URL. The only data sent in the request body are the properties to be updated. It is unnecessary to send the full document across the wire because Mongoose will apply the deltas appropriately. Once the request body is deserialized, the album ID and updated fields are passed to `findByIdAndUpdate()`. If the update operation succeeds, the updated document will be passed to the final query callback, assuming no errors occur.

The `curl` command in Listing 9-54 creates a PUT request with a simple JSON payload that specifies a new value for `releaseDate`. When the request finishes, the printed response shows the updated album data.

Listing 9-54. Finding and Updating an Album by ID with curl

```
example-010$ curl -X PUT http://localhost:8080/
album/54f66ed2fa4af12b43fee49b \
> -d '{"releaseDate": "2013-08-15T05:00:00.000Z"}' \
> -H "Content-Type: application/json"
{"_id":"54f66ed2fa4af12b43fee49b"..."releaseDate":"2013-08-
15T05:00:00.000Z"... }
```

Model.findByIdAndRemove()

To remove a document from MongoDB, the `DELETE` route uses the `Album.findByIdAndRemove()` method to look up the MongoDB document and then remove it from the `albums` collection. The removed album is passed to the final callback in Listing 9-55 if the operation is successful.

Listing 9-55. Finding and Removing an Album by ID

```
// example-010/album-routes.js

/**
 * DELETE /album/{id}
 * @param req
 * @param cb
 */
routes.DELETE['^\/album\/([a-z0-9]+)$'] = function (req, cb) {
```

```
  cb = httpd.asJSON(cb);
  var albumID = req.params[0];
  Album.findByIdAndRemove(albumID)
    .lean(true)
    .exec(function (err, album) {
      if (err) return cb(500, err);
      cb(200, album);
    });
};
```

```
example-010$ curl -X DELETE http://localhost:8080/
album/54f3aa9447429f44763f2603
{"_id":"54f66ed2fa4af12b43fee49b","composer":"Aphelion","title":"Memento"... }
```

A document instance also has a `remove()` method that can be invoked much like its `save()` method. In Listing 9-56 an album instance is fetched by ID. `Query.lean()` is *not* called this time because it is the document, not its plain JSON representation, that will possess a `remove()` method. Once the instance is fetched, `remove()` is called with a callback that will receive an error on failure or a copy of the removed document instance if successful.

Listing 9-56. Removing a Document Instance

```
Album.findById(albumID)
  .exec(function (err, albumInstance) {
    albumInstance.remove(function (err, removedAlbum) {
      // album has been removed
    });
  });
```

Model.count( )

Another useful model method is `count()`, which receives the same type of criteria objects as the `find*()` methods, but returns a simple record count instead of full objects. The HTTP route in Listing 9-57 uses the same query parameters as the general album search and returns the result count in the HTTP response.

Listing 9-57. Counting Albums That Match Criteria

```
// example-011/album-routes.js

/**
 * GET /album/count(?composer={string}&title={string})
 * @param req
 * @param cb
 */
routes.GET['^\/album\/count(?:\\?.+)?$'] = function (req, cb) {
  cb = httpd.asJSON(cb);
  var criteria = {};
  if (req.query.composer) {
    criteria.composer = req.query.composer;
  }
  if (req.query.title) {
    criteria.title = req.query.title;
  }
  Album.count(criteria)
    .exec(function (err, count) {
      if (err) return cb(500, err);
      cb(200, count);
    });
};

example-011$ curl -X GET http://localhost:8080/album/count
4

example-011$ curl -X GET http://localhost:8080/album/
count?composer=Jessica%20Curry
1
```

Query.Populate()

Earlier, in Listing 9-28, a script was used to add a music library to MongoDB. The library schema defined an array property, albums, that contained references to album documents, shown in Listing 9-58.

Listing 9-58. Album References in the Library Schema

```
var librarySchema = mongoose.Schema({
  // ...
  albums: [{type: mongoose.Schema.Types.ObjectId, ref: 'Album'}],
  // ...
});
```

Mongoose documents with foreign references can be fetched with or without resolving those references to other document objects. The route in Listing 9-59 fetches a library by ID, then calls the `Query.populate()` method to eagerly fetch the associated albums for the library. Mongoose is smart enough to know that, even though `albums` is technically an array, the objects it contains actually refer to other album documents.

Listing 9-59. Populating Albums with a Library Model

```
// example-011/library-routes.js

/**
 * GET /library/(id)
 * @param req
 * @param cb
 */
routes.GET['^\/library\/([a-z0-9]+)$'] = function (req, cb) {
  cb = httpd.asJSON(cb);
  var libraryID = req.params[0];
  Library.findById(libraryID)
    .populate('albums')
    .lean(true)
    .exec(function (err, library) {
      if (err) return cb(500, err);
      if (!library) return cb(404, {
        message: 'no library found for ID ' + libraryID
      });
      cb(200, library);
    });
}
```

Figure 9-1 shows a formatted version of the HTTP response. Each album in the `albums` collection has been fully dereferenced. Because `Query.lean()` was also called in the query chain, Mongoose converted the library *and* album data into plain JSON objects.

```
▾ {
    _id: "54ed249312c06b3726d3abcd",
    owner: "Nicholas Cloud",
    albums: ▾ [
        ▾ {
            _id: "54ed1dcb6fb525ba25529bd1",
            composer: "Kerry Muzzey",
            title: "Renaissance",
            price: 4.95,
            releaseDate: "2014-01-13T06:00:00.000Z",
            inPublication: true,
            tracks: ▸ [ {title: "The Looking Glass", _id: "54ed1dcb6fb525ba25529bd6", duration: {m:  3,…],
            genre: ▸ ["Classical", "Trailer Music", "Soundtrack"],
            __v: 0
        },
        ▸ {_id: "54ed1dcb6fb525ba25529bd7", composer: "Audiomachine", title: "Tree of Life",…},
        ▸ {_id: "54ed1dcb6fb525ba25529bf2", composer: "Jessica Curry", title: "Dear Esther",…}
    ],
    __v: 0
}
```

Figure 9-1. *Library population results*

Finding Documents with Query Operators

At this point the album and library routes consist of basic CRUD operations (create, read, update, and delete) that form the basis of many web APIs, but more could be done to make the API robust. MongoDB supports a number of helpful query operators that serve to filter data in specific ways.

The $lt and $gt Operators

The `$lt` and `$gt` operators can be used to find documents with values that are less than (`$lt`) or greater than (`$gt`) some value. The route in Listing 9-60 allows clients to search for albums that have been released on, before, or after a specific date that is passed to the route as a query parameter.

Listing 9-60. Finding Albums by Release Date

```
// example-011/album-routes.js

/**
 * GET /album/released/MM-DD-YYYY
 * GET /album/released/MM-DD-YYYY/before
 * GET /album/released/MM-DD-YYYY/after
 * @param req
 * @param cb
 */
routes.GET['^\/album\/released\/([\\d]{2}-[\\d]{2}-[\\d]{4})(?:\/
(before|after))?$'] = function (req, cb) {
  cb = httpd.asJSON(cb);
  var date = req.params[0];
  var when = req.params[1];

  var criteria = {releaseDate: {}};
  if (when === 'before') {
    criteria.releaseDate.$lt = new Date(date);
  } else if (when === 'after') {
    criteria.releaseDate.$gt = new Date(date);
  } else {
    when = null;
    criteria.releaseDate = new Date(date);
  }

  Album.find(criteria)
    .select('composer title releaseDate')
    .lean(true)
    .exec(function (err, albums) {
      if (err) return cb(500, err);
      if (albums.length === 0) {
        return cb(404, {
          message: 'no albums ' + (when || 'on') + ' release date ' + date
        });
      }
```

```
        cb(200, albums);
    });
};
```

To find albums released *on* a specific date, a normal criteria object is used to map the date value to the releaseDate property:

```
{releaseDate: new Date(...)}
```

If searching for albums before or after the date, however, the criteria object uses the $lt or $gt operator, respectively:

```
{releaseDate: {$lt: new Date(...)} }
```

```
// or
```

```
{releaseDate: {$gt: new Date(...)} }
```

To find albums that were released before, and up to, a specific date, the $lte ("less than or equal") operator could be used. Likewise, the $gte operator would find albums released from a specific date onward. To find all albums that were released on any date *but* the date provided, the $ne ("not equal") operator would filter accordingly. Its inverse, $eq, if used alone is functionally equivalent to setting the releaseDate value on the criteria object directly.

To keep the response small, the Query.select() method is invoked before the query is executed. This method limits the properties returned from each result object. In this case, the query selects only the composer, title, and releaseDate properties, all included in a space-separated string. All other properties are ignored.

Listing 9-61 shows the filtered JSON data returned for each kind of release date query.

Listing 9-61. Using curl to Find Albums by Release Date

```
example-011$ curl -X GET http://localhost:8080/album/released/01-01-2013
{"message":"no albums on release date 01-01-2013"}
```

```
example-011$ curl -X GET http://localhost:8080/album/released/01-01-2013/
before
[{"_id":"54ed1dcb6fb525ba25529bf2","composer":"Jessica Curry","title":"Dear
Esther","releaseDate":"2012-02-14T06:00:00.000Z"},{"_id":"54f3a4d
```

f056601726f867685","composer":"nervous_testpilot","title":"Frozen
Synapse","releaseDate":"2012-09-06T05:00:00.000Z"}]

example-011$ curl -X GET http://localhost:8080/album/released/01-01-2013/after
[{"_id":"54ed1dcb6fb525ba25529bd1","composer":"Kerry Muzzey","title
":"Renaissance","releaseDate":"2014-01-13T06:00:00.000Z"},{"_id":"5
4ed1dcb6fb525ba25529bd7","composer":"Audiomachine","title":"Tree of
Life","releaseDate":"2013-07-16T05:00:00.000Z"}]

Notice that even though the Query.select() filter did *not* specify the _id property
for inclusion, it is still present in each response. To omit this property, a negation needs
to be added to the select string. Prefixing the _id property with a minus sign will prevent
it from being selected:

```
Album.find(...)
  .select('-_id composer title releaseDate')
  // ...
```

Note   The _id property is the only property that may be specified for exclusion
when an inclusive select (one that specifies the properties to be fetched) is
performed. Otherwise, excluded and included properties *may not be mixed.* A query
is either selecting only specific properties or excluding only specific properties, but
not both. If any property in a Query.select() string is negated (except for _id),
all specified properties must be negated or an error will be raised.

The $in and $nin Operators

It is often helpful to select documents with property values that match some subset
of possibilities. The $in operator (and its inverse, $nin) tests a document property
value against each element in an array. The document fulfills the criteria if its property
matches at least one of the elements in the array. To find albums from two composers,
for example, the criteria object in Listing 9-62 might be used.

Listing 9-62. Using the $in Query Operator to Filter by Composer

```
{composer: {$in: ['Kerry Muzzey', 'Jessica Curry']}}
```

The $nin operator does the exact opposite: it will match only if the property value is *not* included in the specified set.

Both $in and $nin work for properties with scalar values (like strings, numbers, dates, etc.), but they can also be used to search within collections. The web route in Listing 9-63 accepts a music genre as a URL parameter and returns related genres in the HTTP response.

Listing 9-63. Using the $in Query Operator to Filter by Genre

```
// example-011/album-routes.js

/**
 * GET /album/genre/(genre)/related
 * @param req
 * @param cb
 */
routes.GET['^\/album\/genre\/([a-zA-Z]+)/related$'] = function (req, cb) {
  cb = httpd.asJSON(cb);
  var principalGenre = req.params[0];
  var criteria = {
    genre: {$in: [principalGenre]}
  };
  Album.find(criteria)
    .lean(true)
    .select('-_id genre')
    .exec(function (err, albums) {
      if (err) return cb(500, err);
      var relatedGenres = [];
      albums.forEach(function (album) {
        album.genre.forEach(function (albumGenre) {
          // don't include the principal genre
          if (albumGenre === principalGenre) return;
          // ensure duplicates are ignored
          if (relatedGenres.indexOf(albumGenre) < 0) {
```

```
            relatedGenres.push(albumGenre);
          }
        });
      });
      cb(200, {genre: principalGenre, related: relatedGenres});
    });
};
```

```
example-011$ curl -X GET http://localhost:8080/album/genre/Dance/related
{"genre":"Dance","related":["Electronica","Soundtrack"]}
```

To determine what constitutes a "related" genre, the criteria object selects albums that have the principal genre as an element in each document's genre array. It then compiles a list of all other genres that have been assigned to albums in the result set and returns that list to the client. Though Album.genre is an array, MongoDB knows to traverse it for values that match the elements in the $in operator. The Query.select() method excludes the _id property and includes only the genre property, since it alone contains the data in which this route is interested.

The $in operator is useful for finding elements in arrays of scalar values, but a different approach is needed when searching arrays of complex objects. Each subdocument in Album.tracks has its own properties and values, for example. To search for albums with tracks that meet some criteria, properties for tracks can be referenced with their full property paths, starting from the album itself. In Listing 9-64, albums will be fetched that possess any track with a title property that matches the value for tracks.title in the criteria object.

Listing 9-64. Using a Subdocument Path in a Criteria Object

```
// example-012/album-routes.js
/**
 * GET /album(?composer={string}&title={string}&track={string})
 * @param req
 * @param cb
 */
routes.GET['^\/album(?:\\?.+)?$'] = function (req, cb) {
  cb = httpd.asJSON(cb);
  var criteria = {};
```

```
// ...
if (req.query.track) {
  criteria['tracks.title'] = req.query.track;
}
// ...
Album.find(criteria)
  .lean(true)
  .exec(function (err, albums) {
    if (err) return cb(500, err);
    cb(200, albums);
  });
};
```

```
example-012$ curl -X GET http://localhost:8080/album?track=The%20Looking%20Glass
[{"_id":"54ed1dcb6fb525ba25529bd1","composer":"Kerry Muzzey","title":"Renai
ssance"... }
```

The $and and $or Operators

Simple criteria objects can query a property by using normal object notation. For example, to find an album that is in publication, the simple criteria object in Listing 9-65 would be sufficient.

Listing 9-65. Simple Criteria Object

```
Album.find({inPublication: true}, function (err, albums) {/*...*/});
```

This approach is insufficient for complicated, compound queries, however, such as the pseudo-query in Listing 9-66.

Listing 9-66. Painful Pseudo-Query

```
(select albums that
  (
    (are in publication and were released within the last two years) or
    (are categorized as classical and priced between $9 and $10)
  )
)
```

Fortunately, the $and and $or operators can be used to construct a criteria object that will produce the desired set of albums. Both operators accept an array of criteria objects that may contain simple queries or complex queries that *also* contain $and, $or, or any other valid query operators. The $and operator performs a logical AND operation using each criteria object in its array, selecting only documents that match *all* specified criteria. In contrast, the $or operator performs a logical OR operation, selecting documents that match *any* of its criteria.

In Listing 9-67, the album recommendations route composes a criteria object that uses *both* compound operators. Note that whereas the keys in simple criteria objects are property names, in compound criteria objects the keys are the compound operators followed by arrays of simple and/or complex criteria objects.

Listing 9-67. Using $and and $or to Find Album Recommendations

```
// example-012/album-routes.js
/**
 * GET /album/recommended
 * @param req
 * @param cb
 */
routes.GET['^\/album\/recommended$'] = function (req, cb) {
  cb = httpd.asJSON(cb);
  var nowMS = Date.now();
  var twoYearsMS = (365 * 24 * 60 * 60 * 1000 * 2);
  var twoYearsAgo = new Date(nowMS - twoYearsMS);

  var criteria = {
    $or: [
      // match all of these conditions...
      { $and: [{inPublication: true}, {releaseDate: {$gt: twoYearsAgo}}] },
      // OR
      // match all of these conditions...
      { $and: [{genre: {$in: ['Classical']}}, {price: {$gte: 5, $lte: 10}}] }
    ]
  };

  Album.find(criteria)
```

```
    .lean(true)
    .select('-_id -tracks')
    .exec(function (err, albums) {
      if (err) return cb(500, err);
      cb(200, albums);
    });
};
```

```
example-012$ curl -X GET http://localhost:8080/album/recommended
[{"composer":"Kerry Muzzey","title":"Renaissance","price":4.95... },
 {"composer":"Audiomachine","title":"Tree of Life","price":9.49... },
 {"composer":"Jessica Curry","title":"Dear Esther","price":6.99... }]
```

The $regex Operator

Often, searching for documents that match a precise text field query yields suboptimal results. Regular expressions can be used to broaden these searches so that documents are selected with fields that *resemble* a particular query parameter. In SQL-based languages, the like operator can be used for this purpose, but MongoDB favors regular expressions. The $regex operator adds a regular expression to a criteria object property, selecting documents that match the regular expression and excluding those that do not. It is often paired with the $options operator which may contain any valid regular expression flag such as i (case-insensitive). The route in Listing 9-68 accepts a query parameter, owner, which is converted to a regular expression and applied against the owner property of every library document.

Listing 9-68. Finding a Library with a Regular Expression

```
// example-012/library-routes.js
/**
 * GET /library?
 * @param req
 * @param cb
 */
routes.GET['^\/library(?:\\?.+)?$'] = function (req, cb) {
  cb = httpd.asJSON(cb);
  var criteria = {};
```

```
  if (req.query.owner) {
    criteria.owner = {
      $regex: '^.*' + req.query.owner + '.*$',
      $options: 'i'
    }
  } else {
    return cb(404, {message: 'please specify an owner'});
  }
  Library.find(criteria)
    .populate('albums')
    .exec(function (err, libraries) {
      if (err) return cb(500, err);
      cb(200, libraries);
    });
};
```

The criteria object specifies the property against which the regular expression will be applied and an object that includes both the expression (the $regex property) and any options to apply while matching (the $options property). In Listing 9-69 the curl command uses the owner cloud as a query string parameter. Since the regular expression in Listing 9-68 surrounds the query parameter with the regular expression wildcard .*, and since the regular expression options specify the case-insensitive option i, the route will return the only library in MongoDB, owned by Nicholas Cloud. Listing 9-69 shows the curl command and HTTP response output.

Listing 9-69. Finding a Library by Owner with cURL

```
curl -X GET http://localhost:8080/library?owner=cloud
[{"_id":"54ed249312c06b3726d3abcd","owner":"Nicholas Cloud"... ]
```

Advanced Query Operators

There are many more MongoDB operators that may be used in Mongoose queries, and while an in-depth analysis of each warrants many more pages, Table 9-3 provides a high-level overview of additional advanced query operators.

Table 9-3. *Additional Advanced Query Operators*

Operator	Description
$not, $nor	Negative logical operators that combine query clauses and select documents that match accordingly
$exists	Selects documents where the specified property exists (remember, MongoDB documents are technically schemaless)
$type	Selects documents where the specified property is of a given type
$mod	Selects documents where a modulo operator on a specified field returns a specified result (e.g., select all albums where the price is divisible evenly by 3.00)
$all	Selects documents with an array property that contains all specified elements
$size	Selects documents with an array property of a given size
$elemMatch	Selects documents where a subdocument in an array matches more than one condition

Summary

MongoDB is schemaless and extremely flexible by design, but application developers often add constraints on data in application code to enforce business rules, ensure data integrity, conform to existing application abstractions, or achieve any number of other goals. Mongoose recognizes and embraces this reality, and rests snugly between application code and the data store.

Mongoose schemas add constraints to otherwise free-form data. They define the shape and validity of the data to be stored, enforce constraints, create relationships between documents, and expose the document life cycle via middleware.

Models provide a full but extensible query interface. Criteria objects that conform to MongoDB query syntax are used to find specific data. Chainable query methods give developers control over the property selection, reference population, and whether full documents or plain JSON objects are retrieved. Custom static methods that encapsulate complicated criteria objects and more involved queries can be added to models to keep application concerns properly segregated.

Finally, Mongoose documents can be extended with custom instance methods that contain domain logic and custom getters and setters that aid in computed property manipulation.

CHAPTER 10

Knex and Bookshelf

The report of my death was an exaggeration.

—Samuel Langhorne Clemens (Mark Twain)

In this chapter, we will explore two libraries that work together to ease many of the difficulties that Node.js developers often encounter when working with relational databases. The first, Knex, provides a flexible and consistent interface for interacting with several well-known SQL platforms such as MySQL and PostgreSQL. The second, Bookshelf, builds on this foundation by providing developers with a powerful object-relational mapping (ORM) library that simplifies the process of modeling the entities that comprise an application's data structure, along with the various relationships that exist between them. Readers who are familiar with Backbone.js and its emphasis on structuring data within Models and Collections will quickly find themselves at home with Bookshelf, as the library follows many of the same patterns and provides many of the same APIs.

In this chapter, you will learn how to do the following:

- Create SQL queries with the Knex query builder

- Create complex database interactions without resorting to nested callback functions, with the help of promises

- Ensure the integrity of your application's data through the use of transactions

- Manage changes to your database's schema with the help of Knex migration scripts

- Bootstrap your database with sample data using Knex seed scripts

© Sufyan bin Uzayr, Nicholas Cloud, Tim Ambler 2019
S. bin Uzayr et al., *JavaScript Frameworks for Modern Web Development*,
https://doi.org/10.1007/978-1-4842-4995-6_10

- Define one-to-one, one-to-many, and many-to-many relationships between Bookshelf models

- Use eager loading to efficiently retrieve complex object graphs based on Bookshelf relationships

---

Note   Most of the examples in this chapter make heavy use of the promise-based and Underscore-inspired APIs that both Bookshelf and Knex provide.

Knex

Knex provides a database abstraction layer (DBAL) for MySQL, PostgreSQL, MariaDB, and SQLite3, a unified interface through which developers can interact with each of these Structured Query Language (SQL) databases without having to concern themselves with minor variations in syntax and response format that exist between each platform. Applications backed by such relational databases can benefit from a number of Knex features, including these:

- A promise-based interface that allows for cleaner control of asynchronous processes

- A stream interface for efficiently piping data through an application as needed

- Unified interfaces through which queries and schemas for each supported platform can be created

- Transaction support

In addition to the library itself, Knex also provides a command-line utility with which developers can do the following:

- Create, implement, and (when necessary) revert database migrations, scripted schema changes that can then be committed with an application's source code

- Create database "seed" scripts, a consistent method by which an application's database can be populated with sample data for local development and testing

Each of these subjects will be covered in more detail throughout this chapter.

Installing the Command-Line Utility

Before going any further, you should ensure that you have installed the command-line utility provided by Knex. Available as an npm package, the installation process is shown in Listing 10-1.

Listing 10-1. Installing the knex Command-Line Utility via npm

```
$ npm install -g knex
$ knex -version
Knex CLI version:  0.16.3
```

Adding Knex to Your Project

In addition to installing the knex command-line utility, you will also need to add the knex npm module as a local dependency within each project in which you intend to use it, along with a supported database library, as shown in Listing 10-2.

Listing 10-2. Installing Knex and a Supported Database Library As a Local Project Dependency via npm

```
$ npm install knex --save
# Supported database libraries include (be sure to --save):
$ npm install mysql
$ npm install mariasql
$ npm install pg
$ npm install sqlite3
$ npm install mysql2
$ npm install oracle
```

Note   SQLite implements a self-contained, serverless database within a single file on your disk and requires no additional tools. If you don't have access to a database server such as MySQL at the moment, the sqlite3 library will provide you with a quick and easy way to begin experimenting with Knex without requiring additional setup. *The examples referenced throughout this chapter will use this library.*

Configuring Knex

With your dependencies now in place, all that remains is to initialize Knex within your project. Listing 10-3 shows what that process looks like if you happen to be using MySQL, PostgreSQL, or MariaDB, while Listing 10-4 shows how to initialize Knex for use with SQLite3.

Listing 10-3. Initializing Knex for Use with MySQL, PostgreSQL, or MariaDB (Substitute `mysql` for `pg` or `mariasql` As Needed)

```
var knex = require('knex')({
    'client': 'mysql',
    'connection': {
        'host': '127.0.0.1',
        'user': 'user',
        'password': 'password',
        'database': 'database'
    },
    'debug': false // Set this to true to enable debugging for all queries
});
```

Listing 10-4. Initializing Knex for Use with SQLite3

```
// example-sqlite-starter/lib/db.js

var knex = require('knex')({
    'client': 'sqlite3',
    'connection': {
        'filename': 'db.sqlite'
    }
});
```

As you can see, the configuration settings required for SQLite3 are quite a bit simpler than those required for other, more full-featured solutions. Instead of providing connection settings, we simply provide the name of a file (`db.sqlite`) in which SQLite will store its data.

The SQL Query Builder

The primary focus of Knex is on providing developers with a unified interface through which they can interact with multiple, SQL-based databases without having to worry about minor variations in syntax and response format that exist between each of them. To that end, Knex provides a number of methods, most of which fall into one of two categories: query builder methods and interface methods.

Query Builder Methods

Query builder methods are those that aid developers in the creation of SQL queries. Examples of such methods include `select()`, `from()`, `where()`, `limit()`, and `groupBy()`. At last count, Knex provides more than 40 such methods, with which platform-agnostic queries can be created. Listing 10-5 shows a simple SQL query, along with an example demonstrating how such a query can be created using Knex.

Listing 10-5. Example Demonstrating the Creation of a Simple SQL Query Using Knex

```
// example-sqlite-starter/example1.js
// SELECT id, name, postal_code FROM cities;knex.select('id', 'name',
'postal_code').from('cities');
```

While the example shown in Listing 10-5 demonstrates the basic method by which SQL queries can be created with Knex, it does little to convey the true value of the library. That value should start to become more apparent as we take a look at the various interface methods that Knex provides. It is with these methods that we can begin to submit our queries and process their resulting data.

Interface Methods

Knex provides a number of interface methods that allow us to submit and process our queries in several convenient ways. In this section, we'll take a look at two of the most useful approaches that are available to us.

Promises

The event-driven nature of JavaScript makes it well suited for efficiently handling complex, asynchronous tasks. Traditionally, JavaScript developers have managed asynchronous control flow through the use of callback functions, as shown in Listing 10-6.

Listing 10-6. Simple Callback Function

```
var request = require('request');
request({
    'url': 'http://mysite.com',
    'method': 'GET'
}, function(err, response) {
    if (err) throw new Error(err);
    console.log(response);
});
```

Callback functions allow us to defer the execution of a particular sequence of code until the appropriate time. Such functions are easy to understand and implement. Unfortunately, they are also very difficult to manage as applications grow in complexity. Imagine a scenario in which additional asynchronous processes must run after the initial response is received in Listing 10-6. To do so would require the use of additional, nested callback functions. As additional asynchronous steps are added to this code, we begin to experience what many developers refer to as "callback hell" or the "pyramid of doom," terms that describe the unmaintainable mass of spaghetti code that frequently results from such an approach.

Fortunately, JavaScript promises provide developers with a convenient solution to this problem—a solution that Knex makes extensive use of through its promise-based interface for submitting and processing queries. Listing 10-7 shows this API in action.

Listing 10-7. Demonstration of the Promise-Based API Provided by Knex

```
// example-sqlite-starter/example2.js

knex.pluck('id').from('cities').where('state_id', '=', 1)
    .then(function(cityIds) {
        return knex.select('id', 'first_name', 'last_name').from('users')
        .whereIn('city_id', cityIds);
    })
```

```
        .then(function(users) {
            return [
                users,
                knex.select('*').from('bookmarks').whereIn('user_id',
                _.pluck(users, 'id'))
            ];
        })
        .spread(function(users, bookmarks) {
            _.each(users, function(user) {
                user.bookmarks = _.filter(bookmarks, function(bookmark) {
                    return bookmark.user_id = user.id;
                });
            });
        console.log(JSON.stringify(users, null, 4));
        })
        .catch(function(err) {
            console.log(err);
        });
```

In this example, three queries are submitted in succession:

1. Cities within a particular state are selected.

2. Users who live within the returned cities are selected.

3. Bookmarks for each of the returned users are selected.

After our final query has returned, we then attach each bookmark to the appropriate user and display the result, which you can see in Listing 10-8.

Listing 10-8. Data Logged to the Console As a Result of the Code in Listing 10-7

```
[
    {
        "id": 1,
        "first_name": "Steve",
        "last_name": "Taylor",
        "bookmarks": [
            {
```

```
            "id": 1,
            "url": "http://reddit.com",
            "label": "Reddit",
            "user_id": 1,
            "created_at": "2015-03-12 12:09:35"
        },
        {
            "id": 2,
            "url": "http://www.theverge.com",
            "label": "The Verge",
            "user_id": 1,
            "created_at": "2015-03-12 12:09:35"
        }
    ]
  }
]
```

Thanks to the promise-based interface provided by Knex, at no point does our
code ever reach beyond one level of indentation, thereby ensuring that our application
remains easy to follow. More importantly, should an error occur at any point during this
process, it would be conveniently caught and handled by our final `catch` statement.

Note   JavaScript promises are a powerful tool for writing complex, asynchronous
code in a manner that is easy to follow and maintain.

Streams

One of the biggest benefits to writing applications with Node.js is the platform's ability
to execute I/O-intensive procedures in a very efficient manner. Unlike synchronous
languages such as PHP, Python, or Ruby, Node.js is capable of handling thousands
of simultaneous connections within a single thread, allowing developers to write
applications capable of meeting enormous demands, while using minimal resources.
Node.js provides several important tools for accomplishing this feat, one of the most
important of which is streams.

Before we take a look at streams, let's examine another example of a traditional JavaScript callback function, as shown in Listing 10-9.

Listing 10-9. JavaScript Callback Function That Accepts the Contents of a Loaded File

```
var fs = require('fs');
fs.readFile('data.txt', 'utf8', function(err, data) {
    if (err) throw new Error(err);
    console.log(data);
});
```

In this example, we use the `readFile()` method of the native `fs` library available within Node.js to read the contents of a file. Once that data is loaded into memory (in its entirety), it is then passed to our callback function for further processing. This approach is simple and easily understood. However, it's not very efficient, as our application must first load the entire contents of the file into memory before passing it back to us. This isn't a terrible problem for smaller files, but larger files may begin to cause issues, depending on the resources available to the server that happens to be running this application.

Node.js streams resolve this issue by piping data through one or more functions in multiple, smaller chunks. By doing so, streams allow developers to avoid dedicating large portions of a server's available resources for any single request. The example shown in Listing 10-10 accomplishes the same goal of our previous example, without loading the contents of the entire file into memory all at once.

Listing 10-10. Pair of Node.js Streams Working Together to Efficiently Load and Display the Contents of a File

```
// example-read-file-stream/index.js

var fs = require('fs');
var Writable = require('stream').Writable;
var stream = fs.createReadStream('data.txt');
var out = Writable();
```

```
out._write = function(chunk, enc, next) {
    console.log(chunk.toString());
    next();
};
stream.pipe(out);
```

Streams are a relatively underutilized feature of Node.js, which is unfortunate, as they happen to be one of the more powerful aspects of the platform. Fortunately, Knex provides a streaming interface for consuming query results that allows us to take advantage of these benefits, as shown in Listing 10-11.

Listing 10-11. Processing the Results of a Query via the Streaming Interface Provided by Knex

```
var Writable = require('stream').Writable;
var ws = Writable();
ws._write = function(chunk, enc, next) {
    console.dir(chunk);
    next();
};
var stream = knex.select('*').from('users').stream();
stream.pipe(ws);
```

In this example, the results of our query on the users table (which could be quite large for some applications) are streamed in smaller chunks to our writable stream, instead of being passed along in their entirety. This approach can also be paired with the library's promise interface to create a more robust implementation, as shown in Listing 10-12.

Listing 10-12. Combining the Streaming and Promise-Based Interfaces Provided by Knex for Better Error Handling

```
var Writable = require('stream').Writable;
var ws = Writable();
ws._write = function(chunk, enc, next) {
    console.dir(chunk);
    next();
};
```

```
knex.select('*').from('users').stream(function(stream) {
    stream.pipe(ws);
}).then(function() {
    console.log('Done.');
}).catch(function(err) {
    console.log(err);
});
```

In this example, we combine the power of the streaming and promise-based interfaces provided by Knex. When a callback function is passed to the library's `stream()` method, that callback function receives the generated promise as opposed to being returned directly. Instead, a promise is returned, which is resolved once the stream is complete.

Note   The streaming interface provided by Knex is compatible with MySQL, PostgreSQL, and MariaDB databases.

Transactions

One of the biggest benefits to using ACID-compliant, relational databases lies in their ability to group multiple queries into a single unit of work (i.e., a "transaction") that will either succeed or fail as a whole. In other words, should a single query within the transaction fail, any changes that may have occurred as a result of previously run queries within the transaction would be reverted.

By way of an example, consider a financial transaction that occurs at your bank. Suppose you wanted to send $25 to your cousin on her birthday. Those funds would first have to be withdrawn from your account and then inserted into your cousin's account. Imagine a scenario in which the application enabling that exchange of funds were to crash for any number of reasons (e.g., a faulty line of code or a larger system failure) after those funds were removed from your account, but before they were inserted into your cousin's account. Without the safety net provided by transactions, those funds would have essentially vanished into thin air. Transactions allow developers to ensure that such processes only ever happen in full—never leaving data in an inconsistent state.

Note   The acronym ACID (Atomicity, Consistency, Isolation, Durability) refers to a set of properties that describe database transactions. Atomicity refers to the fact that such transactions can either succeed in their entirety or fail as a whole. Such transactions are said to be "atomic".

Previous examples within this chapter have demonstrated the process of creating and submitting database queries with Knex. Before we continue, let's review another example that does not take advantage of transactions. Afterward, we'll update this example to take advantage of the peace of mind that transactions provide.

In the example shown in Listing 10-13, a moveFunds() function is declared that, when called, uses the knex object to move the specified amount of funds from one account to another. This function returns a promise that is either resolved or rejected once this process completes, depending on the success or failure of the call. A glaring error exists here—can you spot it?

Listing 10-13. moveFunds() Function Demonstrating the Process of Moving Funds from One Account to Another Without the Security of Transactions

```
// example-financial/bad.js

/**
 * Moves the specified amount of funds from sourceAccountID to destAccountID
 */
var moveFunds = function(sourceAccountID, destAccountID, amount) {

    return knex.select('funds').from('accounts')
        .where('id', sourceAccountID)
        .first(function(result) {
            if (!result) {
                throw new Error('Unable to locate funds for source account');
            }
            if (result.funds < amount) {
                throw new Error('Not enough funds are available in account');
            }
            return knex('accounts').where('id', sourceAccountID).update({
                'funds': result.funds - amount
```

```
        });
    }).then(function() {
        return knex.select('funds').from('accounts')
            .where('id', destAccountID);
    }).first(function(result) {
        if (!result) {
            throw new Error('Unable to locate funds for destination
            account');
        }
        return knex('accounts').where('id', destAccountID).update({
            'funds': result.funds + amount
        });
    });
};


/* Move $25 from account 1 to account 2. */
moveFunds(1, 2, 25).then(function(result) {
    console.log('Transaction succeeded.', result);
}).catch(function(err) {
    console.log('Transaction failed!', err);
});
```

In this example, the following steps are required to accomplish the goal of moving funds from a source account to a destination account:

1. The total funds currently available within the source account are determined.

2. If insufficient funds are available to complete the process, an error is thrown.

3. The funds to be transferred are deducted from the source account.

4. The total funds currently available within the destination account are determined.

5. If the destination account cannot be found, an error is thrown.

6. The funds to be transferred are added to the destination account.

If you haven't spotted the mistake already, a glaring problem presents itself at step 5. In the event that the destination account cannot be found, an error is thrown, but at this point the funds to be moved have already been deducted from the source account! We could attempt to solve this problem in a number of ways. We could catch the error within our code and then credit the funds back to the source account, but this would still not account for unforeseen errors that could arise due to network problems or in the event that our application server were to lose power and completely crash in the middle of this process.

It is at this point that the power of database transactions starts to become evident. In Listing 10-14, our moveFunds() function is refactored to wrap this entire procedure into a single, "atomic" transaction that will either succeed or fail as a whole. Note the creation of the trx object, from which our transaction-aware queries are built.

Listing 10-14. Transaction-Aware Implementation of Listing 10-13

```
// example-financial/index.js

/**
 * Moves the specified amount of funds from sourceAccountID to destAccountID
 */
var moveFunds = function(sourceAccountID, destAccountID, amount) {

    return knex.transaction(function(trx) {

        return trx.first('funds')
            .from('accounts')
            .where('id', sourceAccountID)
            .then(function(result) {
                if (!result) {
                    throw new Error('Unable to locate funds for source
                    account');
                }
                if (result.funds < amount) {
                    throw new Error('Not enough funds are available in
                    account');
                }
                return trx('accounts').where('id', sourceAccountID)
                    .update({
```

```
                    'funds': result.funds - amount
                });
            })
            .then(function() {
                return trx.first('funds')
                    .from('accounts')
                    .where('id', destAccountID);
            })
            .then(function(result) {
                if (!result) {
                    throw new Error('Unable to locate funds for destination
                    account');
                }
                return trx('accounts').where('id', destAccountID)
                    .update({
                        'funds': result.funds + amount
                    });
            });
    });
};

/* Move $25 from account 1 to account 2. */
displayAccounts()
    .then(function() {
        return moveFunds(1, 2, 25);
    }).then(function() {
        console.log('Transaction succeeded.');
    }).catch(function(err) {
        console.log('Transaction failed!', err);
    });
```

As you can see, the transaction-aware example shown in Listing 10-14 largely resembles that shown in Listing 10-13, but it does differ in one important way. Instead of creating our query by calling builder methods directly on the knex object, we first initiate a transaction by calling knex.transaction(). The callback function that we provide is then passed a "transaction-aware" stand-in (trx) from which we then begin to create our series of queries. From this point forward, any queries that we create from the trx object will either succeed or fail as a whole. The knex.transaction() method returns a promise that will be resolved or rejected once the transaction as a whole is complete, allowing us to easily integrate this transaction into an even larger series of promise-based actions.

Migration Scripts

Just as an application's source code is destined to change over time, so too is the structure of the information that it stores. As such changes are made, it is important that they be implemented in a way that can be repeated, shared, rolled back when necessary, and tracked over time. Database migration scripts provide developers with a convenient pattern for accomplishing this goal.

A Knex migration script is composed of two functions, up and down, as shown in Listing 10-15. The script's up function is responsible for modifying a database's structure in some desired way (e.g., creating a table, adding a column), while its down function is responsible for restoring the database's structure to its previous state.

Listing 10-15. Knex Migration Script with up Function Creating a New Table and down Function Dropping the Table

```
// example-sqlite-starter/migrations/20150311082640_states.js

exports.up = function(knex, Promise) {
    return knex.schema.createTable('states', function(table) {
        table.increments().unsigned().primary().notNullable();
        table.string('name').notNullable();
        table.timestamp('created_at').defaultTo(knex.fn.now()).
        notNullable();
    });
};

exports.down = function(knex, Promise) {
    return knex.schema.dropTable('states');
};
```

Configuring Your Project for Migrations

The Knex command-line utility provides developers with simple tools for creating and managing migration scripts. To get started, you'll first need to create a special configuration file by running the following command within the root folder of your project:

```
$ knex init
```

After running this command, a file (knexfile.js) will be created with contents similar to those shown in Listing 10-16. You should alter the contents of this file as needed. Whenever a Knex migration script is run, Knex will determine its connection settings based on the contents of this file and the value of the NODE_ENVIRONMENT environment variable.

Note   On OS X and Linux, environment variables are set from the terminal by running export ENVIRONMENT_VARIABLE=value. The command to be used within the Windows command line is set ENVIRONMENT_VARIABLE=value.

Listing 10-16. knexfile.js

```
// example-sqlite-starter/knexfile.js

module.exports = {

    'development': {
        'client': 'sqlite3',
            'connection': {
                'filename': './db.sqlite'
        }
        },
        'seeds': {
            'directory': './seeds'
        }
    },
```

```
    'staging': {
        'client': 'postgresql',
            'connection': {
                'database': 'my_db',
            'user': 'username',
            'password': 'password'
        },
        'pool': {
            'min': 2,
            'max': 10
            }
        }
    }
};
```

Creating Your First Migration

With our Knex configuration file now in place, we can move forward with the creation of our first migration script. The command for doing so is shown here:

```
$ knex migrate:make users_table
```

When creating your own migrations, substitute the users_table portion of the command with a term that describes the change your migration implements. After running this command, Knex will create a migration script for you that resembles the one shown in Listing 10-17.

Listing 10-17. New Knex Migration Script

```
exports.up = function(knex, Promise) {
};

exports.down = function(knex, Promise) {
};
```

After creating your first migration script, your project's file structure should resemble that shown in Listing 10-18.

Listing 10-18. Excerpt of Project's File Structure After Creating First Migration

```
.
├── knexfile.js
└── migrations
    └── 20141203074309_users_table.js
```

Note   Knex migration scripts are stored in a `migrations` folder at the root level of a project. If this directory does not exist, Knex will create it for you. Knex automatically prepends a timestamp to the file name of migration scripts, as shown in Listing 10-18. This ensures that a project's migrations are always sorted by the order in which they were created.

It is now up to us to modify the up and down functions within our newly created migration script. Let's take a look at two alternative approaches.

Defining Schema Updates with Schema Builder Methods

In addition to providing methods for constructing queries, Knex also provides methods for defining a database's underlying structure (schema). With the help of these "schema builder" methods, developers can create platform-agnostic blueprints that describe the various tables, columns, indexes, and relationships that make up a database. These blueprints can then be applied to any supported platform to generate the desired database. The migration script shown in Listing 10-15 shows the Knex schema builder in action, while Listing 10-19 shows the query generated by the script's up method.

Listing 10-19. SQL Query Generated Through the Use of Schema Builder Methods, As Shown in Listing 10-15

```
// example-raw-migration/migrations/20150312083058_states.js

CREATE TABLE states (
  id integer PRIMARY KEY AUTOINCREMENT NOT NULL,
  name varchar(255) NOT NULL,
  created_at datetime NOT NULL DEFAULT(CURRENT_TIMESTAMP)
);
```

CHAPTER 10   KNEX AND BOOKSHELF

Schema builder methods are useful, in that they allow developers to easily define schemas in a way that can be applied to each of the platforms supported by Knex. They also require a minimal amount of knowledge regarding raw SQL queries, making it possible for developers with little experience working directly with SQL databases to get up and running quickly. That said, schema builder methods are also limiting. To provide a generic interface for defining database schemas that work across multiple platforms, Knex must make certain decisions for you—a fact that you may not be comfortable with. Developers with more experience working directly with SQL databases may wish to bypass the schema builder methods entirely, opting instead to craft their own SQL queries. This is easily accomplished, as we are about to see.

Defining Schema Updates with Raw SQL Queries

In Listing 10-20, we see a Knex migration script that creates a new users table through the use of raw SQL queries. This is accomplished through the use of the knex.schema. raw() method. When called, this method returns a promise that will be either resolved or rejected, depending on the success or failure of the query that it receives.

Listing 10-20. Knex Migration Script Defined with Raw SQL Queries

```
// example-raw-migration/migrations/20150312083058_states.js

var multiline = require('multiline');

exports.up = function(knex, Promise) {

    var sql = multiline.stripIndent(function() {/*
        CREATE TABLE states (
            id integer PRIMARY KEY AUTOINCREMENT NOT NULL,
            name varchar(255) NOT NULL,
            created_at datetime NOT NULL DEFAULT(CURRENT_TIMESTAMP)
        );
    */});
    return knex.schema.raw(sql);

};
```

```
exports.down = function(knex, Promise) {
    return knex.schema.raw('DROP TABLE states;');
};
```

Note   The example shown in Listing 10-20 makes use of an additional library that is unrelated to Knex: `multiline`. The `multiline` library is quite useful because it allows us to define large chunks of text that span multiple lines without requiring that each line end with a continuation character.

Running Knex Migrations

With our newly created migration script now defined and ready for use, our only remaining task is to run the migration, bringing our database up to date with our desired changes. The command for doing so is shown here:

```
$ knex migrate:latest
```

This command will instruct Knex to run all available migration scripts that have not yet been run, in the order in which they were created. Once complete, our database will have been brought fully up to date with our desired changes. If you're curious as to how Knex keeps track of which migrations have and have not been run, the answer lies in the `knex_migrations` table that Knex automatically creates for itself (see Figure 10-1). Within this table, Knex maintains a running list of which migrations have been implemented. The name of this table can be changed by modifying the configuration file we created via the `knex init` command.

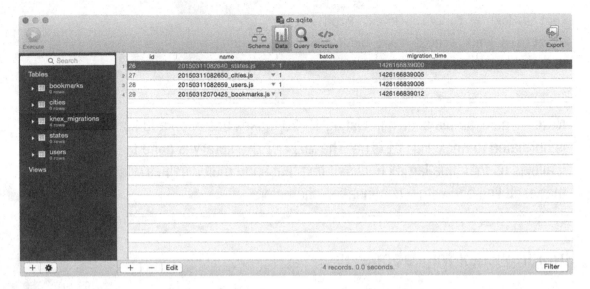

Figure 10-1. *The* `knex_migrations` *table used by Knex to track which migration scripts have already been applied to your database*

Reverting Knex Migrations

The act of running Knex migration scripts is not a one-way street. They can also be undone, which is particularly important during development. The command for doing so is as follows:

```
$ knex migrate:rollback
```

This command will instruct Knex to revert all migration scripts that were run as a result of the most recent execution of `knex migrate:latest`. To verify the status of your database in regard to your migration scripts, you can run the following command to determine your database's current migration version:

```
$ knex migrate:currentVersion
```

Seed Scripts

In the previous section, you learned how Knex migration scripts can empower you to script changes to a database's structure—scripts that can be shared with others, reverted when necessary, and tracked within version control. Knex seed scripts serve a similar purpose, but with a focus on data rather than structure. Seed scripts provide a consistent way in which to specify how a newly created database can be filled with sample data, to get a new development environment up and running. Listing 10-21 shows the contents of a seed script included with one of this chapter's example projects.

Listing 10-21. Simple Knex Seed Script That Removes All Existing Records from the states Table and Inserts Two New Ones

```
// example-sqlite-starter/seeds/01-states.js

exports.seed = function(knex, Promise) {

    return Promise.join(
        knex('states').del(),
        knex('states').insert([
            {
                'id': 1,
                'name': 'Georgia'
            },
            {
                'id': 2,
                'name': 'Tennessee'
            }
        ]);
    );
};
```

Creating Seed Scripts

You can instruct Knex to create a new seed script using the following command:

```
$ knex seed:make users
```

By default, Knex saves newly created seed scripts to the seeds folder at the root path of your project. You can customize this folder by modifying the contents of your project's knexfile.js configuration file (see Listing 10-16).

Running Seed Scripts

After creating seed scripts for your application, you can populate your database with them by running this command:

```
$ knex seed:run
```

Note   Seed scripts are always run in alphabetical order. If the order in which your seeds are run is important, take care to name them appropriately to ensure they run in the desired order.

Bookshelf

Bookshelf builds on the foundation laid by Knex to provide a flexible ORM library that simplifies the process of creating classes ("models") to represent the various objects that make up an application. This section explores the various ways in which developers can use Bookshelf to accomplish the following:

- Create classes ("models") to represent the various tables used within an application's database

- Extend models with custom behavior unique to the needs of their application

- Define complex relationships between models (one-to-one, one-to-many, many-to-many)

- Easily navigate through the various relationships that exist between models without resorting to complex SQL queries, with the help of "eager loading"

Developers who are familiar with Backbone will quickly find themselves at home with Bookshelf, as it follows many of the same patterns and implements many of the same APIs. You could easily describe Bookshelf as "Backbone for the server," and you wouldn't be far off base.

What Is Object-Relational Mapping?

Relational databases store information as a series of rows within one or more tables, each table having one or more columns that describe the various attributes of the records they contain—just as you might go about structuring information within a spreadsheet. In most applications, separate tables are created to represent each type of available entity (e.g., "Account," "User," "Comment"). The various relationships that exist between each of these entities are then defined through the use of "foreign key" columns, as shown in Figure 10-2.

accounts

id	name	created_at	updated_at
Integer	String	Timestamp	Timestamp

users

id	account_id	first_name	last_name	email	created_at	updated_at
Integer	Integer	String	String	String	Timestamp	Timestamp

Figure 10-2. *Here, the relationship between users and accounts (an account has one or more users, users belong to accounts) is described via the* account_id *foreign key column within the* users *table*

This approach to storing information is powerful and serves as the predominant method by which applications store data, for many good reasons (all of which extend well beyond the scope of this book). Unfortunately, this approach is also at odds with the object-oriented approach with which most applications tend to view data.

Object-relational mapping (ORM) tools such as Bookshelf allow developers to interact with the flat tables of information stored within relational databases as a series of interconnected objects, with which they can interact and navigate through to achieve some desired goal. In effect, ORM libraries provide developers with a "virtual object database" that allows them to more easily interact with the flat records contained within relational database tables.

Creating Your First Bookshelf Model

A Bookshelf model can be thought of as a class that, when instantiated, represents a record within a database. In their simplest form, Bookshelf models serve as data containers, providing built-in functionality for getting and setting attribute (i.e., column) values and for creating, updating, and destroying records. As we'll soon see, however, Bookshelf models become much more useful when we extend them with our own custom methods and define the relationships that exist between them.

Bookshelf models are defined via the `bookshelf.Model.extend()` method, as shown in Listing 10-22. In this simple example, a `User` model is defined whose records will be persisted to our database's `users` table.

Listing 10-22. Simple Bookshelf Model That Represents an Application's Users

```
// example-bookshelf1/lib/user.js

var knex = require('./db');
var bookshelf = require('bookshelf')(knex);

var User = bookshelf.Model.extend({
    'tableName': 'users',
    'idAttribute': 'id' // The primary key for our table. Defaults to: 'id'
});

module.exports = User;
```

Creating New Instances

In Listing 10-23, a new instance of the `User` model is created, modified, and then saved to the database.

Listing 10-23. Saving a New Instance of `User` to the Database

```
// example-bookshelf1/create.js

var User = require('./lib/user');
var user = new User();

user.set({
    'first_name': 'Steve',
```

```
    'last_name': 'Taylor',
    'email': 'steve.taylor@mydomain.com'
});

// Individual attributes can also be set as shown below
// user.set('first_name', 'Steve');

user.save().then(function(user) {
    // user has been saved
    console.log('User saved', user.toJSON());
    /*
    {
      first_name: 'Steve',
      last_name: 'Taylor',
      email: 'steve.taylor@mydomain.com',
      id: 1
    }
    */
});
```

Bookshelf provides a convenient `forge()` method that allows us to simplify this example just a bit, as shown in Listing 10-24. This method does nothing more than create and return a new instance of `User` behind the scenes for us, allowing us to forego the use of the new keyword.

Listing 10-24. Creating a New Instance of the `User` Model via the `forge()` Method

```
// example-bookshelf1/forge.js

User.forge({
    'id': 1,
    'first_name': 'John'
}).fetch().then(function(user) {

    /* An object containing every attribute / value for
    this model can be retrieved via the 'toJSON' method. */
    console.log(user.toJSON());
});
```

Fetching Instances

Instances of the User model can be retrieved in a similar manner. In Listing 10-25, a new instance of User is created with a value of 1 for its id attribute. When fetch() is called, Bookshelf will use any attributes set on the model to build the query used to fetch the desired record. In this example, the query used will be

```
SELECT * FROM users WHERE 'id' = 1;
```

Listing 10-25. Retrieving an Instance of the User Model from the Database

```
// example-bookshelf1/fetch.js

User.where({
    'id': 1
}).fetch().then(function(user) {
    // Individual attributes get be retrieved with the get method
    // console.log('first_name', user.get('first_name'));
    console.log(user.toJSON());
});
```

Destroying Instances

Just as model instances can be saved, they can also be deleted via the destroy() method, as shown in Listing 10-26.

Listing 10-26. Deleting an Instance of the User Model

```
// example-bookshelf1/destroy.js

User.where({
    'id': 1
}).fetch().then(function(user) {
    return user.destroy();
}).then(function() {
    console.log('User destroyed.');
});
```

In this example, destroy is called as an instance method on user. We could, however, instruct Bookshelf to simply seek out and destroy the record without first fetching the instance ourselves, as shown in Listing 10-27.

Listing 10-27. Instructing Bookshelf to Destroy the Specified Record

```
User.where({
    'id': 1
}).destroy().then(function() {
    console.log('User destroyed.');
});
```

Fetching Multiple Models (Collections)

In addition to retrieving a single instance of our model via the fetch() method, we can also retrieve multiple instances via the fetchAll() method, as shown in Listing 10-28.

Listing 10-28. Fetching All Instances of User with a Value of John for first_name

```
// example-bookshelf1/fetch-collection.js

User.where({
    'last_name': 'Doe'
}).fetchAll().then(function(users) {
    console.log(JSON.stringify(users.toJSON(), null, 4));
    /*
    [{
        "id": 3,
        "first_name": "John",
        "last_name": "Doe",
        "email": "john.doe@mydomain.com"
    },
    {
        "id": 4,
        "first_name": "Jane",
```

```
        "last_name": "Doe",
        "email": "jane.doe@mydomain.com"
    }]
    */
});
```

In this example, our call to `fetchAll()` returns a promise that resolves to a collection of multiple users. This collection provides a number of built-in methods specifically designed for interacting with multiple models. Given Bookshelf's strong focus on following Backbone patterns, most of the same methods available within Backbone collections are also available here. Listing 10-29 demonstrates a few common use cases.

Listing 10-29. Commonly Used Bookshelf Collection Methods

```
/* Iterate through a collection */
users.each(function(user, index) {
    console.log(user, index);
});

/* Create an array composed of models matching more specific criteria */
users = users.filter(function(user, index) {
    if (user.get('last_name') === 'Smith') return true;
});

/* A simpler method for filtering models, when a function call is not
   needed */
users = users.where({
    'last_name': 'Smith'
});

/* Return the first entry matching the specified criteria */
var johnSmith = users.find(function(user) {
    if (user.get('last_name') === 'Smith') return true;
});

/* Returns an array containing the first name of every user */
var firstNames = users.pluck('first_name');
```

Extending with Custom Behavior

In their simplest state, Bookshelf models do little more than serve as containers for records within a database, providing built-in methods for reading and writing attribute values and performing save or destroy operations. While this is useful, Bookshelf models begin to reach their full potential only when we begin to extend them with their own unique behavior as befitting the needs of our application.

An example of such behavior is demonstrated in Listing 10-30. Here, we update the User model seen in previous examples to include a sendEmail() method. Doing so allows us to abstract away the complexity involved with sending e-mail to registered users of our application.

Listing 10-30. Extending the User Model with a Method for Sending Outbound E-mails from Our Application

```
var Promise = require('bluebird');
var Handlebars = require('handlebars');

var User = bookshelf.Model.extend({
    'tableName': 'users',
    /**
     * Sends an e-mail to the user. Requires an `options` object
     * with values for `subject` and `message`. These values will be
     * compiled as Handlebars templates, passed this user's attributes,
     * and the result(s) will be used to generate the outgoing message.
     */
    'sendEmail': function(options) {
        var self = this;
        return Promise.resolve().then(function() {
                var subject = Handlebars.compile(options.subject)(self.
                toJSON());
                var message = Handlebars.compile(options.message)(self.
                toJSON());
            // Use your e-mail library of choice here, along with the
            // appropriate connection settings.      });
    }
});
```

```
User.where({
    'id': 1
}).fetch().then(function(user) {
    return user.sendEmail({
        'subject': 'Welcome, {{first_name}}',
        'message': 'We are happy to have you on board, {{first_name}}
        {{last_name}}.'
    });
});
```

In addition to those methods inherited from Backbone, Bookshelf collections also provide several methods of their own. Listing 10-31 demonstrates the use of the invokeThen() method, allowing us to easily invoke methods on each of the models contained within the collection.

Listing 10-31. Invoking an Imagined sendEmail() Method on Each Model Contained Within a Collection

```
// example-bookshelf1/invoke-then.js

User.where({
    'last_name': 'Doe'
}).fetchAll().then(function(users) {
    return users.invokeThen('sendEmail', {
        'subject': 'Congratulations on having such a great name, {{first_
        name}}.',
        'message': '{{first_name}} really is a great name. Seriously - way
        to go.'
    });
}).then(function(users) {
    console.log('%s users were complimented on their name.', users.length);
});
```

The invokeThen() method demonstrated in this example returns a promise of its own, which will be resolved only after all the calls to sendEmail() on our collection's models have themselves been resolved. This pattern also provides us with a convenient method for interacting with multiple models simultaneously.

Performing Validation

Those familiar with Backbone will find Bookshelf's event system quite familiar. In regard to validation, of particular interest are the saving and destroying events emitted by Bookshelf. By tapping into these events, Bookshelf models can be customized with unique behavior to either allow or deny these actions, based on some desired criteria. Listing 10-32 shows an example in which users with an e-mail address containing the string "hotmail.com" are prevented from being saved to the database.

Listing 10-32. Demonstration of Bookshelf's Event System, Which Allows for Implementation of Custom Validation Rules

```
// example-bookshelf1/lib/user.js

var User = bookshelf.Model.extend({
    'tableName': 'users',
    'initialize': function() {
        this.on('saving', this._validateSave);
    },
    '_validateSave': function() {
        var self = this;
        return Promise.resolve().then(function() {
            if (self.get('email').indexOf('hotmail.com') >= 0) {
                throw new Error('Hotmail email addresses are not allowed.');
            }
        });
    }
});
```

To prevent calls to save or destroy from succeeding, simply tap into the model's saving or destroying events, passing a reference to your own custom validation functions. If an error is thrown, the call will be prevented. Asynchronous validation is also possible through the use of promises. In Listing 10-33, a custom validation function returns a promise that is ultimately rejected.

Listing 10-33. Custom Validation Function That Returns a Promise

```
// example-bookshelf1/validation.js

User.forge({
    'first_name': 'Jane',
    'last_name': 'Doe',
    'email': 'jane.doe@hotmail.com'
}).save().then(function() {
    console.log('Saved.');
}).catch(function(err) {
    /* Our call to `save` will result in an error, due to this user's
    hotmail.com e-mail address. */
    console.log(err);
});
```

Customizing the Export Process

Previous examples have shown the use of the toJSON() method, which (by default) returns an object containing every available attribute/value for the model on which it is called (or for every available model, if called on a collection). Should you wish to customize the data returned by this method, you can do so by overriding the toJSON() method, as shown in Listing 10-34.

Listing 10-34. Customizing the Data Returned by Our Model's toJSON() Method

```
var User = bookshelf.Model.extend({
    'tableName': 'users',
    'toJSON': function() {
        var data = bookshelf.Model.prototype.toJSON.call(this);
        data.middle_name = 'Danger';
      return data;
    }
});
```

Within this example's overridden toJSON() method, we first call the prototype's toJSON() method, giving us the data that this method would have originally returned, had it not been overwritten. We then strip out the data we wish to hide, add some additional information of our own, and return it.

A common scenario in which this pattern is often seen involves the use of a User model, within which sensitive password information is held. Modifying the model's toJSON() method to automatically strip out such information, as shown in Listing 10-34, helps to prevent this information from unintentionally leaking out over an API request.

Defining Class Properties

Bookshelf's extend() method, which we've seen in previous examples, accepts two parameters:

- An object of instance properties to be inherited by created instances of the model

- An object of class properties to be assigned directly to the model

Previous examples within this chapter have demonstrated the process of assigning instance properties via extend(), but we have yet to look at an example demonstrating the use of class properties. Listing 10-35 shows class properties in action.

Listing 10-35. Defining the getRecent() Class Method on the User Model

```
// example-bookshelf1/lib/user.js

var User = bookshelf.Model.extend({
    'tableName': 'users'
}, {

    /**
     * Returns a collection containing users who have signed in
     * within the last 24 hours.
     */
    'getRecent': function() {
        return User.where('last_signin', '>=', knex.raw("date('now',
        '-1 day')")).fetch();
        }

});
```

```
// example-bookshelf1/static.js

User.getRecent().then(function(users) {
    console.log('%s users have signed in within the past 24 hours.', users.
    length);
    console.log(JSON.stringify(users.toJSON(), null, 4));
});
```

Class-level properties provide a convenient location in which we can define
various helper methods related to the model in question. In this contrived example, the
getRecent() method returns a promise that resolves to a collection containing every
user who has signed in within the last 24 hours.

Extending with Subclasses

Bookshelf's extend() method correctly sets up the prototype chain. As a result, in
addition to creating models that inherit directly from Bookshelf's Model class, developers
can also create models that inherit from each other, as shown in Listing 10-36.

Listing 10-36. Creating a Base Model That Extends Directly from Bookshelf's
Model Class, from Which Other Models Can Also Extend

```
// example-bookshelf-extend/lib/base.js

/**
 * This model serves as a base from which all other models
 * within our application extend.
 *
 * @class Base
 */
var Base = bookshelf.Model.extend({
    'initialize': function() {
        this._initEventBroadcasts();
    },
    'foo': function() {
        console.log('bar', this.toJSON());
    }
});
```

```
// example-bookshelf-extend/lib/user.js

/**
 * @class User
 */
var User = Base.extend({
    'tableName': 'users'
});

// example-bookshelf-extend/index.js

var User = require('./lib/user');
User.where({
    'id': 1
}).fetch().then(function(user) {
    user.foo();
});
```

Having the ability to create models that extend across multiple levels of inheritance provides some useful opportunities. Most of the applications in which we use Bookshelf follow the lead shown in Listing 10-36, in which a Base model is created from which all other models within the application extend. By following this pattern, we can easily add core functionality to all models within our application simply by modifying our Base class. In Listing 10-36, the User model (along with every other model that extends from Base) will inherit the Base model's foo() method.

Relationships

ORM libraries such as Bookshelf provide convenient, object-oriented patterns for interacting with data stored in flat, relational database tables. With Bookshelf's help, we can specify the relationships that exist between our application's models. For example, an account may have many users, or a user may have many bookmarks. Once these relationships have been defined, Bookshelf models open up new methods that allow us to more easily navigate through these relationships.

Table 10-1 lists some of the more commonly used relationships.

Table 10-1. *Commonly Used Bookshelf Relationships*

Association	Relationship Type	Example
One-to-one	hasOne	A User has a Profile
One-to-one	belongsTo	A Profile has a User
One-to-many	hasMany	An Account has many Users
One-to-many	belongsTo	A User belongs to an Account
Many-to-many	belongsToMany	A Book has one or more Authors

In the following sections, you will discover the differences between these relationships, how they are defined, and how they can best be put to use within an application.

One-to-One

A one-to-one association is the simplest form available. As its name suggests, a one-to-one association specifies that a given model is associated with exactly one other model. That association can take the form of a hasOne relationship or a belongsTo relationship, based on the direction in which the association is traversed.

The database schema behind the example that we will soon see is shown in Figure 10-3. In this example, the profiles table has a user_id foreign key column with which it is related to the users table.

users				
id	**first_name**	**last_name**	**created_at**	**updated_at**
Integer	String	Timestamp	Timestamp	Timestamp

profiles						
id	**user_id**	**twitter_handle**	**city**	**state**	**created_at**	**updated_at**
Integer	Integer	String	String	String	Timestamp	Timestamp

Figure 10-3. *The database schema behind our one-to-one relationships*

hasOne and belongsTo

A hasOne relationship specifies that a model "has one" of another model, while the belongsTo relationship specifies just the opposite, that it is owned by or "belongs to" another model. In other words, a belongsTo relationship serves as the inverse of the hasOne relationship. The process by which these relationships are defined with Bookshelf is shown in Listing 10-37.

Listing 10-37. Defining the hasOne and belongsTo Bookshelf Relationships

```
// example-bookshelf-relationships1/lib/user.js

/**
 * @class User
 *
 * A User has one Profile
 */
var User = bookshelf.Model.extend({
    'tableName': 'users',
    /**
     * Bookshelf relationships are defined as model instance
     * methods. Here, we create a 'profile' method that will
     * allow us to access this user's profile. This method
     * could have been named anything, but in this case -
     * 'profile' makes the most sense.
     */
    'profile': function() {
        return this.hasOne(Profile);
    }
});

// example-bookshelf-relationships1/lib/profile.js

/**
 * @class Profile
 *
 * A Profile belongs to one User
 */
```

```
var Profile = bookshelf.Model.extend({
    'tableName': 'profiles',
    'user': function() {
        return this.belongsTo(User);
    }
});
```

Bookshelf relationships are defined through the use of special instance methods, as shown in Listing 10-37. With these relationships defined, we can now begin to use them in several convenient ways. For starters, see Listing 10-38, which demonstrates the process of loading a relationship within a model that has already been instantiated. The output from running this example is shown in Listing 10-39.

Listing 10-38. Loading a Relationship on a Model That Has Already Been Instantiated

```
// example-bookshelf-relationships1/index.js

User.where({
    'id': 1
}).fetch().then(function(user) {
    return user.load('profile');
}).then(function(user) {
    console.log(JSON.stringify(user.toJSON(), null, 4));
});
```

Listing 10-39. The Resulting Output from Listing 10-38

```
{
    "id": 1,
    "first_name": "Steve",
    "last_name": "Taylor",
    "created_at": "2014-10-02"
    "profile": {
    "id": 1,
    "user_id": 1,
    "twitter_handle": "staylor",
    "city": "Portland",
```

```
    "state": "OR",
    "created_at": "2014-10-02"
    }
}
```

In Listing 10-38, an instance of the User model is retrieved. When fetched, the default behavior of a Bookshelf model is to retrieve only information about itself, not about its related models. As a result, in this example we must first load the model's related Profile via the load() method, which returns a promise that is resolved once the related model has been fetched. Afterward, we can reference this user's profile via the user's related instance method.

Bookshelf relationships become even more useful when we begin to look at the manner in which they can be "eagerly loaded," as shown in Listing 10-40. In this example, we fetch an instance of the User model *as well as* its related Profile. We can do so by passing the fetch() method an object of options in which we specify one or more relationships that we are also interested in. The returned promise resolves to an instance of User that already has its profile relationship populated.

Listing 10-40. Using "Eager Loading" to Fetch Our User, and Its Related Profile, with a Single Call

```
// example-bookshelf-relationships1/eager.js

User.where({
    'id': 1
}).fetch({
    'withRelated': ['profile']
}).then(function(user) {
    console.log(JSON.stringify(user.toJSON(), null, 4));
});
```

One-to-Many

The one-to-many association forms the basis for the most commonly encountered relationships. This association builds on the simple one-to-one association we just saw, allowing us to instead associate one model with many other models. These relationships can take the form of a hasMany or a belongsTo relationship, as we will soon see.

The database schema behind the examples we are about to review is shown in Figure 10-4. In this example, the `users` table has an `account_id` foreign key column with which it is related to the `accounts` table.

accounts			
id	**name**	**created_at**	**updated_at**
Integer	String	Timestamp	Timestamp

users						
id	**account_id**	**first_name**	**last_name**	**email**	**created_at**	**updated_at**
Integer	Integer	String	String	String	Timestamp	Timestamp

Figure 10-4. *The database schema behind our one-to-many relationships*

hasMany and belongsTo

A `hasMany` relationship specifies that a model may have multiple (or none at all) of a particular model. The `belongsTo` relationship, which we have already seen in previous examples, is also applicable in one-to-many associations. The process by which these relationships are defined with Bookshelf is shown in Listing 10-41. Listing 10-42 demonstrates their usage.

Listing 10-41. Defining the `hasMany` and `belongsTo` Bookshelf Relationships

```
// example-bookshelf-relationships2/lib/account.js

/**
 * @class Account
 *
 * An Account has one or more instances of User
 */
var Account = bookshelf.Model.extend({
    'tableName': 'accounts',
    'users': function() {
        return this.hasMany(User);
    }
});
```

```
// example-bookshelf-relationships2/lib/user.js

/**
 * @class User
 *
 * A User belongs to an Account
 * A User has one Profile
 */
User = bookshelf.Model.extend({
    'tableName': 'users',
    'account': function() {
        return this.belongsTo(Account);
        },
        'profile': function() {
            return this.hasOne(Profile);
        }
});

// example-bookshelf-relationships2/lib/profile.js

/**
 * @class Profile
 *
 * A Profile belongs to one User
 */
Profile = bookshelf.Model.extend({
    'tableName': 'profiles',
    'user': function() {
        return this.belongsTo(User);
    }
});
```

Listing 10-42. Loading an Instance of the Account Model, Along with All of Its Related Users

```
// example-bookshelf-relationships2/index.js

Account.where({
    'id': 1
}).fetch({
    'withRelated': ['users']
}).then(function(account) {
    console.log(JSON.stringify(account.toJSON(), null, 4));
});

{
    "id": 1,
    "name": "Acme Company",
    "created_at": "2014-10-02",
    "users": [
    {
        "id": 1,
        "account_id": 1,
            "first_name": "Steve",
        "last_name": "Taylor",
        "email": "steve.taylor@mydomain.com",
        "created_at": "2014-10-02"
    },
    {
        "id": 2,
            "account_id": 1,
        "first_name": "Sally",
        "last_name": "Smith",
            "email": "sally.smith@mydomain.com",
        "created_at": "2014-10-02"
    }
    ]
}
```

In Listing 10-42, we see another example of Bookshelf's "eager loading" functionality, with which we can fetch a model *as well as* any of its related models that we also happen to be interested in. The concept of "eager loading" becomes even more interesting when we discover that we can also load nested relationships—those that exist deeper within the object(s) we wish to fetch. Only when we begin to utilize Bookshelf's eager loading functionality can we begin to appreciate the "virtual object database" that it and similar ORM tools provide. The example shown in *Listing* 10-43 should help to clarify this concept.

Listing 10-43. Eagerly Loading an Account, All of Its Users, and the Profile for Each User

```js
// example-bookshelf-relationships2/nested-eager.js

Account.where({
    'id': 1
}).fetch({
    'withRelated': ['users', 'users.profile']
}).then(function(account) {
    console.log(JSON.stringify(account.toJSON(), null, 4));
});

/*
{
    "id": 1,
    "name": "Acme Company",
    "created_at": "2014-10-02",
    "users": [
    {
        "id": 1,
            "account_id": 1,
            "first_name": "John",
            "last_name": "Doe",
            "email": "john.doe@domain.site",
            "created_at": "2014-10-02",
```

```
            "profile": {
                "id": 1,
                "user_id": 1,
                "twitter_handle": "john.doe",
                "city": "Portland",
                "state": "OR",
                "created_at": "2014-10-02"
            }
        },
        {
            "id": 2,
            "account_id": 1,
            "first_name": "Sarah",
            "last_name": "Smith",
            "email": "sarah.smith@domain.site",
            "created_at": "2014-10-02",
            "profile": {
                "id": 2,
                "user_id": 2,
                "twitter_handle": "sarah.smith",
                "city": "Asheville",
                "state": "NC",
                "created_at": "2014-10-02"
            }
        }
    ]
}
*/
```

Many-to-Many

Many-to-many associations differ from the one-to-one and one-to-many associations
this chapter has already covered, in that they allow one record to be associated with
one or more records of a different type, *and vice versa*. To help clarify this point, see
Figure 10-5, which illustrates a commonly cited example involving authors and books.

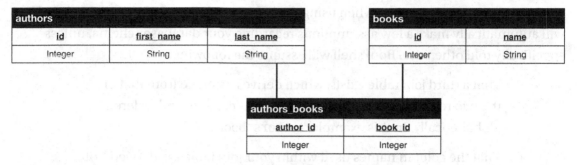

Figure 10-5. *A many-to-many association made possible through the use of a third join table. In this example, an author can write multiple books, and a book can have multiple authors.*

A single foreign key column, as seen in previous examples (see Figure 10-5), would not suffice here. In order to model this relationship, a third join table (`authors_books`) is required, in which multiple relationships for any given record can be stored.

belongsToMany

The database schema shown in Figure 10-5 can be modeled with Bookshelf via the belongsToMany relationship, as shown in Listing 10-44.

Listing 10-44. Modeling a belongsToMany Relationship with Bookshelf

```
// example-bookshelf-relationships3/lib/author.js

var Author = bookshelf.Model.extend({
    'tableName': 'authors',
    'books': function() {
        return this.belongsToMany(require('./book'));
    }
});

// example-bookshelf-relationships3/lib/book.js

var Book = bookshelf.Model.extend({
    'tableName': 'books',
    'authors': function() {
        return this.belongsToMany(require('./author'));
    }
});
```

423

It is important to note that when using the belongsToMany relationship, Bookshelf will automatically make a few assumptions regarding your database schema, unless specifically told otherwise. Bookshelf will assume the following:

- That a third join table exists, which derives its name from that of the two related tables, separated by an underscore, and ordered alphabetically. In this example: authors_books

- That the column names used within your join table are derived from the singular versions of the two related tables, followed by _id. In this example: author_id and book_id

If you prefer to follow a different naming convention, you can do so by modifying the call to this.belongsToMany as shown in Listing 10-45.

Listing 10-45. Modeling a belongsToMany Relationship with Bookshelf While Providing Specific Table and Column Names

```
var Author = bookshelf.Model.extend({
    'tableName': 'authors',
    'books': function() {
        return this.belongsToMany(
            require('./book'), 'authors_books', 'author_id', 'book_id');
    }
});

var Book = bookshelf.Model.extend({
    'tableName': 'books',
    'authors': function() {
        var Author = require('../author');
        return this.belongsToMany(Author, 'authors_books', 'book_id',
        'author_id');
    }
});
```

The process of using this relationship is shown in Listing 10-46.

Listing 10-46. Example Usage (and Resulting Output) of Code from Listing 10-45

```javascript
// example-bookshelf-relationships3/index.js

Book.fetchAll({
    'withRelated': ['authors']
}).then(function(books) {
    console.log(JSON.stringify(books.toJSON(), null, 4));
});

/*
[
    {
        id: 1,
        name: 'Pro JavaScript Frameworks for Modern Web Development',
        authors: [{
            id: 1,
            first_name: 'Tim',
            last_name: 'Ambler',
            _pivot_book_id: 1,
            _pivot_author_id: 1
        }, {
            id: 2,
            first_name: 'Nicholas',
            last_name: 'Cloud',
            _pivot_book_id: 1,
            _pivot_author_id: 2
        }]
    }
]
*/
```

Summary

If you were to quickly survey the database landscape over the past several years, it would be easy to walk away with the impression that so-called "NoSQL" storage platforms have largely supplanted the old guard of relational databases such as MySQL and PostgreSQL, but nothing could be further from the truth. Much like Mark Twain's prematurely reported death in 1897, the death of the relational database is also an exaggeration.

Relational databases offer a number of compelling features, the vast majority of which lie far outside the scope of this chapter. Many wonderful books are available that devote themselves entirely to this subject, and we encourage you to read a few of them before making critical decisions regarding how and where a project stores its information. That said, a key feature to look for in such systems (and one which was covered earlier in the chapter) is support for transactions: the process by which multiple queries can be grouped into a single unit of work that will either succeed or fail as a whole. The examples involving a financial exchange that we looked at in Listings 10-13 and 10-14 demonstrated the important role this concept has in mission-critical applications.

The platform-agnostic API provided by Knex, combined with its promise-based interface, transaction support, and migration manager, provides developers with a convenient tool for interacting with relational databases. When paired with its sister application, Bookshelf, an ORM that is instantly familiar to those with prior Backbone experience, a powerful combination is formed that simplifies the process of working with complex data.

Related Resources

- Knex: `http://knexjs.org`

- Bookshelf: `http://bookshelfjs.org`

- Backbone.js: `http://backbonejs.org`

- Underscore.js: `http://underscorejs.org`

- MySQL: `www.mysql.com`

- PostgreSQL: `www.postgresql.com`

- MariaDB: `http://mariadb.org`

- SQLite: `www.sqlite.org`

- Multiline: `https://github.com/sindresorhus/multiline`

PART VI

Managing Control Flow

CHAPTER 11

Async.js

Always something new, always something I didn't expect, and sometimes it isn't horrible.

—Robert Jordan

We are now familiar with libraries and frameworks such as KnexJS and RequireJS, among many others. This chapter discusses Async.js, a callback-driven JavaScript library that provides a suite of powerful functions to manage asynchronous collection manipulation and control flow.

When it comes to asynchronous programming, it is often a standard practice to adapt a callback-oriented approach. Async.js library too *embraces* the callback-driven approach to asynchronous programming, however, but in such a way that many of the downsides presented by callback-driven code (such as nested callbacks) are avoided.

Many of the Async.js control flow functions follow a similar pattern:

1. The first argument to each control flow function is typically an array of functions to be executed as tasks. Task function signatures will vary a bit based on the exact Async.js control flow function used, but they will always receive a Node.js-style callback as a last argument.

2. The last argument to each control flow function is a final callback function to be executed when all tasks are complete. The final control flow function also receives a Node.js-style callback and may or may not receive additional arguments as well.

© Sufyan bin Uzayr, Nicholas Cloud, Tim Ambler 2019
S. bin Uzayr et al., *JavaScript Frameworks for Modern Web Development*,
https://doi.org/10.1007/978-1-4842-4995-6_11

> **Note**   A Node.js-style callback is simply a callback function that always expects
> an error as its first argument. When the callback is invoked, either an error object
> is passed as its only argument or `null` is passed in for the error value and any
> further values are passed in as additional arguments.

Listing 11-1 shows how this pattern is typically applied.

Listing 11-1. Flow Control Function Pattern

```
var tasks = [
  function (/*0..n args, */ cb) {/*...*/},
  function (/*0..n args, */ cb) {/*...*/},
  function (/*0..n args, */ cb) {/*...*/}
];

function finalCallback (err, result) {/*...*/};

async.someFlowControlFunction(tasks, finalCallback);
```

The rest of the chapter will examine a number of control flow functions, and how
they vary, if at all, from this general pattern. Since all flows organize tasks and handle
errors and values in a similar way, it becomes easier to understand each by contrast.

> **Note**   The meaning of *async* in Async.js relates to organizing asynchronous
> operations. The library itself does not **_guarantee_** that task functions execute
> asynchronously. If a developer uses Async.js with synchronous functions, each will
> be executed synchronously. There is one semi-exception to this rule. The `async.`
> `memoize()` function (which has nothing to do with control flow) makes a function
> cacheable, so that subsequent invocations won't actually *run* the function but
> will return a cached result instead. Async.js forces each subsequent invocation
> to be asynchronous because *it assumes that the original function was itself
> asynchronous.*

Sequential Flow

A sequential flow is one in which a series of steps must be executed in order. A step may not start until a preceding step finishes (except for the first step), and if any step fails, the flow fails as a whole. The functions in Listing 11-2 are the steps for changing a fictitious user's password, the same scenario used to introduce sequential flows in Chapter 12. These steps are slightly different, however.

First, each is wrapped in a factory function that takes some initial data and returns a callback-based function to be used as a step in the sequential flow.

Second, the first step (the task wrapped in the changePassword() function) actually passes new credentials to its callback as an operation result. Steps in a sequential flow are not required to generate results, but if a step does pass a result to its callback, it has no bearing on the other steps in the sequence. If some (or all) steps rely on results from previous steps, a pipeline flow is needed. (Pipelines are discussed later in the chapter.)

Listing 11-2. Sequential Steps

```
// example-001/async-series.js
'use strict';
var async = require('async');
var userService = require('./user-service');
var emailService = require('./email-service');
var nothingToSeeHere = require('./nothing-to-see-here');

function changePassword(email, password) {
  return function (cb) {
    process.nextTick(function () {
      userService.changePassword(email, password, function (err, hash) {
        // new credentials returned as results
        cb(null, {email: email, passwordHash: hash});
      });
    });
  };
}

function notifyUser(email) {
  return function (cb) {
```

```
    process.nextTick(function () {
      // the email service invokes the callback with
      // no result
      emailService.notifyPasswordChanged(email, cb);
    });
  };
}

function sendToNSA(email, password) {
  return function (cb) {
    process.nextTick(function () {
      // the nothingToSeeHere service invokes the
      // callback with no result
      nothingToSeeHere.snoop(email, password, cb);
    });
  }
}
```

In Listing 11-3, each factory function is executed with its initial data, returning task functions that are added to a `steps` array. This array becomes the first argument to `async.series()`, followed by a final callback that receives any error generated during the execution of the series, or an array of results populated by each step in the series. If any results are generated, they are stored according to the order of their corresponding steps in the `steps` array. For example, the result from `changePassword()` will be the first element in the `results` array because `changePassword()` was invoked as the first task.

Listing 11-3. Sequential Flow

```
// example-001/async-series.js
var email = 'user@domain.com';
var password = 'foo!1';

var steps = [
  //returns function(cb)
  changePassword(email, password),
  //returns function(cb)
  notifyUser(email),
  //returns function(cb)
```

```
  sendToNSA(email, password)
];
async.series(steps, function (err, results) {
  if (err) {
    return console.error(err);
  }
  console.log('new credentials:', results[0]);
});
```

Because these steps are asynchronous, they can't be invoked one at a time in the same way that synchronous functions can be called. But Async.js tracks the executing of each step internally, invoking the next step only when the previous step's callback has been invoked, thus creating a sequential flow. If any step in the sequential flow passes an error to its callback, the series will be aborted and the final series callback will be invoked with that error. When an error is raised, the results value will be undefined.

The factory functions used in this chapter are convenient ways to pass initial data to each step, but they are not necessary. The factories could be eliminated in favor of JavaScript's native function binding facilities, as in Listing 11-4, but the code becomes more difficult to read when the steps are actually added to the array. For simple scenarios in which no initial data or bindings are necessary, anonymous task functions may be declared directly within the steps array. (It is always a good idea to name your functions and declare them in a way that promotes readability and maintainability, however.)

Listing 11-4. Series Steps with Argument Binding

```
function changePassword(email, password, cb) {/*...*/}

function notifyUser(email, cb) {/*...*/}

function sendToNSA(email, password, cb) {/*...*/}

var steps = [
  changePassword.bind(null, email, password),
  notifyUser.bind(null, email),
  sendToNSA.bind(null, email, password)
];
```

For the rest of this chapter, we'll be using factory functions instead of bind(), but developers are free to choose whatever approach feels most natural to them.

Parallel Flow

Sometimes it is helpful to run independent tasks in parallel and then aggregate results after all tasks are finished. JavaScript is an asynchronous language, so it has no true parallelism, but scheduling long, nonblocking operations in succession will release the event loop to handle other operations (like UI updates in a browser environment or handling additional requests in a server environment). Multiple asynchronous tasks can be scheduled in one turn of the event loop, but there is no way to predict at which future turn each task will complete. This makes it difficult to collect the results from each task and return them to calling code. Fortunately, the `async.parallel()` function gives developers the means to do just that.

Listing 11-5 shows two functions that wrap jQuery GET requests. The first fetches user data for a given `userID`, and the second fetches a list of US states. It is easy to imagine that these functions may be part of a user's profile page on which the user would be able to update personal information such as phone numbers, postal addresses, and so forth. When the page loads, it makes sense to fetch this information all at once. These are two different API calls, though, so even if they are scheduled simultaneously, the results need to be handled at some future point in time.

Listing 11-5. Parallel Steps

```
// example-002/views/async-parallel.html
function getUser(userID) {
  return function (cb) {
    $.get('/user/' + userID).then(function (user) {
      cb(null, user);
    }).fail(cb);
  };
}

function getUSStates(cb) {
  $.get('/us-states').then(function (states) {
    cb(null, states);
  }).fail(cb);
}
```

In Listing 11-6, Async.js is imported into a fictitious web page with a standard `<script>` tag. Tasks are scheduled using the `async.parallel()` function, which, like `async.series()`, accepts an array of task functions to be executed and a final callback function that will receive an error or the aggregated results. Parallel tasks are simply functions that accept a single callback argument that should be invoked once the asynchronous operation within a task function is completed. All callbacks conform to the Node.js callback convention.

The `getUser()` function in Listing 11-6 is a factory that accepts a `userID` argument and returns a function that accepts a conventional Node.js-style callback. Because `getUSStates()` has no actual arguments, it need not be wrapped in a factory function but is used directly instead.

Both functions fetch data with jQuery's AJAX API. AJAX promises pass data from successful AJAX calls to any callback passed to the promise's `then()` method, whereas errors are passed to any callbacks passed to the promise's `fail()` method. Because the signature of a `fail()` callback accepts a single error argument, the callback passed to each task from Async.js can also be used as the callback to `fail()`.

Listing 11-6. Parallel Flow

```
<!-- example-002/views/async-parallel.html -->
<h1>User Profile</h1>
<form>
  <fieldset>
    <div>
      <label>First Name</label>
      <input type="text" id="first-name" />
    </div>
    <div>
      <label>US States</label>
      <select id="us-states"></select>
    </div>
  </fieldset>
</form>

<script>
(function (async, $) {
```

```
  function getUser(userID) {
    return function (cb) {
      $.get('/user/' + userID).then(function (user) {
        cb(null, user);
      }).fail(cb);
    };
  }

  function getUSStates(cb) {
    $.get('/us-states').then(function (states) {
      cb(null, states);
    }).fail(cb);
  }

  var userID = 1001;

  async.parallel([
    getUser(userID),
    getUSStates
  ], function (err, results) {
    if (err) {
      return alert(err.message);
    }
    var user = results[0],
      states = results[1];
    $('#first-name').val(user.firstName);
    // ...
    $('#us-states').append(states.map(function (state) {
      return $('<option></option>')
        .html(state)
        .attr('value', state);
    }));
  });

}(window.async, window.jQuery));
</script>
```

The Async.js library will iterate over each task in the tasks array, scheduling them one after the other. As each task completes, its data is stored, and once all tasks have finished, the final callback passed to async.parallel() is invoked.

Results are sorted according to the order of tasks passed to async.parallel(), *not* the order in which tasks are actually resolved. If an error occurs in any parallel task, that error will be passed to the final callback, all unfinished parallel tasks will be ignored once they complete, and the results argument in the final callback will be undefined.

Pipeline Flow

When tasks in a series each depend on a value from a preceding task, a pipeline flow (or waterfall) is needed. Listing 11-7 represents tasks for a fictitious corporate rewards program in which a user's age is calculated (based on date of birth), and if the user's age meets certain thresholds, the user is awarded a cash prize.

Each function receives some input and then passes some output to its callback. The output of each function becomes the input for the next function in the series.

1. The getUser() factory function accepts a **userID** and returns another function that, when invoked, looks up a **user** record. It passes the **user** record to its callback.

2. The calcAge() function accepts a **user** argument and invokes its callback with the calculated **age** of the user.

3. The reward() function accepts a numeric **age** argument and invokes its callback with the selected **reward** if the **age** meets certain thresholds.

Listing 11-7. Waterfall (Pipeline) Steps

```
// example-003/callback-waterfall
'use strict';
var db = require('./database');

function getUser(userID, cb) {
  process.nextTick(function () {
    // pass cb directly to find because
    // it has the same signature:
    // (err, user)
```

```
    db.users.find({id: userID}, cb);
  });
}

function calcAge(user, cb) {
  process.nextTick(function () {
    var now = Date.now(),
      then = user.birthDate.getTime();
    var age = (now - then) / (1000 * 60 * 60 * 24 * 365);
    cb(null, Math.round(age));
  });
}

function reward(age, cb) {
  process.nextTick(function () {
    switch (age) {
      case 25: return cb(null, '$100');
      case 35: return cb(null, '$150');
      case 45: return cb(null, '$200');
      default: return cb(null, '$0');
    }
  });
}
```

This pipeline would be rather hideous and difficult to maintain if organized with nested callbacks. If additional steps are ever added to the reward program, the code will need to be teased apart and restructured to accommodate new steps in the pipeline flow. Trapping errors and propagating them through callbacks also happen manually. The example code in Listing 11-8 shows how these tasks would be run *without* Async.js.

Listing 11-8. A Waterfall of Nested Callbacks

```
// example-003/callback-waterfall
function showReward(userID, cb) {
  getUser(userID, function (err, user) {
    if (err) {
      return cb(err);
    }
```

```
  calcAge(user, function (err, age) {
    if (err) {
      return cb(err);
    }
    reward(age, cb);
  });
})
}

showReward(123, function (err, reward) {
  if (err) {
    return console.error(err);
  }
  console.log(reward);
});
```

Fortunately, Async.js makes it relatively painless to organize a pipeline flow that is both maintainable and handles errors gracefully. The code in Listing 11-9 uses `async.waterfall()` to organize the series of tasks to be executed, then provides a final callback to capture any error raised by pipeline tasks or to receive the final reward value if no errors occur.

Listing 11-9. Waterfall (Pipeline) Flow

```
// example-003/async-waterfall.js
'use strict';
var async = require('async');
var db = require('./database');

function getUser(userID) {
  // using a factory function to pass in
  // the userID argument and return another
  // function that will match the callback
  // signature that async.waterfall expects
  return function (cb) {
    process.nextTick(function () {
      // pass cb directly to find because
      // it has the same signature:
```

```
    // (err, user)
    db.users.find({id: userID}, cb);
  });
};
}

// the calcAge and reward functions
// do not change

async.waterfall([
  getUser(1000),
  calcAge,
  reward
], function (err, reward) {
  if (err) {
    return console.error(err);
  }
  console.log('reward:', reward);
});
```

Like async.series() and async.parallel(), an error passed to a callback in *any* waterfall task will immediately halt the pipeline and invoke the final callback with the error.

Reusing a Pipeline

Pipelines are so helpful for processing data that async.seq() will take a series of functions, just like async.waterfall(), and combine them into a single, reusable pipeline function that can be called multiple times. This could be done manually, of course, by using a closure to wrap async.waterfall(), but async.seq() is a convenience function that saves developers the trouble.

Listing 11-10 shows a series of functions used to process a make-believe cellular phone bill. The createBill() function accepts a calling plan and creates a bill object with both the plan and the normal monthly rate. carrierFee() appends a chunk of change to this amount just because the phone company can. The prorate() function then determines if some amount is to be credited to the user (e.g., if the user started a new plan in the middle of a billing cycle). And finally, govtExtortion() appends a calculated tax onto the bill before it is delivered.

Listing 11-10. Sequence (Pipeline) Steps

```javascript
// example-004/async-seq.js
'use strict';
var async = require('async');
var dateUtil = require('./date-util');

function createBill(plan, cb) {
  process.nextTick(function () {
    var bill = {
      plan: plan,
      total: plan.billAmt
    };
    cb(null, bill);
  });
}

function carrierFee(bill, cb) {
  process.nextTick(function () {
    bill.total += 10;
    cb(null, bill);
  });
}

function prorate(bill, cb) {
  if (!bill.plan.isNew) {
    return cb(null, bill);
  }
  process.nextTick(function () {
    bill.plan.isNew = false;
    var days = dateUtil().daysInMonth();
    var amtPerDay = bill.plan.billAmt / days;
    var prorateAmt = ((bill.plan.billDay - 1) * amtPerDay);
    bill.total -= prorateAmt;
    cb(null, bill);
  });
}
```

```
function govtExtortion(bill, cb) {
  process.nextTick(function () {
    bill.total = bill.total * 1.08;
    cb(null, bill);
  });
}
```

Creating a pipeline with `async.seq()` is very similar to using `async.waterfall()`, as shown in Listing 11-11. The primary difference is that `async.seq()` does not invoke the steps immediately but returns a `pipeline()` function that will be used to run the tasks later. The `pipeline()` function accepts the initial arguments that will be passed to the *first* step, eliminating the need for factory functions or binding values to the first step when the pipeline is defined. Also, unlike most other `async` functions, `async.seq()` is variadic (accepts a varying number of arguments). It does not accept an array of tasks like `async.waterfall()`, but instead accepts each task function as an argument.

In Listing 11-11 the `pipeline()` function is created and then invoked with two parameters: a `plan` object, which will be passed to `createBill()`, and a final callback to receive either an error or a final `bill` object for the user.

Listing 11-11. Sequence (Pipeline) Flow

```
// example-004/async-seq.js
var pipeline = async.seq(
  createBill,
  carrierFee,
  prorate,
  govtExtortion
);

var plan = {
  type: 'Lots of Cell Minutes Plan!+',
  isNew: true,
  billDay: 15,
  billAmt: 100
};
```

```
pipeline(plan, function (err, bill) {
  if (err) {
    return console.error(err);
  }
  //bill = govtExtortion(prorate(carrierFee(createBill(plan))))
  console.log('$', bill.total.toFixed(2));
});
```

Loop Flow

Flows that repeat until some condition is met are called *loops*. Async.js has several
looping functions that help coordinate the asynchronous code to be executed and the
conditions to be tested within them.

Looping While Some Condition Remains True

The first two functions, async.whilst() and async.doWhilst(), parallel the well-known
while and do/while looping constructs in many programming languages. Each loop
runs *while* some condition evaluates to true. Once the condition evaluates to false, the
loops halt.

The async.whilst() and async.doWhilst() functions are nearly identical, except
that async.whilst() performs the condition evaluation before any code in the loop is
run, whereas async.doWhilst() executes one iteration of the loop *before* performing
evaluating the condition. Looping code in async.doWhilst() is guaranteed to run at
least once, whereas looping code in async.whilst() may not run at all if the initial
condition is false.

Listing 11-12 shows async.whilst() being used to call an API ten times to get a
random "winner" for some contest. Before the loop runs, an array of names is examined
to determine if ten winners have already been selected. This process is repeated until the
array has a length of ten. If an error occurs during one of the API calls within the loop,
the async.whilst() flow is terminated and the final callback is invoked with the error;
otherwise the final callback will be invoked once the loop condition evaluates to false.

Listing 11-12. Looping While Some Condition Remains True

```html
<!-- example-005/views/async-whilst.html -->
<h1>Winners!</h1>
<ul id="winners"></ul>

<script>
(function (async, $) {

  function pickWinners(howMany, cb) {
    var winners = [];

    async.whilst(
      // condition test:
      // continue looping until we have enough winners
      function () { return winners.length < howMany; },
      // looping code
      function (cb) {
        $.get('/employee/random').done(function (employee) {
          var winner = employee.firstName + ' ' + employee.lastName;
          // avoid potential duplicates
          if (winners.indexOf(winner) < 0) {
            winners.push(winner);
          }
          cb(null);
        }).fail(function (err) {
          cb(err);
        });
      },
      // final callback
      function (err) {
        // if there is an error just ignore it
        // and pass back an empty array, otherwise
        // pass the winners
        cb(null, err ? [] : winners);
      }
    );
  }
```

```
  pickWinners(3, function (err, winners) {
    $('ul#winners').append(winners.map(function (winner) {
      return $('<li></li>').html(winner);
    }));
  });

}(window.async, window.jQuery));
</script>
```

The code in Listing 11-13 shows an abbreviated modification of the `async.whilst()` loop using `async.doWhilst()` instead. Notice that the order of arguments has changed. The looping function is now the first argument to `async.doWhilst()` and the condition test is the second. This structurally mirrors do/while loop syntax.

Listing 11-13. Looping Once and Then Continuing While Some Condition Remains True

```
<!-- example-005/views/async-dowhilst.html -->
<h1>Winners!</h1>
<ul id="winners"></ul>

<script>
(function (async, $) {

  function pickWinners(howMany, cb) {
    var winners = [];

    async.doWhilst(
      // looping code
      function (cb) {
        $.get('/employee/random').done(function (employee) {
          var winner = employee.firstName + ' ' + employee.lastName;
          // avoid potential duplicates
          if (winners.indexOf(winner) < 0) {
            winners.push(winner);
          }
```

```
        cb(null);
      }).fail(function (err) {
        cb(err);
      });
    },
    // condition test is now the second function
    // argument
    function () { return winners.length < howMany; },
    // final callback
    function (err) {
      // if there is an error just ignore it
      // and pass back an empty array, otherwise
      // pass the winners
      cb(null, err ? [] : winners);
    }
  );
}

pickWinners(3, function (err, winners) {
  $('ul#winners').append(winners.map(function (winner) {
    return $('<li></li>').html(winner);
  }));
});

}(window.async, window.jQuery));
</script>
```

Looping Until Some Condition Becomes False

Closely related to the async.whilst() and async.doWhilst() functions are the async.until() and async.doUntil() functions, which follow similar execution patterns but, instead of performing a loop when some condition is *true*, perform loops until some condition tests *false*.

The code in Listing 11-14 shows how a simple HTTP heartbeat can be created in the browser to test an API endpoint for availability. The Heartbeat() constructor function creates a loop with async.until() that will execute repeatedly until the value of the _isStopped property is set to true. Heartbeat() exposes a stop() method that, when invoked sometime after the object is created, will prevent the loop from continuing. Each turn of the loop makes an HTTP request to the server, and if the request succeeds, the loop sets the isAvailable property to true; if it fails, isAvailable is set to false. To create a delay between iterations of the loop, a setTimeout() function wraps the callback invocation within the loop, scheduling future iterations of the loop to run at a later time (every 3 seconds in this example).

Listing 11-14. Looping Until Some Condition Becomes False

```html
<!-- example-006/views/async-until.html -->
<section id="output"></section>

<script>
(function (async, $) {

  var output = document.querySelector('#output');

  function write() {
    var pre = document.createElement('pre');
    pre.innerHTML = Array.prototype.join.call(arguments, ' ');
    output.appendChild(pre);
  }

  function Heartbeat(url, interval) {
    var self = this;
    this.isAvailable = false;
    this.isStopped = false;
    this.writeStatus = function () {
      write(
        '> heartbeat [isAvailable: %s, isStopped: %s]'
          .replace('%s', self.isAvailable)
          .replace('%s', self.isStopped)
      );
    };

    async.until(
      // test condition
      function () { return self.isStopped; },
```

```
      // loop
      function (cb) {
        $.get(url).then(function () {
          self.isAvailable = true;
        }).fail(function () {
          self.isAvailable = false;
        }).always(function () {
          self.writeStatus();
          // delay the next loop by scheduling
          // the callback invocation in the
          // future
          setTimeout(function () {
            cb(null);
          }, interval);
        });
      },
      // final callback
      function (/*err*/) {
        self.isAvailable = false;
        self.writeStatus();
      }
    );
  }

  Heartbeat.prototype.stop = function () {
    this.isStopped = true;
  };

  var heartbeat = new Heartbeat('/heartbeat', 3000);

  setTimeout(function () {
    // 10 seconds later
    heartbeat.stop();
  }, 10000);
}(window.async, window.jQuery));
</script>
```

The `async.doUntil()` function behaves like `async.doWhilst()`: it runs the loop first before evaluating the test condition. Its signature also swaps the order of the test condition function and the looping function.

Retry Loops

A common use case for loops is the *retry loop*, where a task is attempted up to a given number of times. If the task fails but hasn't met the retry limit, it is executed again. If the retry limit is met, the task is aborted. The `async.retry()` function simplifies this process by handling the retry logic for developers. Setting up a loop is as simple as specifying a retry limit, a task to execute, and a final callback that will handle errors or receive a result.

Listing 11-15 demonstrates a simple API call for reserving a seat at some concert or movie. The available seats are listed in an array, most preferable to least preferable. The execution limit is the length of the array. Each time the task runs, it shifts the array, removing the first (most preferable) seat from the collection. If the reservation fails, it continues this process until there are no more seats left.

Listing 11-15. Retry Loop

```
<!-- example-007/views/async-retry -->
<section id="output"></section>

<script>
(function (async, $) {

  var output = document.querySelector('#output');

  function write() {
    var pre = document.createElement('pre');
    pre.innerHTML = Array.prototype.join.call(arguments, ' ');
    output.appendChild(pre);
  }

  function reserve(name, availableSeats) {
    console.log(availableSeats);
    return function (cb) {
      var request = {
```

```
          name: name,
          seat: availableSeats.shift()
        };
        write('posting reservation', JSON.stringify(request));
        $.post('/reservation', request)
          .done(function (confirmation) {
            write('confirmation', JSON.stringify(confirmation));
            cb(null, confirmation);
          }).fail(function (err) {
            cb(err);
          });
      };
    }

    var name = 'Nicholas';
    var availableSeats = ['15A', '22B', '13J', '32K'];

    async.retry(
      availableSeats.length,
      reserve(name, availableSeats),
      function (err, confirmation) {
        if (err) {
          return console.error(err);
        }
        console.log('seat reserved:', confirmation);
      }
    );
}(window.async, window.jQuery));
</script>
```

Each time the task is run, it invokes its callback. If the task succeeds and passes a value to the callback, the final `async.retry()` callback is invoked with that value (in this case, `confirmation`). If an error occurs, the loop is repeated until it reaches the loop limit. The last error is passed to the final callback; previous errors are lost unless accumulated manually. Listing 11-16 demonstrates a potential way to accomplish this by collecting errors in an array, then passing the array itself as the `err` argument to the callback. If the retry loop fails, the final callback's error will be an array of every error generated during each turn of the loop.

Listing 11-16. Accumulating Errors in a Retry Loop

```
function reserve(name, availableSeats) {
  var errors = [];
  return function (cb) {
    // ...
    $.post('/reservation', body)
      .done(function (confirmation) {
        cb(null, confirmation);
      }).fail(function (err) {
        errors.push(err);
        cb(errors);
      });
  };
}
```

Infinite Loops

Infinite loops are bad news in synchronous programming because they arrest the CPU and prevent any other code from executing. But asynchronous infinite loops don't suffer from this downside because, like all other code, they are scheduled for future turns of the event loop by the JavaScript scheduler. Other code that needs to be run can "butt in" and request to be scheduled.

An infinite loop can be scheduled with `async.forever()`. This function takes a task function as its first argument and a final callback as its second. The task will continue to run indefinitely unless it passes an error to its callback. Scheduling asynchronous operations back to back using `setTimeout()` with a wait duration of 0 or `setImmediate()` can create near nonresponsive code in a loop, so it is best to pad each asynchronous task with a longer wait duration, at least in the hundreds of milliseconds.

The loop in Listing 11-17 makes an HTTP GET request during each turn of the infinite loop, loading stock information for the user's dashboard. Each time the GET request succeeds, the stock information is updated and the loop waits for 3 seconds before executing again. If an error occurs during the loop, the final callback is invoked with the error and the loop is terminated.

451

Listing 11-17. Infinite Loop

```
<!-- example-008/views/async-forever.html -->
<ul id="stocks"></ul>

<script>
(function (async, $) {
  $stockList = $('ul#stocks');

  async.forever(function (cb) {
    $.get('/dashboard/stocks')
      .done(function (stocks) {
        // refresh the stock list with new stock
        // information
        $stockList.empty();
        $stockList.append(stocks.map(function (stock) {
          return $('<li></li>').html(stock.symbol + ' $' + stock.price);
        }));
        // wait three seconds before continuing
        setTimeout(function () {
          cb(null);
        }, 3000);
      }).fail(cb);
  }, function (err) {
    console.error(err.responseText);
  })
}(window.async, window.jQuery));
</script>
```

Batch Flow

The last type of control flow this chapter covers is batching. Batches are created by partitioning some data into chunks, and then operating on each chunk one at a time. Batches have some threshold that defines how much data can be put into a chunk. Data added to a batch flow after work has commenced on a chunk is queued until work is complete, then gets processed in a new chunk.

Asynchronous Queue

An asynchronous queue is one way to process items in a batch flow. A queue can be created by calling async.queue() with two parameters. The first is a task function that will be executed for each data item that will be added to the queue. The second is a number that represents *the maximum number of task workers that the queue will schedule concurrently* to process data. In Listing 11-18 a queue is created to make HTTP requests for any URL added to the queue. The result of each HTTP request will be added to the results hash when each request has been completed. The maximum number of HTTP requests that can be running at any one time is three. If additional URLs are added to the queue while three requests are in progress, they will be held for future processing. As workers are released (when requests complete), they will be assigned to queued URLs as needed. There will never be more than three HTTP requests in progress at a given time.

Listing 11-18. Using Queue for Sequential Batches

```
// example-009/index.js
'use strict';
var async = require('async');
var http = require('http');

var MAX_WORKERS = 3;
var results = {};

var queue = async.queue(function (url, cb) {
  results[url] = ";
  http.get(url, function (res) {
    results[url] = res.statusCode + ' Content-Type: ' + res.
    headers['content-type'];
    cb(null);
  }).on('error', function (err) {
    cb(err);
  });
}, MAX_WORKERS);

var urls = [ // 9 urls
  'http://www.appendto.com',
  'http://www.nodejs.org',
```

```
  'http://www.npmjs.org',
  'http://www.nicholascloud.com',
  'http://www.devlink.net',
  'http://javascriptweekly.com',
  'http://nodeweekly.com',
  'http://www.reddit.com/r/javascript',
  'http://www.reddit.com/r/node'
];

urls.forEach(function (url) {
  queue.push(url, function (err) {
    if (err) {
      return console.error(err);
    }
    console.log('done processing', url);
  });
});
```

The queue will emit a number of events at certain points in its life cycle. Functions may be assigned to corresponding event properties on the queue object to handle these events. These event handlers are optional; the queue will operate correctly with or without them.

The first time the queue has reached the maximum number of active workers, it will invoke any function assigned to `queue.saturated`. When the queue is handling all items and no other items are queued, it will call any function assigned to `queue.empty`. Finally, when all workers have completed and the queue is empty, any function assigned to `queue.drain` will be called. The functions in Listing 11-19 handle each of these raised events.

Note   The empty and drained events differ subtly. When empty is triggered, workers may still be active though no items remain in the queue. When drained is triggered, all workers have ceased and the queue is completely empty.

Listing 11-19. Queue Events

```
// example-009/index.js
queue.saturated = function () {
  console.log('queue is saturated at ' + queue.length());
};

queue.empty = function () {
  console.log('queue is empty; last task being handled');
};

queue.drain = function () {
  console.log('queue is drained; no more tasks to handle');
  Object.keys(results).forEach(function (url) {
    console.log(url, results[url]);
  });
  process.exit(0);
};
```

Asynchronous Cargo

The `async.cargo()` function is similar to `async.queue()` in that it queues up items to be processed by some task function. They differ, however, in how the workload is divided. `async.queue()` runs multiple *workers* up to a maximum concurrency limit—its saturation point. `async.cargo()` runs a single worker at a time, but splits up the queued items to be processed into payloads of a predetermined size. When the worker is executed, it will be given one payload. When it has completed, it will be given another, until all payloads have been processed. The saturation point for cargo, then, is when a *full* payload is ready to be processed. Any items added to the cargo after the worker has started will be grouped into the next payload to be processed.

A cargo is created by supplying the task function as the first argument to `async.cargo()` and a maximum payload size as the second. The task function will receive an array of data (with a length up to the maximum payload size) to be processed and a callback to be invoked once the operation is complete.

The code in Listing 11-20 shows how `async.cargo()` can be used to package a series of database updates into a fictitious transaction, one payload at a time. The task function iterates over the "update" objects supplied to it, converting each into an UPDATE query

455

in some imaginary relational data store. Once all the queries have been added to a transaction, the transaction is committed and the callback is invoked.

Listing 11-20. Using Cargo for Parallel Batches

```
// example-010/index-01.js
'use strict';
var async = require('async');
var db = require('db');

var MAX_PAYLOAD_SIZE = 4;
var UPDATE_QUERY = "UPDATE CUSTOMER SET ? = '?' WHERE id = ?;";

var cargo = async.cargo(function (updates, cb) {
  db.begin(function (trx) {
    updates.forEach(function (update) {
      var query = UPDATE_QUERY.replace('?', update.field)
        .replace('?', update.value)
        .replace('?', update.id);
      trx.add(query);
    });
    trx.commit(cb);
  });
}, MAX_PAYLOAD_SIZE);

var customerUpdates = [ // 9 updates to be processed in payloads of 4
  {id: 1000, field: 'firstName', value: 'Sterling'},
  {id: 1001, field: 'phoneNumber', value: '222-333-4444'},
  {id: 1002, field: 'email', value: 'archer@goodisis.com'},
  {id: 1003, field: 'dob', value: '01/22/1973'},
  {id: 1004, field: 'city', value: 'New York'},
  {id: 1005, field: 'occupation', value: 'Professional Troll'},
  {id: 1006, field: 'twitter', value: '@2cool4school'},
  {id: 1007, field: 'ssn', value: '111-22-3333'},
  {id: 1008, field: 'email', value: 'urmom@internet.com'},
  {id: 1009, field: 'pref', value: 'rememberme=false&colorscheme=dark'}
];
```

```
customerUpdates.forEach(function (update) {
  cargo.push(update, function () {
    console.log('done processing', update.id);
  });
});
```

The cargo object has the same event properties as the queue object, shown in Listing 11-21. The main difference is that the cargo's saturation limit is reached once a maximum number of payload items has been added, at which point the worker will commence.

Optional function handlers may be assigned to event properties as needed.

Listing 11-21. Cargo Events

```
// example-010/index-01.js
cargo.saturated = function () {
  console.log('cargo is saturated at ' + cargo.length());
};

cargo.empty = function () {
  console.log('cargo is empty; worker needs tasks');
};

cargo.drain = function () {
  console.log('cargo is drained; no more tasks to handle');
};
```

Note   Both async.queue() and async.cargo() schedule the task function to run in the next immediate tick of the event loop. If items are added to a queue or cargo *synchronously*, one after the other, then the thresholds of each will be applied as expected; the queue will throttle the maximum number of workers, and the cargo will divide the maximum number of items to be processed. If items are added to each *asynchronously*, however—if items are added *after* the next immediate turn of the event loop—the task functions may be invoked at less than their maximum capacities.

The code in Listing 11-22 pulls each update out of the `customerUpdates` array and pushes it to the cargo, then schedules the next push to happen 500 milliseconds later, in a future turn of the event loop. Because cargo schedules its task immediately, the `UPDATE` query will run with one—maybe two—updates each time, depending on how long it takes for a task to finish and for the next task to be scheduled.

Listing 11-22. Adding Items to Cargo Asynchronously

```
// example-010/index-02.js
(function addUpdateAsync() {
  if (!customerUpdates.length) return;
  console.log('adding update');
  var update = customerUpdates.shift();
  cargo.push(update, function () {
    console.log('done processing', update.id);
  });
  setTimeout(addUpdateAsync, 500);
}());
```

To guarantee that the maximum thresholds are met for both queue and cargo, push items to each *synchronously*.

Summary

This chapter has covered a number of common synchronous control flows and demonstrated how Async.js can be used to adapt these patterns for asynchronous code. Table 11-1 shows each flow and the corresponding Async.js functions that were covered.

Table 11-1. *Flows and Corresponding Async.js Functions*

Flow	Async.js Function(s)
Sequential	`async.series()`
Parallel	`async.parallel()`
Pipeline	`async.waterfall()`, `async.seq()`
Loop	`async.whilst()`/`async.doWhilst()`, `async.until()`/`async.doUntil()`
	`async.retry()`, `async.forever()`
Batch	`async.queue()`, `async.cargo()`

Sequential and parallel flows allow developers to execute multiple independent tasks, then aggregate results as needed. Pipeline flows can be used to chain tasks together, where the output of each task becomes the input of a succeeding task. To repeat asynchronous tasks a given number of times, or according to some condition, looping flows may be used. Finally, batching flows are available to divide data into chunks to be processed asynchronously, one batch after the next.

By cleverly organizing asynchronous function tasks, coordinating the results of each task, and delivering errors and/or task results to a final callback, Async.js helps developers avoid nested callbacks and brings traditional synchronous control flow operations into the asynchronous world of JavaScript.

PART VII

Further Useful Libraries

CHAPTER 12

Underscore and Lodash

You must be the kind of [person] who can get things done. But to get things done, you must love the doing, not the secondary consequences.

—Ayn Rand

JavaScript is a pragmatic utility language, useful in no small part because of its simple APIs and sparse type system. It is an easy language to learn and master because its surface area is so small. And while this characteristic lends itself nicely to productivity, sadly it means that JavaScript types have historically lacked advanced features that would make the language stronger, such as functional iteration constructs native to collections and hashes.

To fill this gap, Jeremy Ashkenas created a library in 2009 called Underscore.js, a collection of over 100 functions used to manipulate, filter, and transform hashes and collections. Many of these functions, such as `map()` and `reduce()`, embody concepts common to functional languages. Others, like `isArguments()` and `isUndefined()`, are specific to JavaScript.

As the presence of Underscore became ubiquitous in many web applications, two exciting things happened. First, the ECMAScript 5 specification was published in the same year. It features a number of Underscore-like methods on native JavaScript objects such as `Array.prototype.map()`, `Array.prototype.reduce()`, and `Array.isArray()`. While ECMAScript 5 (and to a lesser degree ECMAScript 6 and 7) expands the APIs of several key types, it only includes a fraction of the functionality that Underscore.js provides.

Second, Underscore was forked into a new project called Lodash with the goal of dramatically improving the performance and expanding its API. Since Lodash implements all of Underscore's functions while adding its own, Underscore is a subset of Lodash. All of the corresponding ECMAScript spec functions are part of Lodash as well.

© Sufyan bin Uzayr, Nicholas Cloud, Tim Ambler 2019
S. bin Uzayr et al., *JavaScript Frameworks for Modern Web Development*,
https://doi.org/10.1007/978-1-4842-4995-6_12

Table 12-1 shows Underscore and Lodash functions mapped to their native ECMAScript counterparts.

Table 12-1. *Underscore and Lodash Functions Compared to Current (and Proposed) Native JavaScript Implementations*

ECMAScript 5	Underscore/Lodash
`Array.prototype.every()`	`all()/every()`
`Array.prototype.filter()`	`select()/filter()`
`Array.prototype.forEach()`	`each()/forEach()`
`Array.isArray()`	`isArray()`
`Object.keys()`	`keys()`
`Array.prototype.map()`	`map()`
`Array.prototype.reduce()`	`inject()/foldl()/reduce()`
`Array.prototype.reduceRight()`	`foldr()/reduceRight()`
`Array.prototype.some()`	`some()`
ECMAScript 6	**Underscore/Lodash**
`Array.prototype.find()`	`find()`
`Array.prototype.findIndex()`	`findIndex()`
`Array.prototype.keys()`	`keys()`
ECMAScript 7	**Underscore/Lodash**
`Array.prototype.contains()`	`include()/contains()`

Because Underscore and Lodash share an API, Lodash can be used as a drop-in replacement for Underscore. The inverse isn't necessarily the case, however, because of the extra functionality that Lodash supplies. For example, while both Underscore and Lodash have a `clone()` method, only Lodash implements a `cloneDeep()` method. Often developers choose Lodash over Underscore because of these extra features, but the performance benefit is tangible as well. According to a function-by-function performance benchmark, Lodash is 35% faster on average than Underscore. It achieves this performance gain by favoring simple loops over native delegation for functions like `forEach()`, `map()`, `reduce()`, and so forth.

This chapter focuses mostly on features of Underscore and Lodash *that are not already (or are scheduled to be) implemented in JavaScript* (the functions in Listings 12-1 and 12-2). Mozilla's excellent documentation covers each of the native functions, and the Underscore and Lodash API documentation covers each of their implementations as well.

But Underscore and Lodash offer a great deal more than just a few handy functions for objects and collections, several of which will be explored in this chapter.

Note   For brevity, the remainder of this chapter simply refers to Underscore, but understand that, unless otherwise noted, Underscore and Lodash are interchangeable.

In essence, Lodash provides more consistent iteration support for arrays, strings, and objects. As compared to Underscore, Lodash is more of a superset—it offers better API behaviors, features such as AMD support, deep merge, and more.

Other than that, Lodash (also written as Lo-Dash) is more flexible and has been performance tested to run in Node, PhantomJS, and other libraries/frameworks. If you are familiar with Backbone.js, it might be a better idea to use Lodash as it comes with multiple Backbone boilerplates by default.

Lastly, Lodash is more frequently updated as compared to Underscore.

Installation and Usage

Underscore may be directly imported as a library in the web browser or any server-side JavaScript environment, such as Node.js. It has no external dependencies.

You can download the Underscore.js script directly from the Underscore web site (http://underscorejs.org) or install it with a package manager like npm, Bower, or Component.

In the browser, you can include Underscore directly as a script or load it with an AMD- or CommonJS-compatible module loader (such as RequireJS or Browserify). In Node.js the package is simply required as a CommonJS module.

Accessing the Underscore object (on which its utility functions live) depends on how the library is loaded. When Underscore is loaded in the browser with a `script` tag, the library will attach itself to `window._`. For variables created by module loaders in any environment, it is convention to assign the actual underscore character to the module, as shown in Listing 12-1.

Listing 12-1. Loading the Underscore Library in a Node.js Module

```
// example-001/index.js
'use strict';
var _ = require('underscore');

console.log(_.VERSION);
```

All Underscore functions live on the _ ("underscore") object. Because Underscore is a utility library, it holds no state other than a handful of settings (but we'll cover more on that later in the chapter). All functions are *idempotent*, which means passing a value to any function multiple times will yield the same result each time. Once the Underscore object is loaded, it may be used immediately.

Underscore's utility functions operate mostly on collections (arrays and array-like objects, such as arguments), object literals, and functions. Underscore is most commonly used to filter and transform data. Many Underscore functions complement each other and can work together to create powerful combinations. Because this can be so useful, Underscore has built-in support for function chains that create terse pipelines that apply multiple transformations to data at once.

Aggregation and Indexing

Pieces of data in a collection often share similar schemas, yet have an identifying attribute that makes each unique. It can be helpful to distinguish these two types of relationships in a set of data—commonality and individuality—in order to quickly filter and work with a subset of objects that matches aggregation criteria.

Underscore has a number of functions that perform these tasks, but three specific functions can be tremendously beneficial when working with collections: countBy(), groupBy(), and indexBy().

countBy()

Counting objects that share some characteristic is a common way to generalize data. Given a collection of URLs, one can imagine some analytic process that determines how many URLs belong to specific top-level domains (e.g., .com, .org, .edu, etc.). Underscore's countBy() function is an ideal candidate for this task. It invokes a callback on each element in an array to determine which category the element fits into (in this example, which top-level domain the URL occupies). The callback returns some string value that represents this category. The final result is an object with keys that represent all categories returned from the callback and numeric counts representing the number of elements that fall into each category. Listing 12-2 shows a primitive implementation that yields an object with a count of two .org domains and one .com domain.

Listing 12-2. Counting Elements by Some Criteria

```
// example-002/index.js
'use strict';
var _ = require('underscore');

var urls = [
  'http://underscorejs.org',
  'http://lodash.com',
  'http://ecmascript.org'
];

var counts = _.countBy(urls, function byTLD(url) {
  if (url.indexOf('.com') >= 0) {
    return '.com';
  }
  if (url.indexOf('.org') >= 0) {
    return '.org';
  }
  return '?';
});

console.log(counts);
// { '.org': 2, '.com': 1 }
```

If the items in a collection are objects with properties, and the values for a specific property represent the data to be counted, an iterator function is not required. The name of the property to be tested may be used as a substitute. Note that in Listing 12-3 the keys in the final result will be the *values* for the property examined on each object.

Listing 12-3. Counting Elements by Some Property

```
// example-003/index.js
'use strict';
var _ = require('underscore');

var urls = [
  {scheme: 'http', host: 'underscorejs', domain: '.org'},
  {scheme: 'http', host: 'lodash', domain: '.com'},
  {scheme: 'http', host: 'ecmascript', domain: '.org'},
];

var counts = _.countBy(urls, 'domain');

console.log(counts);
// { '.org': 2, '.com': 1 }
```

If one or more objects in the collection lack the property to be tested, the final result object will contain an undefined key paired with the number of those objects as well.

groupBy()

Underscore's groupBy() function is similar to countBy(), but instead of reducing results to numeric counts, groupBy() places elements into categorized collections in the result object. The URL objects in Listing 12-4 are each placed into collections for each corresponding top-level domain.

Listing 12-4. Grouping Elements by Some Property

```
// example-004/index.js
'use strict';
var _ = require('underscore');

var urls = [
```

```
  {scheme: 'http', host: 'underscorejs', domain: '.org'},
  {scheme: 'http', host: 'lodash', domain: '.com'},
  {scheme: 'http', host: 'ecmascript', domain: '.org'},
];

var grouped = _.groupBy(urls, 'domain');

console.log(grouped);

/*
{
  '.org': [
    { scheme: 'http', host: 'underscorejs', domain: '.org' },
    { scheme: 'http', host: 'ecmascript', domain: '.org' }
  ],
  '.com': [
    { scheme: 'http', host: 'lodash', domain: '.com' }
  ]
}
*/
```

Note   The groupBy() function may also use an iterator function as its second argument (instead of a property name) if a greater degree of control is required to categorize elements.

It is worth mentioning that counts may easily be derived from grouped objects by simply querying the length of each grouped array. It may be advantageous, depending on application context, to prefer grouping over counting. Listing 12-5 shows how to get the count for a single set of grouped data as well as a function for creating an object of counts from groupBy() results.

Listing 12-5. Deriving Counts from Grouped Objects

```
// example-005/index.js
'use strict';
var _ = require('underscore');

var urls = [
  {scheme: 'http', host: 'underscorejs', domain: '.org'},
  {scheme: 'http', host: 'lodash', domain: '.com'},
  {scheme: 'http', host: 'ecmascript', domain: '.org'},
];

var grouped = _.groupBy(urls, 'domain');
var dotOrgCount = grouped['.org'].length;
console.log(dotOrgCount);
// 2

function toCounts(grouped) {
  var counts = {};
  for (var key in grouped) {
    if (grouped.hasOwnProperty(key)) {
      counts[key] = grouped[key].length;
    }
  }
  return counts;
}

console.log(toCounts(grouped));
// { '.org': 2, '.com': 1 }
```

indexBy()

It can also be useful to identify differences among data in a collection, especially if those differences can serve as unique identifiers. Fishing a single object out of a collection by a known identifier is a pretty common scenario. Done manually, this would require looping over each element in the collection (perhaps with a while or for loop) and returning the first that possesses a matching unique identifier.

Imagine an airline web site on which a customer selects departure and destination airports. The user chooses each airport via drop-down menus and is then shown additional data about each airport. This additional data is loaded from airport objects in an array. The values chosen in each drop-down menu are the unique airport codes, which are then used by the application to find the full, detailed airport objects.

Fortunately, the developer who created this application used Underscore's indexBy() function to create an index object from the airports array, shown in Listing 12-6.

Listing 12-6. Indexing Objects by Property

```
// example-006/index.js
'use strict';
var _ = require('underscore');

var airports = [
  {code: 'STL', city: 'St Louis', timeZone: '-6:00'},
  {code: 'SEA', city: 'Seattle', timeZone: '-8:00'},
  {code: 'JFK', city: 'New York', timeZone: '-5:00'}
];

var selected = 'SEA';

var indexed = _.indexBy(airports, 'code');
console.log(indexed);
/*
{
  STL: {code: 'STL', city: 'St Louis', timeZone: '-6:00'},
  SEA: {code: 'SEA', city: 'Seattle', timeZone: '-8:00'},
  JFK: {code: 'JFK', city: 'New York', timeZone: '-5:00'}
}
*/

var timeZone = indexed[selected].timeZone;
console.log(timeZone);
// -8:00
```

The `indexBy()` function behaves a bit like `groupBy()`, except that each object has a unique value for the indexed property, so the final result is an object whose keys (which must be unique) are the values of each object for a specified property and whose values are the objects that possess each property. In Listing 12-6 the keys for the `indexed` object are each airport code, and the values are the corresponding airport objects.

Keeping an indexed object with relatively stable reference data in memory is a fundamental caching practice. It incurs a one-time performance penalty (the indexing process) to avoid multiple iteration penalties (having to traverse the array each time an object is needed).

Being Choosy

Developers often extract wanted data, or omit unwanted data, from collections and objects. This might be done for legibility (when data will be shown to a user), for performance (when data is to be sent over a network connection), for privacy (when data returned from an object or module's API should be sparse), or for some other purpose.

Selecting Data from Collections

Underscore has a number of utility functions that select one or more elements from a collection of objects based on some criteria. In some circumstances, this criteria may be a function that evaluates each element and returns true or false (whether the element "passes" the criteria test). In other circumstances, the criteria may be a bit of data that will be compared to each element (or a part of each element) for equality, the success or failure of which determines whether the element "matches" the criteria used.

filter()

The `filter()` function uses the criteria function approach. Given an array of elements and a function, `filter()` applies the function to each element and returns an array consisting only of elements that passed the criteria test. In Listing 12-7 an array of playing cards is filtered so that only spades are returned.

Listing 12-7. Filtering an Array with a Criteria Function

```
// example-007/index.js
'use strict';
var _ = require('underscore');

var cards = [
  {suite: 'Spades', denomination: 'King'},
  {suite: 'Hearts', denomination: '10'},
  {suite: 'Clubs', denomination: 'Ace'},
  {suite: 'Spades', denomination: 'Ace'},
];

var filtered = _.filter(cards, function (card) {
  return card.suite === 'Spades';
});

console.log(filtered);
/*
[
  { suite: 'Spades', denomination: 'King' },
  { suite: 'Spades', denomination: 'Ace' }
]
*/
```

where()

The where() function is similar to filter() but uses the comparison criteria approach instead. Its first argument is an array of objects, but its second argument is a criteria object whose keys and values will be compared to the keys and values of each element in the array. If an element contains all the keys and corresponding values in the criteria object (using strict equality), the element will be included in the array returned by where().

In Listing 12-8, a set of board game objects is filtered by an object that specifies a minimum player count and play time. *Pandemic* is excluded because it does not match the playTime value of the criteria object, though it does match the minPlayer value.

473

Listing 12-8. Filtering an Array by Criteria Comparison

```
// example-008/index.js
'use strict';
var _ = require('underscore');

var boardGames = [
  {title: 'Ticket to Ride', minPlayers: 2, playTime: 45},
  {title: 'Pandemic', minPlayers: 2, playTime: 60},
  {title: 'Munchkin Deluxe', minPlayers: 2, playTime: 45}
];

var filtered = _.where(boardGames, {
  minPlayers: 2,
  playTime: 45
});

console.log(filtered);
/*
[
  { title: 'Ticket to Ride', minPlayers: 2, playTime: 45 },
  { title: 'Munchkin Deluxe', minPlayers: 2, playTime: 45 }
]
*/
```

find() and findWhere()

The `filter()` and `where()` functions always return collections. If no object passes the criteria test, each returns an empty set. A developer could use these functions to find an individual object within a set (e.g., by some unique identifier), but would then have to fish that object from the result array by using index zero. Fortunately, Underscore provides `find()` and `findWhere()` functions that complement `filter()` and `where()`. They each return the *first* object to pass the criteria check or return `undefined` if no objects in the set pass. In Listing 12-9 a collection is searched twice for specific entries. Note that even though multiple items would fulfill the {what: 'Dagger'} criteria object passed to `findWhere()`, only the first match in the collection is returned.

Listing 12-9. Finding a Single Item in a Collection

```
// example-009/index.js
'use strict';
var _ = require('underscore');

var guesses = [
  {who: 'Mrs. Peacock', where: 'Lounge', what: 'Revolver'},
  {who: 'Professor Plum', where: 'Study', what: 'Dagger'},
  {who: 'Miss Scarlet', where: 'Ballroom', what: 'Candlestick'},
  {who: 'Reverend Green', where: 'Conservatory', what: 'Dagger'}
];

var result = _.find(guesses, function (guess) {
  return guess.where === 'Ballroom';
});

console.log(result);
// { who: 'Miss Scarlet', where: 'Ballroom', what: 'Candlestick' }

result = _.findWhere(guesses, {what: 'Dagger'});

console.log(result);
// { who: 'Professor Plum', where: 'Study', what: 'Dagger' }
```

Selecting Data from Objects

The Underscore functions covered up to this point all filter larger collections into focused, smaller ones (or even a single object) when a portion of data is unnecessary to the application. Objects are also collections of data, indexed by string keys instead of ordered numbers; and like arrays, filtering data in individual objects can be quite useful.

pluck()

A developer could get a property's value from each object in a collection by looping over each element and capturing the desired property value in an array or by using `Array.prototype.map()` (or Underscore's equivalent, `map()`). But a faster, more convenient option is to use Underscore's `pluck()` function, which takes an array as its first argument and the name of the property to lift from each element as its second. The `pluck()`

function is used in Listing 12-10 to extract the numbers that landed face up from a roll of three dice. These values are then summed (with `Array.prototype.reduce()`) to determine the total value of the roll.

Listing 12-10. Plucking Properties from Objects in a Collection

```
// example-010/index.js
'use strict';
var _ = require('underscore');

var diceRoll = [
  {sides: 6, up: 3},
  {sides: 6, up: 1},
  {sides: 6, up: 5}
];

var allUps = _.pluck(diceRoll, 'up');

console.log(allUps);
// [ 3, 1, 5 ]

var total = allUps.reduce(function (prev, next) {
  return prev + next;
}, 0);

console.log(total);
// 9
```

While `pluck()` is quite useful for selecting individual properties from objects, it only operates on collections and is not very useful for dealing with individual objects.

values()

The ECMAScript 5 specification introduced the `keys()` function on the `Object` constructor, a handy utility for turning the keys of any object literal into an array of strings. Underscore has a corresponding `keys()` implementation but *also* has a `values()` function that, sadly, has no counterpart in native JavaScript. The `values()` function is used to extract all property values from an object, and is arguably most *valu*able (dad joke) for objects that hold a collection of "constants," or serve as an enumeration would in another language. Listing 12-11 demonstrates how this extraction takes place.

Listing 12-11. Extracting Values from an Object Literal

```javascript
// example-011/index.js
'use strict';
var _ = require('underscore');

var BOARD_TILES = {
  IND_AVE: 'Indiana Avenue',
  BOARDWALK: 'Boardwalk',
  MARV_GARD: 'Marvin Gardens',
  PK_PLACE: 'Park Place'
};

var propertyNames = _.values(BOARD_TILES);

console.log(propertyNames);
// [ 'Indiana Avenue', 'Boardwalk', 'Marvin Gardens', 'Park Place' ]
```

Reference data (e.g., a hash of US state abbreviations and names) is often retrieved and cached all at once. This data will typically be dereferenced by key so that some particular value can be extracted, but sometimes it is useful to work with all values regardless of key, as the Underscore template in Listing 12-12 demonstrates. (Underscore templates will be discussed later in this chapter, but Listing 12-12 should give you enough to grasp basic usage.) Each value in the BOARD_TILES hash (the tile name) is rendered as a list item in an unordered list. The keys are inconsequential; only the values matter, a perfect scenario for the values() function.

Listing 12-12. Extracting Values from an Object Literal

```html
<!-- example-011/index.html -->

<div id="output"></div>

<script id="tiles-template" type="text/x-template">
<ul class="properties">
  <% _.each(_.values(tiles), function (property) { %>
  <li><%- property %></li>
  <% }); %>
</ul>
</script>
```

```
<script>
(function (_) {
  var template = document.querySelector('#tiles-template').innerHTML;
  var bindTemplate = _.template(template);
  var BOARD_TILES = {
    IND_AVE: 'Indiana Avenue',
    BOARDWALK: 'Boardwalk',
    MARV_GARD: 'Marvin Gardens',
    PK_PLACE: 'Park Place'
  };
  var markup = bindTemplate({tiles: BOARD_TILES});
  document.querySelector('#output').innerHTML = markup;
}(window._));
</script>
```

pick()

Finally, to whittle an object down to a subset of its keys and values, developers can use
Underscore's pick() function. When passing in a target object and one or more property
names, pick() will return another object composed solely of those properties (and
their values) from the target. In Listing 12-13 the name and numPlayers properties are
extracted from a larger hash of board game details with pick().

Listing 12-13. Picking Properties from an Object Literal

```
// example-012/index.js
'use strict';
var _ = require('underscore');

var boardGame = {
  name: 'Settlers of Catan',
  designer: 'Klaus Teuber',
  numPlayers: [3, 4],
  yearPublished: 1995,
  ages: '10+',
  playTime: '90min',
  subdomain: ['Family', 'Strategy'],
```

```
  category: ['Civilization', 'Negotiation'],
  website: 'http://www.catan.com'
};

var picked = _.pick(boardGame, 'name', 'numPlayers');

console.log(picked);
/*
{
  name: 'Settlers of Catan',
  numPlayers: [ 3, 4 ]
}
*/
```

omit()

The inverse of pick() is omit(), which returns an object composed of all properties *except* the ones specified. The properties designer, numPlayers, yearPublished, ages, and playTime are all eliminated from the result object created by omit() in Listing 12-14.

Listing 12-14. Omitting Properties from an Object Literal

```
// example-013/index.js
'use strict';
var _ = require('underscore');

var boardGame = {
  name: 'Settlers of Catan',
  designer: 'Klaus Teuber',
  numPlayers: [3, 4],
  yearPublished: 1995,
  ages: '10+',
  playTime: '90min',
  subdomain: ['Family', 'Strategy'],
  category: ['Civilization', 'Negotiation'],
  website: 'http://www.catan.com'
};
```

```
var omitted = _.omit(boardGame, 'designer', 'numPlayers',
  'yearPublished', 'ages', 'playTime');

console.log(omitted);
/*
{
  name: 'Settlers of Catan',
  subdomain: [ 'Family', 'Strategy' ],
  category: [ 'Civilization', 'Negotiation' ],
  website: 'http://www.catan.com'
}
*/
```

In addition to property names, both `pick()` and `omit()` accept a predicate that will evaluate each property and value instead. If the predicate returns `true`, the property will be included in the resulting object; if it returns `false`, the property will be excluded. The predicate for `pick()` in Listing 12-15 will only add properties to the result object for values that are arrays; in this case, the properties `numPlayers`, `subdomain`, and `category`.

Listing 12-15. Picking Properties from an Object Literal with a Predicate Function

```
// example-014/index.js
'use strict';
var _ = require('underscore');

var boardGame = {
  name: 'Settlers of Catan',
  designer: 'Klaus Teuber',
  numPlayers: [3, 4],
  yearPublished: 1995,
  ages: '10+',
  playTime: '90min',
  subdomain: ['Family', 'Strategy'],
  category: ['Civilization', 'Negotiation'],
  website: 'http://www.catan.com'
};
```

```
var picked = _.pick(boardGame, function (value, key, object) {
  return Array.isArray(value);
});

console.log(picked);
/*
{
  numPlayers: [ 3, 4 ],
  subdomain: [ 'Family', 'Strategy' ],
  category: [ 'Civilization', 'Negotiation' ]
}
*/
```

Chaining

Underscore contains a number of utility functions that are frequently used together to create transformation pipelines for data. To begin a chain, an object or collection is passed to Underscore's chain() function. This returns a chain wrapper on which many Underscore functions may be called in a fluent manner, each compounding the effects of the preceding function call.

Listing 12-16 shows an array of coffee shops and the hours during which each is open. The whatIsOpen() function accepts a numeric hour and a period ('AM' or 'PM'). These are then used to evaluate the coffee shops in the collection and return the names of the coffee shops that are open during that time.

Listing 12-16. Chaining Functions on a Collection

```
// example-015/index.js
'use strict';
var _ = require('lodash');

/*
Note that lodash, not underscore, is used for
this example. The cloneDeep() function below
is unique to lodash.
*/
```

```
var coffeeShops = [
  {name: 'Crooked Tree', hours: [6, 22]},
  {name: 'Picasso\'s Coffee House', hours: [6, 24]},
  {name: 'Sump Coffee', hours: [9, 16]}
];

function whatIsOpen(hour, period) {
  return _.chain(coffeeShops)
    .cloneDeep()                              // #1
    .map(function to12HourFormat (shop) {  // #2
      shop.hours = _.map(shop.hours, function (hour) {
        return (hour > 12 ? hour - 12 : hour);
      }
      return shop;
    })
    .filter(function filterByHour (shop) { // #3
      if (period === 'AM') {
        return shop.hours[0] <= hour;
      }
      if (period === 'PM') {
        return shop.hours[1] >= hour;
      }
      return false;
    })
    .map(function toShopName (shop) {        // #4
      return shop.name;
    })
    .value();                                // #5
}

console.log(whatIsOpen(8, 'AM'));
// [ 'Crooked Tree', 'Picasso\'s Coffee House' ]

console.log(whatIsOpen(11, 'PM'));
// [ 'Picasso\'s Coffee House' ]
```

After `chain()` wraps the `coffeeShops` array in a fluent API, the following functions are called to manipulate and filter the collection until the desired data has been produced:

1. `cloneDeep()` recursively clones the array and all objects and their properties. In step 2 the array data is actually modified, so the array is cloned to preserve its original state.

2. `map(function to12HourFormat() {/*...*/})` iterates over each item in the cloned array and replaces the second 24-hour number in the `hours` array with its 12-hour equivalent.

3. `filter(function filterByHour() {/*...*/})` iterates over each modified coffee shop and evaluates its `hours` based on the period (`'AM'` or `'PM'`) specified: the first element for the opening hour and the second for the closing hour. The function returns `true` or `false` to indicate whether the coffee shop should be retained or dropped from the results.

4. `map(function toShopName() {/*...*/})` returns the name of each remaining coffee shop in the collection. The result is an array of strings that will be passed to any subsequent steps in the chain.

5. Finally, `value()` is called to terminate the chain and return the final result: the array of names of coffee shops that are open during the hour and period provided to `whatIsOpen()` (or an empty array if none match the criteria).

This may seem like a lot to grasp, but Underscore chains can be reduced to a few simple principles that are easy to remember:

- Chains can be created with any initial value, though *object* and *array* are the most typical starting points.

- Any Underscore function that operates on a value is available as a chained function.

- The return value of a chained function becomes the input value of the next function in the chain.

- The first argument of a chained function is always the value on which it operates. For example, Underscore's `map()` function normally accepts two arguments, a collection and a callback, but when invoked as a chained function, it only accepts a callback. This pattern holds for all chained functions.

- Always invoke the `value()` function to terminate a chain and retrieve its final, manipulated value. If a chain does not return a value, this is unnecessary.

Chaining functions for a collection or object might seem natural and obvious, but Underscore also has a number of functions that work on primitives. Listing 12-17 shows how a chain can wrap the number 100 to eventually generate the lyrics to "99 Bottles of Beer."

Listing 12-17. Chaining Functions on a Primitive

```
// example-016/index.js
'use strict';
var _ = require('underscore');

_.chain(100)
  .times(function makeLyrics (number) {
    if (number === 0) {
      return ";
    }
    return [
      number + ' bottles of beer on the wall!',
      number + ' bottles of beer!',
      'Take one down, pass it around!',
      (number - 1) + ' bottles of beer on the wall!',
      '♫ ♪ ♫ ♪ ♫ ♪ ♫ ♪ ♫ ♪ ♫',
    ].join('\n');
  })
  .tap(function orderLyrics (lyrics) {
    // reverse the array so the song is in order
    lyrics.reverse();
  })
```

```
  .map(function makeLoud (lyric) {
    return lyric.toUpperCase();
  })
  .forEach(function printLyrics (lyric) {
    console.log(lyric);
  });
```

The `times()` function takes a number as its first argument and a callback to be invoked for each decremented value of that number. In this example, the callback `makeLyrics()` will be invoked starting with the number 99 (not 100) and ending with the number 0, for 100 total iterations. For each invocation, one refrain of "99 Bottles" is returned. This creates an array of strings, which is then passed to the next function in the chain.

Because the final chained function `forEach()` creates side effects instead of returning a value, there is no need to terminate the chain by calling `value()`. Instead, Listing 12-18 shows the results that are printed to the console.

Listing 12-18. The Song to Ruin All Road Trips

```
99 BOTTLES OF BEER ON THE WALL!
99 BOTTLES OF BEER!
TAKE ONE DOWN, PASS IT AROUND!
98 BOTTLES OF BEER ON THE WALL!
♫ ♪ ♫ ♪ ♫ ♪ ♫ ♪ ♫ ♪ ♫
98 BOTTLES OF BEER ON THE WALL!
98 BOTTLES OF BEER!
TAKE ONE DOWN, PASS IT AROUND!
97 BOTTLES OF BEER ON THE WALL!
♫ ♪ ♫ ♪ ♫ ♪ ♫ ♪ ♫ ♪ ♫
        ...
```

Function Timing

Functions execute when they are scheduled on JavaScript's internal event loop. Native functions like `setTimeout()`, `setInterval()`, and Node's `setImmediate()` give developers a degree of control over when these functions run—which turn of the event loop will handle their invocations. Underscore augments these primitives with a number of control functions that add flexibility to function scheduling.

defer()

Underscore's `defer()` function mimics the behavior of `setImmediate()` in a Node.
js environment; which is to say, `defer()` schedules a function to execute on the next
immediate turn of the event loop. This is equivalent to using `setTimeout()` with a delay
of 0. Since `setImmediate()` is not a JavaScript standard function, using Underscore's
`defer()` in both browser and server environments can provide a greater degree of
consistency than polyfilling `setImmediate()` in the browser.

The example code in Listing 12-19 demonstrates the value of `defer()` in a user
interface. It loads a large data set of playing card information for the popular card game
Dominion, then populates an HTML table with card details.

While the data is fetched from the server and then processed, the user sees the
message, "Please be patient while cards are loading!" Once the GET request has
completed, the `processCards()` handler begins to process almost 200 cards in blocks
of 10. For each block (except the first), the handler *defers* processing, which has two
beneficial effects. First, it allows the UI time to paint the previous 10 processed rows in
the table, and second, it allows the user to scroll in between window paints. Because the
block size is so small, the scroll speed is relatively normal for the user. If `processCards()`
attempted to render all table rows at once, the UI would freeze until all DOM elements
had been added to the table.

Listing 12-19. Deferring a Function

```
<!-- example-017/views/defer.html -->
<p id="wait-msg">Please be patient while cards are loading!</p>
<table id="cards">
  <thead>
    <tr>
      <th>Name</th>
      <th>Expansion</th>
      <th>Cost</th>
      <th>Benefit</th>
      <th>Description</th>
    </tr>
  </thead>
  <tbody></tbody>
</table>
```

```
<script>
$(function () {
  var $waitMsg - $('#wait-msg');
  var $cards = $('#cards tbody');

  function processCards(cards) {
    var BLOCK_SIZE = 10;

    // process the first chunk of 10 cards
    (function processBlock() {
      if (!cards.length) {
        $waitMsg.addClass('hidden');
        return;
      }

      // take the first 10 cards from the array;
      // splice() will reduce the length of the array
      // by 10 each time
      var block = cards.splice(0, BLOCK_SIZE);

      _.forEach(block, function (card) {
        var $tr = $('<tr></tr>');
        $tr.append($('<td></td>').html(card.name));
        $tr.append($('<td></td>').html(card.expansion));
        $tr.append($('<td></td>').html(card.cost));
        $tr.append($('<td></td>').html(card.benefits.join(', ')));
        $tr.append($('<td></td>').html(card.description));
        $cards.append($tr);
      });

      // defer the next block of 10 cards to
      // allow the user to scroll and the UI to
      // refresh
      _.defer(processBlock);
    }());
  }
```

```
  // kick off the process by loading the data set
  $.get('/cards').then(processCards);
}());
</script>
```

debounce()

"Debouncing" is the practice of ignoring duplicate invocations, requests, messages, and so forth in a system for some period of time. In JavaScript, debouncing a function can be very helpful if a developer anticipates that duplicate, identical function calls may be made in quick succession. A common scenario for a debounced function, for example, is preventing a form's submit handler from being called more than once when a user accidentally clicks a Submit button multiple times on a web page.

A custom debounce implementation would require a developer to track the invocations of a function over a short period of time (perhaps only hundreds of milliseconds) using setTimeout() and clearTimeout() for each duplicate invocation. Fortunately, Underscore provides a debounce() function that handles this plumbing for developers, as demonstrated in Listing 12-20.

Listing 12-20. Debouncing a Function

```
<!-- example-018/debounce.html -->
<button id="submit">Quickly Click Me Many Times!</button>
<script>
(function () {
  var onClick = _.debounce(function (e) {
    alert('click handled!');
  }, 300);

  document.getElementById('submit')
    .addEventListener('click', onClick);
}());
</script>
```

In Listing 12-20 an onClick() function is created by invoking debounce(). The first argument to debounce() is the function that will actually be run once all duplicate invocations have stopped. The second argument is a duration, in milliseconds, that must elapse between invocations for the callback to finally be triggered. For example, if a user clicks the #submit button once, and then clicks it again within the 300-millisecond time span, the first invocation is ignored and the wait timer is restarted. Once the wait period has timed out, the debounce() callback will be invoked, alerting the user that the click has been handled.

Note   Each time a debounced function is invoked, its internal timer is reset. The specified time span represents the minimum time that must pass between the last invocation and its preceding invocation (if any) before the callback function executes.

In Figure 12-1, a debounced function with a timeout of 300ms is called three times. After the first call at point A, 250ms elapse, at which point another call happens at point B and the wait timer is reset. The interval between B and the next call, C, is shorter: 100ms. Again, the wait timer resets. At point C a third call is made, after which the wait duration of 300ms is met. At point D the debounced function's callback is invoked.

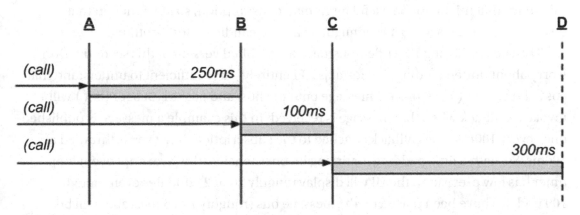

Figure 12-1. *A debounced function invoked multiple times*

The debounced function's callback will receive any arguments passed to the debounce() function itself. For example, in Listing 12-20, jQuery's event object e is forwarded to the debounced function's callback. While each invocation may pass different arguments, it is important to realize that *only the arguments passed during the last invocation within the wait period* will actually be forwarded to the callback. The debounce() function receives an optional third, immediate parameter which may be true or false. Setting this parameter to true will invoke the callback for the *first* invocation instead, ignoring all subsequent duplicates for the wait period. If the arguments passed to the debounced function vary, capturing the first parameters passed instead of the last might be strategically beneficial.

throttle()

Underscore's throttle() function is similar to debounce(). It ignores subsequent invocations of a function for a specified period of time, but does *not* reset its internal timer with each function call. It effectively ensures that only one invocation happens *during* a specified period, whereas debounce() guarantees that only one invocation will happen sometime *after* the last invocation of a debounced function. Throttling a function can be particularly useful if a function is likely to be called many times with the same arguments, or when the granularity of the arguments is such that it is not useful to account for every invocation of the function.

The in-memory JavaScript message bus, postal.js, is a useful library for routing messages through an application. Some application modules send messages at a frequency that might not be useful for human consumption, so any function that displays these messages to a user might be a good candidate for throttling.

The code in Listing 12-21 demonstrates a simplified version of this scenario. Don't worry about understanding the postal.js API entirely—it is sufficient to understand that postal.publish() will place a message onto the bus, and postal.subscribe() will invoke a callback when that message is received. In this example a message is published once every 100ms. The callback attached to the subscription, however, is throttled at 500ms. So, with a little padding for timing inconsistencies (the JavaScript event loop timer has low precision), the UI will display roughly 20 or 21 updates even though 100 updates have been placed on the message bus (roughly 1 in 5 messages will be displayed).

Listing 12-21. Using a Throttled Function to Control Status Updates

```
<!-- example-019/throttle.html -->
<section id="friends"></section>

<script>
$(function () {
```

```
  var $friends = $('#friends');

  function onStatusUpdate(data) {
    var text = data.name + ' is ' + data.status;
    $friends.append($('<p></p>').html(text));
  }

  /*
   * subscribing to status updates from friends
   * with a throttled callback that will only
   * fire *once* every 500ms
   */
  postal.subscribe({
    channel: 'friends',
    topic: 'status.update',
    callback: _.throttle(onStatusUpdate, 500)
  });
}());
</script>

<script>
  $(function () {
    var i = 1;
    var interval = null;

    /*
     * publishing a status update from a
     * friend every 100ms
     */
    function sendMessage() {
      if (i === 100) {
        return clearInterval(interval);
      }
      i += 1;
      postal.publish({
        channel: 'friends',
        topic: 'status.update',
```

```
      data: {
        name: 'Jim',
        status: 'slinging code'
      }
    });
  }

  setInterval(sendMessage, 100);
}());
</script>
```

Figure 12-2 illustrates how `throttle()` differs from `defer()`. Once a throttled function is invoked at point A, it will ignore all further invocations (at points B and C) until its wait duration has passed—in this case, 300ms. Once elapsed, the next call at point D will invoke the throttled function.

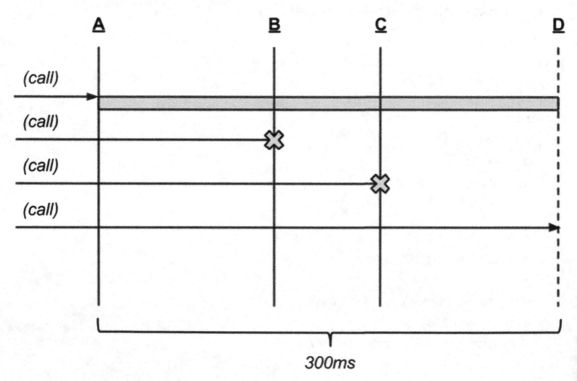

Figure 12-2. A throttled function invoked multiple times

Templates

Underscore offers a micro-templating system that compiles a template string (typically HTML) into a function. When this function is invoked with some data, it uses the template string's binding expressions to populate the template, returning a new HTML string. Developers who have used templating tools like Mustache or Handlebars will be familiar with this process. Unlike these more robust templating libraries, however, Underscore's templates have a much smaller feature set and no real template extension points. Underscore can be a strong choice as a template library when the templates in an application are fairly trivial and you have no desire or need to incur the overhead of a template-specific library in an application.

Template systems usually begin with some markup, and Underscore is no exception. Data binding expressions are added to a template with "gator tags" (so named because the opening and closing elements, <% and %>, look kind of like alligators). Listing 12-22 shows a simple block of HTML that will later be bound to an object literal containing two properties, title and synopsis.

Listing 12-22. Template with "Gator Tags"

```
<h1><%- title %></h1>
<p class="synopsis"><%- synopsis %></p>
```

Gator tags come in three varieties. The tags used in Listing 12-22 generate safe HTML output by escaping any HTML tag sequences. If the movie synopsis contained an HTML tag such as <strong>, it would be converted to <strong>. In contrast, the gator tag <%= may be used to output unescaped strings with HTML markup intact. The third gator tag is the JavaScript evaluation tag, and it simply begins with <% (more on this tag will be covered in a bit). All gator tags share the same closing tag, %>.

To turn the HTML in Listing 12-22 into a populated template, the HTML string is first compiled by passing it to Underscore's template() function. A reusable binding function is returned. When a data object is passed to this binding function, any properties that match the binding expressions in the original template string will be substituted in the final, computed output. Under the hood Underscore uses JavaScript's with keyword to magically bring these properties into the template's scope. Listing 12-23 demonstrates how to bind a simple template string to a data object and shows the HTML that is produced as a result.

Listing 12-23. Binding an Underscore Template

```html
<!-- example-020/index.html -->
<div id="output"></div>

<script>
(function (_) {
  var markup =
    '<h1><%- title %></h1>' +
    '<p class="synopsis"><%- synopsis %></p>';

  // compile the string into a function
  var compiledTemplate = _.template(markup);

  // invoke the function with data to
  // get the rendered string
  var rendered = compiledTemplate({
    title: 'Sunshine',
    synopsis: 'A team of scientists are sent to re-ignite a dying sun.'
  });

  document.querySelector('#output').innerHTML = rendered;

}(window._));
</script>
<div id="output">
  <h1>Sunshine</h1>
  <p class="synopsis">A team of scientists are sent to re-ignite a dying
  sun.</p>
</div>
```

Once a template string is compiled to a function, it may be invoked any number of times with different data to produce different rendered markup. It is common for applications to compile template strings into functions during page load (or during application startup, if Node.js is the runtime environment), then call each as needed during the lifetime of the application. If template strings do not change, there is no need to recompile them.

Loops and Other Arbitrary JavaScript in Templates

Many templating libraries include shorthand tags for common templating chores like iterating over a collection. To keep its templating system thin, Underscore forgoes syntactical sugar and, instead, allows developers to write template loops in plain, valid JavaScript.

In Listing 12-24 an unordered list of actors is created by using Underscore's `each()` function within the template. There are two important things to note here. First, plain JavaScript is evaluated within gator tag code blocks. These blocks are created by using gator tags *without* a hyphen symbol in the opening tag (e.g., <% %> instead of <%- %>). Second, the `each()` loop is split in the middle, where valid templating markup is used to render the `actor` variable, created by the loop itself, in a list item element. Finally, the loop is terminated by a closing brace, parenthesis, and semicolon, as if it were a normal JavaScript loop.

Listing 12-24. Looping in a Template

```
<!-- example-021/index.html -->
<div id="output"></div>

<script>
(function (_) {
  var markup =
    '<h1><%- title %></h1>' +
    '<p class="synopsis"><%- synopsis %></p>' +
    '<ul>' +
    '<% _.each(actors, function (actor) { %>' +
    '  <li><%- actor %></li>' +
    '<% }); %>' +
    '</ul>';

  // compile the string into a function
  var compiledTemplate = _.template(markup);

  // invoke the function with data to
  // get the rendered string
  var rendered = compiledTemplate({
    title: 'Sunshine',
```

```
  synopsis: 'A team of scientists are sent to re-ignite a dying sun.',
  actors: ['Cillian Murphy', 'Hiroyuki Sanada', 'Chris Evans']
});

document.querySelector('#output').innerHTML = rendered;

}(window._));
</script>
<div id="output">
  <h1>Sunshine</h1>
  <p class="synopsis">A team of scientists are sent to re-ignite a dying
  sun.</p>
  <ul>
    <li>Cillian Murphy</li>
    <li>Hiroyuki Sanada</li>
    <li>Chris Evans</li>
  </ul>
</div>
```

JavaScript evaluation tags can also be used to execute arbitrary JavaScript code. The template in Listing 12-25 calculates a rating percentage for the movie based on X out of Y stars awarded to it by critics. The template uses Underscore's internal print() function to render the result of the calculation in the template output, an alternative to gator tag interpolation that is sometimes used in more complex expressions.

Listing 12-25. Arbitrary JavaScript Within a Template

```
<!-- example-022/index.html -->
<div id="output"></div>

<script>
(function (_) {
  var markup =
    '<p>' +
    '<%- voted %> out of <%- total %> stars!' +
    ' (<% print((voted / total * 100).toFixed(0)) %>%)' +
    '</p>';
```

```
var compiledTemplate = _.template(markup);

var rendered = compiledTemplate({
  voted: 4, total: 5
});

document.querySelector('#output').innerHTML = rendered;
}(window._));
</script>
<div id="output">
  <p>4 out of 5 stars! (80%)</p>
</div>
```

Note   Generally it is bad practice to perform calculations in a template (the application's "view"). Instead, the actual calculated value should be part of the data passed to the compiled template function. Listing 12-25 should be considered for demonstration purposes only.

Living Without Gator Tags

Gator tags can be a bit unruly in nontrivial templates. Fortunately, Underscore allows developers to change the syntax of template tags with regular expressions. Setting the `templateSettings` property on the Underscore object to a hash of key/value settings alters the behavior of Underscore for the lifetime of your page (or Node.js process), and affects all rendered templates.

Listing 12-26 shows how to change Underscore's gator tag syntax into a more terse Mustache/Handlebars syntax. In this case, the three different types of tags (evaluation, interpolation, and escaped interpolation) are each assigned a regular expression on the global settings object.

Listing 12-26. Changing Template Syntax

```html
<!-- example-023/index.html -->
<div id="output"></div>

<script>
(function (_) {
  _.templateSettings = {
    // arbitrary JavaScript code blocks: {{ }}
    evaluate: /\{\{(.+?)\}\}/g,
    // unsafe string interpolation: {{= }}
    interpolate: /\{\{=(.+?)\}\}/g,
    // escaped string interpolation: {{- }}
    escape: /\{\{-(.+?)\}\}/g
  };

  var markup =
    '<h1>{{- title }}</h1>' +
    '<p class="synopsis">{{- synopsis }}</p>' +
    '<ul>' +
    '{{ _.each(actors, function (actor) { }}' +
    '  <li>{{- actor }}</li>' +
    '{{ }); }}' +
    '</ul>';

  var compiledTemplate = _.template(markup);

  var rendered = compiledTemplate({
    title: 'Sunshine',
    synopsis: 'A team of scientists are sent to re-ignite a dying sun.',
    actors: ['Cillian Murphy', 'Hiroyuki Sanada', 'Chris Evans']
  });

  document.querySelector('#output').innerHTML = rendered;
}(window._));
</script>
```

Any markup compiled by the template system must now support the specified Mustache syntax. Templates that still contain gator tags will not be rendered correctly.

Table 12-2 is a convenient reference for matching template settings to syntax and the regular expressions that enable each syntax.

Table 12-2. *Global Template Settings*

Setting	Template Syntax	Regular Expression
evaluate	{{ ... }}	/{{(.+?)}}/g
interpolate	{{= ... }}	/{{=(.+?)}}/g
escape	{{- ... }}	/{{-(.+?)}}/g

Accessing the Data Object Within a Template

As mentioned, Underscore uses JavaScript's with keyword to evaluate a data object's properties in a template's scope as "first class" variables. But the object itself may also be referenced through the obj property in the template. To modify a previous example, in Listing 12-27 the template tests for the data property obj.percent in an if/else block before attempting to calculate a percentage. If the percent property exists on the data object, it is rendered; otherwise the calculated value is rendered.

Listing 12-27. The "obj" Variable

```
<!-- example-024/index.html -->
<div id="output"></div>

<script>
(function (_) {
  var markup =
    '<%- voted %> out of <%- total %> stars!' +
    '<% if (obj.percent) { %>' +
    ' (<%- obj.percent %>%)' +
    '<% } else { %>' +
    ' (<% print((voted / total * 100).toFixed(0)) %>%)' +
    '<% } %>';
```

```
    var compiledTemplate = _.template(markup);

    var rendered = compiledTemplate({
      voted: 4, total: 5, percent: 80.2
    });

    document.querySelector('#output').innerHTML = rendered;

}(window._));
</script>
```

As a micro-optimization (and perhaps a security feature), the scoped object can be given a name so that the with keyword is avoided altogether. This makes the templating function run slightly faster, but also requires that *all* properties in the template be referenced as properties of the named data object. To specify a name for the data object, an options object may be passed to Underscore's template() function when compiling the template. This object's variable property will assign the data object's variable name, which may then be referred to in the template. Listing 12-28 shows this setting in action.

Listing 12-28. Setting the Data Object's Variable Name

```
<!-- example-025/index.html -->
<div id="output"></div>

<script>
(function (_) {
  var markup =
    '<%- movie.voted %> out of <%- movie.total %> stars!' +
    '<% if (movie.percent) { %>' +
    ' (<%- movie.percent %>%)' +
    '<% } else { %>' +
    ' (<% print((movie.voted / movie.total * 100).toFixed(0)) %>%)' +
    '<% } %>';

  var settings = {variable: 'movie'};
  // settings is the *third* parameter
  var compiledTemplate = _.template(markup, null, settings);
```

```
var rendered = compiledTemplate({
  voted: 4, total: 5, percent: 80.1
});

document.querySelector('#output').innerHTML = rendered;
}(window._));
</script>
```

Note   The `variable` property may be set in Underscore's global settings.
However, giving variables good and relevant names is important, so it makes more
sense to name a variable according to its context. Instead of defining some generic
variable like `data` or `item`, the examples in this section use the variable name
`movie` and apply it by passing a settings object to `template()` when the movie
template is compiled.

Default Template Data

While not part of its templating system, Underscore's `defaults()` function can be used
to ensure that a template always has default data. This will prevent binding failures
in the event that a data object is missing one or more referenced properties. The first
parameter to the `defaults()` function is an object with potentially missing properties.
Any following arguments may be objects with properties set to default values, which
will fill in any missing properties on the first object. The return value is an object that
represents the "merged" properties of all arguments. Listing 12-29 shows this effect on a
data object that is missing its `synopsis` property. When the `data` and `DEFAULTS` objects
are passed to the `defaults()` function, the returned object contains the title from `data`
and the synopsis from `DEFAULTS`.

Listing 12-29. Default Template Values

```
<!-- example-026/index.html -->
<div id="output"></div>

<script>
(function (_) {
  var markup =
    '<h1><%- title %></h1>' +
    '<p class="synopsis"><%- synopsis %></p>';

  // compile the string into a function
  var compiledTemplate = _.template(markup);

  var DEFAULTS = {
    title: 'A Great Film',
    synopsis: 'An epic hero defeats and evil villain and saves the world!'
  };

  var data = {
    title: 'Lord of the Rings'
  };

  // fill in any missing data values with defaults
  var merged = _.defaults(data, DEFAULTS);

  var rendered = compiledTemplate(merged);

  document.querySelector('#output').innerHTML = rendered;
}(window._));
</script>
```

If multiple default objects are passed to `defaults()`, they are evaluated from first to last. Once a missing property is found on a default object, it will be ignored on any following default objects.

Summary

Modern and future implementations of ECMAScript have given developers a great many utility functions on primitive types like `String`, `Array`, `Object`, and `Function`. Unfortunately, the world moves faster than specifications come to fruition so libraries like Underscore and Lodash occupy the intersection of developer needs and language maturity.

With over 100 utility functions and a micro-templating system, Underscore enables developers to manipulate, transform, and render data in objects and collections. Underscore can be used in browser and server environments and has no dependencies. It can be added to a web page with a simple `script` tag or imported as an AMD or CommonJS module. Popular package managers like Bower, npm, component, and NuGet can all download prebuilt Underscore packages for a developer's platform of choice.

Underscore's strong feature set and ubiquitous availability make it an ideal and unobtrusive Swiss Army knife for JavaScript projects.

Related Resources

- Underscore: `http://underscorejs.org/`
- Lodash: `https://lodash.com/`

PART VIII

Front-End Development

CHAPTER 13

React

So far in this book, we have covered a diverse selection of JavaScript frameworks. Many of these frameworks serve a specific purpose and cater to a particular niche. Many others, on the other hand, have a more diversified plethora of functions and can perform various tasks and actions.

Similarly, many JavaScript frameworks that we have talked about during the course of this book have a smaller user base and community. On the contrary, some of the JavaScript frameworks mentioned in these pages are really popular with a large user base and dedicated community.

In this chapter, we will be turning our attention toward another rather popular JavaScript framework that has risen to fame in a comparatively smaller amount of time—React.

React Overview

Speaking purely in textbook terms, React is not even a proper "framework" per se. Instead, it is a JavaScript library meant for building user interfaces.

However, owing to its sheer popularity, and the fact that it is now being used in projects of diverse nature, React is now almost as large and as component based as any other framework. This is why it is no longer uncommon to see React being mentioned wherever JavaScript frameworks are discussed.

In the simplest of words, React is a JavaScript library for building user interfaces (Figure 13-1). It is maintained by Facebook, alongside a community of developers and companies.

507

© Sufyan bin Uzayr, Nicholas Cloud, Tim Ambler 2019
S. bin Uzayr et al., *JavaScript Frameworks for Modern Web Development*,
https://doi.org/10.1007/978-1-4842-4995-6_13

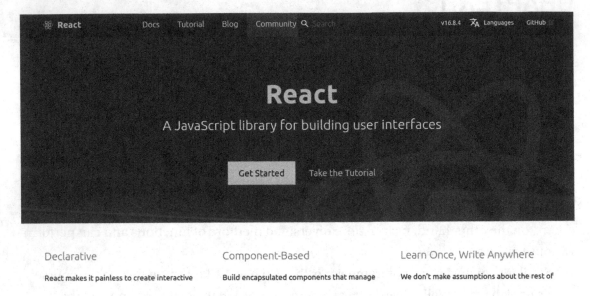

Figure 13-1. *React is a JavaScript library for building user interfaces*

Keeping in mind that React enjoys the backing of Facebook, it has grown in stature over time. Today, React is often employed by developers to empower user interfaces of both big and small projects.

Even more so, React has grown beyond the simplified textbook definition of being a "library" or "framework." Nowadays, React is often used in assonance with other technologies and scripting languages to power complex web apps. For instance, even though its core is in PHP, WordPress has shown a paradigm shift toward React for powering its new block-based editor (named Gutenberg) as well as its desktop apps for the WP.com hosted solution.

React was first released in 2013, and since then, it has consistently risen in terms of popularity.

What Makes React Special?

React is component based. This implies that parts of the app are wrapped within self-contained and highly encapsulated modules known as Components. Furthermore, since the components' data is written in JavaScript, it is possible for developers to pass rich data through their apps and keep the state out of the DOM.

React makes use of one-way binding and Flux control to control the application workflow. Beyond that, React components, in general, are written using JSX. This makes for more legible and easier to understand code and is also a less steep learning curve for many developers.

JSX stands for JavaScript XML, which is an extension to the JavaScript language syntax. It provides a way to write code in a manner or style that is slightly similar to HTML, making it easier for many developers to comprehend the syntax within minutes.

In React, for every DOM object, there is also a corresponding virtual DOM object. This virtual DOM is a copy or representation of the original DOM, thereby helping out with one-way binding. The DOM is updated only when a change is detected in virtual DOM—there is no need to re-render the entire page. It is worth bearing in mind that manipulating the virtual DOM is faster than actually modifying the original DOM as no data is drawn onscreen.

React can be used to create highly interactive and very dynamic user interfaces for a wide variety of purposes, such as web sites, mobile applications, and more. Developers can create simplified views for various states, and React can update and modify the relevant components as and when the state changes. Such declarative coding can save a good deal of time and effort.

Well, that is what React brings to the table. But how do we get started with React?

Getting Started with React

The first step, obviously, is to add React to our project in order to use its features. There are more than one way to do it, but the most recommended and simplest method is to add React to HTML pages by means of a <script> tag.

How to Add React to Web Pages?

Adding React to our HTML pages is very simple. The first step is to add an empty <div> tag in the HTML page, right where we want the React component to appear.

For example:

```
<!-- ... some HTML ... -->
<div id="my_react_component"></div>
<!-- ... some HTML ... -->
```

The next step is to add <script> tags to the same HTML page. These should ideally be placed just before the closing </body> tag.

For example:

```
<!-- ... some HTML ... -->
<script src="https://unpkg.com/react@16/umd/react.development.js"
crossorigin></script>
 <script src="https://unpkg.com/react-dom@16/umd/react-dom.development.js"
 crossorigin></script>
  <!-- React component. -->
  <script src="super_react.js"></script>
</body>
```

Lastly, we create the React component. It is noteworthy that the file name must be the same as specified in the <script> tag earlier; in our case, it will be super_react.js

The React component file will then pass on the component to the HTML. Voila! We have successfully added React to our web page, and can now start working with it.

Obviously, this was a fairly simple and theoretical example of adding React. But before seeing a React app in action, let us also cover the traditional method of installing React.

Installation

Sometimes, adding React to an HTML page by means of <script> tags may not suffice. This is especially true if we are trying to integrate React with an existing workflow, say a component library or a server-side project, and so on.

Similarly, if we are trying to build a single-page web app, using Create React App might be a better choice. This will enable us to make use of the latest React features and also set us up with an environment ideal for building Single Page Apps in React as well as learning React.

To install, we will use npm:

```
npm install create-react-app
```

The installation process should not take a lot of time to complete (Figure 13-2).

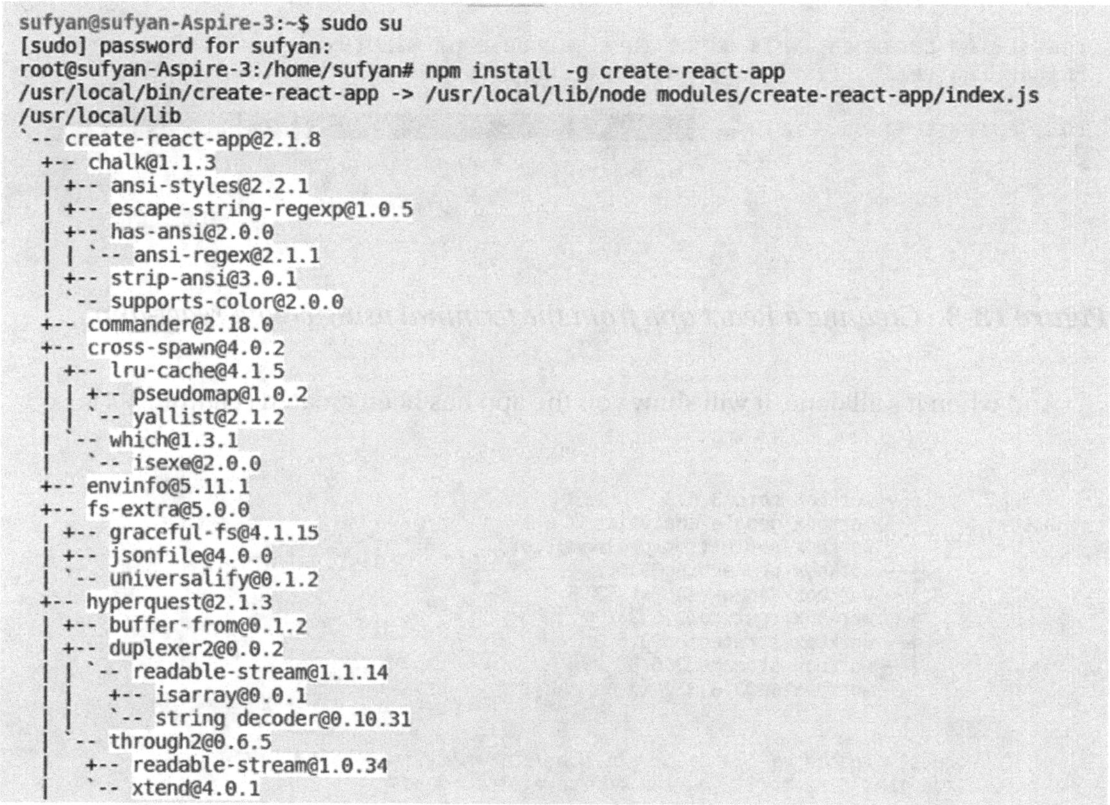

```
sufyan@sufyan-Aspire-3:~$ sudo su
[sudo] password for sufyan:
root@sufyan-Aspire-3:/home/sufyan# npm install -g create-react-app
/usr/local/bin/create-react-app -> /usr/local/lib/node modules/create-react-app/index.js
/usr/local/lib
`-- create-react-app@2.1.8
  +-- chalk@1.1.3
  | +-- ansi-styles@2.2.1
  | +-- escape-string-regexp@1.0.5
  | +-- has-ansi@2.0.0
  | | `-- ansi-regex@2.1.1
  | +-- strip-ansi@3.0.1
  | `-- supports-color@2.0.0
  +-- commander@2.18.0
  +-- cross-spawn@4.0.2
  | +-- lru-cache@4.1.5
  | | +-- pseudomap@1.0.2
  | | `-- yallist@2.1.2
  | -- which@1.3.1
  |   `-- isexe@2.0.0
  +-- envinfo@5.11.1
  +-- fs-extra@5.0.0
  | +-- graceful-fs@4.1.15
  | +-- jsonfile@4.0.0
  | `-- universalify@0.1.2
  +-- hyperquest@2.1.3
  | +-- buffer-from@0.1.2
  | +-- duplexer2@0.0.2
  | | `-- readable-stream@1.1.14
  | |   +-- isarray@0.0.1
  | |   `-- string decoder@0.10.31
  | `-- through2@0.6.5
  |   +-- readable-stream@1.0.34
  |     `-- xtend@4.0.1
```

Figure 13-2. *Installing Create React App using npm*

> Create React App requires Node.js 6.0 or higher and npm version
> 5.2 or hig her.

Thereafter, we can create our React application as under:

```
create-react-app app_name_comes_here
```

For example:

```
create-react-app my-react-one
```

The preceding command will create an application name my-react-one, as shown in Figure 13-3.

```
sufyan@sufyan-Aspire-3:~$ create-react-app my-react-one

Creating a new React app in /home/sufyan/my-react-one.

Installing packages. This might take a couple of minutes.
Installing react, react-dom, and react-scripts...

loadDep:parse-json → netw ▆ ▐
▐
```

Figure 13-3. *Creating a React app from the terminal using create-react-app*

And when it's all done, it will show you the app has been created (Figure 13-4).

```
        ── workbox-core@3.6.3
        ── workbox-google-analytics@3.6.3
        ── workbox-navigation-preload@3.6.3
        ── workbox-precaching@3.6.3
        ── workbox-range-requests@3.6.3
        ── workbox-routing@3.6.3
        ── workbox-strategies@3.6.3
        ── workbox-streams@3.6.3
        └─ workbox-sw@3.6.3

Success! Created my-react-one at /home/sufyan/my-react-one
Inside that directory, you can run several commands:

  npm start
    Starts the development server.

  npm run build
    Bundles the app into static files for production.

  npm test
    Starts the test runner.

  npm run eject
    Removes this tool and copies build dependencies, configuration files
    and scripts into the app directory. If you do this, you can't go back!
```

Figure 13-4. *App successfully created*

Once our application is set up, we can launch it to preview in browser.

First, we need to change the directory to navigate to the root folder of the project.

```
cd my-react-one
```

And then, we can serve the app as

```
npm start
```

This preceding command should inform us of the app's state when it is ready (Figure 13-5).

```
Compiled successfully!

You can now view my-react-one in the browser.

  Local:            http://localhost:3000/
  On Your Network:  http://192.168.43.212:3000/

Note that the development build is not optimized.
To create a production build, use npm run build.
```

Figure 13-5. *Launching the React app*

Furthermore, it will also automatically launch the web browser and open localhost:3000—that's where our application is running (Figure 13-6)!

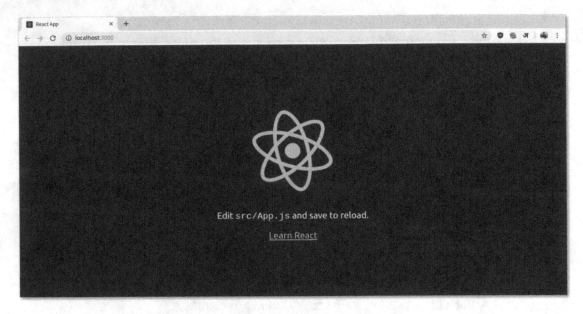

Figure 13-6. *App successfully running at localhost:3000*

Great, we have now successfully created a sample React application.

Now, it is time to do something more with it.

Building a To-Do Application

Notice that the application tells us to open src/App.js file? Well, that is the main file of the application.

Here is what its contents look like, by default:

```
import React, { Component } from 'react';
import logo from './logo.svg';
import './App.css';

class App extends Component {
  render() {
    return (
      <div className="App">
        <header className="App-header">
          <img src={logo} className="App-logo" alt="logo" />
```

```
        <p>
          Edit <code>src/App.js</code> and save to reload.
        </p>
        <a
          className="App-link"
          href="https://reactjs.org"
          target="_blank"
          rel="noopener noreferrer"
        >
          Learn React
        </a>
      </header>
    </div>
  );
  }
}
export default App;
```

Furthermore, the src/App.js file inherits CSS styling from the src/App.css file. Its contents are as follows:

```
.App {
  text-align: center;
}

.App-logo {
  animation: App-logo-spin infinite 20s linear;
  height: 40vmin;
  pointer-events: none;
}

.App-header {
  background-color: #282c34;
  min-height: 100vh;
  display: flex;
  flex-direction: column;
  align-items: center;
  justify-content: center;
```

```
  font-size: calc(10px + 2vmin);
  color: white;
}

.App-link {
  color: #61dafb;
}

@keyframes App-logo-spin {
  from {
    transform: rotate(0deg);
  }
  to {
    transform: rotate(360deg);
  }
}
```

We can leave the CSS classes as is and even use them in our application.

Now, let us try building a very simple to-do application in React. Our src/App.js file uses JSX notation, which we have discussed earlier.[1]

We can place the following code in the App.js file to replace its existing code:

```
import React, { Component } from 'react';
import './App.css';

class MyToDoList extends React.Component {
  constructor(props) {
    super(props);
    this.state = { items: [], text: " };
    this.valChange = this.valChange.bind(this);
    this.valSubmit = this.valSubmit.bind(this);
  }
```

---

[1]Some functions of the to-do app were based on the demo app at ReactJS web site:
https://reactjs.org/

```
render() {
  return (
    <div className="App-header">
      <h1>MY FANCY TO DO LIST</h1>
      <TodoList items={this.state.items} />
      <form onSubmit={this.valSubmit}>
        <label htmlFor="new-todo">
          What should we do next....?
        </label>
        <input
          id="new-todo"
          onChange={this.valChange}
          value={this.state.text}
        />
        <button>
          Add #{this.state.items.length + 1}
        </button>
      </form>
    </div>
  );
}

valChange(e) {
  this.setState({ text: e.target.value });
}

valSubmit(e) {
  e.preventDefault();
  if (!this.state.text.length) {
    return;
  }
  const newItem = {
    text: this.state.text,
    id: Date.now()
  };
```

```
    this.setState(state => ({
      items: state.items.concat(newItem),
      text: "
    }));
  }
}

class TodoList extends React.Component {
  render() {
    return (
      <ul>
        {this.props.items.map(item => (
          <li key={item.id}>{item.text}</li>
        ))}
      </ul>
    );
  }
}
export default MyToDoList;
```

What does the preceding code do?

- First, it imports the necessary components.

- Then, it creates a class MyToDoList that makes use of the React component to generate a to-do handler.

- Then, we render the to-do input field and the button, along with an H1 tag.

- Lastly, we are exporting the result to the display.

We can now save the file, and then the app preview at localhost:3000 should refresh automatically. Figure 13-7 shows how it looks (notice that we have inherited the App.css styling in the <div> tag).

Figure 13-7. *To-do application preview*

We can also add our tasks, as shown in Figure 13-8.

Figure 13-8. *To-do application in action*

There we have it! We've built our first React to-do app. For your reference, Figure 13-9 shows the src/App.js file in code editor.

```
File  Edit  Selection  View  Go  Debug  Terminal  Help

JS App.js    ×

  1   import React, { Component } from 'react';
  2   import './App.css';
  3
  4   class MyToDoList extends React.Component {
  5     constructor(props) {
  6       super(props);
  7       this.state = { items: [], text: '' };
  8       this.valChange = this.valChange.bind(this);
  9       this.valSubmit = this.valSubmit.bind(this);
 10     }
 11
 12     render() {
 13       return (
 14         <div className="App-header">
 15           <h1>MY FANCY TO DO LIST</h1>
 16           <TodoList items={this.state.items} />
 17           <form onSubmit={this.valSubmit}>
 18             <label htmlFor="new-todo">
 19               What should we do next....?
 20             </label>
 21             <input
 22               id="new-todo"
 23               onChange={this.valChange}
 24               value={this.state.text}
 25             />
 26             <button>
 27               Add #{this.state.items.length + 1}
 28             </button>
 29           </form>
 30         </div>
 31       );
 32     }
```

Figure 13-9. *src/App.js file preview*

You can find the code for the to-do application over at this book's GitHub repo.

Summary

In this chapter, we have covered what is React and what makes it different from the other JavaScript frameworks and libraries.

When it comes to React, the ecosystem is so vast that there is no dearth of learning resources or literature. Ranging from tutorials to books and even video courses, there is no shortage of good content pertaining to React development.

Since React is often used for front-end UI development, it might be a good idea to use it in assonance with a Node.js framework, such as Next.js or Sails.js for more complex projects.

That said, the official React documentation is fairly large and very well updated for any learner looking to brush up his or her React skills. Beyond that, community-run blogs and other publications are not hard to find and even a simple Google search should suffice for the most part.

- React Web site: `https://reactjs.org/`

- React Documentation: `https://reactjs.org/docs/getting-started.html`

- React Community on reddit: `www.reddit.com/r/reactjs/`

Lastly, it is worth pointing out again that since React is under the aegis of the likes of Facebook, it is not very likely that this particular JavaScript library will fall out of favor anytime soon. As such, for building rich web applications and web sites, React is a very sensible choice.

CHAPTER 14

Vue.js

So far in this book, we have covered various JavaScript frameworks that serve different purposes. Most of these JS frameworks have a more or less noticeable ecosystem and have been around for years.

But what about a newer JavaScript framework? One that is rising at a really impressive pace and, in spite of being a lesser known and relatively younger entity, is as powerful as any other framework in its league?

Yes, we are talking about Vue.js which is a progressive and really popular front-end JavaScript framework.

So now, it is time to get started with Vue. In this chapter, we will be learning about Vue.js framework, what it is about, and more importantly, what makes it special.

Furthermore, we will also be creating a simple Vue application so as to better understand the functionality and methodology of this JS framework.

Vue.js Overview

First up, what exactly is Vue.js and why should we be interested in it? It is worth noting that in spite of being relatively newer to the playground, Vue.js has risen in popularity and is steadily growing in stature. Surely, that has to be something worth the effort about it, isn't it?

So, what makes this framework tick?

What Is Vue.js?

Vue is a progressive JavaScript framework that is fairly tiny in size (20 KB in size, approx.).

Notice the word "progressive"? What exactly does it mean in this context? Progressive implies that the framework in question is implemented as an additional markup to existing HTML.

In other words, Vue.js being a progressive framework means it is a template model that is in turn bound to a data model, and the framework "reacts" to the model's updates.

Here is how the Vue GitHub page describes itself[1]:

> Vue (pronounced /vjuː/, like view) is a progressive framework for building user interfaces. It is designed from the ground up to be incrementally adoptable and can easily scale between a library and a framework depending on different use cases. It consists of an approachable core library that focuses on the view layer only and an ecosystem of supporting libraries that helps you tackle complexity in large single-page applications.

What Is Vue Meant For?

Vue has been designed especially with adaptability in mind—so much so that the core library consists of just the "view" layer (noticed the name "Vue," which can be pronounced as "view"?). This very layer can be bound to or integrated with other libraries and projects.

In other words, if we have an existing project coded in some other JS framework, we can easily use Vue.js to build user interfaces for our existing project, wherein Vue will handle the front-end view of the UI, whereas any other framework can be used for server-side rendering and data handling (Figure 14-1).

---

[1]Vue.js on GitHub: `https://github.com/vuejs/vue`

The Progressive JavaScript Framework

Special Sponsor

Standard Library

Build APIs you need in minutes instead of days, for free.

Approachable	Versatile	Performant
Already know HTML, CSS and JavaScript? Read the guide and start building things in no time!	An incrementally adoptable ecosystem that scales between a library and a full-featured framework.	20KB min+gzip Runtime Blazing Fast Virtual DOM Minimal Optimization Efforts

Figure 14-1. *Vue.js is a progressive JavaScript framework for building user interfaces*

Owing to its simplicity and ease of use, as well as the comparatively easier learning curve, Vue has risen in popularity for smaller projects as well. This implies the likes of single-page web apps, which can be entirely powered by Vue.js.

Beyond that, Vue has earned a reputation for being far less opinionated than the likes of Angular and more nimble and modern than many other JS frameworks out there. This, of course, is more of an opinion-based verdict, and not everyone may find Vue to have an edge over other frameworks. With that said, very few JS frameworks or libraries have risen in popularity in this decade as Vue has. Naturally, the reputation is not without good reasons.

So, how do we get started with Vue.js?

Getting Started with Vue.js

The first step, obviously, is to install Vue in order to use it in our projects and applications.

Installation

Installing Vue.js is, basically, a no-brainer. We can choose to either include it directly with the <script> tag or go the usual way and install via npm.

If we are including Vue in our projects via the <script> tag, Vue will be registered as a global variable.

The procedure is simple. We just need to reference the required CDN URL in our tags, for example:

```
<script src="https://cdn.jsdelivr.net/npm/vue@2.6.10/dist/vue.js"></script>
```

Or

```
<script src="https://unpkg.com/vue@2.6.1"></script>
```

It might be a smart idea to pay attention to the version numbering and build system, as using an experimental Vue version in a production-level project can break things. The Vue.js documentation has detailed info on which build of Vue to use and when.[2]

The second way of installing Vue.js is to do so via npm. As we have learned by now, npm refers to the Node Package Manager. We will need to have Node.js up and running on our system in order to use npm, and if you have been following the chapters of this book so far, there are very good chances you already have Node.js and npm all set up.

The installation command is fairly simple:

```
npm install vue
```

Using npm for installing Vue.js is ideal if we are attempting to use Vue in a large project and intend to integrate it with other libraries or tools. For instance, if we are using tools such as Webpack, installing Vue via npm will pair it nicely with Webpack automatically (Figure 14-2).

---

[2]See https://vuejs.org/v2/guide/installation.html#Explanation-of-Different-Builds

```
sufyan@sufyan-Aspire-3:~$ sudo su
[sudo] password for sufyan:
root@sufyan-Aspire-3:/home/sufyan# npm install vue
/home/sufyan
+-- aurelia-cli@1.0.0-beta.3
+-- socket.io@2.1.1
+-- svelte@2.14.3
+-- vue@2.6.10
`-- webix@6.0.9
```

Figure 14-2. *Installing Vue.js using npm*

Installing Vue via npm will also give us access to the Vue.js CLI (assuming we have a compatible version of Node.js on our system; as long as we have the latest build of Node, we should be fine). The minimum supported version of Node is >=8.

The Vue CLI can easily help us set up projects and build applications quickly (Figure 14-3). It can create basic skeleton apps or provide scaffolding that we can customize to build complex and larger applications. We will soon be creating a project using Vue CLI, though if needed, you can find detailed information about the CLI on the concerned web site.[3]

Vue CLI

✂ Standard Tooling for Vue.js Development

Get Started →

Figure 14-3. *Vue CLI provides a set of standard tools for rapid Vue.js app development*

---

[3]Vue CLI Homepage: https://cli.vuejs.org/

We can easily install Vue CLI using npm, as under:

```
npm install -g @vue/cli
```

It might take a while to fetch and install, but once done, we are ready to use Vue CLI in our development workflow (Figure 14-4).

```
sufyan@sufyan-Aspire-3:~$ sudo su
[sudo] password for sufyan:
root@sufyan-Aspire-3:/home/sufyan# npm install -g @vue/cli
npm WARN deprecated cross-spawn-async@2.2.5: cross-spawn no longer requires a build toolchain, use it instead
loadDep:ws -> headers     | |############################----------------------------------
/usr/local/bin/vue -> /usr/local/lib/node_modules/@vue/cli/bin/vue.js

> protobufjs@6.8.8 postinstall /usr/local/lib/node_modules/@vue/cli/node_modules/protobufjs
> node scripts/postinstall


> nodemon@1.18.10 postinstall /usr/local/lib/node_modules/@vue/cli/node_modules/nodemon
> node bin/postinstall || exit 0

Love nodemon? You can now support the project via the open collective:
 > https://opencollective.com/nodemon/donate

/usr/local/lib
`-- @vue/cli@3.5.1
  +-- @vue/cli-shared-utils@3.5.1
  | +-- joi@14.3.1
  | | +-- hoek@6.1.2
  | | +-- isemail@3.2.0
  | | | `-- punycode@2.1.1
  | | `-- topo@3.0.3
  | +-- launch-editor@2.2.1
  | | `-- shell-quote@1.6.1
  | |   +-- array-filter@0.0.1
  | |   +-- array-map@0.0.0
  | |   +-- array-reduce@0.0.0
```

Figure 14-4. *Installing Vue CLI via npm*

Building Our First Vue App

In order to create a Vue app, we first need to set up our project. The command for the same is

```
vue create my-vue-project
```

wherein the project is named as "my-vue-project" and can be changed to anything of your liking (Figure 14-5).

```
sufyan@sufyan-Aspire-3:~$ vue create my-vue-project


Vue CLI v3.5.1
? Please pick a preset: default (babel, eslint)


Vue CLI v3.5.1
⚡ Creating project in /home/sufyan/my-vue-project.
🗃 Initializing git repository...
⚙ Installing CLI plugins. This might take a while...

loadDep:find-up → 304      ▌ ▐███████████████████████████▒
▊
```

Figure 14-5. *Creating our first Vue.js application using Vue CLI*

The installer will ask us to select some options, and unless there is something custom needed, we can go with the default linter, and so on. Again, it can take some time to load all the required dependencies.

Once the project is set up, we can actually launch the app and preview in a browser.

First, we need to change the directory:

```
cd my-vue-project
```

And then, run the application:

```
npm run serve
```

The output in the terminal will be as shown in Figure 14-6.

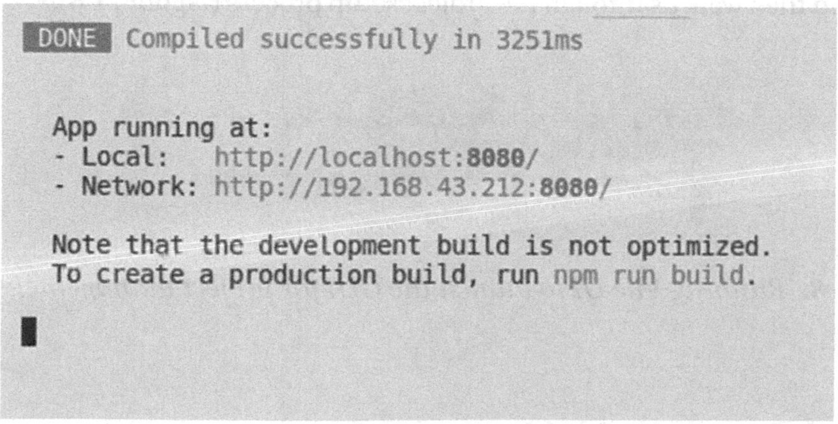

```
 DONE  Compiled successfully in 3251ms


  App running at:
  - Local:   http://localhost:8080/
  - Network: http://192.168.43.212:8080/

  Note that the development build is not optimized.
  To create a production build, run npm run build.

▊
```

Figure 14-6. *Running our first Vue application*

As we can see, the localhost port number is displayed in the terminal. When we navigate to localhost:8080 in the web browser, we will find our sample application up and running, as shown in Figure 14-7.

Figure 14-7. *Previewing the Vue app in the web browser*

Alternatively, we can also choose to use

```
vue ui
```

The preceding command will launch a graphical user interface (GUI) in the web browser, and then walk us through the project setup process (Figure 14-8).

```
sufyan@sufyan-Aspire-3:~$ vue ui
🦋 Starting GUI...
🎯 Ready on http://localhost:8000
```

Figure 14-8. *Running Vue UI to launch the GUI for project management in Vue.js*

We first need to select the location to create our new project (or load an existing one). See Figure 14-9.

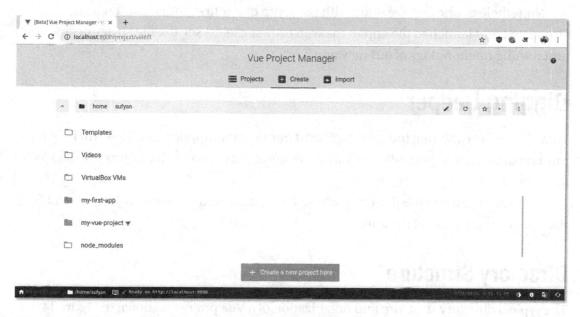

Figure 14-9. *Selecting location of project in Vue UI*

And then, we will specify the usual details, such as package manager, project name, linter, other details, and so on (Figure 14-10).

Figure 14-10. *Creating a new project using Vue UI in the browser*

For those of us who are not the most comfortable working with the command line, using Vue UI for project creation is an ideal choice.

Nonetheless, once we are done with the setup of our first project, and having also tested and launched the app in the web browser, let us see the file structure and functioning methodology of our new app.

Digging Deeper

We will now be exploring the specific files of our new Vue application. This will help us understand how Vue.js handles its various components and how it outputs the data to the browser.

Upon navigating to the directory where we have created our new project, we will find the directory structure of the app.

Directory Structure

The typical directory structure and organization of a Vue project is shown in Figure 14-11.

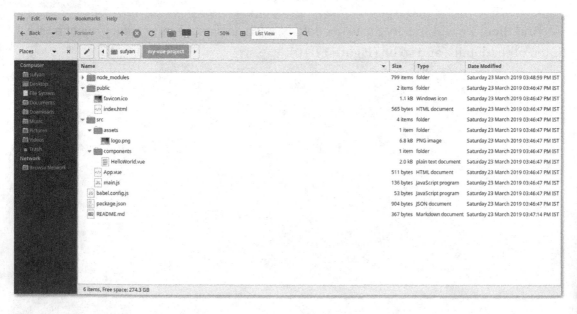

Figure 14-11. *Directory structure showing file hierarchy in a Vue project*

Most of the preceding directories are fairly self-explanatory. For instance, the public folder contains some assets and an index.html file that is to render the app in the browser.

Let us look at the src directory in greater detail.

We find the following within the src directory:

- An assets directory, containing images and other media assets

- A components directory, which, for the sample app generated earlier, contains the HelloWorld.vue file

- Two files, namely, App.vue and main.js

src/main.js File

This particular file is what drives our app. Upon inspecting, its contents look something like this:

```
import Vue from 'vue'
import App from './App.vue'
Vue.config.productionTip = false
new Vue({
  render: h => h(App),
}).$mount('#app')
```

Figure 14-12 is the file preview in the code editor.

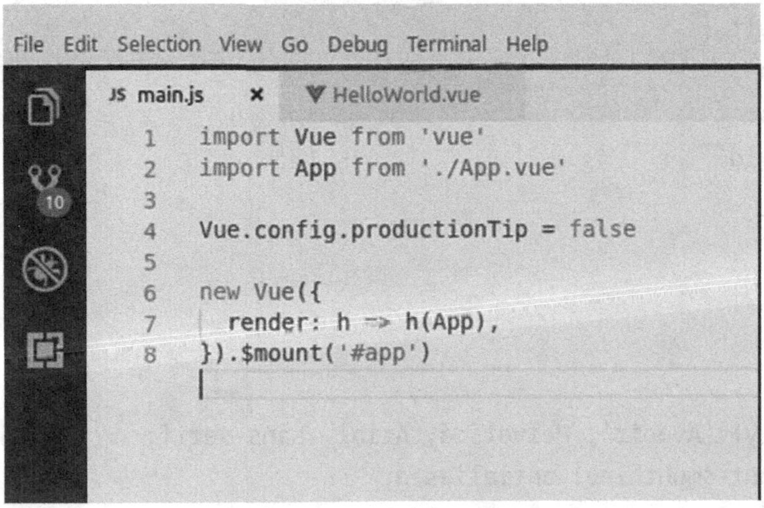

Figure 14-12. *src/main.js file of the Vue application*

In the given file, we are first importing the Vue library and then the App component from App.vue.

Thereafter, we are setting the productionTip to false, so that Vue will not output "Development Mode" in the console.

Next, we are creating our Vue instance and assigning it to the DOM element that is identified by #app, so as to use the App component.

src/App.vue File

This particular file is a Single File Component, containing HTML, CSS, as well as JS code.

In other words, the App.vue file is a stand-alone component that has all of its stuff in one file only. Following are its contents, which can be viewed in our code editor, as well:

```
<template>
  <div id="app">
    <img alt="Vue logo" src="./assets/logo.png">
    <HelloWorld msg="Welcome to Your Vue.js App"/>
  </div>
</template>

<script>
import HelloWorld from './components/HelloWorld.vue'

export default {
  name: 'app',
  components: {
    HelloWorld
  }
}
</script>

<style>
#app {
  font-family: 'Avenir', Helvetica, Arial, sans-serif;
  -webkit-font-smoothing: antialiased;
  -moz-osx-font-smoothing: grayscale;
  text-align: center;
```

```
  color: #2c3e50;
  margin-top: 60px;
}
</style>
```

The CSS code of this file is self-explanatory, as it provides the styling for the code. The script tag, however, is importing a component from the components/HelloWorld. vue file. Let us, therefore, turn our attention toward the said file itself.

components/HelloWorld.vue File

The components/HelloWorld.vue file might seem to be slightly larger at first, but even a slight look at its contents will be enough to comprehend the way it operates.

Here is what the file should contain by default, which can also be viewed in the code editor:

```
<template>
  <div class="hello">
    <h1>{{ msg }}</h1>
    <p>
      For a guide and recipes on how to configure / customize this project,<br>
      check out the
      <a href="https://cli.vuejs.org" target="_blank" rel="noopener">vue-
      cli documentation</a>.
    </p>
    <h3>Installed CLI Plugins</h3>
    <ul>
      <li><a href="https://github.com/vuejs/vue-cli/tree/dev/packages/
      %40vue/cli-plugin-babel" target="_blank" rel="noopener">babel</a></li>
      <li><a href="https://github.com/vuejs/vue-cli/tree/dev/packages/
      %40vue/cli-plugin-eslint" target="_blank" rel="noopener">eslint</a>
      </li>
    </ul>
    <h3>Essential Links</h3>
    <ul>
      <li><a href="https://vuejs.org" target="_blank" rel="noopener">Core
      Docs</a></li>
```

```
    <li><a href="https://forum.vuejs.org" target="_blank"
    rel="noopener">Forum</a></li>
    <li><a href="https://chat.vuejs.org" target="_blank"
    rel="noopener">Community Chat</a></li>
    <li><a href="https://twitter.com/vuejs" target="_blank"
    rel="noopener">Twitter</a></li>
    <li><a href="https://news.vuejs.org" target="_blank"
    rel="noopener">News</a></li>
  </ul>
  <h3>Ecosystem</h3>
  <ul>
    <li><a href="https://router.vuejs.org" target="_blank"
    rel="noopener">vue-router</a></li>
    <li><a href="https://vuex.vuejs.org" target="_blank"
    rel="noopener">vuex</a></li>
    <li><a href="https://github.com/vuejs/vue-devtools#vue-devtools"
    target="_blank" rel="noopener">vue-devtools</a></li>
    <li><a href="https://vue-loader.vuejs.org" target="_blank"
    rel="noopener">vue-loader</a></li>
    <li><a href="https://github.com/vuejs/awesome-vue" target="_blank"
    rel="noopener">awesome-vue</a></li>
  </ul>
  </div>
</template>

<script>
export default {
  name: 'HelloWorld',
  props: {
    msg: String
  }
}
</script>
```

```
<!-- Add "scoped" attribute to limit CSS to this component only -->
<style scoped>
h3 {
  margin: 40px 0 0;
}
ul {
  list-style-type: none;
  padding: 0;
}
li {
  display: inline-block;
  margin: 0 10px;
}
a {
  color: #42b983;
}
</style>
```

This file contains our HelloWorld component that is in turn included in the App component. When we preview the app in the browser, we can see that this file's component outputs a set of links with some explanatory text and other info.

In the preceding code, it is noteworthy that CSS is "scoped." This means any CSS added to the HelloWorld component is not global in nature and will not be applied to other components.

The message or info that this component will output is stored in the data property of the Vue instance.

So now, we have seen that the HelloWorld component is used to output the contents of our app, and with scoped attributes being set, the CSS is not leaked onto the other components.

Further, the HelloWorld component is imported by the App.vue file, and the App component itself is imported by the main.js file.

At this point, we can safely turn to the index.html file.

---

public/index.html File

The index.html file is, in simple words, the main file for our app and can be viewed in the code editor. Here is what it contains:

```html
<!DOCTYPE html>
<html lang="en">
  <head>
    <meta charset="utf-8">
    <meta http-equiv="X-UA-Compatible" content="IE=edge">
    <meta name="viewport" content="width=device-width,initial-scale=1.0">
    <link rel="icon" href="<%= BASE_URL %>favicon.ico">
    <title>my-vue-project</title>
  </head>
  <body>
    <noscript>
      <strong>We're sorry but my-vue-project doesn't work properly without
      JavaScript enabled. Please enable it to continue.</strong>
    </noscript>
    <div id="app"></div>
    <!-- built files will be auto injected -->
  </body>
</html>
```

All of the code here is fairly obvious to understand. We can see that the file, in the body, contains one element:

```html
<div id="app"></div>
```

This is the element that the Vue application will use to attach to the DOM.

And there we have it! These are the major files that our sample app runs on. We have read and understood the way each component is handled and imported, and it might be worthwhile to refer to the app output once again here to better visualize the app's functioning.

Summary

In this chapter, we familiarized ourselves with Vue.js, plus we also learned how to install this JS framework, what specialty it has to offer, as well as how to create a sample app.

Next, we learned about the major files and components within a Vue.js application, how its projects are handled, as well as which file or component serves a particular purpose.

Next Steps

To learn more about Vue.js, a good place to start might be the official documentation itself. Both the Style Guide and the API docs are fairly well laid out and detailed in nature. Beyond that, Vue.js ecosystem also has a job board and a news portal, to help developers get the most out of their skills and also stay updated with the latest insight and information.

Here are some of the channels that you can use to stay updated with Vue.js and also learn the maximum about it:

- Official Vue.js Documentation: `https://vuejs.org/v2/guide/`

- Vue.js Cookbook: `https://vuejs.org/v2/cookbook/`

- Vue.js Job Board: `https://vuejobs.com/`

- Vue.js News Board: `https://news.vuejs.org/`

- Vue.js Examples: `https://vuejs.org/v2/examples/`

In addition to that, it might also be worth the effort to check out the Awesome Vue repository on GitHub that shares a curated list of some of the most interesting tools and stuff related to Vue.js—you may visit the repository at `https://github.com/vuejs/awesome-vue`.

Lastly, it is a good idea to give VuePress a shot. It is a static site generator built in Vue.js and is a good example of how to harness the power of the Vue template engine. Since static site generators in themselves are beyond the scope of this book per se, we'd leave you with just a couple of handy links to help you learn more about VuePress:

- VuePress Homepage: `https://vuepress.vuejs.org/`

- VuePress Intro and Installation Tutorial: `https://codecarbon.com/vuepress-static-site-generator/`

Index

A

Aggregation and indexing
    countBy(), 467, 468
    groupBy(), 468, 470
    indexBy(), 470–472
Album.create() method, 317, 332
Album.findByIdAndUpdate()
    method, 360
Album.find() method, 355
Angular, 8, 210
    vs. angularJS, 209
    aspects, 210
    CLI using npm, 213
    components file, 218
    CSS changes, 220, 221
    Dependency Injection, 221–223
    directory structure, 215, 216
    first app, 215
    installation, 211
    local host, 217
    Node.js, 212
    output update, 219
    recompiling changes, 220
    serve command, 217
    title in browser, 219
    web app, 210
    workspace creation, 213, 214
Asynchronous module
    definition (AMD), 92, 133, 134

Async.js
    batch flow
        asynchronous cargo, 455–458
        asynchronous queue, 453–455
    flow control function
        pattern, 429, 430
    flows and functions, 459
    loop flow
        condition, false, 446, 447, 449
        condition, true, 443–446
        infinite loop, 451, 452
        retry loop, 449–451
    parallel flow, 435, 437
        steps, 434
    pipeline flow
        async.waterfall(), 439, 440
        calcAge() function, 437
        getUser() factory function, 437
        nested callbacks, 438, 439
        pipeline() function, 442
        reward() function, 437
        steps, 437, 438, 441
    sequential flow, 431–433
async.parallel() function, 434, 435
async.retry() function, 449
async.series(), 435
Automated JavaScript linting, Grunt, 27
Automated Sass stylesheet compilation,
    Grunt, 28
Automated unit testing, Grunt, 29

541

Printed in the United States
By Bookmasters